Leap of Faith

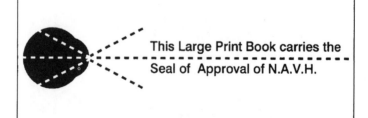

This Large Print Book carries the
Seal of Approval of N.A.V.H.

LEAP OF FAITH

Memoirs of an Unexpected Life

QUEEN NOOR

LARGE
PRINT
PRESS

Waterville, Maine

Published in 2005 by arrangement with Miramax Books,
a division of Miramax Film Corp., c/o Hyperion, an imprint of
Buena Vista Books, Inc.

The text of this Large Print edition is unabridged.
Other aspects of the book may vary from the original edition.

Set in 16 pt. Plantin.

Printed in the United States on permanent paper.

ISBN 1-58724-466-7 (lg. print : hc : alk. paper)
ISBN 1-59413-070-1 (lg. print : sc : alk. paper)

For my beloved Hussein,
light of my life.

*"Work for life on this earth
as if you are to live forever,
and work for the life after in heaven
as if you are to die tomorrow."*

National Association for Visually Handicapped
-- serving the partially seeing

As the Founder/CEO of NAVH, the only national health agency solely devoted to those who, although not totally blind, have an eye disease which could lead to serious visual impairment, I am pleased to recognize Thorndike Press★ as one of the leading publishers in the large print field.

Founded in 1954 in San Francisco to prepare large print textbooks for partially seeing children, NAVH became the pioneer and standard setting agency in the preparation of large type.

Today, those publishers who meet our standards carry the prestigious "Seal of Approval" indicating high quality large print. We are delighted that Thorndike Press is one of the publishers whose titles meet these standards. We are also pleased to recognize the significant contribution Thorndike Press is making in this important and growing field.

Lorraine H. Marchi, L.H.D.
Founder/CEO
NAVH

★ Thorndike Press encompasses the following imprints: Thorndike, Wheeler, Walker and Large Print Press.

contents

acknowledgments

I always imagined that if I were to try to tell my story that I would do so in a quiet reflective period toward the end of my active life when there might be an almost complete story to tell. However, after my husband's death, many people encouraged me to share my memories and my perspective on Hussein's legacy at a time when it might be of particular relevance.

This book was written in the spirit of reconciliation, which I hope will contribute to a greater awareness, especially in the West, of events that have shaped the modern Middle East, and encourage a deeper understanding of contemporary challenges facing the Arab world as well as an appreciation for the true values of Islam. I have often spoken about the need to build bridges between cultures as a way to promote constructive dialogue; it is my fervent hope that this book will inspire some of its readers to put those ideals into practice. I do not claim to be a political scientist, historian, or theologian; I have tried to write accurately and from firsthand experience whenever possible.

The responsibility for the views expressed in these pages is, of course, mine alone, but they were refined in the course of many spirited conversations with friends and advisers. These are my views, however, and should not be construed as the official Jordanian government position.

Memoirs are by definition a deeply personal undertaking requiring reflection and a measure of introspection. This book was no exception. During this sometimes painful and often painstaking endeavor, I was very fortunate to have the assistance of many exceptional and creative minds. In the initial research and information-gathering stage, Linda Bird Francke and I spent many hours reviewing primary source materials, especially my daily journals of the past twenty-five years. Linda traveled to Jordan where she interviewed our family, friends, and my working colleagues. Victoria Pope has been an invaluable and indefatigable guide and friend throughout the critical culmination of the project, lending her many editorial talents to shaping the final text. The manuscript also benefited from Peter Guzzardi's deft line-editing. Hania Dakhgan deserves special thanks for her crucial involvement in the last, hectic months before deadline, researching and co-ordinating the project while giving many thoughtful suggestions on how to improve the book's flow. Ghadeer Taher and Basma Lozi also contributed in many meaningful ways.

I am grateful to Robert B. Barnett, Tina Brown, and Jonathan Burnham for believing in this book from the start. My thanks go also to Caroline Migdadi, Manal Jazi, Carol Adwan, Gail Nash Brown, Elizabeth Corke, Dianne Smith, Carlo Miotti, Jennifer Georgia, Tufan Kolan, Christine Anger, Liesa Segovia, Janell Bragg, Susan Mercandetti, Hilary Bass, Jill Ellyn Riley, Kristin Powers, and Kathie Berlin.

Family members and friends also offered much-appreciated advice and support. My parents, Doris and Najeeb Halaby, my brother, Chris, my sister, Alexa, and my cousins Rodrigo and Pedro Arboleda all helped to piece together our family story in the first chapters. Hussein's and my children, Feisal, Hamzah, Hashim, Iman, Raiyah, and Abir, and our nephews Prince Talal and Prince Ghazi, Prince Raad and Princess Majda, Prince Ali Bin Nayef and Princess Wijdan, and Prince Zeid Bin Shaker (who supported and comforted so many of us after Sidi's death until he left us too soon to join his dearest friend and brother), and Leila Sharaf my valued friend and counsel, all helped me by sharing happy memories, as well as valuable historical and cultural perspectives. Many friends kindly lent their support, Queen Sofia, Empress Farah, King Constantine and Queen Anne-Marie, Swanee Hunt, Camille Douglas, Marion Freeman, Tessa Kennedy, Melissa Mathison, Sarah Pillsbury, Lucky Roosevelt, Gillian Rowan, Steven Spielberg, and Nadine Shubailat. Thank you.

I am especially indebted to the researchers as well as several dear friends who helped check and recheck facts on the region, including Moustapha Akkad, Aysar Akrawi, Fouad Ayyoub, Lina Attel, Adnan Badran, Dr. Sima Bahous, Ghazi Bisheh, Timoor Daghastani, Ali Ghandour, Sheikh Ahmed Hllayel, Rana Husseini, Khaled Irani, Ibrahim Izzedin, Abdul Kareem Kabariti, Rami Khouri, Lina Kopti, Ali Mahafza, Ashraf Malhas, Hussein Majali, Suleiman Al Moussa, Sheikh Walid Al Said, Rebecca Salti, Kamel Sharif, Hana Shaheen, Ali Shukri, Jafar Toukan, Abla Zureikat, Dr. Fouad Ajami, Kareem Fahim, Katherine Johnston Hutto, Dr. Sheila Johnson, Alison McIntyre, Megan Ring, Burdett Rooney, Jerry White, and Richard Verrall.

Finally, I would like to especially thank my children for their patience with my near-total immersion in the creation of this book over the last few years. It was their support and the memory of their father that kept me moving forward even when the task seemed over-whelming. God bless you all.

chapter one

First Impressions

I first met my future husband through the lens of a camera. I was standing with my father on the tarmac at the airport in Amman, Jordan, when King Hussein strolled over to greet us. Never one to hold back, my father thrust his camera into my hands. "Take my picture with the King," he said. Mortified, I nonetheless dutifully took the photograph, which caught the two men standing side by side, with the King's eldest daughter, Princess Alia, in the background. Afterward my father and the King exchanged a few words. Then King Hussein called his wife, Queen Alia, over to meet us.

It was the winter of 1976, and my father had asked me to join him on a brief visit to Jordan, where he had been invited to attend a ceremony marking the acquisition of the country's first Boeing 747. My father, Najeeb Halaby, a former airline executive and head of the Federal Aviation Administration, was chairman of the International Advisory Board for the Jordanian airline. He was also in Amman laying the groundwork for a pan-Arab aviation university, an ambitious project aimed at reducing the region's dependence on foreign manpower and training. This undertaking, still in its infant stages, was the brainchild of King Hussein, my father, and other aviation dreamers in the Middle East. Since I was at loose ends, having recently completed a job in Tehran, I welcomed an opportunity to travel to Jordan, which I had visited briefly for the first time earlier that year. Another trip to this part of the Middle East would bring me back to the land of my ancestors and, I hoped, reconnect me with the Arab roots of my Halaby family.

I distinctly recall my first impressions of Jordan. I had been en route to the United States from Iran, where I was working for a British urban planning firm. From the window of my aircraft, I had found myself spellbound by the serene expanse of desert landscape washed golden by the retreating sun at dusk. I was overwhelmed by an extraordinary sensation of belonging, an almost mystical sense of peace.

It was spring, a magical season in Jordan, when the winter-browned hills and valleys turn green from the winter rains, and wild anemones spring from the earth like red polka dots. Oranges, bananas, strawberries, tomatoes, and lettuces were being sold along the road through the lush fields and orchards of the Jordan River Valley, and city families from the high, cool Amman Plateau were picnicking along the warm shores of the Dead Sea. There was a warmth and joy in everyone and everything I saw, and I was entranced by the delightful harmony of past and present, of sheep grazing in fields and empty lots adjacent to sophisticated office buildings and state-of-the-art hospitals. I remember in particular the sight of students walking in the open fields at the edge of Amman, textbooks in hand, completely absorbed in their studies for the *Tawjihi*, a general government exam that Jordanians must take in the final year of high school.

I knew from looking at maps how close Jordan was to Israel and the occupied Palestinian territories, but I had not fully understood it until I stood on the Jordanian shore of the Dead Sea and looked across at the ancient city of Jericho on the occupied West Bank. Jordan, in fact, had a longer border with Israel than any other country; it ran some 400 miles from Lake Tiberius or the Sea of Galilee in the north to the Gulf of Aqaba in the south. Despite the enduring beauty of the landscape, World War II, three Arab-Israeli wars, and countless border skirmishes had left Jordan and Israel's cease-fire line — a sacred tract of land where the prophets once walked — riddled with land mines.

My knowledge of Jordan then was limited to

what I had read in newspapers or picked up in conversations, but I was aware of King Hussein's unique position in the region. He was a pan-Arabist with a deep understanding of Western culture, a consistent political moderate, and a dedicated member of the Nonaligned Movement. Jordan, I knew, was a linchpin for Middle East peace efforts, strategically located between Israel, Saudi Arabia, Syria, and Iraq. While in Jordan, I also learned that the King was a Hashimite — a direct descendant of the Prophet Muhammad, *Peace Be Upon Him* — and therefore held a special position of respect for Muslims.

The Jordan I visited for the first time in early 1976 was a fascinating blend of modernity and tradition. The Emirate of Transjordan was founded in 1921 and became the independent Hashimite Kingdom of Jordan in 1946. The country had been transformed by King Abdullah, its founder, and then by his grandson, King Hussein, and had steadily developed into a modern state. Having lost its historic access through Palestine to the commercial seaports of the Mediterranean due to the creation of Israel, Jordan had developed Aqaba as a port for traffic on the Red Sea and beyond to the Indian Ocean.

When I first came to know Jordan, the government was initiating an ambitious overhaul of the country's telecommunications. At the time it would take hours to call within Amman, and the capital did not even have international direct-dialing. Birds alighting on the system's copper wires could cut telephone connections, but soon there would be a state-of-the-art network of telephone services linking the country in even its most remote areas.

Smooth new roads had been built, mostly from north to south, to complement the traditional trade routes west through Palestine. You could easily drive, as I did, from Jordan's northern border with Syria all the way to Aqaba on the modern Desert Road. Traveling through the desert I saw nomadic Bedouin tending to their livestock, and children darting in and out of the distinctive black goat-hair tents known as *beit esh-sha'ar*. As day faded into night, I was transfixed by the rosy golden glow of the setting sun on the rocky hillsides, where herds of sheep looked almost iridescent in the waning light of day.

The Desert Road was the fastest and most direct road to the south, but my favorite route was the scenic Kings' Highway, which followed the ancient trade routes. The Three Wise Men are thought to have traveled at least part of the way to Bethlehem on the Kings' Highway, and Moses used it to lead his people toward Canaan. "We will stay on the Kings' Highway until we are out of your territory," reads Numbers 21:21–22 in the Bible, referring to Moses' request to King Sihon for permission to cross his kingdom, which was denied. Alternating between the two Nikon cameras I wore constantly around my neck, I took photograph after photograph of Mount Nebo, near where Moses is said to be buried, and of the magnificent mosaics I saw in nearby churches, just off the Kings' Highway.

Earlier civilizations kept the dirt track cleared of stones to hasten the passage of donkeys and camel caravans laden with gold and spices, and the Romans paved sections of the Kings' Highway with cobblestones to allow travel by chariot. Evidence of ten thousand years of history is scattered along or near the Kings' Highway, from striking plaster neolithic statues with darkly lined eyes, the oldest representations of the human form, to the Iron Age capital of the Ammonites, Rabbat-Ammon, which forms the nucleus of Jordan's present-day capital, Amman.

The archaeological treasures I saw in Jordan during this early visit were stunning, among them the classical walled city of Jerash in the hills of Gilead, with its colonnaded streets, temples, and theaters. Lakes once covered the eastern desert, where fossilized lions' teeth and elephants' tusks can be found in the sand. On the road to Baghdad loom the 1,300-year-old Islamic "Desert Castles" of the Umayyads — an Islamic dynasty established by the caliph Muawiyah I in 661 B.C. — with their colorful frescoes and mosaics of birds, animals, and fruits, and heated indoor baths.

A few hours to the south lies the ancient Nabataean city of Petra, carved into multi-colored sandstone cliffs. Hidden to the Western world for 700 years until Swiss explorer Johann Burckhardt stumbled on it in 1812, Petra is entered through a mile-long, narrow *Siq,* a natural gorge that cuts through the cliffs to emerge into a breathtaking marvel of shrines, temples, and tombs carved into the stone. It has a palette of natural colors and designs that no artist could duplicate, ancient caves and monuments whose floors and walls blaze with swirls of red, blue, yellow, purple, and gold veins of rock.

On that first trip, I explored Amman on foot. Shepherds crossed the downtown streets with their flocks, herding them from one grassy area to another. They were such an ordinary part of life in Amman that no one honked or lost their patience waiting for the streets to clear; animals and their minders had the right of way. I wandered through the marketplace admiring the beautiful inlaid mother-of-pearl objects — frames, chests, and backgammon boards — as well as the cobalt blue, green, and amber vases known as Hebron glass.

Amman looked classically Mediterranean with its white limestone buildings and villas ranging over and beyond the seven fabled hills that Roman general Ptolemy II Philadelphus had conquered in the third century B.C. In my room in the Inter-Continental Hotel, situated on a hill between two valleys, I lay awake each

19

morning in the predawn stillness, listening to the call to early morning prayers, *Al Fajr*. I was completely captivated by the rhythmic sound of the muezzin calling to the faithful as it echoed off the surrounding hills. Jordan's capital was peaceful and calm, so different from the growing restiveness I had witnessed in the last months of my job in Tehran.

On that fateful day when my father introduced me to King Hussein on the tarmac, a dense cluster of people surrounded the monarch: members of his family, the Royal Court, and government officials, including the CEO of the Jordanian airline, Ali Ghandour, an old friend of my father who had invited us to the ceremony. A lifelong aviator, the King was celebrating an exciting step forward for his beloved airline, which he considered a vital Jordanian link to the world. No doubt he simply longed to head for the cockpit of the country's first 747 and take off. Instead he was surrounded by courtiers, officials, guards, and family members. It was as if an invisible string were holding them all together; when the King moved, the entire group would sway with him.

As I watched, I was struck by the way the King never lost his composure or his smile, despite the overwhelming noise and confusion. For many years I was reminded of that day at the airport by the photograph my father had asked me to take. During my engagement and after I married, I kept it in my office, still in the photo shop's simple paper frame. Sadly, it was lost more than a decade ago, when I asked to have a copy made. I keep hoping that it will fall out of a book or show up in a desk drawer; it is not often that one has a memento of the very first moments spent with someone who would become the most precious part of one's life.

That short stay in Jordan ended with lunch at the King's seaside retreat in Aqaba, which had an appealing simplicity. Instead of living in an imposing vacation palace, the King and his family resided in a relatively modest beach house facing the sea; guests and other family members were housed in a series of small, double-suite bungalows that made up the rest of the royal compound.

The King was traveling at the time but had asked Ali Ghandour to "take my good friend Najeeb to lunch in Aqaba." Over the *mezzah*, an assortment of appetizers including tabouleh, hummus, and marinated vegetables, the conversation veered quickly to politics — to Lebanon and its ongoing bloody civil war. I listened intently, asking many questions, fascinated by the complex political events of the region.

Aqaba was a lovely spot, but our sojourn in Jordan was nearing its end. Soon I would be back in New York, hunting for a job in journalism. I never imagined that I would be returning to Jordan just three months later, nor did I have any inkling of how fateful that return would be. Perhaps I should have taken more seriously a curious prediction made on one of my last evenings in Tehran, just a few months earlier. At the end of a farewell dinner at a restaurant in the city center, an acquaintance at the table had told my fortune in the traditional Middle Eastern way, by reading my coffee cup. He swirled the thick grounds, turned over the cup, flipped it back, and studied the patterns within. "You will return to Arabia," he had predicted. "And you will marry someone highborn, an aristocrat from the land of your ancestors."

chapter two

Roots

I first learned the history of my family when I was six years old in Santa Monica, California. One day, in my parents' bedroom overlooking the ocean, my mother told me about my Swedish and European ancestry on her side of the family and my Arab roots on my father's. I remember sitting there alone after our conversation, staring out the window at the limitless horizon of the ocean. It was as if my world had suddenly expanded. Not only did I have a new sense of identity; I felt connected for the first time to a larger family and a wider world. To my mother's long-standing frustration, I was most intrigued by my Arab roots, but how could my mother's hardworking, hardy forebears compete in my imagination with the dashing brothers Halaby?

My Arab grandfather, Najeeb, and his older brother, Habib, were only twelve and fourteen when they had sailed steerage from Beirut to Ellis Island with their mother, Almas, and younger siblings. They hailed from the Syrian city of Halab, or Aleppo, a great cultural capital and center of learning in the Arab world. My grandfather lived very briefly in the scenic riverside village of Zahle, Lebanon, before joining the family in Beirut for its voyage to the New World. Stored in their oversize carpetbags were oriental rugs, damask fabric, copperware, and jewelry — fine wares from the old country to sell and trade while they adjusted to a new life. The Halaby boys barely spoke English and had no contacts, but they turned out to be as shrewd as they were charming. They took their carpetbags to the summer resort village of Bar Harbor, Maine, where Najeeb met and beguiled Frances Cleveland, the pretty young wife of President Grover Cleveland. The letters of introduction the First Lady gave the young Arab ensured the brothers' initial success.

Habib stayed in New York to work in the import-export business, while Najeeb moved on to Texas in pursuit of oil and cotton money. Darkly handsome, gallant, and exotic in socially conservative Dallas, Najeeb met and married interior decorator Laura Wilkins, the daughter of a local rancher, in 1914. Together they founded Halaby Galleries, which combined his import-export skills with her love of art and decorating. Their business catered to the fashionably rich of Dallas, Houston, and Fort Worth. It was such a huge success that when Stanley Marcus and his partner, Al

Neiman, doubled the size of their department store in downtown Dallas in the mid-1920s, they invited Najeeb and Laura Halaby to rent the top two floors to house the Halaby Galleries. More than half a century ago, that far-sighted troika of Neiman, Marcus, and Halaby created a center for the luxury trade in downtown Dallas.

Perhaps this entrepreneurial instinct was a family trait. Camile, Habib and Najeeb's younger brother, was equally enterprising, though in a less conventional way. While Habib and Najeeb were making their way in the United States, Camile decided to leave Brooklyn for South America. His mother — my father's grandmother, Almas, who barely spoke English — had seen an advertisement in *The New York Times* offering a reward to the person who recovered a sunken dredge full of gold from the Atrato River in the tropical jungles of a remote country called Colombia. The Choco Pacific Gold Mine Company was in dire financial straits due to the accident, and its only hope was to salvage the gold. Speaking not a word of Spanish, Camile arrived in Colombia and gamely made his way into one of the least hospitable rain forests in the world, crossing from the coastal city of Barranquilla through the jungles of the Darien Peninsula. He ended up rescuing the dredge, gaining the reward, and traveling across the Andes to Medellín, where he won the hand of a local beauty. He settled in

25

Colombia and became a successful manufacturer's agent for textile companies, an owner of several textile mills, and co-owner of a boiler factory. He and his family became prominent in Medellín. (Indeed, they have felt the negative repercussions of that prominence quite dramatically; several family members have been kidnapped for ransom, and two were killed by warring Colombian terrorist factions.)

My father, born in Dallas in 1915, was an only child. My grandmother doted on him, and he wanted for nothing. He attended private school and lived in a beautifully appointed house that doubled as a customer showcase for Halaby Galleries. My grandfather, to his credit, never Americanized his family name, as so many immigrants did. He was accepted, nonetheless, and was even invited to join the Dallas Athletic Club despite the many restrictions they placed against the ethnic groups that were flocking to the New World. His only concession to his adopted country, besides taking the nickname Ned, was to allow his wife to convert him from the Greek Orthodoxy of his childhood to the Christian Science faith. From that time onward, my grandfather followed the teachings of Mary Baker Eddy, who emphasized healing through spiritual means. He and my grandmother did not consult doctors and eschewed the use of medicine, which may have contributed to his death at an early age. After waiting for faith to cure what was thought to be a case of strep throat, Najeeb senior was quite weak when he finally went into the hospital, where he developed an infection and died. My father, his son, was only twelve years old.

After her husband's untimely death, Laura Halaby, my paternal grandmother, sold the Halaby Galleries and moved to California. She remarried not long after — this time to an affluent Frenchman from New Orleans. The marriage lasted six or seven years, apparently strained by relations between my father and his stepfather. At least some of the disaffection stemmed from the attention Laura heaped on her son, which made her new husband quite jealous. Indeed, Laura's boy, "Jeeb," did much to make her proud. My father excelled at whatever he tried and lived life with great gusto. He attended Stanford University, where he was captain of the golf team, then went on to Yale Law School. Once he graduated, he became a pioneering aviator, flying the P-38 twin-engine fighters, the Hudson bomber, and the Lockheed Lodestar transport during World War II as a test pilot for Lockheed aviation. As a navy pilot in the Carrier Fighter Test Branch, he would fly more than fifty different types of aircraft, including the first American-built jet.

My father had the temperament so necessary to a test pilot. He was bold, confident in his technical skills, focused, and a risk taker, as well as possessing an aviator's broad perspective and inherent optimism — personality traits

27

he would share with my future husband. One test of my father's character occurred during his stint in the navy, when it fell to him to coax the first primitive jet, the YP-59, up to 46,900 feet, the highest altitude any plane had ever reached. He was so excited to have broken the altitude record that he forgot to check the fuel gauges. Both engines flamed out at 12,000 feet, leaving the plane with no power, no radio, and no way to electronically lower the flaps or landing gear. He had to hand-crank the gear down — exactly 127 turns, he noted later — succeeding with seconds to spare at 100 feet over the runway. He then somehow glided the plane in, for what is known as a dead-stick landing.

Najeeb Halaby met my mother, Doris Carlquist, at a Thanksgiving party in Washington, D.C., in 1945, a few months after the war ended. My mother was tall and blonde, of Swedish descent, and came, as my father did, from the West Coast. They seemed perfectly suited. Both had come east to join the war effort, he as a test pilot, she as an administrative assistant first in the Office of Price Administration, then in the State Department's German-Austrian Occupied Affairs Branch. They quickly discovered they shared an interest in politics. "For the first time I had found a quick and witty girl who enjoyed this give-and-take debating as much as I did," Najeeb observed later. And they were both idealistic. "Like me, she had stars in her eyes about peace and international understanding," he said. They were married three months later.

Married life must have been difficult for my mother. My father was an unapologetic workaholic and was rarely at home. After the war he had joined the office of Research and Intelligence, a new branch of the State Department. He spent the second summer of their marriage in Saudi Arabia, as civil aviation adviser to King Saud Bin Abdul Aziz. When Najeeb returned to Washington, he successfully urged the State Department to increase American military aid and technical assistance to the oil-rich nation.

Other governmental departments were being revamped after the war, including the military. When the Defense Department came into being in 1947, unifying the various competitive military branches, my father left the State Department for the Pentagon to work for the first Secretary of Defense, James Forrestal. After Forrestal's tenure came to an end, my father continued at Defense, helping to organize NATO under Truman and becoming deputy assistant secretary of defense for international security affairs under President Eisenhower. By the time I was born in August 1951, however, he was weary of government service. Money was becoming an issue, and he began to eye the private sector. He met Laurance Rockefeller at a naval reserve officers' dinner in 1953. The largest shareholder in Eastern Airlines, Rockefeller offered my father a job, and that year we moved to New York.

My childhood memories begin around this time. My brother, Christian, was born in 1953, and my sister, Alexa, in 1955. My nursery school was a few blocks from our apartment on East 73rd Street in Manhattan. In that dark, crowded, overheated schoolroom, I was agonizingly torn between competing instincts to join in or maintain a solitary independence from the group. I can never remember not being shy. As a child, I would make myself scarce when my parents' guests would come to our house and I knew I would be expected to exchange pleasantries with them. I had a small number of friends, but we were close, which was what mattered to me.

We moved often during my childhood, and the constant change reinforced my natural reserve. Every few years I would have to adjust to a new, strange home and new friends, as well as new schools, neighborhoods, and cities. Time and again I would find myself on the outside looking in — watching, studying, learning — having to familiarize myself with unfamiliar people and communities.

My father viewed me as "aloof," and my mother, concerned about what she considered my loner temperament, turned to a child psychologist for advice. The psychologist told my mother I would grow out of it, but in truth I

30

never did. To this day, I am most comfortable when a conversation has an intellectual focus. Perhaps this helps explain why I have always felt particularly inept at and impatient with small talk, intrigues, and gossip.

Part of this social awkwardness no doubt stems from a sense of inadequacy, rooted in considerable part in my relationship with my father. He sought perfection and never seemed satisfied. I felt I could never measure up, and as I was the eldest, his expectations for me were the most pronounced. I will never forget one incident in grade school concerning my eyesight, which was extremely poor, though no vision problem had yet been diagnosed. When I could not see the writing on my classroom chalkboard even from the first row, my mother took me to an optician. Back home after the visit, my mother explained to my father how truly weak my sight was. He did not believe it at first — or did not want to believe it. He held up a copy of *Time* magazine and asked me to read it. He held it quite close, but I could not read even the headlines. He still refused to believe I needed eyeglasses. How could one of his children be so flawed?

My father learned a great deal about the aviation business working for the Rockefeller brothers, immersing himself in the corporate financing of airlines and the municipal funding of airports, setting up a task force to reorganize

31

and modernize the country's rapidly growing airways and airport systems. When political infighting kept him from being appointed head of the Civil Aeronautics Association, he decided to leave the Rockefellers. Shortly thereafter he became executive vice president of an electronic subsystems manufacturer, Servo-Mechanisms, Inc., with offices in Long Island and Los Angeles.

I was five when we moved back to California, supposedly for the summer. My mother says the move was particularly traumatic for me, but I suspect those may have been her own feelings about leaving the East Coast, as I have only happy memories of those years. I loved being outdoors, and I learned to swim in the pool of that first house we rented in Brentwood. The house, which had belonged to the actress Angela Lansbury, had a wonderful garden full of orange and lemon trees. To this day I remember its rich citrus smells, the exuberant bougainvillea vines, and the stately palm trees.

We moved to another house in the fall, and then a few months later to an enchanting old Victorian situated on the edge of a Santa Monica bluff overlooking the Pacific. With an expansive, tumbledown garden bordered at the end by a row of dilapidated pigeon cages, it was a wonderful house to grow up in: eccentric and full of character, like an old Maine summer hotel. It had, with its high ceilings, an atrium filled with plants, a billiard room, a porch with a huge swing, and a spacious, romantic attic in which my father, in a burst of domestic energy, assembled a puppet theater swathed in tiny lights, where we spent many happy hours entertaining family and friends.

I contentedly played alone in a vacant lot next to the house, digging in the soil and collecting rocks. I loved to read books under my favorite magnolia tree. It was here, in a little alley near the house, that my father taught me to ride a bicycle. I had to learn quickly, as he had little patience. Perhaps the house's most winning attribute was its proximity to the Pacific Ocean, which I could hear so clearly as it thundered outside my bedroom window, lulling me to sleep, a constant, comforting companion. My preferred refuge was the ocean. I spent hours riding the waves off Santa Monica, often with a favorite raft. The ocean was both freedom and challenge for me, and I was blissfully happy just being out there on my own.

Whenever we moved, my paternal grandmother, Laura, would move with us, in order to be close to her son and his family. Opinionated and flamboyant, she was an integral part of my early memories of Santa Monica. Often, after classes at the Westlake School, I would walk the short distance to her home and immerse myself in her world, at once artistic and unconventional. With her Art Deco jewelry, loose flowing dresses, and intriguing art and memorabilia, she was the most original person I had ever met. She was also a dedicated Christian Scientist, and I was influenced by her to believe in the power of positive thinking — that an optimistic outlook in life can create positive outcomes, not just for oneself, but for others, too. I was still very young, nine or ten at the time, but the two of us would engage in long philosophical discussions about how to live a meaningful and worthy life.

As the oldest child I had to find my own way; nearer in age to each other, my brother and sister shared a room and seemed very close and companionable. I was sleepless for what seemed like hours and hours every night, intensely conscious of my isolation, the only creature still stirring in a peacefully slumbering house. Restlessness drew me to my father's library, where I would spend hours poring through his eclectic collection of books. I particularly remember Khalil Gibran and Nevil Shute, the classics, and the infinitely fascinating *Encyclopaedia Britannica*. I would flip through copies of *National Geographic* and gaze longingly at the globe that helped me chart my parents' international trips.

One day in Santa Monica I decided to run away from home, certain that at age nine I was now perfectly capable of looking after myself in the larger world. I dragged a sheet off my bed and piled all my most precious possessions into it, at the last minute adding my entire collection of Nancy Drew books and an alarm clock to the mix. After hauling this unwieldy cargo down the long winding staircase, across the entrance hall, and out the front door, I paused on the front porch to consider my options. It was a balmy summer evening, with the ocean undulating in the distance while the bright ball of the sun gradually dropped beyond the horizon. I so loved that view that I was lulled into a reverie. Suddenly it was dark. I never made it any farther. My sister loves to tease me about my failed odyssey, saying that several years later when she attempted the same escape she at least made it beyond the front porch and across the street.

We left California when I was ten, to return to Washington, D.C. John F. Kennedy had been elected President in 1960, and my father had been approached soon afterward by two of his former colleagues at Yale Law School — Sargent Shriver, Kennedy's brother-in-law, and Adam Yarmolinsky, a Kennedy talent scout — to take over the Federal Aviation Administration. My father was flattered but reluctant to accept the government post. He had left Servo-Mechanisms to start his own technology company in Los Angeles and was also practicing law. He was finally making good money and was not in a rush to return to the relative penury of public service. It took a private meeting in Washington with the President-elect, the day before he was inaugurated on

January 20, 1961, to convince my father to accept the stewardship of the FAA and to become Kennedy's presidential aviation adviser.

My brother, sister, and I were not at President Kennedy's inauguration on that freezing, snowy day in Washington. We watched it on television in sunny California and saw our parents seated close behind the windblown podium where Kennedy took the oath of office. Nor were we in Washington for my father's Senate confirmation hearings, or for his swearing-in ceremony in the Oval Office on March 3 as only the second administrator of the FAA. He could not afford to bring us to Washington. Overnight his income had dropped by two-thirds, and the federal government did not contribute to the cost of relocation. So, to my great relief, we remained at home in California for the rest of the school year and the summer.

My first inkling of my father's prominence in the Kennedy administration came at a farewell party for him at the Ambassador Hotel in Los Angeles. A helicopter was sent to take us to the lawn at the Ambassador, then on to see my father preside over the ceremonial opening of the new Los Angeles International Airport. I loved my first helicopter ride, which was fortuitous given the integral role helicopters would play in my future. I was less enthusiastic about the ceremonial role I had to play at the airport. It had been decided that I would have the honor of teaming up with Vice President Lyndon

Johnson onstage at the airport to unveil the commemorative plaque. I was almost paralyzed by stage fright, but I did it and was complimented afterward by a sweetly supportive Lady Bird Johnson.

Once in Washington I had further adjustments to make. I had coasted through school in California, but now I was finding the educational system much more rigorous. I was also tall for my age, scrawny and awkward, and dependent on Coke-bottle-thick glasses. I missed California, the sunshine, the ocean, the pungent smell of fresh citrus, the majestic, quirky character of the palms, and the freedom of being outdoors all year round.

Fortunately, my grandmother's home, a farm in nearby Centreville, Virginia, provided a peaceful retreat. I already loved horses and spent hours exploring the countryside on a small pony with my grandmother's German shepherd tagging along behind. It was not far from my grandmother's property that I had my first startling exposure to poverty when I came upon a cluster of dilapidated shacks on the edge of a farming community. I felt absolute shock, fear, and then utter helplessness and guilt as I was confronted by the blank, hopeless stares of migrant children and their families seeking shade from the pitiless noonday sun.

As we children reached adolescence my parents insisted on sending us to private schools. This decision created a further financial burden, but my parents were adamant, and I was sent to the National Cathedral School for Girls. A number of my classmates at NCS were also daughters of transplanted members of the Kennedy administration, and we naturally gravitated to each other, newcomers all. Grace Vance, whose father, Cyrus, the new Secretary of the Army, had attended Yale Law School with my father, became a close friend, as did Carinthia West, whose father, the distinguished general Sir Michael West, was the British representative to NATO in Washington, and Mo Orrick, whose father was an assistant attorney general. Like young girls everywhere we were captivated by the Beatles, the Beach Boys, and other rock and roll groups, but some of us, because of our parents, were even more interested in national politics and the world scene.

The Peace Corps topped the list of career goals in my diary of those Washington years, and there were times, in spite of my friendships at NCS, when I longed to leave the privileged environment of my private girls school for a less rarefied milieu. I urged my parents to allow me to attend Western High, a public school in Washington where I knew I would not be so insulated from the social and economic realities of the world, but to no avail.

I became aware of racism for the first time. Federal laws prohibited racial discrimination in public schools and universities, but several southern states were either ignoring or defying those laws. The new Kennedy administration's commitment to social justice encouraged civil rights leaders, among them Dr. Martin Luther King, Jr., to press for the enforcement of existing legislation and for sweeping new laws to eradicate racial discrimination once and for all. The powerful television images of African Americans — or Negroes, as they were called then — were having a profound impact on me and on many of my classmates. We saw policemen beating protesters for peacefully trying to assert their legal right to vote, to attend school, or even to sit in the front section of a public bus.

I will never forget watching the television news with my grandmother in the fall of 1962 when James Meredith, a young black man, tried to enroll at the University of Mississippi. He had to be escorted through a jeering crowd and up the steps by federal agents and, even so, was turned away time and again by police and state officials. Martin Luther King came on the screen, commenting on the mistreatment of Meredith. Filled with admiration, I said, "Isn't he wonderful?" My grandmother agreed, but it quickly became apparent that she was praising George Wallace, the racist governor of Alabama, who had spoken about the event a few minutes earlier, and the realization triggered an excruciating argument. I stormed off to my room and buried myself in a book until I left the next day. I thought that I would never be able to forgive her, and in some ways our relationship was never quite the same.

A small group of my friends and I supported the civil rights movement through the Student Nonviolent Coordinating Committee (SNCC), which had been founded in 1960 to coordinate student "sit-ins" at segregated lunch counters throughout the South to force their integration. The sit-ins had started informally when four black students in Greensboro, North Carolina, had gone to an F. W. Woolworth store to buy school supplies; when they sat down at the store's segregated lunch counter to eat, they were refused service. More black students returned to Woolworth's the next day, accompanied by a reporter, and soon sit-ins were launched at segregated lunch counters all over the South. By the time I joined SNCC in 1961, the student movement had grown to more than 70,000 participants and had broadened its segregated targets to include public parks, public rest rooms, movie theaters, libraries — anyplace where people assembled. We wore our SNCC pins with pride, marched, and joined protests, adding our youthful voices to the larger call to action. We sang "We Shall Overcome," and we meant it. Images of police dogs attacking children and powerful water cannons knocking them off their feet were viewed constantly on television sets across the country, and before long President Kennedy announced that he was sending sweeping civil rights legislation to Congress. We were so young, yet we felt responsible for contributing our voices and energies to the call for social justice. I vividly remember the massive civil rights march in Washington and the rally at the Lincoln Memorial in August 1963, five days after my twelfth birthday. I could not understand why everyone in the city was not marching that day, or why they were not as inspired by Martin Luther King's "I Have a Dream" speech as I was.

Life in Washington was not just about politics. Horseback riding was my other passion, and, instinctively perhaps, I formed a special bond with a magnificent Arabian stallion, Blackjack. I felt particularly capable and at peace with the world when I was on horseback, and I competed whenever possible in regional equestrian events. When my instructor suggested I was ready to compete nationally, I was filled with pride and determined to commit completely to the sport.

I also loved singing. My chorus teacher encouraged me to take private lessons, giving me the impression that I had a special talent, but in retrospect I realize that her suggestion was probably rooted in a desire to save her ears and the reputation of our school choir. For financial reasons my parents said no to voice and violin lessons, which my mother wisely anticipated would torture the entire household.

I discovered the pleasures of flying as well. A few times during those years my father took me with him on working visits to small-town airports around the country in a small plane. He let me take over the plane's basic navigational controls and work the radio, acting as his copilot. During those rare moments my father and I were in perfect harmony.

My father was rarely home during the four years he ran the FAA, and when he was home he was often distracted. One of my most significant memories was of a conversation we had one sunny Sunday morning in the small garden of our Washington home, when my father seemed particularly distressed. I asked what was troubling him, and he explained that he was struggling under a terrible burden of debt and yet was happier and more fulfilled in public service than in any more lucrative career. I remember being both frightened by his uncharacteristic vulnerability and extremely proud of him. The conversation, perhaps our first adult exchange, had a profound impact on my thinking, my dreams for the future, and my appreciation for sacrifices made for a larger purpose.

We were all raised to be independent, perhaps to a fault. My father now says, looking back, that he and my mother probably encouraged us to be too individualistic, islands unto ourselves rather than part of a whole. Perhaps we reflected the growing and irreparable gulf that was dividing our parents. The constant tension between them permeated the household. My father says now that he and my mother differed in "terms of faith and intellectual beliefs and philosophy," and he has questioned whether they should have had children at all. But they did, and from an early age we all had to deal with the palpable conflict between them. I protected myself as much as possible from the turbulence in their marriage, trying very hard to distance myself from them emotionally.

My father also attributed the seeds of marital disharmony to the very different life experiences my parents had as children, which led to their different expectations as adults. My father considered himself far better educated than my mother, whose father had been in the brokerage business in Spokane, Washington, in 1929 when the stock market crashed, and he had never recovered. Her mother, May Ethel Ackroyd Carlquist, had died when Doris was fifteen. A few years later, she was forced to drop out of college for financial reasons, and instead of living with her father, my mother was passed from relative to relative. Her father had encouraged Doris and her two siblings to be self-sufficient, and my mother had strong professional goals, yet when she married my father she gave up her job, as was customary then for married women. Once her children were out of grade school she dedicated herself to community service, working for a New York settlement house in East Harlem. She also volun-teered with public television as well as with a number of organizations promoting U.S.–Arab relations, social welfare in the Middle East, and support for Palestinian refugees, commitments she honors to this day.

For all the tension in my parents' marriage, my mother was very fond of the Arab side of the family. Though she had never met Najeeb, Sr., she did meet his brother, Camile, who sent her white orchids from his farm in Colombia when she married my father. (I would carry orchids from Camile's farm at my wedding as well.) My mother wanted to name me Camille in his honor, but my great-uncle protested. Like many immigrants to the Americas, he felt pressure to assimilate as thoroughly as possible and to de-emphasize his Arab roots. He wanted my parents to name me Mary Jane. They compromised by giving me a name that I never identified with, Lisa. Once I heard that story, I always thought of myself as Camille.

As much as I loved and admired my father, we had an extremely difficult relationship. I realized at a fairly early age that the frustrations my father took out on his family stemmed from the impossible standards he set for himself. He had clear goals at the FAA, but he was plagued by partisan infighting as he tried to achieve them. He was also beset with financial problems, a troubled marriage, and the added pressure of being an oddity in WASP Washington. I remember a quiz in one of the local papers asking, "What is a Najeeb Elias Halaby: animal, vegetable, or mineral?"

My father's dissatisfaction was a reflection of his unrelenting drive to prove himself. During one particularly intense episode at home I looked up at his face, glowing with rage, and I realized with absolute clarity: This does not have to do with me; this has to do with him. "He is so frustrated that he needs to get it out of his system," I thought to myself. My sister developed a strategy of accommodation, whereas I had a completely different approach: "Take me or leave me as I am." Although I may have seemed defiant, I wanted desperately to be accepted for who I was, on my own merit.

In an interview many years later, I would describe my family as a typical late-twentieth-century, moderately dysfunctional American family, and I believed that to be an honest and diplomatic description. However, my mother was very upset when she read those words. Maintaining the myth of the ideal family was very important to her generation, which is precisely what kept my parents together for far longer than made any sense. I remember as a teenager begging them to divorce for their own sakes — not what most children want their parents to do — but they remained miserably imprisoned by convention until they finally dissolved their marriage in 1974. Ironically, their divorce eventually freed them to rediscover what they had initially so appreciated in each other, and they have become great friends and confidants over the years.

On November 22, 1963, while crossing Woodley Road with my classmates on our way to the athletic field, I heard a devastating report from Dallas, Texas, on the crossing guard's radio. President Kennedy's motorcade had come under fire, and there were concerns that the occupants of his car might have been hit. The news moved like wildfire through the school. When the National Cathedral's bells began to toll their tragic message later in the day, we were devastated. It was inconceivable that our dashing young President could have been in harm's way. The Secret Service whisked away Vice President Johnson's daughters, and the daughters of Kennedy appointees were called into the headmistress's office to be reassured.

President Kennedy's death shattered my world. My father, indeed everyone I knew, was inspired by the President's ideals, his energy, and his ability to attract exceptional talent. His assassination was a crushing blow, especially after such a heady period of optimism and hope. My father continued to head the FAA under the new President, Lyndon Johnson, who had many good qualities — I especially admired his ardent defense of civil rights and his commitment to wage the "War Against Poverty" — but his forcefulness was less appealing when he consistently rebuffed my father's many requests to return to the private sector. My father finally prevailed and moved us to New York in 1965. Heavily in debt after four years at the FAA, he accepted an offer from Juan Trippe, the founder and CEO of Pan American World Airways, to take over Pan Am.

Another new school. Another new environment. I was fourteen and miserable. Moving to New York meant I was deprived of my treasured horseback riding. On top of all this disappointment and insecurity, my first months in the city were haunted by an unusual menace — a young man, an American University student once employed by my mother in Washington as a part-time babysitter, was harassing me with a series of disturbing letters. I was terrified. He wrote that he was watching me, that he was going to visit me and take me away. In those first months in New York, I was certain he was stalking me. I was afraid to leave the apartment building, and when I did, I felt even worse. I finally confided in my mother, who alerted the authorities. The young man was eventually institutionalized, but it would be some time before I could relax.

It was around this time that I went on a classical studies tour of Greece. My Mediterranean Arab instincts surfaced in the marketplaces, where I learned the art of bargaining over every price. On my return to New York, I reflexively continued to use the same approach when making a purchase at Bloomingdale's, to the clerk's total befuddlement. It was not easy to suppress the Halaby brothers' entrepreneurial genes.

In New York my parents insisted on sending me to the one school we visited that I had said I did *not* want to attend: Chapin, an elite private school for girls. My mother and my father were concerned about negative peer pressure and wanted to protect me from the social upheaval of the times. I had no plans to become a flower child and run away to San Francisco, but I was increasingly vocal about my opposition to America's military involvement in Vietnam.

From the beginning Vietnam was different from other wars: It was televised, bringing the wrenching images of war into our student dormitories and people's living rooms; also, its goals were ambiguous, offering little justification, many of us thought, for becoming involved in a civil war thousands of miles away in Southeast Asia. Americans divided quickly into two camps: hawks, who supported military action and saw it as essential to limiting the spread of Communism, and doves, who supported the withdrawal of U.S. troops from Vietnam. Indeed, many students felt U.S. intervention into Vietnam's internal affairs was immoral in light of the corruption and unpopularity of the Vietnamese government;

others were protesting the draft, the use of violence against civilians, and the mounting body count of American soldiers. Yet the military buildup continued. By the end of 1965, the nearly continuous bombing raids over North Vietnam were under way, and there were more than 200,000 U.S. troops in Vietnam.

It was a heady time to be young in America, but not at my school in New York. The world was held at arm's length at Chapin, with no student involvement in the debate over Vietnam or the civil rights movement or, indeed, anything that smacked of dissent. Instead, there were rules and regulations about everything, starting with the school uniform. Chapin girls had only just stopped wearing gloves to school but were still required to wear hats, and in the era of miniskirts, the skirts of our uniforms had to touch the floor when we kneeled. After the stimulating and politically charged environment my friends and I had enjoyed in Washington, Chapin felt like a straitjacket. I deeply resented my parents' unilateral decision to send me there.

Nor was my independent spirit appreciated by school authorities. My election to class office was vetoed by the Chapin administration because I was considered "apathetic and negligent." They might have felt I posed a threat to their well-ordered, meticulously controlled environment. Perhaps I did. Being viewed as a less-than-desirable Chapin student was a distinction I shared with a far more illustrious Chapin rebel, Jacqueline Bouvier, who had attended some twenty years earlier.

To the school's credit, it offered a community service program tutoring non-English-speaking students in a public school in Harlem, and I volunteered to serve. It was a humbling experience. Initially I was frustrated by my inability to make any meaningful progress with the students, many of whom had serious learning disabilities and needed far more support than I or anyone available to them would ever be able to provide. I eventually made some headway, but the most important lesson I took away from the experience was just how difficult it is to break the vicious cycle of ignorance and poverty. Years later I chose to focus my senior architecture and urban planning thesis at Princeton on a community redevelopment scheme in Harlem.

While I struggled at school, my father was having his own difficulties at Pan Am. Juan Trippe was very farsighted — he was the first airline executive to add Boeing 707 and 747 jets to his fleet — but he was also grandiose. He ordered no fewer than twenty-five of the first 747s, which were too heavy for their engines, and approved several extravagantly expensive construction projects. Moreover, for all his promises that he would step aside and make my father CEO of the airline, Trippe continued to rule the company for another four years. When he finally retired, he made my father president but handed the chairmanship of the financially strapped airline to another man.

For all my father's challenges as second in command at Pan Am, there were substantial benefits to us. Since we traveled Pan Am routes for free, during holidays we went wherever Pan Am flew; skiing was more economical for us in Austria or Switzerland, as was studying the Greek language in Greece and French in France. That part of our family life was heaven, but the tension at home was becoming more pronounced. Looking back however, I realize that circumstances at home — my father's unrelenting perfectionism and my mother's courageous if painful struggle for family peace — strengthened me and taught me self-reliance. And I would draw inspiration from their dedication to public service, for the rest of my life.

After years of lobbying my parents to attend boarding school, I finally succeeded in attending Concord Academy, in Concord, Massachusetts, for my remaining two years of high school. The school was one of the most academically prestigious in the country, and I had been particularly impressed in a meeting with the headmaster when he explained that students were disciplined for missing or being late to classes or meals by having to chop the wood that helped heat the dorms in winter — a healthy contrast, I thought, with Chapin's controlling atmosphere. I felt very fortunate to be at Concord Academy. My classmates were a brilliant group of strong, motivated young women. Academic life was extremely stimulating, and expectations were high, but more important to me, the school placed a high premium on individualism and personal responsibility.

It was on a whim that I applied to Princeton University in my senior year at Concord. For years I had planned to return to the West Coast for university, and I particularly loved the campus at Stanford University. Princeton was debating opening its doors to women for the first time in its 222-year history and had indicated they might consider applications for the class of 1973. My college adviser was very enthusiastic and urged me to apply. I did, for a lark; I was going to Stanford if they accepted me. Princeton, traditional and conservative, did not fit my notion of an ideal university, especially during this period of social change and political turmoil.

In the hot competition for places at top-rated universities I did not feel particularly distinguished, although I had good test scores, played several varsity sports, and was captain of my field hockey team. Compared to my talented classmates I was unremarkable, so when my letter of acceptance arrived from Stanford, I was thrilled. I was also one of 150 women, along with my good friend and classmate

Marion Freeman, whom Princeton accepted for its historic first coed class. I was suddenly torn. Part of me was drawn to the unprecedented Princeton challenge, but I was also longing to return to California. I agonized until the last minute of the deadline for postmarking our replies. I stood at a mailbox on a deserted New York City street weighing my options and finally mailed my acceptance to New Jersey, thinking I could always transfer after two experimental years.

That fall, Princeton's first class of women arrived on campus with little sense of what to expect. We found ourselves isolated in a dormitory, Pyne Hall, on the edge of the campus. We were definitely in an awkward situation, one woman to every twenty-two men, males whose previous experience with women on campus was as weekend attractions. We were not dates; we were not made up; we were just going to class at eight in the morning.

Marion and I would room next to each other during our sophomore year and become very close friends. We remain so to this day. Unfortunately, the reserve I had acquired in nursery school to cope with my social awkwardness led to all sorts of misconceptions. One upperclassman told me that at first he had thought of me as a "New York snob," while another labeled me "haughty" and an "ice princess." It did not help that, in a flurry of publicity, my father was finally named the new CEO and president of Pan Am soon after the fall term began, further cementing my "unapproachable" image. One day I was confronted by a couple of upperclassmen who taunted me about my Arab background, one more reason I spent so many Saturday nights of my freshman year alone, reading in my room.

In the midst of all this, my mother began calling me, desperately trying to persuade me to make my society debut in New York that winter. I found the whole idea absurd. The archaic "coming out" party tradition to introduce young women to society, and thus, presumably, to establish their eligibility for marriage, was anathema to me. I sensed that she was being pressured by my father's continuing need to be accepted and assimilated, and by the social priorities of her own New York friends, whose daughters were no doubt being far more accommodating than I.

The Vietnam War was of far greater concern to me at that time than my social eligibility. Antiwar sentiment was in full cry at college campuses across the country, and Princeton was no exception. With the body count of U.S. and Vietnamese casualties mounting daily and a campus filled with draft-age young men, a debutante party seemed not only frivolous and embarrassing, but totally inappropriate. I could not fathom my parents' insensitivity. One day, while my mother sobbed her pleas to me over the phone, I finally relented but declared I would attend only one group event. I understood that my "coming out" party was not about me but about them.

A month after I started at Princeton, 250,000 people, the largest gathering yet, marched on Washington to protest the war. In solidarity, the entire campus observed Vietnam Moratorium Day and fasted while the headline of *The Princetonian* bannered: "Stop the War." The disclosure of America's secret intervention in Cambodia in the spring of 1970 triggered intense campus protests all over the country, including Kent State University, where protesting students were fired on by the Ohio National Guard. Four were killed and nine injured. The TV and newspaper images remain seared in my memory, especially the photograph of a young woman, Mary Ann Vecchio, kneeling by the dead body of a student, her arms outstretched in shock and her face contorted by the screams anyone looking at the photograph could hear.

The outrage was immediate. Violent protests against the Kent State killings erupted across America. The entire Princeton campus went on strike, and exams were canceled. During a protest at the Institute of Defense Analyses we were teargassed by anti-riot police.

It was a seminal moment in shaping my view of American society. While I loved my country, I found my trust in its institutions badly shaken. The war in Vietnam and the rapidity of the social and political changes sweeping the country had simply engulfed us. Many students were dropping out of school or taking leaves of absence at the time to examine and re-sort their priorities. I certainly did not feel I was getting as much out of university as I wanted to, and I did not want to waste the time I was there, so after three distracted semesters I decided to take a year's leave of absence to clear my head. In the winter of 1971 I went to Colorado, thinking I could easily find a job to support myself in a winter resort town. I arrived during a major winter storm and woke up on the floor of a trailer where I had been offered refuge during the blizzard.

My father was furious. He flew to Aspen, where I had found a job cleaning hotel rooms, to accuse me of "running away." But the opposite was true. I needed time and space to set my own priorities and to discover if I could survive on my own. However disappointed my father might have been, a sentiment he expressed in no uncertain terms, I knew the sabbatical was the right thing for me.

I worked as a maid, as a waitress in a pizza parlor, and as a part-time gofer at the Aspen Institute, making enough money to eat and pay my share of the rent in a house I was sharing with other young women. I attended my first Institute conference on "Technological Change and Social Responsibility," which featured the wisdom and expertise of the amazing inventor-architect-genius Buckminster Fuller. And I worked on an innovative architectural project, for an environmental school. Once again, I felt I was intellectually engaged.

I went back to Princeton after a year in Colorado and elected to major in architecture and urban planning. My course of study was an eclectic one, combining history, anthropology, sociology, psychology, religion, arts, physics, and engineering. I loved it. It was a captivating, multidisciplinary approach to understanding and addressing the most basic needs of individuals and communities. Architecture studies also provided me with some very practical skills — a reduced need for sleep, and practice in thinking on my feet when faced with merciless critiques of my work. Both of these would prove very useful in later life.

My father's job at Pan Am was about to end. He had lobbied the members of the Civil Aeronautics Board in Washington for a fair shake for the company, but Richard Nixon, a Republican, was President, and my father, a registered Democrat, could make no headway. Nixon's staff was so partisan that my father was even included in John Dean's White House "enemies list," effectively killing any chance of federal support for Pan Am. (A few months later that paranoia would prove to be Nixon's undoing, as news of the Watergate scandal broke.) Mergers were a possible solution, but for various reasons none came to fruition. There were personnel problems, issues with the board of directors, differences with the top executives, and Pan Am's mounting debt. Finally it was over. On March 22, 1972, the board asked for — and received — my father's resignation.

My father observed later that Alexa, Chris, and I "seemed genuinely pleased" that he was no longer a "big business tycoon." "Whether that meant they wanted to see more of me or that they were embarrassed by trying to explain away Pan Am to their friends, I do not know," he said. I cannot speak for my sister or brother, but it was clear to me that he was far less suited to the cutthroat ways of the business world than he was to his first love — public and international service.

Soon after my father stepped down from Pan Am, the president of Jordan's national airline, Ali Ghandour, invited my parents to visit that country in the spring of 1973. Because my father seemed so tired, Ghandour arranged for my parents to spend a few days by the sea at the royal compound in Aqaba, and it was there that they met King Hussein. The two men hit it off immediately. The King, then thirty-eight, told my father about his plans for expanding civil aviation in Jordan and asked him to act as an adviser. My father readily agreed. For the rest of their time in Jordan, my parents toured the ancient land's remarkable archaeological sites in the King's helicopter.

During my spring break from Princeton, I heard all about my parents' trip, especially their audience with King Hussein. My mother was enchanted by him and showed me a brooch he had given her, fashioned in the shape of a peacock and set with four small stones: sapphire, emerald, ruby, and diamond. He had chosen the different-colored stones, he had told her, because he did not know whether she would be a blonde, a brunette, or a redhead. So it was my mother who first brought King Hussein into my life, and in a very appealing way. "He has," she said, "the most beautiful, kind eyes."

chapter three

Tehran Journal

When I graduated from Princeton in 1974, I decided to take advantage of the Pan Am travel privileges extended to our family and to travel and work abroad in regions of special interest to me. I began in Australia, having been offered a job in the Sydney office of the British planning firm Llewelyn-Davis, but a significant revision of the country's immigration law coincided with my arrival and I was denied a work permit. In an amazing instance of serendipity, while considering my next steps, I happened to run into an old car-pool companion from my elementary school in California one day in Sydney. She was leaving her position at another architectural firm, which had projects in the Middle East. My Arab-American background uniquely qualified me to work on these projects from their Sydney office, making me eligible for the elusive Australian work visa.

After a year working in Australia, I attended an Aspen Institute symposium in Persepolis, near the ancient Persian capital of Shiraz, which was built some 2,500 years ago by King Darius the Great and finished by his son Xerxes. In Persepolis, the ruins came to life in a *son et lumière* show with a narrative about the accomplishments of the early Persian kings who extended the borders of the Persian Empire into Europe and India, built a canal between the Nile and the Red Sea and a network of roads that are still being used today, and even established a postal system. The sound and light show was a beautifully effective blend of music, poetry, and imagery that sent shivers down my spine. I could never have imagined at the time that I would be involved in later efforts to achieve a similar atmospheric and powerful dramatization of history in a sound and light presentation in the Jordanian city of Jerash. At that Aspen Institute conference I met for the first time Empress Farah Diba of Iran, who a few years later would become a dear and respected friend, though at the time our two worlds could not have appeared further apart. The Shahbanou hosted the final evening's banquet, held in grand tents erected five years earlier for the celebration honoring the 2,500th anniversary of the Persian Empire, which had been the largest gathering of heads of state in history.

At the end of the conference, I was offered a fascinating opportunity to join Llewelyn-Davis in Iran. The firm had been hired by the Shah, Reza Pahlavi, to build a model city center on 1,600 acres in north Tehran. Shahestan Pahlavi ("town of the Shah Pahlavi") was an enormously ambitious undertaking and a personal interest of the Shah's. The project was an urban planner's fantasy.

The new city center, with its views of the snowcapped Alborz mountain range, was to feature pedestrian malls, theaters, moving sidewalks, shopping galleries, shaded arcades, and terraced gardens. Government ministry buildings and foreign embassies would rim one of the largest open public spaces in the world, to be called Shah and Nation Square. The scale was monumental: Shah and Nation Square was designed to be larger than Red Square in Moscow, and the Shahanshah Boulevard, the broad, tree-lined avenue through the project's center, was intended to emulate the Champs-Elysées in Paris. My work as a planning assistant entailed surveying and mapping all the buildings in the vast area surrounding the site.

When the Shah initiated the model city scheme, he was inspired by Shah Abbas the Great, a Persian leader and patron of the arts in the sixteenth and seventeenth centuries. Shah Abbas had transformed Esfahan, the former capital of Persia, into one of the world's great cities, with innovative architecture and a sweeping use of space. Located in the center of Iran, it is an island of green amid the vast desert plains, with magnificent buildings, like the Sheikh Lutfullah mosque and the Chehel Sotoon palace, and graced with wide boulevards, an abundance of bridges, and lush aromatic gardens. When I think of Esfahan, I see the intricately designed blue ceramic tiles that decorate so many of its buildings and the ubiquitous tearooms where Iranians would sit for hours, chatting and smoking water pipes.

I arrived in Tehran in the fall of 1975. There were about twenty of us working on the project, living in a cluster of apartments near the site. At twenty-four, I was the youngest of the group and the only woman. Many of my colleagues treated me like a little sister, making brotherly attempts to sophisticate me, encouraging me to use makeup and make more of an effort with my loose, flowing hair. Iranian women living in the city, like their Arab counterparts, tended to be elaborately formal in their appearance, jewelry, and dress. I possessed neither makeup nor jewels, only the bare necessities of an easily packed working wardrobe and jeans, having always assumed that character and professional merit would serve me better than my appearance. Nonetheless I longingly admired the striking, filmy chadors of delicately printed chiffon and other fabrics that enveloped Iranian women of all ages and backgrounds as they moved about in public. I would happily have adopted that style of dress — so intensely feminine and mysteriously modest at the same time.

I loved walking in Tehran, wandering through the tangled maze of the bazaar and down Qajar Street, a pedestrian's delight of magnificent oriental carpets and wall hangings. Nearby, modern buses and automobiles vied for space with donkey carts. It was hard to describe Iran to my friends back in the United States because it defied easy categorization. Under those gossamer chadors, hip young women wore bellbottom jeans and platform shoes. When I traveled up to the vast Shahestan Pahlavi site, I passed by the palatial homes of Tehran's new rich, but in the south of the city I could barely breathe due to air pollution from refineries situated in the middle of neighborhoods where Iran's growing number of poor people lived. The treatment of women was nuanced as well. I never felt pressured or intimidated when traveling alone or moving from one place to another, but I was often stared at strangely, especially if I went to a restaurant alone for a meal. Near the end of my stay, when most of our team had relocated to London, I would go out alone to eat quite often. Those were not easy moments — the embarrassed maitre d' did not quite know what to do when I showed up, and inevitably seated me off in an obscure corner.

My journal from those days describes my feeling that the country seemed to have a split personality. On the one hand, it was very

Western and cosmopolitan, with a large, well-educated middle class, and on the other, it retained an exotic, Middle Eastern flavor and a dynamic folk culture. It was in Iran that I sensed with even greater intensity what had struck me in visits to Mexico and Central America in the early 1970s — the vitality of a country expressed through its handicrafts. Persian carpets are the best-known example, but it was the intricate, finely detailed paintings on lacquered wood, delicate silver boxes with fine enameling, and drawings of historic scenes that captured my imagination. I learned that the Shah's wife, Empress Farah, had supported the handicrafts industry as a way of raising the living standards of the poor. Years later I would recall the Shahbanou's success when I initiated a project to revive and develop this aspect of Jordan's heritage.

It was in the homes of Iranians that I first became aware of the seeds of discontent that would develop into full-blown revolution just three years later. I was more fortunate than many foreigners in Tehran because I had family friends in the city, all of whom were very kind and hospitable. At dinners with Cyrus Ghani, a prominent lawyer and author of several books on Iran, and members of the extensive Farmanfarmaian family, I met artists, actors, and leading intellectuals, as well as government officials, and was exposed to differing perspectives on culture, politics, and social issues.

Many of the young professionals I met supported the direction in which the country was moving. One of the goals of the "White Revolution" the Shah had advanced in 1963 was ambitious land reform that would redistribute the vast holdings of the rich few to the many rural poor. The Shah had also championed women's rights. While I was living in Iran, he had placed Empress Farah in a position of enhanced authority. She put her support behind monthly gatherings of the country's best minds. In time, this group would be referred to as the Empress's think tank. In addition, his sister, Princess Ashraf, was serving as Iran's ambassador to the United Nations. I observed these developments with interest. As a young professional, I was intrigued by the special challenges facing women in their public and private lives, particularly highly visible and active women like the Shahbanou, who so often seemed to draw fire because of opposition to their husbands and for the failings of their society.

Despite these progressive goals, my friends were concerned that Iran was quickly becoming a heavy-handed police state. SAVAK, the Shah's secret police, was beginning to clamp down on any perceived threat to the regime, and I would meet people who were hesitant to say anything that might in any way be construed as critical. One popular employee at Llewelyn-Davis, a young Iranian architect, was summarily picked up off the street by SAVAK and taken off for interrogation. We were not sure whether we would see him again, but he returned the next day, badly shaken. Another morning, during a company meeting, project director Jaquelin Robertson passed a note over his desk for us to read; it indicated that our offices were bugged and that we should be on guard at every moment.

The warning was indicative of a growing restiveness. Conversations began to focus on the government and the image of the Shah and his family. In addition to the prominent and controversial Princess Ashraf, the Shah's wife was a convenient target. One story described her visit to a poor section of Tehran. Evidently, just prior to her arrival the city's mayor had the street paved over and arranged a complete facelift for that part of town. This sparked a great deal of criticism, although most guests at the table, when pressed, acknowledged that the Empress probably was completely unaware that the mayor had whitewashed the situation to make it appear less desperate than it really was.

I learned about public reaction to the 1974 Shiraz Festival. The aim of the Shiraz Festival was perfectly commendable — to spark cross-pollination between Iran and the rest of the world through a program that reflected the latest trends in theater and the performing arts. Unfortunately, this approach backfired badly. A French theater company staged the musical

Hair, which had shocked Western audiences at the time because of its nudity. Needless to say, it had a far more jarring effect in an Islamic culture.

There were other more substantive causes for the growing feeling of unrest. For one thing, the oil money that had started pouring into Iran in 1973 after the third Arab-Israeli war and the Arab oil embargo ended was upsetting the social structure and threatening the country's cultural equilibrium. One could not miss the jolting juxtaposition of conservative and progressive. This incongruous mix was acceptable for the adaptable young middle class, but it was taking place in a society that also had strong conservative and religious underpinnings.

Huge economic gaps were growing between different segments of the society. In the rural areas outside Tehran, people lived very simply yet perhaps better than those in Tehran's growing slum areas, which often had unpaved roads, lacked electricity or sanitation, and offered the unskilled poor no way of bettering their lot. The Shah had instituted an ambitious program to eradicate illiteracy, but many of the poor had no education save what they learned at the *madrasahs*, or religious schools. Just as the government and the Shah were trying to close those gaps, they grew wider: The new oil wealth appeared to be increasingly and conspicuously concentrated in a small segment of the population.

After coming to know the city and its people, I became quite disturbed by the destructive environmental and social impact I imagined the mammoth Shahestan Pahlavi project would have on the only remaining green "lung" in the city's rapidly growing urban sprawl. Surrounded on three sides by mountains, Tehran was a virtual trap for pollution from refineries, car exhaust, and factories. The *jubes* — open canals lining the edges of the streets throughout the city — carried rainwater mixed with garbage and sewage across the city north to south. Traffic gridlocked certain sections of the city for hours. It was alarming to watch the deterioration of Tehran at the hands of rapid industrialization, especially since what had drawn me to the country was its extraordinary beauty.

Living in Tehran, I also became aware of the depth of religious fervor among the Shi'a branch of Islam, which is centered in Iran. I learned that the major difference between the Shi'a and Sunni branches of Islam is the issue of the right of succession from the Prophet Muhammad. When the Prophet died in A.D. 632, a majority of his followers believed that the Prophet's father-in-law, Abu Bakr, should be their spiritual leader. Another group believed that his rightful successor was his cousin and son-in-law, Ali. The latter group eventually formed the Shi'at Ali, the Party of Ali, and persisted in their belief that only Ali, his male heirs, or the members of the Prophet's household could be the rightful spiritual leader, or caliph, of Islam. However, the Sunni Muslims, who greatly outnumbered them, chose the caliph on merit by consensus. Despite the gulf between these two branches of Islam, they both viewed the Hashimites as spiritual leaders.

The rift between Shi'ites and Sunnis escalated into violence in A.D. 680. After Imam Ali died, his son, Imam Hussein, received word in Mecca that the self-proclaimed new Umayyad caliph in Damascus was corrupt and a drunkard, and was not fit to be the spiritual leader of the Muslim world. Despite warnings from his advisers, Imam Hussein left the Hejaz (a region on the western coast of the Arabian Peninsula) with his family and a small army to challenge the spiritually corrupt caliph. In the bloody confrontation that followed, Imam Hussein was ambushed and murdered with seventy of his followers and family at Karbala in southern Iraq. By giving his life for Islam, Hussein became a *shaheed*, or martyr, central to the Shi'ite identity as oppressed and persecuted, and Karbala, where he is buried, became a holy place of pilgrimage. Since then the story of the martyrdom of Imam Hussein has played a key role in Shi'a religious thought and ritual, which also includes the staging of Shi'a Muslim "passion plays" that recount that tragic day in Imam Hussein's life to large crowds on the day of Ashura.

I was in Tehran during Ashura in 1976, and I shall never forget it. Early one morning, alone in my apartment, I heard a strange sound, loud, swelling and completely unrecognizable. It grew louder and louder, building to a roar. Looking out the window, I saw a procession of perhaps fifty men walking through the streets, flailing their bloodied bodies with chains. The sight was terrible and transfixing. At the time I had no idea what I was seeing and hearing. I learned later from Iranian friends that the self-flagellation is an expression of grief and shared suffering with Imam Hussein, whose infant son had been murdered in his arms, and whose head had been cut off and paraded about on the point of a spear.

The same zeal that the Shi'ites brought to their religion was also being channeled into politics. The Shi'ite scholars in the holy city of Qom, who had opposed the Shah's reforms from the beginning, demonized the Western influences that were permeating the culture. The Shah's land reforms were communist, they insisted, and the inclusion of women and non-Muslim minorities in the vote was anti-Islam. Riots had broken out in Qom in 1963, and the army had suppressed them, silencing or exiling the scholars, including the fiery Ayatollah Ruhollah Khomeini.

The growing turmoil eventually affected our

71

Llewelyn-Davis office. When two Americans were shot quite close to the residence of Jaquelin Robertson, we were advised to continually change our routes to the office and the times we normally traveled them. By early in the summer of 1976, the project staff began leaving. Concern for our safety was growing, and there was a professional reason to close the operation down as well. Now that our preliminary work was done, the next stages would take place in London, where production drawings were being created, and in New York, where architects would begin to create models.

Because I was the last one hired and the lowest on the totem pole professionally, I was one of the last employees to leave. When it was my turn, regretfully, to leave Iran, I flew to Jordan, for my first brief visit there, and then on to New York.

My urban planning work in Tehran had exposed me to the social and cultural fabric of a major Middle Eastern Islamic country, and made me aware of a fundamental lack of understanding in the West, especially in the United States, of Middle Eastern culture and the Muslim faith. These experiences reignited my interest in journalism, since forging an understanding between cultures now seemed even more urgent than urban planning. On my trip back to the United States, I decided to contact CBS, PBS, and other media organizations about possible jobs, and I also decided to apply to Columbia University's Graduate School of Journalism. I hoped that I could make a difference in a part of the world that was beginning to mean so much to me.

chapter four

An Audience with the King

"Oh, do come in with us," Marietta urged in her typically persuasive manner. Marietta Tree, the civil rights activist and former U.S. representative to the United Nations Human Rights Commission, was an old friend of my father's, and the two of them were passing through Amman on their way to Beirut. Thinking that Marietta and King Hussein would enjoy meeting each other, my father had requested an audience with the King. Any minute now, that meeting would be taking place. "No, no," I protested vehemently. "The arrangement is for you, not me."

Eight months earlier I had agreed to temporarily work for my father's aviation company in Jordan, Arab Air Services, which provided aviation design, engineering, and technical support to countries throughout the Middle East. My father's manager had taken ill, and I was covering for him until his return. As I was making arrangements to return to Amman, I was shocked to learn that Queen Alia, whom I had met only months before at the Amman airport, had been killed in a helicopter crash. In my first weeks traveling about the city, I would occasionally catch sight of a photo of the late Queen pasted on the rear window of a car and be moved to tears by the image of such a young life lost and mourned.

The director of my father's office had returned to work by mid-1977, but I had stayed on to help him for a while, at the same time conducting research for the pan-Arab aviation university in several Arab capitals. I had been preparing to leave the country when Ali Ghandour approached me with an intriguing job offer: to head a department he was creating within the Jordanian airline to coordinate planning, design, and maintenance of all the airline's facilities in Jordan and throughout the world. As fate would have it, the very next day I received my acceptance letter from Columbia's journalism school.

I weighed my options. Here, finally, was the opportunity to pursue the career in journalism I wanted. But here also was the totally unexpected opportunity to take my architectural and planning training and apply it in a meaningful way. I felt ridiculously underqualified for the position Ali Ghandour was offering me, but I could not resist the challenge.

I had not mentioned to Marietta or my father the fleeting encounters I had had with the

King, usually at the Amman airport, since moving to Jordan. While working, I was often out at the airport on one errand or another. I remember speeding there one day in my rented black VW Golf to pass on a letter to a colleague who was departing for the United States. I arrived, breathless, left my car engine running, and dashed onto the tarmac. The plane had only a couple of minutes before takeoff. A huge crowd of mechanics and men in gray suits had lodged themselves by the wing of the plane, in an area that blocked my access. I broke through the group and nearly careened into King Hussein. "Your Majesty," I gasped, feeling a warm blush cover my face. He smiled. "How are you?" he asked. "Why don't I see more of you?" It was as if we were old friends. I blurted out something incoherent and excused myself to hand off the letter. Afterward I drove to my friend Meliha's office at the airport's civil aviation training center. "You won't believe what just happened to me," I began, and then gave her a description of my excruciatingly awkward performance at the airport.

On another occasion, Cyrus Vance, who had recently been appointed U.S. Secretary of State by President Jimmy Carter, visited Jordan soon after I started working there. Knowing of my interest in a career in journalism, members of the press corps invited me to join them for Vance's press conference with King Hussein. The press bus drove us through a deep fog up the winding road to the royal residence, Hashimya Palace. When Cyrus Vance, one of my family's oldest friends, saw me standing among the journalists, he walked over to greet me, causing everyone in the room to turn and stare at me. It did not help that King Hussein then called out to me as I tried to shrink back into the crowd.

Marietta and my father continued to insist I join them in the royal audience, while I continued to resist. I was relieved when Yanal Hikmat, the Chief of Protocol, arrived to escort them from the sitting room into the King's office chambers at the Diwan, as Jordan's Royal Court is called. My plan was to leave and meet them later at the hotel, but no sooner had they been ushered into the meeting than Yanal returned and asked me to join the group. I knew Yanal through mutual friends, so I felt comfortable telling him that I did not want to intrude on the meeting. He quickly overruled me. "The King requests your presence," he told me, putting emphasis on the word "King."

I slipped into the meeting as unobtrusively as possible. At the end of the audience, the King turned to me and asked if I might be able to visit his residence, Hashimya, to take a look at some of the problems he was having with the construction of the sprawling palace complex. The next thing I knew we had a lunch appointment for the next day. "Hash. 12:30," reads my diary entry for April 7. What it does not say is that I did not get home until 7:30 that evening.

When I arrived at Hashimya, the King warmly welcomed me at the door in a leather jacket and open-necked shirt. He was talkative and relaxed as we sat down for lunch, after which we made a tour of the palace. It is fair to say it was in disastrous shape. Hashimya had been built quickly and sloppily — and it showed. The roof leaked so badly that when it rained, water poured through the light fixtures into the living spaces. The heating, electricity, and plumbing all had abundant glitches that needed fixing. The King asked me if I could take responsibility for the work and looked surprised when I told him that I was not qualified for the job.

As I would later learn, people in positions like the King's are usually the last to be given an accurate assessment of problematic situations. Most people might assure the King of their ability to accomplish whatever he wanted, regardless of their competence or experience, but I did not want to misrepresent my capabilities with him, of all people. Someone in his position should have the best possible help. "The most I can do is try to help you identify what company could provide the kind of expertise you need," I told him.

As I prepared to leave the palace, the King asked if he might introduce his three younger children to me: Prince Ali, who was then two years old; Princess Haya, who was three; and five-year-old Abir, a Palestinian girl that the King's third wife, Alia, had brought into the palace after the child's mother was killed by a plane crash at her refugee camp near the Amman airport. Then the King suggested that we visit the royal stables, home to desert-bred Arabian horses whose pedigrees stretched back through hundreds of years. We drove to the stables, officially known as the Royal Jordanian State Stud, with the security motorcade that escorted the King everywhere.

The horses, which the Bedouin call "drinkers of the wind," were extraordinarily graceful. They seemed to float above the ground as they trotted around the paddock. I had seen Arabian horses in the United States, but here in their home they struck me as even more beautiful. Arabs take great pride in their horses, with the distinctive Arabian "dish" between their wide-set eyes, their small, pointed ears, their thick manes and tails, and short backbones, one vertebra less than other breeds, to better traverse rough country and sandy deserts. Many of the horses we saw that afternoon were descended from those ridden by the Hashimites during the Great Arab Revolt, the struggle, led by Sharif Hussein of Mecca, for independence from the Ottoman Empire. Emir Abdullah, Sharif Hussein's son and King Hussein's grandfather, rode his favorite mare, Johara (jewel), on the day he and the other fighters besieged Medina.

The King knew all the horses by name and loved to show visitors the Stud, which he considered a point of Jordanian pride, especially since so many of the great horse-breeding tribes are Jordanian. Since 1960, a Spanish couple, Santiago and Ursula Lopez, had run the stables, but the King had recently handed over responsibility to his eldest daughter, Princess Alia, who was deeply involved in the breeding of these horses, carefully developing the stock to improve bloodlines while preserving the horses' desert pedigree. Under her direction, the Stud has distinguished itself in regional and international competitions.

Just as we were about to leave, an extraordinary vehicle pulled up. It was a large convertible, a bright blue Excalibur, a recent gift to King Hussein from a Gulf prince. The King suggested that I drive myself home in it — with him in the passenger seat. I tried to refuse, but I could tell that the King thought it would be a great lark. So I offered a compromise. I told him that I would drive home, but in a less flashy car. I could not believe what was happening. I was driving the King of Jordan through the streets of Amman surrounded by security vehicles, with people on the street craning for a look as the royal motorcade passed by. I felt very self-conscious, but the King seemed to revel in the spontaneity of the moment. I would soon discover that Hussein loved to create surprises. (And he loved to make me blush; it was well into my marriage before I was able to control my blushing in the face of his teasing.) I, on the other hand, was counting the streets until I could get to my apartment and flee inside.

I kept my experiences at Hashimya to myself. And I did not tell anyone about the telephone calls the King made to me the next day. I had lived in Jordan long enough to know that his every word, every move, every personal encounter was constantly analyzed and often misinterpreted or exaggerated. Interest in the King's private life was meteoric at the time. At forty-one years old, he was once again a very eligible bachelor, and there was constant speculation about who might be his next wife. Names were being traded around the Amman dinner circuit, every source purporting inside knowledge.

I was flattered, of course, that such a distinguished and accomplished man seemed to enjoy our conversations so much; I was only twenty-six at the time. However, the King was known for his generosity of spirit and concern for everyone living in or just passing through Jordan. Much later he would tell me that he had seen something special in my eyes during the audience at the Diwan, and that he had fallen in love at that moment.

I had made some wonderful friends during my stay in Amman: Meliha Azar, a teacher in the civil aviation school; Fatina Asfour, who was running her family's match factory; Rami Khouri, the young editor in chief of the *Jordan Times*; and Amer Salti, a banker who was a member of a group I occasionally joined for tennis and who was married to an American, Rebecca. I also spent time with Khalid Shoman, Deputy Chairman and the son of the founder of the most prominent Arab bank, and his wife, Suha, an artist. Amman was a very small town, I quickly discovered, and almost everyone seemed to know each other.

I also met my friends' families, which further extended my social circle. At the time most entertaining in Jordan took place within a family context, and my friends' families were always warm and welcoming. I treasured their invitations to dinner. Those family meals were the best I had in Jordan, in terms of both the food and the company. Fatina's mother, a particularly good cook, taught me how to prepare my favorite dishes in the family kitchen: *bamieh*, which was okra, *foul*, which were fava beans, and *fasoulieh*, green beans in tomato sauce, which I would go home and prepare in my little apartment. The rest of the time I was usually on my own. I did not want to overextend my welcome by inviting myself too often to dinner, despite their open invitations and the fact that I was often very lonely. It did not help that I had to walk a mile or so to the Inter-Continental Hotel just to place long-distance calls home.

Jordanian families are very close, and I envied them that. Their households seemed so different from my own family's and, indeed, from many of the families I knew in the West. Arab culture stresses interdependence. In Jordan, children my age, both sons and daughters, did not go off to live on their own but stayed home until they married, so they always had each other for company, supervision, and security. My friends the Asfours had seven daughters; with that many children, they were a world unto themselves. They were not desperately driven by material or social needs because they had everything they needed within their own family. I enjoyed every visit to their home for dinner, where I was welcomed as one of their own.

Jordan is quite a melting pot. For thousands of years, it has been at the crossroads of the Middle East, serving as a vital communication and trading link between states and empires in the region and beyond. In antiquity, it was assimilated into the empires of Assyria, Babylon, Egypt, Greece, Rome, Byzantium, and Persia. The scope of that cross-pollination can be seen in many of the large established families of Amman. They reflect the three main demographic groups in the country: the traditionally semi-nomadic Bedouin who now have largely settled in urban areas; families who came to the young country of Jordan in the first half of the twentieth century from neighboring lands (Syria, Iraq, Palestine, Lebanon, and Saudi Arabia); and the residents of numerous towns, villages, and agricultural hamlets whose ancestors had practiced a settled lifestyle for centuries, even millennia in some cases.

The long tradition of these settled town and village folk is most easily identifiable today at antiquities sites. The unbroken human and architectural legacy of the settlements is of farmers, traders, and craftsmen and -women who lived near reliable water sources, farmed the land and kept herds of animals, communicated locally and regionally across old-as-time trade routes, and provided the strong sense of local cultural identity — in towns such as Kerak, Madaba, Irbid, Azraq, Husn, Ajlun, Anjara, Ma'an, Aqaba, and many others — that would coalesce into the Jordanian identity in the twentieth century.

Jordan also provided refuge over hundreds of years for many ethnic minorities fleeing political persecution and violence. Among those were the Circassians, a small but influential community of non-Arab Sunni Muslims and former refugees from oppression in their homeland in the Caucasus region in central Asia. An ancient race, consisting of twelve tribes, the Circassians fought the Russians for a hundred years, from 1764 to 1864, losing almost half of their population. The superpowers at the time, Turkey and Russia, together forced the migration of the remaining population to three areas in the Ottoman Empire: Turkey, Syria, and Jordan. The first Circassians arrived in 1878, settling first in the Roman ruins at Amman (uninhabited since Roman times) and then spreading to several nearby sites. Four decades later they welcomed King Abdullah to Jordan and instantly backed his regime. After the creation of Transjordan in 1921, the Circassians were stalwarts of the army and the government. The King's honor guard was made up of these typically tall, fair-skinned men, and at least one of my friends, Yanal Hikmat, Chief of Protocol at the Royal Court, was a Circassian as well.

Then there were the Chechens, also Muslims from the Caucasus, who had fled Russian expansion in the 1890s and found a home in what was then the Ottoman Empire. Three of the eighty seats in Jordan's parliament are reserved for Chechens and Circassians. The Chechens, like the Circassians, are famous for their distinctive wedding rituals. I was fascinated by romantic tales of bridal kidnappings from the homes of disapproving parents. I longed to witness one of these dramatic elopements, when the suitor would gallop up to his beloved and sweep her away to the sound of celebratory gunfire.

The Bedouin are the country's traditional "desert dwellers." The Bedouin's ancestors, inhabitants of the Arabian Peninsula, were mentioned in the Old Testament's Book of Genesis as the children of Shem, son of Noah. Over the centuries, the Bedouin roamed their grazing territories and were known to offer safe transit and use of their wells to Christian pilgrims on their way to the Holy Land.

More recently, the Bedouin way of life has changed, and a majority of them have moved to cities like Amman, entering business and serving in the army and government. A dwindling few continue in their traditional lifestyle, moving with the seasons to graze their livestock in the stark beauty of the desert. I admired the Bedouin spirit, envied their freedom, and thought modern man could learn valuable lessons from their total independence from material culture.

Though more than 90 percent of Jordanians are Sunni Muslim, there is also quite a sizable Christian community in Jordan, as evidenced by the 50,000 people who crowded into Amman's sports stadium in 2000 to welcome the Pope. Many are Greek Orthodox, as were my Halaby relatives. And many are descendants of the first Christians in the Holy Land thousands of years ago. Kerak, with its massive Crusader Castle, has an ancient population of Christians, as do Salt and Madaba. The most famous mosaic in the region was uncovered in the Greek Orthodox Church of St. George in Madaba — a detailed sixth-century map of the villages, rivers, and valleys of the whole Holy

Land from Egypt to Syria, with the holy city of Jerusalem at the center.

Since 1948 Palestinians, who trace their ancestry to the ancient Canaanite Arabs — the earliest known inhabitants of Palestine — have comprised a significant proportion of Jordan's population. According to conservative estimates, some 800,000 Palestinians were forcibly uprooted by the creation of the state of Israel in 1948 and dispersed to Jordan, Syria, and Lebanon. Today their diaspora includes many countries throughout the world.

Over the years, roughly 1.5 million Palestinian refugees have sought safe haven in the Hashimite Kingdom of Jordan, where they acquired citizenship after the unification of the West Bank and the East Bank of Jordan, in 1950. The welcome was warm; in fact, King Hussein was the only head of an Arab state to grant these suddenly stateless people citizenship. The forced migration of Palestinians flooding into Jordan — after the 1948 war and again after the 1967 Arab-Israeli war — almost doubled the population.

The strain on Jordan's resources was unmistakable. Where once Amman was comfortably settled on seven hills, I could now count more than fourteen. In the space of thirty years, the open hillsides around the Citadel and the Roman amphitheater in downtown Amman had become stacked from top to bottom with ramshackle houses, one built over another until there was not a square meter of open space.

Some 80,000 less fortunate refugees were living in thirteen crowded refugee camps in Jordan. The refugee crisis reached such magnitude following the 1948 war that the United Nations created a temporary agency, the United Nations Relief and Works Agency for Palestine Refugees in the Near East (UNRWA), to oversee, shelter, and educate more than 3.9 million registered exiled Palestinian refugees in Jordan, Syria, Lebanon, the Gaza Strip, and the West Bank. UNRWA is still struggling to cope with the refugee tragedy today, more than fifty years later. Passing by some of these camps as I traveled around the country, I was amazed by how resourceful those families had to be to survive for so long in conditions everyone had assumed would be short-lived.

It was not until I started working and living in Jordan that I began to understand the enormity of this human tragedy. Second and even third generations of Palestinians were being born in the refugee camps in 1977, with nothing to cling to but memories. Many still lived in tents, unwilling to move into more permanent housing for fear of losing their refugee status and, with it, their longed-for right to return to their homeland. Some had tattered documents they had fled with thirty years earlier, proving ownership of the land and houses they had been forced from, and more than a few still wore their house keys around their necks.

I was fascinated by accounts of the events leading up to the founding of the modern state of Jordan, beginning in 1914 in the holy city of Mecca, in the Hejaz, where Islam was born. Direct descendants of the Prophet Muhammad, the Hashimites had ruled Mecca for more than a thousand years and were the hereditary custodians of Islam's most holy places: Mecca, where Muslims believe Abraham rebuilt the first house of worship devoted to God and where the Prophet was born, and Medina, where in A.D. 662, the Prophet was forced to flee persecution for his beliefs.

At the turn of the last century, the Grand Sharif of Mecca (Sharif and Sharifa are titles carried by men and women who are direct descendants of the Prophet Muhammad through the male line), the Hashimite Hussein Bin Ali, and other prominent Arabs in the region deeply resented the increasingly oppressive policies of the Ottoman Empire, which forbade both the teaching of the Arabic language in schools and its official use. Arab nationalists were being arrested and the tolerance that had for so long characterized the culture was replaced with persecution; in this political climate secret societies of Arabs throughout the region turned to Sharif Hussein for leadership.

World War I presented the Hashimites with an opening: Sharif Hussein saw the war against the Germans and their allies as an opportunity not only to rid Arab land of the Ottomans after 400 years of occupation but, after the war, to create an independent confederation of Arab states out of all the Arab provinces of the Ottoman Empire from Yemen to Syria, including the Arabian Peninsula, Lebanon, Mesopotamia (modern Iraq), and Palestine.

The British, after long negotiations in Cairo with Sharif Hussein's son, Abdullah, were receptive. "If you and His Highness your father still favor a movement such as would lead to the full independence of the Arabs," wrote Ronald Storrs, the British Oriental Secretary, "Great Britain is prepared to assist such a movement by all the means in her power."

With that and other British statements of support for Arab independence from Sir Henry McMahon, the British High Commissioner in Egypt, Sharif Hussein aligned the Hashimites with the English and mobilized a force of 30,000 Arab tribesmen under the command of three of his sons, Ali, Abdullah, and Feisal. In June 1916 the Great Arab Revolt, as it became known, was launched under the leadership of Sharif Hussein, and it helped change the course of World War I in the Middle East.

Over the next two years, the Arabs of the Hejaz under the Hashimite banner liberated Mecca, Taif, Jeddah, and other Ottoman strongholds. The Arabs repeatedly sabotaged the garrisoned Hejaz railroad — the 820-mile link between Damascus and Medina the Ottomans had built in the early 1900s, denuding many of Jordan's forests in the process. One entire section of track was knocked out of operation by Arab fighters, with the help of the British engineer and military strategist Captain T. E. Lawrence. In the most daring military move of the campaign, the Hejazis, led by Feisal and Lawrence, traveled 800 excruciating miles from Mecca to liberate Aqaba with the help of local tribes. The Arabs swept down on the unsuspecting Ottoman armies from the desert the Ottomans had presumed so impassable that their heavy artillery was fixed out to sea.

Though Lawrence's camel tripped during the furious raid and Aqaba was taken before he regained his senses, the legend of Lawrence reached epic proportions in the West, documented first by American journalist Lowell Thomas, then in every retelling of the Great Arab Revolt, including Lawrence's book *Seven Pillars of Wisdom* and the film *Lawrence of Arabia*. I remember seeing the film when it first came out in 1962 and marveling at what appeared to be the one-man defeat of the Turks by the eccentric Lawrence. The Arab forces he "advised," actually the armies of Hussein's sons Feisal, Ali, and Abdullah, were depicted as ill trained, undisciplined, and incapable of defeating the Turks on their own. The film had struck a deep chord in me as an adolescent, at a time when I had just become conscious of my

Arab roots and had few references for learning about the history and culture of my heritage. The glorification of Lawrence in the West incensed many Arabs, I later learned, who felt their own leaders were unfairly robbed of rightful credit for a great victory. And they also found a racist subtext in the West's version of the events: The message seemed to be that it took a white man, an Englishman, to make the Arab dream of independence come true.

Having liberated Aqaba and the Hejaz, the Arab army drove north until it captured Amman. The Great Arab Revolt culminated in a victorious march with their European allies into Damascus on October 1, 1918, leading to the Allies' armistice with Turkey thirty days later. What was an undeniable Hashimite triumph in war, however, would not survive the peace.

Sharif Hussein, who was proclaimed King of the Hejaz, naturally expected the British to carry out their pledge of support for Arab independence. So did the other Arabs. Three months after the Hashimite forces rode into Damascus, the Arab Syrian Congress proclaimed Sharif Feisal King of an independent Syria, while a group of Iraqi leaders chose Sharif Abdullah to be King of newly created Iraq (ancient Mesopotamia).

But the Hashimites had been betrayed. In 1916, while they were launching their rebellion against the Ottoman Empire, Britain was already secretly negotiating with France to divide, after the war, the Arab lands whose independence the Hashimites were fighting for. In what became known as the Sykes-Picot Agreement, the French carved out Syria and Lebanon for themselves and the British took Palestine, Iraq, and the region east of the Jordan River known as Transjordan.

While the British supported Sharif Feisal as the Hashimite King of Syria, the French refused to recognize his government and in 1920, after twenty-one months of his rule, drove him forcibly from the throne and into exile. At a 1921 conference in Cairo presided over by Winston Churchill, then England's Colonial Secretary, Feisal became the King of Iraq, while Sharif Abdullah became the leader of Transjordan. Churchill rejected Abdullah's entreaties to merge Palestine and Transjordan into one country.

Sharif Hussein had committed his sons and his volunteer forces to overthrowing the Turks on the understanding with Britain that all the Arab nations under Turkish occupation, including Palestine, would form a united state after the war. Sir Arthur James Balfour, the British Foreign Secretary, had other ideas. Instead of supporting self-determination for the Arabs — who constituted nearly all of Palestine's population and had lived there for centuries, in some cases millennia — he promised their land to the Jewish people as a "national home." The Balfour Declaration, the 1917 document that made these fateful moves policy, also stated clearly that "nothing shall be done that may prejudice the civil and religious rights of existing non-Jewish communities in Palestine."

I was familiar, of course, with the story of the creation of Israel and its turbulent history before I came to Jordan. I was very sympathetic, and still am, to the persecution of the Jewish people through the ages and sickened by the atrocities committed by Nazi Germany against the Jews during World War II. Everyone I knew, including my new friends in Jordan, expressed horror at the realities of the Holocaust. But they resented, as I was growing to, how Arabs were cast as the aggressors in the dispute between Israel and the Arab countries, when it was their land that had been seized to resolve a European political problem.

Jews, Muslims, and Christians had lived peacefully in the Middle East and indeed in Palestine for centuries. It was not until the rise of Zionism and the creation of Israel that animosities took root. Theodor Herzl, the father of modern Zionism, was a Hungarian-born Jewish journalist who posited that Jews, however patriotic or good citizens, would never be integrated into the life of any European country because of abiding anti-Semitism and were in fact a "nation without a land." His solution to this dilemma: the creation of a Jewish nation.

Herzl did not insist on Palestine being the only territory for a Jewish nation. He suggested Argentina as well. The British would later offer the Zionists Uganda as a possible homeland, but the offer was rejected. While Herzl and like-minded nationalists might have settled for any territorial solution, the more religious Jews in the Zionist ranks wanted only the Holy Land — Palestine and what is now Jordan.

It would take fifty bloody years to proclaim the state of Israel. The process begun by the Balfour Declaration, which King Hussein called "the root cause of almost all the bitterness and frustration in our Arab world today," took a giant step in 1920 when the newly formed League of Nations confirmed Britain's postwar trusteeship of Palestine. The British Mandate, as it was universally called, would last until 1948 and was doomed from the beginning. Promising independence to the Arabs in the wave of postwar Arab nationalism while at the same time promising a homeland to the Jews, the British Mandate made for an impossible situation. The Arabs feared, and it turned out rightly, that some of the Zionist Jews beginning to arrive in Palestine had no intention of sharing the land but wanted to own it all. In 1901 the well-funded World Zionist Organization, set up in Basel, established the Jewish National Fund, which immediately began buying up large tracts of Arab land in Palestine, mostly from absentee landlords in Syria and Lebanon. I would meet Palestinians in Jordan who had farmed for many years in Palestine, only to be evicted from their land and their homes. And so the pattern of Palestinian displacement began.

Between 1919 and 1921, the acquisition of more and more land, combined with the arrival in Palestine of 18,000 Jewish immigrants, set off riots in Jerusalem and Jaffa. Another 10,000 arrived from Europe in 1928, triggering more riots. The steady influx of Jewish immigrants became a flood after the Nazis took over Germany in 1933. Jewish immigration jumped to 30,000 in 1933, 42,000 in 1934, and 61,000 in 1935, setting off an Arab revolt that would last for three years before it was brutally suppressed by the British.

The pain of the Palestinians did not escape world leaders. "Palestine belongs to the Arabs in the same sense that England belongs to the English or France to the French," Mahatma Gandhi said. "What is going on in Palestine today cannot be justified by any moral code of conduct." But there was to be no break in the conflict. Fighting resumed again following the end of World War II as thousands of illegal refugees came to Palestine.

In 1947 the British turned the fate of the region over to the United Nations. On November 29 the UN General Assembly, at the recommendation of Britain, voted to partition Palestine into two states — one Arab, one Jewish — with Jerusalem to be placed under international control. The Arab and non-Arab Muslim member countries, which had countered with a proposal to keep Palestine united as one, voted adamantly against partition. UN Resolution 181 awarded the Jews 55 percent of the land, though they represented only one-third of Palestine's population and owned only 6 percent of the land. The Arab countries refused to honor the UN resolution, which passed by only two votes, and walked out of the General Assembly in fury. Once again, the future of an Arab people was being decided by European and Western countries. Palestine erupted into a deadly civil war.

Many conflicts have an emblematic atrocity that comes to symbolize the war's horror. In Vietnam it was the massacre of civilians by U.S. soldiers at My Lai. In India it was the 1919 slaughter of 400 civilians by British troops at Jallinwala Bagh in Amritsar. In Palestine it was Deir Yassin.

I had never heard of Deir Yassin until I came to Jordan. I knew that the Arabs called the tragic events of 1948 *aam al nakba,* which translates as "the year of the catastrophe," but I did not know any of the details until I started studying the history of Palestine. I soon discovered that there was not a single Palestinian I met who did not know all about Deir Yassin and the massacre of its inhabitants in April

1948 by the Stern gang, a Jewish terrorist group of several hundred members founded in 1940, and the Irgun, the military arm of the Revisionist Party, under the command of Menachem Begin, a future Prime Minister of Israel.

Though the leaders of Deir Yassin had made a peace pact with neighboring Jewish villages, Israeli terrorist forces entered the village on the morning of April 9, 1948, and, after overcoming initial resistance, went house to house, shooting the people inside at close range, then blowing up some of the houses. No one knows the exact number of Palestinians who died that day. The gangs said they killed hundreds. Over the next few days, members of the International Red Cross found bodies dumped in four cisterns, stacked in a pit, and buried in the rubble of houses. Most were old men, women, and children.

News of the massacre at Deir Yassin rippled through Palestine and had the desired effect of intimidating the population. Palestinian families began to flee their homes all over the country and to seek temporary refuge in neighboring countries. The plan of the radical Zionists to drive out the Palestinians was working.

Were it not for the testimony of eyewitnesses, the report of a member of the International Red Cross, and a few brave Jewish scholars who pressed for access to primary sources in Israeli archives, the scope of the tragedy might never have been known. Some key documents are still "classified" by the Israeli government, including photographs of the aftermath of the attack. Some Zionists even go so far as to deny the massacre ever happened.

One bloodbath, of course, led to another. A few days after the massacre at Deir Yassin, Arabs retaliated by ambushing a convoy of Jewish medical personnel. Other atrocities were committed by both sides in the countdown to the withdrawal of the British and the declaration of the state of Israel in May 1948. It was clear that David Ben-Gurion and other Zionist leaders had no intention of allowing the Palestinians to be part of the Jewish state. Jewish military forces had been steadily and systematically depopulating Arab villages for months, driving out the inhabitants and then bulldozing their houses to the ground. Almost all the Palestinian communities between Haifa and Jaffa on the coast had been "cleared"; Palestinian villages had been captured along the road between Tel Aviv and Jerusalem; the Palestinian populations of Haifa and Tiberius had fled; and Arab West Jerusalem had been occupied and the Palestinians driven out.

When I was growing up in the United States, the prevailing view of the 1948 Arab-Israeli war was that Israel was forced to defend itself against hordes of bloodthirsty Arabs pouring across its borders. But now that I was living in Jordan, I was discovering that the Arab view was quite the opposite: Israel had been on the offensive, demonstrated by the fact that most of the fighting was not within the territory partitioned to Israel but in the territory partitioned to the Palestinians. The Arab "armies," which were hardly armies save for Jordan's Arab Legion, crossed into Palestine to come to the aid of their Palestinian Arab brethren and to try to prevent Israeli forces from taking more territory. They failed. By the end of the "year of the catastrophe," Israel had captured 78 percent of the land assigned to the Arab state, thereby gaining nearly one-third more of the territory than the UN had originally granted in UN General Assembly Resolution 181, which partitioned Palestine.

Israel also ignored UN Resolution 194, passed in December 1948 and reaffirmed many times since, acknowledging the rights of the Palestinians to receive compensation for properties seized and the right of return to their homes. Instead, the Israelis, who by then had depopulated some 500 Arab villages and settlements, leveled the majority of villages and repopulated them with Jewish immigrants. Homeless Palestinians lived in caves and makeshift tents during the cold winter months of 1949, some just miles from their former homes and orchards in the new state of Israel. I remember my mother telling me later that she cried when she saw their suffering during a visit she took to the region with my father.

★ ★ ★

The tiny Hashimite Kingdom of Jordan survived the upheaval but would suffer greatly
from the demographic, economic, and political
turmoil that came in its wake. This tragic history suffused every aspect of King Hussein's
life. For him, matters of state were also matters
of the heart. But there were times when he
would put aside these pressing issues and relax,
and his seaside home in Aqaba was where he
was most able to unwind. One week after our
first lunch at Hashimya, the King invited me to
Aqaba for the weekend with his children and a
group of friends. I was struck at once by how
informal he could be. Were it not for the fact
that King Hussein was addressed by all, including family, as *Sidi* (meaning "sir," informally), *Sayidna* ("my lord," more formally), or
Jalalet El Malek ("Your Majesty"), and that everyone stood out of respect when he came into
a room, it would have been easy to forget that
he was, in fact, one of the world's longest-
serving and most respected monarchs. He took
obvious pleasure in creating a festive, relaxing
atmosphere among his guests. He took us all
out on his motorboat and tried to persuade us
to go water skiing, even though it was April and
the water was still chilly. There was a float in
the water just off the beach, and he spent quite
a lot of time enticing his children to dog-paddle
their way out to it, a surreptitious way of teaching them to swim. We watched movies every

night after dinner in the little theater he had had built in the compound.

We spent four idyllic days in Aqaba. The sunsets were particularly lovely, turning the turquoise sea pink and the mountains along the coastline lavender. Even the tankers anchored offshore had a certain charm, especially at night when they were limned in lights. It was the peak of the oil boom and the port of Aqaba was full.

Added to Aqaba's beauty was its historical significance. Long valued for its coastal location on trade and pilgrimage routes and its abundance of fresh water just below ground level, Aqaba had been conquered and reconquered since the tenth century B.C. From the beach you could see how close were friend and foe. Saudi Arabia was to the southeast and Egypt to the southwest; between Egypt and the royal property at Aqaba was Israel and its resort town of Eilat, just a few miles away down the coast to the west. The barbed-wire border with Israel was barely half a mile along the beach from the stone jetty on King Hussein's property. One of the more incongruous sights was to see Jordanian soldiers in full gear patrolling one side of the border and Israeli soldiers the other, with sunbathers on the beaches in the background.

I would later become accustomed to the thuds of Israeli depth charges just offshore to discourage enemy frogmen from slipping ashore at night. The Israelis unfortunately destroyed the coral reef off Eilat in the process, killing the habitat for the wide variety of tropical fish in the Gulf. Thankfully, Aqaba's coral reefs remain essentially intact and a favorite international destination for scuba divers and tourists in glass-bottom boats.

I was so engrossed in discovering Aqaba that I was unaware of the personal tensions that were unfolding over the weekend in the royal entourage. Among the houseguests was an English photographer, a woman who had been living and working in Jordan for a period of time. She had met the King through friends in England. Someone in the King's entourage told me that she was not happy I was there, a sentiment that I found puzzling, oblivious as I was to the fierce competition for the King's attention.

We returned to Amman on April 16, and the King began inviting me to Hashimya for dinner. Although his life there was decidedly more constrained than in Aqaba, over meals we had enough privacy to talk at length about a wide range of subjects, including our childhoods. We found that we had led oddly parallel lives. Oldest children, we were both shy and had few trusted friends. We had both been sent to a bewildering succession of schools, Hussein to seven and I to five. We had both emerged from our family experiences and disjointed schooling with a determination to be self-reliant. We also discovered that we had both had difficult relationships with our fathers and special relationships with a grandparent, he with his grandfather, King Abdullah, and I with my paternal grandmother. His bond with his grandfather, however, was profoundly significant and had been cruelly broken under dramatic circumstances.

In 1951 young Prince Hussein had been in Jerusalem, standing ten feet away from King Abdullah, when his grandfather was assassinated by a Palestinian for his efforts to explore a political solution with Israel. Hussein was sixteen at the time and many years later still found it hard to talk about that shocking moment at the Al Aqsa mosque, where King Abdullah had taken him for Friday prayers. A gunman had suddenly stepped out from behind a pillar and shot the King point-blank in the head. Hussein could still see his grandfather's white turban roll to a stop in front of his feet, see his grandfather's entourage flee for their own safety, see the gunman turn, aim his pistol at the young Prince's chest — and fire. Only the medal on the military uniform, a decoration that his grandfather had insisted he wear that morning, saved his life by deflecting the bullet.

Hussein became Crown Prince and his father, Talal, became King — but for only twelve months. King Talal was a victim of schizophrenia, characterized by erratic and mercurial behavior. Hussein had great regard for his father's intelligence and sensitivity, but as much as he loved him, he feared for him and despaired over his deepening decline into mental illness. The King always seemed so sad when he spoke about his father, whom he had loved deeply. He admired the courage it had taken for King Talal to try to reign as King and the enormous contribution he had made to the country when he ushered in a democratic Constitution that was revolutionary for its time and remains the country's legal blueprint to this day. But his health could not withstand the pressure. On August 11, 1952, after being examined by three Jordanian doctors and two foreign specialists, King Talal was removed from the throne by a vote in Parliament.

Crown Prince Hussein was in Switzerland on holiday from the Harrow School, outside London, when he abruptly heard the news. "There was a knock on the door, and the hotel page delivered a cablegram from the Royal Court in Jordan, addressed to 'His Majesty, King Hussein,'" he remembered. He was just shy of his seventeenth birthday. He finished at Harrow and undertook a condensed course to receive his commission from the Royal Military Academy Sandhurst. By the age of eighteen, Hussein was Jordan's full-time ruler.

Hussein's life had been amazing. I could not help being impressed by his intelligence and valor. I was drawn, too, to his vitality and huge store of energy. But there were quiet moments alone in my flat when I worried where it was all going. It was a delight, a privilege really, to spend time with him. But we had begun spending a great deal of time together, and I was starting to wonder whether our idyll would become more complicated. What if he made an overture for a more intimate relationship — how would I deal with that? Gossip had it that the King was a playboy, and I did not want this precious friendship to lead to a stereotypical royal affair. I could not imagine myself in such a situation and hoped that our uncomplicated friendship would go on forever.

My father was somewhat uneasy as well. When he passed briefly through Amman en route to the United States, he cautioned me to be careful. I will never forget him standing by my car in the Inter-Continental Hotel parking lot saying, "Take care, Lisa. The Royal Court is full of intrigues, and this society can be vicious. I like King Hussein very much, as you know, but I don't want you to be hurt."

I was surprised by his words and gave him a searching look, thinking that his concern was misplaced. "You know, there's nothing for you to worry about," I said. "This is not like other courts. There are no intrigues here." I would look back on that conversation in later years with wry amusement.

For the moment I was enjoying the King's company, and evidently he was enjoying mine. The day after my father left, my diary entry reads: "Surprise visit." Then his words to me when he stopped by unexpectedly: "I miss you." I realize now that he was sending obvious signals that had been going over my head. At the time I did not question the evenings we spent with his three youngest children, reading to them, hearing their prayers at night, and putting them to bed. We dined and watched the original bulky NTSC video films every night in his spacious sitting room. (Hussein had the first video machine I had ever seen, and he also screened films playing in the local cinemas.) His favorites were John Wayne films (*The Quiet Man*, in particular), Peter Sellers's *The Party*, and heroic films like Charlie Chaplin's *Limelight*, because, he explained, "one man survives against all the bad guys." One film, *The Day of the Dolphin*, became a source of great amusement between us. George C. Scott plays a scientist training a pair of dolphins and manages to get them to speak and understand English, albeit with a very limited vocabulary. Hussein would make me laugh by mimicking the dolphin voice in the film: "Fa loves Be," with its playful suggestion of our own budding affections.

Perhaps our most private moments were long motorcycle rides throughout Amman and the surrounding countryside. One lovely spring evening, the King adroitly managed to "lose" his security detail on Amman's narrow streets, and we spent an evening alone touring the city.

I felt an exhilarating sense of freedom, however briefly. What fun it was to savor the life of ordinary people out on the town.

One day we flew out to the Dead Sea, to scout out an area that might make a good tourist resort, with Hussein at the controls of his favorite helicopter, an Alouette; its bubble-shaped cockpit provides such extraordinary visibility that I felt as though I were flying unencumbered through the air. I sat in the front passenger seat next to King Hussein as we floated above the Amman Plateau, then out over the valleys, known as *wadis,* and waterfalls that plunge down to the desert, then into a field by the Dead Sea, the lowest point on earth.

The days and evenings I spent with the King were exciting on both an intellectual and a personal level, but also quite exhausting. I was waking every morning at 6:00 to go to work, and the evenings I spent with the King always involved a long dinner followed by a film, sometimes more than one. Often I would not return home until 1 or 2 A.M. At best, I was getting four or five hours of sleep. I was also losing weight. King Hussein ate his meals very rapidly, a habit that he had developed during his days at Sandhurst and that was reinforced later as a survival strategy in his fast-paced official life. While he ate at supersonic speed, I ate slowly, in part because that was my habit and in part because we were having such interesting conversations. He would finish an entire meal while I was still trying to finish my soup. I felt it would be impolite to continue eating once he had finished, so very often that would be all I would get. And with most of my free time taken up with our meetings at Hashimya, I never had a moment to stock my own kitchen. I lost between ten and fifteen pounds, not that I minded. I thought I had learned a great deal from my reading and from meetings with foreign correspondents who would come through the region, but with King Hussein I was receiving a doctorate degree.

His greatest sorrow, he told me, was the disastrous 1967 Arab-Israeli war and Israel's subsequent military occupation of Jerusalem and the West Bank. As he recounted the unfolding events of the war, a tale of great deceit and squandered opportunities, he had tears in his eyes. I was fascinated to learn of King Hussein's apprehensive role in the 1967 war, which was not unlike King Abdullah's in the 1948 war. They both knew that the Arab armies were no match for the better equipped and better trained Israeli forces. More important, they understood that the only lasting solution would have to be political, not military.

The countdown had begun two years earlier, in an already very tense Middle East, when Israeli settlers started plowing land in the demilitarized zone between Israel and Syria near the Sea of Galilee. In the view of many, Israel's strategy was to provoke the Syrians into shooting at the settlers so the Israeli army could justify a disproportionate reprisal. "If they didn't shoot, we would tell the tractor to advance further, until in the end the Syrians would get annoyed and shoot," Moshe Dayan, Israel's Defense Minister, would be quoted in *The New York Times* as saying. "And then we would use artillery and later the air force also." The pivotal provocation occurred in April 1967. Soon after the anticipated Syrian response began, Israel went on its planned offensive, inflicting heavy casualties on the ground and shooting down six Syrian MiG-21s, some over Damascus.

Amid rumors that the Israeli Defense Forces, commanded by Yitzhak Rabin, were massing tanks near the Syrian border, Egypt, which had a defense pact with Syria, called on the United Nations to remove its peacekeeping troops on the Egyptian side of the border with Israel, then replaced them shortly thereafter with Egyptian troops and closed the Straits of Tiran to Israeli shipping. No one knows to this day whether Egypt's President Gamal Abdel Nasser was bluffing or not. In the countdown to war, Israel assured King Hussein that Israeli forces would not attack Jordan if it remained neutral — despite the fact that in November Israeli troops had overrun the Jordanian West Bank village of Sammou', destroying 125 houses, a clinic, and its school, killing and wounding innocent civilians. (UN Security Council Resolution 228 censured Israel for the attack.) It was an offer King Hussein could not accept. "I was in an impossible situation," he told me more than a decade later.

Acting on their own, Palestinian commandos in Jordan were staging raids against Israel, bringing heavy Israeli retaliation against Arab villages on the West Bank. The Palestinian population in Jordan was enraged by the Israeli attacks, and many focused their fury at King Hussein for not protecting them. In weighing the balance of whether or not to go to war with Israel, he was damned if he did and damned if he didn't. The reality was that the Jordanian army was outmanned and outgunned by the Israeli forces both on the ground and in the air. "I risked military defeat if we fought Israel," he told me. "I risked endangering Jordan's security and stability if we didn't."

King Hussein flew to Egypt to see President Nasser and reluctantly joined the military alliance with Egypt and Syria, agreeing that Jordanian troops would fall under Egyptian command. He assembled his army officers, among them three members of the royal family. He wanted them to know the truth. "We are being forced into a war with Israel, and though I know you will do your best, we are going to lose," he told them, assessing the dismal balance of power. But the officers, including his first cousin, Prince Ali Bin Nayef, refused to accept his conclusion. "As soldiers, we thought we were much better than the Israelis," Prince Ali later recalled. "We were tougher, we were stronger, we were better trained, and we were more courageous. But they had more equipment, ammunition, and petrol for their tanks."

There were conflicting views as to how the war actually started, but in all the debate one fact is indisputable: Israel struck the first blow. The war was essentially over before it began, though no one, including King Hussein, knew it. On June 5, 1967, the Israeli air force launched a surprise attack, flying under Egyptian radar and destroying virtually every one of Egypt's fighter plane units from Cairo to Alexandria while they were still on the ground. The Israeli planes then proceeded to strafe unprotected Egyptian ground forces in the Sinai, opening the way for Israeli troops to invade Egypt and rout the retreating Egyptians.

The looming disaster for Jordan was cemented by an inexplicable radio announcement that morning from the Egyptian commander in chief, Field Marshall Abdul Hakim Amer, that it was the Egyptian air force that had been victorious. Not only had Egyptian planes shot down 75 percent of the Israeli air force, he postured, but Egyptian ground forces were advancing into Israel. President Nasser, who apparently had not been fully informed, repeated this to King Hussein over the phone some hours later. It would be days, in fact, before the citizens of Jordan and Egypt would know the truth. But the damage had long since been done.

Three hours after the demolition of the Egyptian air force, that same Egyptian commander in chief in Cairo ordered Jordanian forces into a war that had already been lost. It was a disaster from the beginning. Jordan had only sixteen pilots trained to fly its twenty-two Hunter Hawk fighter planes. They completed one bombing run, but when the planes returned to Jordan to refuel, the Israeli air force crossed the border and destroyed them all on the ground. The Israelis then took aim at Amman, one missile finding its mark through the wall at Basman Palace, where King Hussein then resided, and destroying a chair in the King's study. Jordanian ground forces did not fare much better, although they fought bravely. Without any air or ground support from the Egyptians, the Jordanian troops exposed in the desert were being wiped out by the Israeli air force.

Time and again, King Hussein put himself at risk, traveling to the front and encouraging his troops. He had several narrow escapes, one with his cousin, Prince Raad, on the second day of the war. After meeting with the Prime Minister, King Hussein had insisted on going to visit the army high command, which was north of Amman. To get there, he had to pass by the Iraqi army's encampment near Suweileh, which had been bombed by the Israelis the day before, at around the same time, with many casualties. "I pleaded with him not to go at that time, arguing that the Israeli air force might make another bombing run at the Iraqis," Prince Raad later told me. "But he looked at me with a fury I'd never seen before in his eyes. So we went."

Prince Raad is convinced that God protected King Hussein. Low clouds suddenly came in along their route and covered them as they passed the dangerous intersection and continued on to army headquarters. They were having coffee at the headquarters when the clouds parted, and they saw sunlight reflecting off the Israeli planes, bright and sparkling, as once again they bombed the Iraqi positions. The two men returned safely to Amman, where King Hussein resumed his vigil, circulating among his troops, keeping radio contact, meeting with his generals and government. "I didn't sleep for forty-eight hours," he told me.

King Hussein appealed to the UN Security Council for a cease-fire on June 6, just twenty-four hours into what became known as the Six-Day War; however, arguments over the wording of the cease-fire delayed its adoption for another critical twenty-four hours. The delay gained the Israelis their objective of seizing as much territory as they could, just as they had in 1948. Even after King Hussein formally accepted the cease-fire proposal on June 7 — the cease-fire announcement was broadcast regularly over Radio Amman — Israeli forces continued to fight Jordanians in Jerusalem and to seize control of the West Bank.

Israeli forces then set their sights on the Golan Heights, ignoring, as they had with Jordan and Egypt, a UN-sponsored cease-fire with Syria. An American electronic intelligence ship, the USS *Liberty*, was steaming off the coast of Gaza on June 8, the fourth day of the Six-Day War, listening to and relaying Israeli preparations for the invasion of Syria, when the ship's communication channels were suddenly jammed and the ship was just as suddenly attacked, first by unmarked Israeli fighter planes, then by torpedo boats. Thirty-four American sailors were killed, another 175 wounded. Israel quickly apologized for the attack, insisting it was an accident, but others disagree. Many, including senior U.S. officials, expressed outrage that Israeli forces could have deliberately attacked the *Liberty* to halt the flow of intercepted messages and mask Israel's intentions to seize more territory.

Hours after Syria accepted the Security Council's cease-fire on the morning of June 9, the Golan Heights fell to Israel's massive air and artillery attack, cementing Israel's goal. In less than a week, Israel had seized enough territory to more than triple its land. The entire area of Palestine originally allocated to the Palestinians under the British Mandate and the United Nations was now under Israeli control.

The war took a terrible toll on Jordan and its people. Seven hundred soldiers were killed, and more than 6,000 were wounded or missing. One of the missing was Prince Ali, who was presumed dead by King Hussein and the rest of the royal family. Prince Ali's wife, Princess Wijdan, told me of her anguish as she went to the army hospital every day to look for his body. "The dead and wounded were coming in trucks, horribly burned by napalm," she told me. "I volunteered to feed the wounded because they couldn't feed themselves." As each new truckload came in she would call out, "Anybody in the Third Brigade? Anybody in the Third Brigade?" Finally one of the wounded soldiers said yes, and that he had seen Prince Ali two days earlier "still sitting on a tank with a machine gun aimed at the Israeli planes overhead." Three days later, Prince Ali came home. "We were ashamed to come back, having lost the war," Prince Ali told her. "So we just stayed there."

King Hussein was crushed — he would always take Jordan's losses very personally. In less than a week, the Hashimite Kingdom of Jordan had lost half its territory: the Palestinian lands it had assumed responsibility for protecting in 1950, including Jerusalem, Bethlehem, Hebron, Jericho, Nablus, and Ramallah.

The entire West Bank and its fertile farmland were occupied by Israel, sending a new wave of some 400,000 Palestinian refugees into Jordan. The country's economy, which was one of the most promising in the Arab world, was in tatters. The flourishing tourist industry completely dried up, foreign investment slowed, and development projects were shelved. Those six days of war, the King told me, "were the worst days of my life."

His cousin, Sharif Abdul Hamid Sharaf, told me that the King, in a private moment, had wept bitterly over the loss of Jerusalem, the holy city his grandfather had fought for and saved for Arabs and Muslims. It was the first time he had ever seen the King cry. "I cannot accept that Jerusalem is lost in my time," the King had lamented.

From that moment, the King said, he had put all his energies into trying to rebuild what had been lost and to secure a just and comprehensive peace not only for the Palestinians but for the stability of the entire region and, by extension, the world. His journey had taken him to New York in November 1967, just five months after the war, where the United Nations, too, was trying to find a peaceful and equitable resolution to the ongoing Arab-Israeli conflict.

King Hussein stayed at the Waldorf Hotel, as did Egypt's Foreign Minister Mahmoud Riad, Israel's Foreign Minister Abba Eban, and Arthur Goldberg, the U.S. ambassador to the

United Nations. Meeting separately around the clock in secret with Goldberg, the men eventually agreed to the wording of what would become UN Resolution 242 when it was unanimously adopted by the Security Council on November 22. Resolution 242 laid out the principles for peace in the Middle East, emphasizing "the inadmissibility of the acquisition of territory by war" (a basic premise of the UN charter) and calling for the "withdrawal of Israeli armed forces from territories occupied in the recent conflict," in exchange for "acknowledgment of the sovereignty, territorial integrity, and political independence of every state in the area and their right to live in peace within secure and recognized boundaries free from threats or acts of force."

After being given assurances by U.S. Secretary of State Dean Rusk and President Lyndon Johnson that Israel would return a substantial portion of the West Bank to Jordan within six months, King Hussein accepted Resolution 242 and its formula of "land for peace." "I was assured by the Americans that Israel was 'on board,'" King Hussein said. "They told me that six months would be the outside limit for its implementation. I believed them." But just as his great-grandfather had been deceived in 1917, so was King Hussein let down in 1967.

As we lingered over dinner at Hashimya in 1978, Israel still had not withdrawn from the Arab lands it had seized more than a decade earlier. From the terrace of the palace, we could look over and see the lights of historic Jerusalem nearly obscured by the lights of the encircling settlements and developments that the Israelis had built around the holy city. The reminders of the impasse were everywhere, from the Palestinians in refugee camps all over Jordan to the daily newspapers, which used the dateline "Occupied West Bank" or "Occupied Jerusalem" for any story emanating from the other side of the Jordan River. Yet King Hussein remained optimistic. The implementation of Resolution 242 would become a mainstay of our life and work together as he tried again and again to reach a lasting peace with Israel and justice for the Palestinians. This quest would take us to many places, and it would test the mettle of our marriage. But it was a mission I would come to embrace with all my heart and soul.

chapter five

A Leap of Faith

"I want to see your father," reads one sentence in my journal entry of April 25, 1978, quoting what King Hussein had said to me earlier that evening. I had not yet fathomed the full importance of his remark. I did know that King Hussein was planning a spring trip to the United States, as he did every year. Perhaps he wished to discuss some aviation matters with my father? It had not occurred to me that King Hussein, with his Old World manners, was obliquely telling me that he intended to ask my father for my hand in marriage. It had been barely three weeks since I had joined my father and Marietta Tree for the audience with the King.

I remember the moment when the meaning of his comment began to sink in. It was after dinner one evening at the palace, as I was cutting up an apple, his favorite dessert, for us to share. Hussein repeated his intention to visit the United States and speak with my father.

This time there was something in the way he said it and the way he looked at me that lent his words a special weight. I was so stunned that I did not respond except to say, "Have another piece of apple," as I cut first one slice, then another, then another.

Too much of a gentleman to press his case, the King dropped me off at my apartment soon after. He was leaving on an official visit to Yugoslavia in the morning and gave me two gifts as he bade me farewell. When I was alone, I opened them. One was a diamond-trimmed cigarette lighter, the other a gold ring encrusted with tiny white and yellow diamonds. I was completely overwhelmed. The next day, I wore the ring to the office, concealing it on a chain around my neck under my shirt. I could just imagine the reaction if I suddenly appeared in the office or among friends with the ring on my finger.

For the next two days the only contact I had with King Hussein was by tuning in to the evening news. It was the first time we had been separated for any amount of time, and as I watched the coverage of his official state visit to Yugoslavia, I was taken aback by how much I missed him and by how connected I felt to the man on the TV screen. Once back from his travels, he persisted in mentioning my father in almost every conversation. Then, with a few well-chosen words, he proposed marriage. My days of avoiding the subject were over.

King Hussein was one of the world's most eligible bachelors at the time. Families in Jordan, not to mention other countries in the region, would delight at the thought of having a daughter marry the King; the advantages of such a union would be enormous. During an official visit to the United States, shortly after his third wife's death, the King had traveled to Texas and had come away with the impression that every single young woman in the community had been paraded in front of him as if, he said later, they were competing to be the next Grace Kelly. The idea of material or social advantage deriving from one's choice of husband was not something that I would have considered under any circumstances, let alone now. My generation married for love.

I agonized over my decision for the next two weeks, trying to work out in my mind whether I should question his judgment in considering me to be the right choice for him and for the country. Although none of his previous wives had been born in Jordan either, what might be the negative implications for him in the Arab world if he married me? Would it matter that I was born in the United States? Was I suitable? I had lived an independent life, traveled in many different countries. I had a free, open spirit. Would I have the self-discipline necessary to make a good wife for a king? The responsibility was daunting. And what about my own role? I had always worked, not only out of necessity, but also because it was important to me to contribute to society.

It concerned me that I had not spent that much time talking to King Hussein about my life before Jordan. I knew how the international media could pick apart public figures. And I wanted Hussein to be wise about his choice. I did not want him to ever have to pay a price for choosing someone that might further complicate his life. On a more personal level, I wondered where I would find the strength for the difficult times that were bound to come. Would I be able to cope? My mind was ablaze with questions and worries.

I also had to think through what little I knew about the King, and sort through all the rumors and the gossip about his personal life. I will not deny that the idea of being his fourth wife, or anybody's fourth wife, was troubling to me. He had told me about his first, eighteen-month marriage to Sharifa Dina Abdel Hamid (who became Queen Dina), a distant Hashimite cousin seven years older than he with whom he had a daughter, Alia; his second marriage in 1961 was to a young English-woman, Antoinette Gardiner, who became Princess Muna. They had two sons, Abdullah and Feisal, and twin daughters, Zein and Aisha. He divorced Muna after eleven years to marry Alia Toukan, from a Palestinian family, who died tragically after four years. If I accepted his proposal, I would be stepmother to his eight

123

children, including Queen Alia's very young children. That seemed an enormous responsibility, but in my idealistic view it was one that I could gladly embrace.

There were other considerations. America had long since replaced Britain as the major influence in the region, and its unflinching political support for Israel was highly unpopular in the Arab world, including Jordan. Might his own people feel antagonistic toward their King, even betrayed, by his choice of an American woman, albeit one with Arab roots? This was not a frivolous concern. The King's image had already been deeply affected in the region when an article in *The Washington Post* the year before alleged that he was on the United States Central Intelligence Agency payroll — a critical charge in a region where anti-American sentiment ran so high. The last thing I wanted to do was add any fuel to this kind of damaging slander.

Given the present tension in the region, it would have been very easy to do. Much of that tension was due to Egyptian President Anwar Sadat. I had been passing through Paris on a working visit for the airline when President Sadat made his historic visit to Israel in November 1977 to address the Knesset, Israel's Parliament, and to pray at the Al Aqsa mosque, the third holiest shrine in Islam, the site where the Prophet Muhammad's Night Journey, or ascension to heaven, occurred. I recall the live

124

coverage of Sadat's arrival in Tel Aviv and descent from the aircraft and holding my breath as he reached Israeli soil. It was an extraordinary sight. I remember thinking idealistically that Sadat's gesture offered hope for peace, but the Lebanese friends I was with were horrified.

Our divergent responses reflected the controversy that would swirl around Sadat's visit. While many in the West considered Sadat a hero, the Arab world was incensed. There were riots in Damascus and bombs thrown at the Egyptian embassy; Arab students stormed the Egyptian embassy in Athens; and a group of Palestinians broke into and temporarily held the Egyptian embassy in Madrid. While there was no violence in Amman, the public mood was dark.

The nightmare for Hussein was that Israel would weaken the Arab position by dividing and co-opting its leaders, and leaving the Palestinians hanging in the balance. For the Israelis, the most powerful, largest, most populous state with the least problematic occupied territory was Egypt. The Sinai, which Israel had seized from Egypt in the 1967 war, would be relatively easy to return if the Israelis could convince President Sadat to abandon Arab solidarity and go it alone, although Sadat kept publicly insisting that would never happen.

Sadat's unexpected announcement that he would visit Jerusalem and speak before the Knesset in November 1977 had caused such concern in Jordan that King Hussein had called an emergency cabinet meeting. Hussein, however, muted his criticism of the Egyptian President's historic trip and called on the Arab states to reserve judgment. The King feared that an outright rejection of the Egyptian initiative might provoke an alienated Sadat to seek a separate agreement with Israel. He also saw many positive elements in Sadat's opening statement to the Knesset, such as his rejection of a separate settlement to the Palestinian problem. King Hussein, as ever, insisted on holding out hope that some good could come out of Sadat's intentions. Not giving up on anyone, I was learning, was a defining characteristic of his. He had a tenacious faith that man's better angels would prevail. However, his relatively mild reaction to Sadat's announcement infuriated some Jordanians, who felt the Egyptian leader deserved harsher treatment.

One such Jordanian was the wife of the Chief of the Royal Court. "All that Sadat does, and this is your statement?" she said at the time to her husband. His reply echoed King Hussein's own words. "You either want to get Sadat back in the Arab fold or you want to drive him away."

Prior to Sadat's visit to Israel, the newly installed Carter administration in Washington, D.C., had been negotiating with Israel and the Arab countries to convene an international

Middle East peace conference in Geneva. In the first months of our friendship, King Hussein was working day and night with the United Nations, traveling constantly to Egypt, Syria, Saudi Arabia, and other Gulf states to win support for the peace conference with Israel and a solution based on UN Resolution 242. He would return from his journeys physically exhausted but full of hope. He believed that Arab unity was the greatest strength in the negotiating position of the Arab countries, not only to the benefit of each but particularly to the Palestinians, whose tragedy was at the heart of the conflict.

In retrospect, I find it somewhat astonishing that during those days Hussein was able to carve out so much time to spend with me. Although I had asked for time to consider his proposal, we continued to meet for dinner at Hashimya and would often listen to music and watch films. His favorite singers were the beautiful Lebanese singer Fairuz; Farid Al Atrache, a Syrian-born musician, singer, and actor (the Maurice Chevalier of the Arab world); Johnny Mathis; and the Swedish group Abba. Sometimes Hussein would sing to me. Though I was not as drawn to Abba as he was, to say the least, I was quite charmed when he would croon "Take a Chance on Me." My heart was melting.

On some of these evenings, a few of his

friends would join us. I vividly recall the first time I met Leila Sharaf, a native of Lebanon who had spent the last nine years in Washington, D.C., and New York with her husband, Sharif Abdul Hamid Sharaf, who had been Jordan's ambassador to the United States and permanent representative to the United Nations. I was immediately drawn to Leila's sharp wit and canny political skills. Her husband, who would become Prime Minister after serving as Chief of the Royal Court, had a brilliant mind and a progressive intellect. They would quickly become my close friends and advisers.

In one of our first conversations Leila explained the significance of an event I had witnessed earlier. While walking down a main thoroughfare of the city I had become caught up in a sudden swirl of official motorcades, royal guards, and police barriers outside the entrance of the historic Parliament building, a modest two-story structure. The commotion was caused by the King's convening the National Consultative Council, Jordan's interim representative body. Leila explained that since the union of the West Bank with Jordan in 1950 at the request of Palestinian leaders seeking protection from Israeli expansionism, members of the Jordanian Parliament had been elected in equal numbers from the West and East Banks of the Jordan River. As a direct repercussion of the 1967 war, Parliament was suspended because Israel prevented the members living on the occupied West Bank from crossing easily into Jordan to attend the sessions. Even if the elected officials did manage to get across, they no longer represented constituencies under Jordanian jurisdiction. "Who would run the elections under occupation?" Leila said. "And holding elections would essentially mean accepting the occupation." So with half of Parliament gone, the elected body had been suspended, leaving Jordan without a representative legislative body until the moment I had observed.

The members of the new National Consultative Council were appointed from all parts of the population in terms of geography, ethnicity, profession — and gender. For the first time women were officially included in a national decision-making body. Elections would have to wait for the mandated return of the West Bank and the right of self-determination for the Palestinians, but the National Consultative Council was an important and inclusive step forward for Jordan.

The King and I were following what had by now become a routine of seeing each other and the children every evening. On one occasion he arrived to pick me up at my apartment with Abir. She was five at the time, with curly black hair, big brown eyes, and an irrepressible personality. She disappeared into my bedroom, then into my closet, pulling on my boots, and strode across my living room in them, to my amusement and Hussein's chagrin. Haya, age three, who came over another afternoon, was lively, too, but dainty and adorably coquettish, a little ballerina. Both girls liked to play with my hair endlessly, when not absorbed with their extensive collection of Barbie and Cindy dolls. And two-year-old Ali was a little bundle of joy, cuddly, with chubby cheeks and a wonderfully impish grin. Often overshadowed by his two older sisters, he reached out to me for attention and affection.

In the meantime, I felt a growing need to respond to the King's proposal. It would have been helpful to have someone to talk with, to help me sort things out, but there are no secrets in Amman. It was not that I doubted the discretion of my few close friends; however, I instinctively felt that it would be an infringement of his privacy for me to speak about him to anyone. Apart from his inner circle and his sister, Princess Basma, and her husband, Major Timoor Daghastani, whom we visited occasionally in the evenings, no one knew I was seeing him. Nor did I feel this decision was something I could thrash out with friends and family in the United States over the telephone. It would have to be my decision alone.

About ten days after the King proposed marriage, I wavered. We had just spent a weekend at the King's seaside home in Aqaba with Empress Farah of Iran. The Shahbanou was not the problem. Hussein was. The moment we arrived in Aqaba, I watched the King change before my eyes from the sensitive, relaxed, warm person I had come to know and love to a virtual stranger who was tense and distant. He seemed to fixate on every detail of the visit, double- and triple-checking even the most minor arrangements. Once the guests arrived, he also became a different person around the Empress and her entourage — formal and stiff — a dramatic departure from his usual easy way with friends and family.

Empress Farah's supremely sophisticated lifestyle and circumstances were quite a contrast to the relatively no-frills life I had seen inside the Jordanian court. Hussein so clearly admired her that I could not help but wonder if he might be completely mistaken about me and the image I could project as his wife. I went through the motions all weekend, accompanying King Hussein and his Iranian guests to an elaborately catered dinner down the coast beyond the small Saudi coastal village of Hagl, where tents had been set up on the beach. On another day we went by helicopter to Wadi Rum, where there were more tents and another banquet. On the bus returning to Aqaba, I was quiet, and Hussein's sister, Basma, seemed to read my thoughts. She strongly advised me to consider marriage to her brother very carefully.

Everything returned more or less to normal after the guests left, but I could not help thinking about the other Hussein I had seen

131

during the royal visit. Over time I would come to understand how entertaining honored guests was almost a sacred duty to my husband. To begin with, the ideal of the perfect host was deeply embedded in the King's culture. Throughout the Arab world, visitors to one's home are given every attention, and even enemies who seek refuge are provided safe haven. Among Jordan's Bedouin, for example, a tribesman will slaughter his last head of cattle or offer the food off his own plate to a guest. In the case of the Shah's wife, she was a guest among guests, since my husband had known the Shah and his family for almost twenty years. In the years to come, I began to appreciate the enormous responsibility he felt with guests such as the Iranians, who had not only hosted my husband's family in legendary style but had been extremely supportive of Jordan's development over many years.

After our guests left, Hussein confided in me something that helped explain his preoccupation. The Shahbanou had taken him aside and asked him, "If anything happens to us, will you be guardian to our children?" She may have been thinking about her husband's battle with cancer, which none of us knew about at the time, or she may have been concerned about the growing unrest in her homeland. Pressure on the Shah was building from the Shi'ite scholars in the holy city of Qom, where there had been a riot just three months earlier. The

Shah's security forces had successfully contained the violence, but the restiveness that I had sensed and occasionally felt while I lived in Iran was continuing.

Hussein was moved by her request and concerned by the rising religious fervor among Iran's religious class. He told the Shahbanou that he would talk to Imam Moussa Sadr, a prominent moderate Shi'ite scholar in Lebanon, to see if he would serve as an intermediary to help quell the mounting conflict. If anyone could play a constructive role, it would be the influential Imam. King Hussein invited him to Jordan for a meeting at Hashimya, where the Imam told His Majesty that revolution was imminent and there would be bloodshed unless there was a real effort at reconciliation. Sadr recommended that the Shah invite Ayatollah Ruhollah Khomeini back home from exile in Iraq and try to come to a peaceful solution. After the meeting, King Hussein went to Tehran and told the Shah what he had learned. The Shah's head of intelligence, who was at the meeting, said, "Sadr is a liar. He and Khomeini are two snakes. The people are content, and there is no fear of revolution." After the visit, the King told Ali Ghandour, "I am afraid Imam Sadr is right, and the price of ignoring him will be very high."

The King also sent a letter to Khomeini, who was living in exile in Paris and leading the opposition against the Shah. Khomeini responded politely, but it was obvious he was not open to negotiations with the Shah's regime.

On the drive back to Amman from Aqaba, we stopped along the way in the Jordan Valley at the farm of Hussein's cousin, Sharif Zeid Bin Shaker, and his wife, Nawzad. Sharif Zeid was a year older than Hussein and was one of his oldest and dearest friends. He had been at the prestigious Victoria College secondary school in Alexandria, Egypt, with Hussein and a year ahead of him at Sandhurst; he then went into the Jordanian army and was now Commander in Chief of the Armed Forces. He would go on to become the Chief of the Royal Court and Prime Minister for three terms, after which the King would bestow on him the honorary title of Prince.

We had a delicious, impromptu picnic lunch on the farm, which was just the respite I needed after the weekend in Aqaba. We ate in a gaily colored cotton tent set up in a field and discussed the family's forays into agricultural production. We met again a few days later when the King invited me to attend a traditional welcoming military "Beat the Retreat" ceremony in honor of the visiting President of Mauritania. The King picked me up from my apartment and drove to Sharif Zeid's house in the military headquarters compound, where it was arranged that I would continue on to the event with Nawzad. We arrived at the ceremony just before the King and were escorted to our seats along the seemingly interminable length of the parade ground in front of the expectant official audience. I was acutely self-conscious in such a public setting but thankfully oblivious to the fact that apparently all eyes were on me.

Later I learned that as we reached our seats near the King's, somewhere in the middle of the front row, someone in the crowd had looked questioningly at the King's aide-de-camp while pointing at me. The aide-de-camp responded by outlining a crown over his head and saluting. Other friends reported later that they had seen the way the King looked at me when he arrived, as if, one said, "the light of the sun was coming out of his eyes." The collective opinion was that I was certain to become King Hussein's wife. "They are definitely going to marry," Leila Sharaf told her close friend Nawzad Shaker as the two women drove away together after the ceremony.

Hussein began to press me for an answer. "We cannot go on like this," he said. I tried to tell him more about my life before I had come to Jordan and discuss the problems our marriage might cause. "I really do not want to know," he told me. He was so sure about our future life together that his confidence was infectious. His unfailing conviction was beginning to win me over.

I already had tremendous personal respect for him and admiration for all he stood for and was trying to achieve. The gossip and rumors aside, I knew the man as he really was, full of character, decency and conviction. I was also deeply attracted to him. Still, I knew that this would be no ordinary union.

I had an incomplete picture of what the future might be, but I knew that no matter what happened, I would always have my work and the contributions I could make to the country to see me through. The King had let me know in so many words that he was offering me a partnership. That realization, too, helped me make up my mind. I had a job to do for a country I already loved, and an extraordinary man as a partner. Together we could make a difference.

"Shall I call your father?" he asked me again on May 13, eighteen days after he had first proposed. We were at Hashimya in the early afternoon, having just put the children down for a nap. I looked at him across the room, seeing the sincerity in his gaze, hearing the certainty in his voice. My mother was right about those eyes. "Yes," I said.

"Slightly amazed" were the words my father used to describe the moment when he picked up the phone in his kitchen in his house in Alpine, New Jersey, and heard King Hussein say in his deep, rich voice: "I have the honor to ask for the hand of your daughter in marriage." The last encounter my father knew about was our March audience with King Hussein and the invitation he had extended for me to inspect Hashimya. "I thought it was just for lunch," he blurted out. My mother was equally stunned when we telephoned her afterward on the secure phone in the King's radio room in Hashimya. I told her that I was in love and going to marry the man with the beautiful eyes. There was silence on the line until she collected herself and said how happy she was for me. Both of my parents counseled me to carefully consider my decision, knowing nothing of my long internal debate. Their loving concern meant a great deal to me. Rather than considering prestige or any kind of benefit that might accrue to them at any level, they were focused on my personal happiness. They both liked King Hussein very much but were apprehensive about the challenges I would face as his wife.

My mother did not like the idea of me living so far away, and she expressed her concern that our culturally different backgrounds might prevent us from finding a common language. I told her about our long conversations and that I had never met anyone easier to talk to. My father's anxieties were more political. He wondered whether I was ready to handle the Byzantine ways of a royal family and court. He was also concerned about my safety, given the turbulence in the Middle East. Threats to the King's life were well documented, and he feared I would face the same danger.

In fact, attempts against King Hussein were the stuff of legend. On one occasion in the late 1950s, his plane had been flown almost into the ground in Syria by MiG jets, the attack planes coming so close to his that his uncle, who was traveling with him, exchanged an obscene gesture with one of the Syrian pilots. Other attempts on his life, especially during the early years of his monarchy, seemed positively medieval. On one occasion, Hussein's Egyptian valet filled the King's bottle of nose drops with acid, a potentially fatal substitution discovered when the bottle accidentally broke after falling in the sink and the contents ate through the enamel. Poison was the weapon of choice for another would-be assassin, an assistant cook at the court who had been bribed by a cousin in Syrian intelligence. The plot was uncovered when dead cats began appearing around the palace in Amman. Since he was not familiar with poison, the cook had been practicing on local strays.

There had been various other, more conventional attempts on the King's life in Jordan, one an ambush on the road from the airport, another on the road to his farm in Hummar. His maternal uncle, Sharif Nasser, had the bad luck to be involved in both those incidents as well as the MiG attack. In the first case, he had pushed Hussein out of the car and into a ditch when the shooting started, then had thrown himself over him. King Hussein always laughed about it later, saying he had been in more danger from being smothered by his rather stout uncle than dying from the bullets. In the second incident, it was Sharif Nasser who was almost killed. Both he and the King drove Buick convertibles and the gunmen mistakenly fired on Sharif Nasser's car, shattering the windshield and puncturing a tire but, amazingly, missing him.

The King had had many other close calls over the years, but they did not disturb him. He believed in fate and in the will of Allah. Like all Muslims, he subscribed to the view that God, and God alone, would decide when and how he would die. He always wore a gun, a habit he had adopted as a teenager after the assassination of his grandfather, King Abdullah. He also made sure his security detail was one of the best trained and best equipped in the world. While he was careful, he did not let security concerns circumscribe his activities.

Every bit as legendary as the assassination attempts was his ability to forgive his enemies. It was remarkable, especially in a region where political enemies were not treated kindly. One general in the Jordanian army, Ali Abu Nuwar, who tried to overthrow King Hussein, was not only pardoned but eventually became Jordan's ambassador to France.

The media was far more interested than I was in whatever danger surrounded the King. Most of my early interviews began with questions about threats to his life and whether the possibility of violence had given me pause in accepting his proposal. But the truth was that I had never given my own security any thought. I could not imagine myself being a political target.

Though my parents had misgivings, they blessed the union. My mother made plans to quietly meet me in Paris so that I could look for a wedding dress and some proper clothes. My entire wardrobe at the time consisted of three skirts, some shirts, two blazers, and several pairs of blue jeans, which even I, a dedicated minimalist, knew would no longer be adequate. We decided to keep the engagement a secret until I returned from Paris, realizing that once it became public, I would no longer have any freedom of movement, but our plan was immediately foiled.

King Hussein, I discovered, did not like to keep good news to himself. The very next morning in his office at the Diwan he mentioned our engagement to his cousin, Prince Raad, who, evidently not able to keep secrets either, immediately started to ululate throughout the Diwan. By noon, the news was all over Amman and that was the end of it. I was not able to travel to meet up with my mother or organize anything. Instead, by the time of the official announcement two days later, I was more or less captive in Amman. It is stunning even now to remember how quickly everything I owned was packed up and moved to Al Ma'Wa, a small house in the Basman Royal Court compound. The house had been a favorite retreat of King Hussein's beloved grandfather, King Abdullah, a respite from the pressures of family and work that held a special attachment for his grandson. Hussein affectionately remembered quiet afternoons praying in the garden, or challenging his grandfather to a game of chess. The peaceful, reflective space had been greatly changed, however. The façade was now a bastardized version of the original simple stone structure, and inside the floors were covered in wall-to-wall shag carpeting in relentless shades of brown.

Life as I had known it was over. I was assigned a court driver, and wherever I went by car, as either a passenger or a driver, a security vehicle would follow. For security reasons I was not able to visit my office even one last time, nor did I ever return to my apartment. The suddenness with which I stopped working was particularly hard to accept. I knew my staff was more than capable, but I still felt terrible about leaving them in the lurch. The decision, however, was out of my hands. It was not as if I was never going to work again, I consoled myself. It just meant that I was making an adjustment.

A press conference was called, but otherwise the court supported my desire to have minimal contact with the media. I felt strongly that the personal and private aspect of the situation should be safeguarded, yet my efforts did not stop the media speculation. A great deal was made of our age difference. He was forty-two and I was twenty-six, but I was not conscious of that at all. We seemed so naturally connected, and I appreciated his wisdom and experience. Much would also be made about the difference in our heights, given that he was two inches shorter than I. This, too, seemed ridiculous to me. My only concern, which would never entirely dissipate, was whether I would be adequate to the role of his wife and consort and worthy of his faith in me.

The press was persistent, though. Time and again journalists managed to circumvent the palace's switchboard and ring through directly to Al Ma'Wa. When this would happen, I would pretend to be someone else while the reporter on the other end of the phone used all manner of ruses to finagle some contact with the King's fiancée. How ironic to be engaged in this cat-and-mouse game with the press, given my goal not so very long ago to be a journalist. I divulged nothing, but the persistence of the media was so taxing that I asked Meliha Azar, my close friend from the Civil Aviation Academy, if she might be able to come work for me. Mercifully she accepted and, among other things, shielded me from the voracious press.

I was not a prisoner. I could come and go as I pleased. Hussein had provided a car for me — a silver Lancia, which had been a gift to him; to this day, the smell of new car leather evokes fond memories of that period of my life. I drove myself a lot of the time, as I continued to do throughout my married life.

The most precious gift the King ever gave me was my name. One possibility, suggested by Ali Ghandour, was Allyyessar, a Phoenician queen whose name encompassed Lisa, but the King decided it sounded too much like "Al Yasar," an Arabic term for someone politically to the left. (In fact, it might not have been entirely inappropriate, as I was certainly more liberal than most of the people around him.) One day while sitting with me in Hashimya, the King suddenly said, "Noor."

Noor. It means "light" in Arabic. My name would be Noor Al Hussein, the "Light of Hussein." Over the next few weeks and months, a transition gradually took place in my mind, in my dreams. I became Noor.

My family had much more trouble accepting my new name, especially my mother. That was understandable, of course. She had named me, after all, and for twenty-six years she had known me as Lisa. I gave her license for a while, but after several years I became quite adamant. I felt she was making a statement by continuing to call me Lisa, refusing in her way to accept my new identity and life. What she did not understand, until I explained it quite forcefully, was that I had made a lifelong commitment when I embarked on marrying King Hussein, and if she loved me and supported me, she had to recognize and accept that commitment as well. She never called me Lisa again.

I knew I was going to become a Muslim, so I spent a great deal of time in that little house learning more about Islam. The Jordanian Constitution does not mandate that the monarch's wife be a Muslim. It does require the King to be a Muslim and to be a descendant of Sharif Hussein Bin Ali, the leader of the Great Arab Revolt, but the King, like all Muslim men, is free to marry a woman of any monotheistic faith, described in the Quran as "the people of the book."

My parents had not brought me up in any particular religion and had always encouraged me to choose my own spiritual path. The Muslim faith was the first religion I had been truly drawn to. I admired Islam's emphasis on a believer's direct relationship with God, the fundamental equality of rights of all men and women, and the reverence for the Prophet Muhammad as well as all the Prophets and messengers who came before him, since Adam, to Abraham, Moses, Jesus, and many others. Islam calls for fairness, tolerance, and charity: "Let there be no compulsion in religion," the Quran commands (2:256). And "Not one of you is a true believer until he desires for his brother what he desires for himself," reads one of the sayings of the Prophet Muhammad. I

144

was attracted, too, by its simplicity and call for justice. Islam is a very personal belief system. There are prayer leaders and religious scholars but no intermediaries or bureaucrats, as in other monotheistic religions. No Muslim is better than any other Muslim except by piety. Honesty, faithfulness, and moderation are a few of the virtues that Islam calls for, and by which one Muslim can have merit over another.

Hussein did not tell me I had to become a Muslim. He never even asked me. The decision would be mine and mine alone. (Adopting a belief system is an important decision — one that, on principle, I would not make for convenience.) There was simply no question about it in my mind. For the first time in my life, I felt a sense of belonging to a larger community. I felt humbled and grateful. The call to prayer that had beckoned to me from my first days in Tehran now had a deeply personal meaning.

I lived by myself in Al Ma'Wa and asked for books on Islam and Jordanian history so I could study and learn as much as possible. I had been studying Arabic since I first arrived in Jordan, and now I redoubled my efforts.

King Hussein and I continued to come to know each other, and unburdened by my prior caution and self-examination, I fell deeply in love with him. I spent a lot of quiet time with his youngest children. When Hussein told Haya that we were going to be married and she would have a new mother, she said in her prayers before going to bed, "Please, God, make her live long." Those children had suffered such loss in their young lives. I understood why her two-year-old brother, Prince Ali, often clutched my hand and would not let go.

Looking back now on that period before our marriage, I realize that those were the most golden, carefree weeks of my life. The King and I had little to do with the details of the wedding, which spared me all the frenzy that so often accompanies such occasions. Our only directive to the Royal Court, which made all the arrangements through Royal Protocol, was to keep the wedding utterly simple. In the Middle East, weddings can be extravagant three-day affairs, with banquets, musicians, and dancers. But like many women of my generation, I always thought I would be married barefoot on a mountaintop or in a field of daisies. I had never wanted an elaborate wedding. Also, being keenly aware of the criticism of the extravagance of the 1970s oil-boom period in many Arab countries, I hoped that we could strike a simpler balance.

Gradually, during this period, Hussein introduced me to other members of his family. I met his brother, Prince Mohammed, one day at tea on the terrace at Hashimya. He had been designated Crown Prince from 1952 to 1962, and in 1971 became head of the Council of Tribal Chiefs. I was very touched by the way Prince

Mohammed welcomed me so warmly into the family. I was also introduced to the King's younger brother, Crown Prince Hassan, and his wife, Sarvath, who came from a prominent Pakistani family. King Hussein had appointed his Oxford-educated brother Crown Prince in 1965 out of concern for the succession during those turbulent years of so many attempts on the King's life. Crown Prince Hassan served as a deputy and adviser to the King and as regent during his absences from the country. He played a valuable role in Jordan — overseeing the country's development strategy and founding the Royal Scientific Society — and would passionately promote interfaith and cross-cultural understanding. Hassan had a lively sense of humor and a bellowing, infectious laugh, and I loved to watch the two brothers laughing uproariously in their rare moments of relaxation together. His wife, I discovered over tea, was very interested in education and would found an excellent private school with programs in special education for the mentally disabled, as well as Jordan's first center for learning difficulties.

On one of our trips to Aqaba, Hussein arranged for me to accompany his sister, Princess Basma, on a visit to a Bedouin community in Wadi Rum. It was the first time I had seen the Hashimite family in this traditional role of engaging with local communities, in this case a southern tribe. In the stifling sun, under a *beit esh-sha'ar,* we received members of the tribe one by one, hearing their requests for help with a sick child or for better schools, housing, or transport. Many would bring written petitions, as was the custom, to members of the royal family. I was full of admiration for Princess Basma's patience and grace as she greeted all with a smile and patiently listened to their requests. After his third wife's death, the King had asked his sister to run a fund to support programs that the late Queen had shown interest in. Princess Basma would expand the fund considerably beyond that mandate and eventually establish a number of social welfare centers around the country. She also would become increasingly engaged in women's issues in Jordan and internationally in later years.

Hussein traveled frequently during our engagement, which fell in that critical period between President Sadat's trip to Jerusalem and the Camp David Accords a year later. Our evenings together were constantly interrupted by telephone calls related to meetings with other Arab leaders. I was struck by the intensity of the King's sense of personal responsibility to achieve a final consensus among the Arabs about the Geneva Conference. He would often return to Amman from these meetings confident that the Middle East was on the verge of a breakthrough.

We tried to create a regular routine despite

the press of events. When we were not together, we would often communicate using two-way radios. The King always had one of these handheld radios with him so that he could be in instant communication with the royal guards, his Prime Minister, and the Chief of the Royal Court. After our engagement, Hussein gave me one, along with the code name November Hussein for Noor Al Hussein. His was Hotel Tango for Hussein Talal. In the evenings after dropping me off at Al Ma'Wa he would radio that he had arrived safely home. This was how we said good-night.

Hussein wanted us to marry as soon as possible but was persuaded to allow time for our families to gather in Amman. We set our wedding for June 15, the day after his mother, Queen Zein, was scheduled to return from her biannual trip to Europe, which did not leave us much time to get organized. First, there was the matter of a wedding dress. Hussein's secretary of many years made the decision to commission a wedding dress from Dior in London, and two Dior designers flew into Amman with sketches of elaborate dresses that I would never wear. I wanted the dress to be very simple, not extravagant. I showed them a favorite Yves Saint Laurent boutique dress, somewhat bohemian in character, that I had recently splurged my salary on, and I asked them to use it as a model. The result was a supremely simple white silk dress.

The shoes were more problematic. The fashion of the time was very high platform shoes, which I thought were both hideous and impractical. Apparently there were no low-heeled shoes to be found anywhere in Jordan, and I did not want to tower over my husband. I often wore Dr. Scholl's sandals, but they would not do. In the end, a friend helped me to arrange for a pair of shoes to be made in Beirut. We were not sure whether they would arrive on time or whether I would be a barefoot bride after all. The shoes arrived on the morning of my wedding, still smelling of glue when we unpacked them.

A few days earlier, Hussein had driven me to the airport to welcome my family to Jordan. It was the first visit for my brother, Christian, and my sister, Alexa, and their first encounter with my fiancé. My sister remembers me glowing with happiness and "floating on a cloud," unable to coherently answer any of her questions about the arrangements or, for that matter, anything else.

I became a Muslim on the morning of my wedding. Hussein appeared at the door of Al Ma'Wa around 9 A.M. "I just realized that you have not formally joined the faith yet," he said. So we went into the sitting room and I proclaimed the testimony of faith, *ash-shahada: "Ashhadu anna la ilaha illa Allah, wa anna Muhammadun rasoolu Allah"* — I declare there is no God but Allah and Muhammad is His messenger.

After that I began to prepare for the ceremony. It might well have been the simplest royal wedding ever. A hairdresser, provided for me, arranged my hair as simply as I could persuade him to. I wore no makeup. I did interject a little Western tradition by wearing something borrowed, something blue: The blue was my father's wedding present, a sapphire stickpin from Tiffany; something new was a pair of earrings from a magnificent set of jewelry which included a necklace of a diamond-framed pendant of an image of Hussein that had arrived that morning from Crown Prince Fahd of Saudi Arabia. (The Crown Prince told my husband that he had given each of us something to represent the other.) They were stunning drop earrings, but since I had never worn anything quite that dramatic before, I decided to wear only the tops.

The wedding was to be at Zahran Palace, the home of King Hussein's mother, Queen Zein. She and I were introduced at the airport the day before the wedding, when we welcomed her back from Switzerland. The Queen Mother invited me to prepare for the wedding ceremony in her home, where Princess Basma met me the next morning to help and to steady my nerves. Like any bride, I was in a state of high anxiety that was compounded by the suffocating heat of the day. The Queen Mother whispered words of encouragement as I descended the large circular staircase to where my husband was waiting to escort me into the small but beautifully furnished oriental sitting room where we were to be married.

I was the only woman present. In Islam, marriage is essentially a contract, which both parties agree to and sign in front of witnesses. Though I did not know it at the time, I was the first Hashimite bride in Jordan to represent herself at the religious ceremony (the *Katb Al Kitab*). Even Hussein's daughters would adopt the more traditional approach of having a close male relative stand in for the bride. Prince Mohammed, who to this day has been a dear and true brother, was my guardian.

The ceremony took only five minutes and would have been very relaxed were it not under such scrutiny. Once I had been escorted to my seat next to King Hussein, a damask settee intricately inlaid with mother of pearl, I greeted his brothers, Prince Mohammed and Crown Prince Hassan. My father and brother and other male members of the royal family were all but obscured by the frenzy of flashing camera bulbs and the blinding television lights of the international and Arab media, which, I realized with shock, filled the far end of the long narrow room.

With great effort I concentrated on repeating the simple marriage vows that I had been practicing in Arabic. Looking at the King, I said, "I have betrothed myself to thee in marriage for the dowry agreed upon." He replied, "I have accepted thee as wife, my wife in marriage for the dowry agreed upon." We sealed our vows by clasping our right hands and looking at each other. No rings were exchanged. The sheikh conducting the ceremony recited verses from the Quran; then we walked into an adjoining room, where we were joined by our families and guests shouting, "*Mabrouk,* congratulations!" Abir, Haya, and Ali were the first to embrace us.

Looking now at the pictures of us that appeared on the front page of newspapers around the world, I see a young woman flushed with optimism and hope, smiling with all her heart at a handsome bearded man who is responding in kind. The rest of my wedding day is a jumble of memory fragments: our struggle to cut the wedding cake — no one had pointed out that the bottom layer was cardboard; our impatience to leave the reception to be alone; and our walk to the front courtyard of the Palace, where we adroitly avoided the elaborately decorated Excalibur to leap into Hussein's car and escape to the airport for our precious refuge in Aqaba.

I invited all eight children to join us in Aqaba for the few days we were there before leaving for our honeymoon in Scotland. I wanted them to feel part of our new life together as soon as possible. I knew it would not be easy. Three mothers were involved. Some of Hussein's older children were fully grown adults, and the youngest, Ali, was only two. But all the children adored their father, and with this common denominator I had every hope we might succeed in creating a loving, secure, nurturing family spirit.

Our brief Aqaba idyll was great fun as far as I was concerned. In spite of the differences in their ages, the children seemed to enjoy one another's company tremendously. There was a lot of laughter, teasing, and games. No doubt they were all checking me out, but I felt very easy and at home in their midst.

It had been on our first night in Aqaba, when my new husband and I were watching the news on television, that I heard the announcement that he was giving me the title of Queen. I do not know why he had not told me himself. Perhaps he wanted to surprise me. I was the only person, it seems, in Jordan and the Western world who was not fixated on what title I would have. The newspapers had been filled with conjecture ever since our engagement had been announced. There had also been concerns that, as an American, I might not be accepted in the region, but there was no Arab outcry, as far as I knew, about our marriage, nor any I was aware of from Jordanians. As a Halaby, I was considered an Arab returning home rather than a foreigner.

Our departure for our honeymoon in Scotland was further delayed by graduation day at Jordan University. My husband always handed out the diplomas to all the graduating students, so two days after our marriage we returned to Amman for what would be our first public event. I was quite nervous, not knowing what to expect. There was tremendous excitement when we arrived at the university and great warmth in the way we were received. I knew that the outpouring of affection for me, including the photos of me throughout the city and on cars and buses, was in fact for Hussein, and I was very touched by it — but also conscious that I should not take that affection as an entitlement: I had to earn it in my own right.

One contribution I did make was simply instinctive. I had become so conscious of the issue of the King's security that every time we went out in public, beginning with the graduation at Jordan University, I would try to subtly position myself to protect him in relation to the crowds. Our children would do the same in later years, but at the beginning of our marriage I reflexively found myself contributing to his front line of protection.

As Hussein and I prepared to leave for Scotland, I was filled with a sense of happiness and calm. I felt life had no boundaries, that every dream and goal was possible. I had committed my life to my husband and to Jordan, with all its demands and responsibilities, its frustrations and setbacks, its victories and disappointments. I had taken a leap of faith, and faith has richly rewarded me.

chapter six

Honeymoon at Gleneagles

We nearly died on our honeymoon. Literally. We were at Gleneagles, the grand old golf resort and hotel in the highlands of Perthshire. My husband and I both loved the wide vistas, rolling green hills, and wild beauty of Scotland, which I had first discovered as a backpacking young high school graduate. The hotel was lovely, too. Sculptured shrubs and silver birches and a high hedge of rhododendrons flanked its long driveway, and wide flowerbeds bursting with peonies in bloom graced the front entrance. It was picture perfect, really, except that it was dreadfully cold. In fact, not only was July 1978 one of the coldest on record in Scotland, but it also poured rain almost every day.

Our accommodations were in a newly built, never-before-occupied, ultra-modern bungalow to the rear of the main hotel. We were shown to it with great pride and fanfare and presented with a golden key as its first occupants. Carpeted in orange and brown shag, it could not

157

have been more different from the atmosphere of the distinguished old hotel, with its high-ceilinged rooms, mahogany four-poster beds, generous fireplaces, and all the distinctive charm of old Scotland.

"Do you smell anything odd?" I asked my new husband one night before we went to bed. He did not. I am normally a very light sleeper, but on this night I struggled for consciousness as I became aware that Hussein was shaking me and pulling me out of the bed. "Get up, get up!" he was saying, as if from a long distance. He half dragged me into the sitting room, and I slowly registered that we needed fresh air to clear the acrid-smelling haze that had enveloped the entire suite. I felt groggy, and my eyes and throat were burning. Hussein looked for a window to open, but they were set high up in the wall and out of reach. The front door was locked from the outside, most likely by our own security. I quickly examined the oversized, baroque-style gold key we had been presented ceremoniously upon our arrival. It was clearly decorative and was not going to open the door, though I could not resist a try just to lighten the mood.

Telephoning for help seemed futile as well. We had not been given any kind of directory for the hotel, nor a contact number for either Jordanian security or the British agents assigned to us from Scotland Yard's Special Branch. We could see their trailer parked at the front of the bungalow, but it was just out of earshot. Our calls for help went unanswered. All we could do was laugh at our absurd predicament.

We tried randomly dialing different combinations of numbers on the telephone until our efforts finally yielded a reply. A startled hotel operator put us through to the trailer, and moments later the guards opened our door. We gulped in fresh air in painful gasps. It turned out that a heater located in the narrow corridor from the sitting room to the bedroom had burned out, filling the room with noxious fumes. Had it started a fire, we would have had no escape route.

It was a ludicrous situation. After all the plots and assassination attempts against my husband in his twenty-seven years on the throne, who would have ever imagined that a faulty heater in a friendly country would create such a close call? The further irony was that we had chosen Scotland for our honeymoon precisely because it was safe and comfortable. Our security in Britain was provided by the professional and unobtrusive Special Branch of Scotland Yard.

Our honeymoon was challenging in more ways than one. I was not yet used to the security that surrounded Hussein, nor to the familiarity everyone, everywhere seemed to feel toward him, and now toward us. The World Cup soccer matches were being played at the time, and no matter where we were — at lunch, at tea, or driving through the countryside — members of our entourage would constantly approach us with updates on the latest developments. My husband did not seem to mind. Not only was he an avid soccer fan and glued to the matches on television on those rainy afternoons in Scotland, he was also used to being surrounded by his entourage and security at all times.

I, a private person by nature, was not. I simply could not understand the constant invasion of our privacy — especially the constant presence of a Special Branch officer in our car when we set out on long drives around the countryside, just about the only activity we could undertake, given the stormy weather conditions. We were already surrounded by both leading and following security vehicles.

My husband's favorite way of relaxing, I was discovering, was to go on long drives, while mine was to do something physically active, preferably outdoors — exercise, tennis, skiing, horseback riding. We compromised somewhat in Scotland. Between rainstorms, I persuaded the King to go for walks with me on the famous Gleneagles golf course or across the Scottish moors. He was obliging, but he still preferred to drive.

Hussein's passion for cars stemmed from his schoolboy years at Harrow. That passion had been stoked, I am sure, by the reluctance of the Royal Court in Jordan to let him get behind the wheel of a car. No one at the Royal Court wanted the responsibility of sanctioning a license for the seventeen-year-old heir to the throne. So he passed his driving exam in England instead and bought the first of many cars.

I was less interested in the car itself than where it would take us, and there arose another difference. I loved exploring little roads and lanes in Scotland, not knowing quite where we were or what we might find. Hussein loved to explore, too, but he was more destination-oriented. One day during our honeymoon, for example, he decided he wanted to show me Sandhurst, where he had completed his military training, and within minutes we were in the car heading for Surrey. Once on the grounds, he proudly showed me the statue of Queen Victoria, to whom Sandhurst cadets, if guilty of some infraction, were ordered to "pay their respects"; while on parade they would run off in disgrace to salute and then return to their fellow cadets on the parade ground.

My husband liked to know exactly where he was and where he was going, which stemmed, I am sure, from his many years behind the controls of helicopters and airplanes. Hussein had been taught to fly by a Scot, Jock Dalgliesh. They had met at a tragic moment. Jock, then a wing commander in the British air force on loan to the Jordanian military, was at the airstrip outside of Jerusalem when sixteen-year-old Hussein arrived in shock after witnessing the murder of his grandfather, King Abdullah. Everyone seemed at a loss as to what to do. Except Jock. He took Hussein over to his grandfather's Dove, a twin-engine aircraft, put him in the copilot's seat, and flew him back to Amman. Hussein never forgot that kindness, and the two men developed a lifelong bond that centered on their mutual passion for flying.

Once again, the Royal Court had disapproved of the Crown Prince's new enthusiasm. Even Jock tried to discourage him by taking Hussein up and putting the plane through so many extreme aerial maneuvers that the young prince got airsick, but Hussein was determined. Not only did he have the same love for flying as he did for cars; his ambition was to build a first-class air force in Jordan. If he flew, then other young men in the kingdom would want to fly. So he continued his flight training and, when he was ready, defied the orders given by the Royal Court to Jock, the other pilots, and every mechanic on the ground: Do not let the Crown Prince fly solo. He simply got into an airplane one day when no one was looking and took off.

You could say that without Jock, I might never have met the King. It was Jock's fixation with flying that had first introduced Hussein to the flying bug. Hussein's passion, my father's passion, and my own love of adventure had combined to put the King and me in the same place at the same time.

Jock and my husband reminisced happily over tea in Jock's cottage outside Edinburgh, reliving another dramatic event — their own near-death experience twenty years earlier in the air over Syria. It was Jock who had taken over the controls of the old Dove during the attack and literally skimmed the plane just over the ground to evade the Syrian fighter jets and escape into Jordanian airspace. My husband told me that it was the closest he had ever come to losing his life.

Hussein never lost touch with his old friends, and Jock held a special place in his affections. When Jock was getting on in years, my husband arranged for his UK helicopter pilot, Richard Verrall, to fly the Dove to Scotland on two occasions so that Jock could fly the aircraft again. Jock was well into his seventies by then and had not been in the plane for more than thirty years, but Richard said his hands worked the levers as if time had stood still.

We both enjoyed the visit with Jock, but there was no getting around the dreary weather. The driving rain was not letting up, and I was uncomfortably cold all the time. I had simply not packed with this contingency in mind. I had been so busy getting together my dress and shoes for the wedding that there had been no opportunity for me to organize a trousseau or even suitable clothes for the honeymoon. A friend of my husband's from London had brought some outfits to Amman, but they were essentially cruise wear for a Caribbean holiday. After four days of terrible weather, and very little privacy, we had our close call with the noxious fumes. That sealed it. We decided to leave the next morning for London, where Hussein owned a house on a private road across from Kensington Palace that had formerly served as the Jordanian embassy. At the time he usually stayed at Claridge's Hotel rather than the house, but over time I persuaded him that Palace Green would be more private and secure.

Palace Green was a large five-story house that the King had bought from the government some years back when they were going to sell it. He had lived in it for a while, had given it to his second wife when they divorced, then had bought it back from her. It was a pattern I would get used to: He rarely sold property; instead he would give it away. Palace Green had family quarters on the upper floors and more formal reception rooms on the ground floor. My husband's English secretary of twenty-five years worked out of one of the guest rooms on the second floor and had set up a typewriter on a dressing table. There was no switchboard, and when the phone rang, my husband would often answer it.

I soon discovered how busy the King would be whenever we spent time in London. On our honeymoon he was quickly inundated by requests from Jordanians, the press, diplomats, and ordinary citizens for audiences. The work-load simply carried over from Amman to London. I found myself alone much of the time and adrift in the midst of the whirlwind of activity. Nothing in my life had prepared me for what I now understood would be an everyday reality: Our marriage would be one in which we would fight to find private time together amid the press of events. In fact, our bathroom would become the only reliable sanctuary for the two of us. Often it was the only place where we could talk with complete freedom.

Given all the stress that King Hussein had lived through and the extraordinary challenges and crises he continued to face, I determined very early in our marriage that as much as possible I would try not to add to that stress by burdening him with problems or needs of my own. It was not always easy to keep that pledge, especially on our honeymoon, when I was still getting to know the man I had married. The demands on his time were so constant and so varied that I felt increasingly frustrated.

I was not only a young bride after a short courtship, but by virtue of my marriage to Hussein, a stepmother to eight children. I already felt close to his three youngest — Abir, Haya, and Ali — with whom I had spent many happy moments during our courtship. After my marriage to their father, they would call me "Mama" or "Mummy." However, I hardly knew his other children — Alia, his eldest, Abdullah and Feisal, and his twins, Zein and Aisha — except for what he had told me about the challenges they had faced in the course of his previous three marriages. Hussein's older children would call me "Abla Noor," which translates to big sister.

Over the years I tried as much as possible to include all the children and, when appropriate, their mothers in family gatherings, hoping that regular contact would bring us closer and reduce whatever tensions might exist. I wish I could say that this strategy was an unequivocal success. In hindsight, I think I was a little naïve. I believed that if I exuded positive feelings, these would be returned in kind. It was not that simple. Misunderstandings would bubble up not infrequently, even though I am convinced that all of us — parents, stepparent, and children alike — wanted the complex situation to work.

One of the most enjoyable aspects of our London stay was meeting some of Hussein's old friends. We spent time with the Jordanian ambassador to Britain, Ibrahim Izzedin, and his wife, Noor; both were bright, positive, and supportive. Ibrahim and Hussein had grown up in the same neighborhood and had learned how to ride a bike together. While they met at the embassy, Noor and I found time to talk, and I was immediately drawn to her gentle wisdom and mischievous sense of humor. She also helped me in my search for an antique prayer rug — a present for my husband.

We also had a delightful day in the country at the home of Tessa Kennedy, a distinguished interior designer in England and a longtime friend of my husband's. She had met Hussein in 1957, introduced by the British ambassador in Amman at the time, Charles Johnston. Her mother, hoping to block her marriage to a young painter whom she considered an unsuitable match, had taken Tessa on an extended trip through the Middle East. It did not work. Seventeen-year-old Tessa created a society scandal when she eloped the day she returned to England. She and Hussein remained close friends through the years. He was godfather to her daughter, Milica, and Tessa and her family often visited Jordan during the Easter holidays or in the summer.

Over lunch at her house in the country, I gave Tessa my account of our honeymoon, which we spent nearly frozen in Scotland, and of our near-death experience. Then we played a spirited game of croquet on the lawn, surrounded by a large cedar of Lebanon, a weeping rowan, and other magnificent trees. The setting, the weather, and the company all made for a perfect occasion. Tessa told me later that my sense of humor about nearly being gassed to death in that bungalow convinced her that the marriage would work. It turned out that Hussein had called her soon after he had met me and said: "I think I've found someone. I have been really miserable, and I am happy at last. My life is going to turn around."

What I found most unsettling from the beginning of our marriage was the drip, drip, drip of gossip about Hussein's friends and family. Upon our arrival in London from Scotland I was introduced to his secretary, a loyal and dedicated woman who was also quite possessive and protective. Shortly after our first meeting, she began to criticize most of the people surrounding the King. Seemingly without inhibition, she scrolled through a list of Hussein's friends. His previous wives and children were also fair game. I tried to veer her onto neutral subjects, but to no avail. I had never been exposed to such gossip, and I began to wonder about the world I had married into.

Another difficult adjustment concerned our personal finances. First of all, I found the whole concept of spending someone else's money difficult to adapt to. I was accustomed to earning and spending my own income. After we married, the Royal Court budgetary systems and my husband's finances seemed both mysterious and beyond my control. All I knew for certain was that I was not supposed to worry about money, but what did that mean? On the one hand, I knew the King would not set limits on me, though he had made references to past extravagance. On the other hand, I had been raised to set responsible limits for myself. It

168

was a puzzlement. I did not know what the requirements were as his wife, as a Queen, so there were the inevitable awkward moments. "Why don't you go shopping with my secretary?" my husband often suggested when he was tied up in meetings during our stay in London. He presumed that I loved to shop, but this was my honeymoon, and I wanted to spend it getting to know my husband.

One day, feeling somewhat overwhelmed by it all, I decided I needed a change in atmosphere and contacted my friend Fatina Asfour, who was newly married and living in London. My husband had several cars garaged at Palace Green and probably drivers standing by as well, but I told his secretary I would be happy to take a cab. However, when it came time for me to return, I realized I did not know the address of the London house or even the phone number! I called the Jordanian embassy, but it had already closed for the day. Somehow, by trial and error, Fatina and I determined where I needed to go, and she drove me back to the gated residence. All the while I was wondering if, having exited the rabbit hole from the surreal world surrounding the King, I could re-enter — and even whether I actually wanted to return. Was it all just a strange dream? There was a decidedly Alice in Wonderland quality to the situation. When we finally arrived, the gates to the house were closed, which only reinforced the sensation. I gulped and rang the doorbell, and a guard let me in.

In truth, the only thing drawing me back to those four walls was my husband. We had been married less than two weeks. I truly loved him, and I believed fervently in his quest for peace. Granted, the quiet rituals we had observed during our courtship — dinners and movies and talking alone together — were now less frequent, but there would be other ways to get to know each other and for me to learn more about his world.

Even now, on our honeymoon, politics had become our constant companion. From those days onward, wherever we would go in the world, a black shortwave radio as large as a briefcase would sit on the nightstand, our waking and nightly connection to current events. I was already familiar with the critical events in the region, but I knew them mainly through books and newspapers, as a series of struggles and crises that seemed to unfold almost inevitably, one event upon another. But now it seemed that the lifeblood of human beings was being spilled or saved with every decision. I could see that to my husband this was living history, and it preoccupied his every hour. He framed his life and work in terms of his Hashimite heritage and the search for peace.

Jordan faced a unique political challenge. Many of its citizens identified strongly with their Palestinian heritage and actively sought the return to the land of their forebears. When the Palestinian Liberation Organization (PLO) was created in 1964, it was only natural that many Jordanians of Palestinian origin supported a political movement that promised to restore their property and rights in Palestine itself. King Hussein hoped that one day a permanent peace settlement in Palestine would give Jordanians of Palestinian origin the choice of either remaining in Jordan or returning to their homeland. That was a goal we all worked for, but in the meantime all Jordanian citizens were viewed as members of a single family, with a shared commitment to build the country.

Hussein continued to press for an Israeli withdrawal from the Occupied Territories. He had welcomed the hundreds of thousands of Palestinians displaced by the Israeli occupation of the West Bank and Gaza after the 1967 war, but he had forbidden the extremists among them to establish bases on Jordanian soil from which to mount guerrilla operations against Israel. The Palestinian guerrilla groups that made up the PLO — among them Fatah, led by Yasser Arafat — were of another mind. Their intent, as the PLO's name made clear, was to reclaim their entire homeland from Israel by any means, including force. "I was sympathetic to their cause, but not to their tactics," King Hussein told me. There were, however, more than enough sympathizers in the Palestinian refugee camps and communities to shelter the *fedayeen,* as the Palestinian freedom fighters were called, and they regularly staged raids against Israel across the border. The Israelis struck back with disproportionate force, destroying Jordanian and Palestinian villages all along the Jordan River Valley.

Then came Karameh. An established and quite prosperous Palestinian community that had begun as a small refugee camp, Karameh was the location of one of Arafat's many command posts in the country. The Palestinians living there had welcomed Arafat and the PLO after the Israelis lobbed artillery shells into Karameh in November 1967, killing several schoolgirls on their way home from school. The cycle of attacks and retaliation continued, until on March 21, 1968, Israel sent a massive armored force of 15,000 men into Jordan to wipe out the PLO in Karameh. Instead they were met head-on by the Jordanian army and its armored units.

In the fierce battle that followed, Jordanian forces had the upper hand and were actually defeating the Israelis on the ground until the Israeli air force was called in. The Israelis managed to raze Karameh, leaving only the mosque, but they paid a heavy price on their retreat to the border. By Jordanian accounts, Jordanian tanks destroyed twenty Israeli tanks and another twenty-five armored personnel carriers, and killed or wounded more than 200 Israeli soldiers, figures Israel quickly disputed. Jordan lost a sizable number of its tanks and took roughly the same number of casualties, but the psychological victory was enormous for Jordanians. What stunned them was that Arafat immediately claimed it for the PLO, announcing that it was they who had repelled the Israelis. Though that claim has always been disputed, the effect of Karameh has not.

Almost overnight, Arafat and his *fedayeen* became heroes throughout the Arab world for facing down the Israelis. Shortly thereafter, full of bluster, the PLO began to move against King Hussein. Listening to Hussein describe the anarchy that had overtaken Jordan in the wake of the battle at Karameh evoked a tragic and terrifying image. Partisan volunteers from all over the Arab world — even from parts of Africa and Cuba — had rushed to Jordan to join the Palestinian resistance. As the Israelis stepped up their retaliations to *fedayeen* raids by bombing and napalming Jordanian villages in the Jordan River Valley, the undisciplined PLO "armies" moved to Amman. Different factions of the PLO set up roadblocks to check identity papers and demand money from motorists. "No one — adult or child — could be sure on leaving home whether anyone would ever see them again," King Hussein told me. Jordanian army officers and police were taunted, kidnapped, and even killed. "Amman became a virtual battlefield," my husband said.

King Hussein came under intense pressure to strike back at the PLO, especially from the armed forces who were being so humiliated. But he held them back. "What did they expect me to do?" he said. "What should I do to a people who were driven from their country, who had lost everything? Shoot them?" He met several times with Arafat to negotiate a return to order, but Arafat claimed he could not control the streets either. Still Hussein held his army back. "I kept hoping the *fedayeen* would come to their senses and remember that the battle was not between fellow Arabs, but against the Israeli occupation," King Hussein said.

In response to the rockets the PLO was now firing across the border, Israeli reprisals grew more violent along the whole Jordan River Valley, from the Dead Sea to the Sea of Galilee. "I was very worried about what was almost perpetual fighting," Hussein recounted. "In some places, the Palestinians had rigged their rocket launchers to timers behind our army lines, setting up the army to take the brunt of the retaliations. In other places, we had to take our army units away from the cease-fire line to try to contain the Palestinians, which left the border very vulnerable."

With his country in jeopardy both internally and externally, Hussein secretly contacted the Israelis in March 1970. "I wanted them to know that it was not an army that was fighting them but people resisting the occupation of their country," King Hussein told me. His meeting with the Israelis continued in the spirit of his grandfather's efforts to explore a negotiated settlement with the Israelis that would not compromise Palestinian rights or Palestinian territory. "He knew and I knew there was no future in war, no future in continued suffering for both our people," my husband told me. "I wanted to have a direct dialogue with the Israelis, whether it led anywhere or not. I could not just sit idly by, not knowing what their thinking was." This approach, best summed up by his oft-mentioned phrase "Engagement is not endorsement," would be one that he would employ over many years of negotiations.

In this instance, King Hussein also wanted to make sure the Israelis were not going to take advantage of the inner turmoil in Jordan. By meeting them, he was putting himself at even greater risk, given the inflamed emotions of 1970, but he believed he had no choice. He was losing control of his own country to the PLO and could not afford an offensive from Israel at the same time.

With a unified army of sorts under the rubric of the Palestinian Resistance Movement and PLO leaders roaring around Amman in motorcades with armed escorts, the *fedayeen* were establishing what was essentially a state within a state in Jordan. They saw King Hussein as an obstacle to the PLO cause because of his commitment to a peaceful settlement with Israel. Twice he came very close to being killed by the PLO in ambushes.

Other members of the royal family were targeted as well. Sharif Zeid Bin Shaker, the King's cousin — whom we all called Abu Shaker — was at army headquarters in June 1970 when his mother's house and the house next door, which belonged to Prince Ali Bin Nayef, came under intense PLO artillery fire. Princess Wijdan, Ali's wife, told me later how she was awakened at 6 A.M. by the sound of shelling and bullets hitting the house. She gathered her terrified children under the dining room table and was trying to calm them when a round hit the house so hard the chandelier fell from the ceiling and smashed onto the table. Soon afterward she heard on the radio that the PLO had agreed to a cease-fire. Why, then, did the shelling of their house continue?

Prince Ali, an intelligence staff officer of the third Royal Armored Division who had been condemned to death by the PLO, happened to be at home that day. He called army headquarters to be told that the PLO did not consider the cease-fire to apply to him or his family. "They told him that the family of Prince Ali did not deserve to live," Wijdan would recall. "I was getting hysterical, and he told me to calm down." Prince Ali then called Arafat, who responded that the shelling was continuing because Jordanian soldiers outside Abu Shaker's house were firing back at the PLO gunmen. Prince Ali telephoned the house; when Abu Shaker's sister, Sharifa Jozah, answered, he told her to tell the Jordanian soldiers outside to hold their fire. "Call to them from downstairs," he told her. "The PLO are shooting down at the house from the minaret in the mosque and the roof is exposed." Sharifa Jozah put the phone down and soon afterward Prince Ali heard a burst of machine-gun fire and a scream. Abu Shaker's mother eventually came back on the line to say that Jozah had gone up on the roof to contact the soldiers and the PLO had shot her. She was dead.

The two families and Sharifa Jozah's body were eventually evacuated by ambulances that continued to be fired upon by the PLO. After delivering the families safely to Civil Defense headquarters, Prince Ali arranged to send his wife and children to London and then returned to work. It was, the 1967 war veteran said, the most difficult day of his life. "The PLO was more in control of Amman than we were," Prince Ali would tell me. "Amman was their city, not ours."

Flush with power, a particularly militant faction of the Palestinians then proceeded to spend the international political capital they had gained at Karameh, replacing it with an unsavory reputation as terrorists. During one week in September 1970, four passenger airplanes were hijacked by the Popular Front for the Liberation of Palestine (PFLP), led by George Habash. Three of the aircraft were forced to land in Jordan. The hijackings infuriated King Hussein, who called them the "shame of the Arabs." Listening to him recount the episode eight years later, I could see he was still deeply troubled by the hostages' ordeal. He considered it an absolute outrage that his country was violated by these hijackers, and as a form of penance and apology he would maintain a lifelong correspondence with people on those planes.

The hijackings gave the West as well as the Arab world a negative view of the PLO. Both Egypt and Iraq withdrew their support of the PFLP, as did Arafat, but the anarchy did not subside. Although the hostages were released, the PFLP blew up all three aircraft. Arafat could not control the PLO extremists in Jordan's cities, and the Jordanian security forces restrained from action were on the verge of mutiny. Ten days after the first hijacking, King Hussein formed a military government headed by a Palestinian brigadier general, Muhammad Daoud. He and other government members contacted Arafat one last time to try to negotiate a return to law and order, but Arafat rebuffed their efforts: "Tell King Hussein the only concession I will give him is twenty-four hours to leave the country." With the gauntlet thrown down by Arafat, Hussein finally ordered the Jordanian army to move against the PLO.

The army began to flush out the PLO city by city, refugee camp by refugee camp, street by street, house by house. The operation would take ten months and would be agonizing for the King, who had tried everything to avoid a situation where Arabs were fighting Arabs. "It was the most difficult year of my life," he told me. The fighting was especially fierce in the center of Amman near the royal palaces. King Hussein's grandfather, King Abdullah I, had forbidden any building on the hillside overlooking the palaces for security reasons, but King Hussein, pressed by the influx of Palestinian refugees, had allowed them to build there. "They had suffered so much already, I could not deny them," he told me.

He almost paid for his kindness with his life. The Basman Palace compound came under heavy PLO shelling from that hillside during the confrontation. The commander of the Palace Guard discovered that one of the palace cooks was giving signals to the PLO as to Hussein's whereabouts in an effort to kill him. King Hussein survived, but the palace was gouged and pockmarked by bullets and rocket shells, constant reminders to us of the Palestinian tragedy that continues to this day.

Electricity and telephone service failed in the violence, shutting off Jordan from the outside world. Foreign journalists holed up in Amman

179

somehow got news out, but because their sources were the PLO, their reports were slanted. It fell to King Hussein, an avid ham radio operator, to use his radio to communicate information on the situation. Sharing information with other ham radio operators around the world, I would soon discover, was a passion of his. Wherever we stayed together, even outside the country, he would always have a small ham radio unit set up in our house, be it in England, the mountains of Austria, or Washington, D.C. During this dangerous period in 1970, his hobby actually played a useful role, as it would again when he saved a ship from sinking off Hong Kong. In that instance, the Port Authority in Hong Kong harbor had no idea that there was a ship in distress 200 miles offshore. For some reason, they could not receive the ship's distress signals, but Hussein did and managed to get the information to the proper authorities. In 1970, however, the radio served as his own lifeline.

Jordan's very survival was hanging in the balance. On September 19, 1970, the second day of the campaign against the PLO, the Jordanian military discovered Syrian tanks massing on the border with Jordan. A Jordanian reconnaissance team sent to the area reported back that the Syrians had written "Palestine Liberation Army" on their tanks, a ruse that fooled no one. "We knew very well the Syrians were manning these tanks," Hussein told me.

Neither King Hussein nor the Jordanian military command thought the Syrians would actually attack. However, using the pretext that Jordan was under orders from America to destroy PLO positions, Syrian tanks did cross the border the next day and threatened to occupy the northern city of Irbid. "It was the gravest threat in our history," my husband told me. Not only did the Syrians invade Jordan with a big armored force, but also to further complicate the situation, there were Iraqi troops in the same area who had come in during the 1967 war to protect Jordanian air bases from the Israelis and had stayed on. "In those hours, we did not know whether the Syrians and the Iraqis would join forces against Jordan," Prince Raad said. "It was touch and go. If they had, we would have been in dire straits."

The Iraqis did not support the Syrian invasion. Neither did the Syrian air force; indeed, its commander, Hafez Al Assad, decided that Israel and possibly the American government — which had placed its troops in Europe on alert — would retaliate if Syria moved into Jordan. Assad would later claim that he had defied the orders of his government because he did not want Arabs fighting other Arabs, but the consensus is that his decision was more pragmatic. What is indisputable is that Jordanian ground forces, with the help of the Jordanian air force, managed to stop the Syrian advance, despite being greatly outnumbered.

"We had to defend ourselves," Abu Shaker would recall. "The enemy is the man who is shooting at you, Arab or not." Two days later the Syrians withdrew.

The operation was over in two weeks, but it would take another ten months, until July 1971, to root out the last of the Palestinian resistance fighters in Jordan. Arafat tried to flee the country, in disguise, but was caught by military intelligence. True to his nature, King Hussein ordered Arafat's release. Hussein was just as forgiving with other captured *fedayeen*. When a group of commandos were brought to him and, in great fear, prostrated themselves in front of him and tried to kiss his feet, he told them to get up, collect their belongings, and leave, free men. "They were my brothers," he told me.

The thousands of captured Palestinian fighters being held in Jordanian camps by the army were also treated tolerantly. A large number had come from Lebanon, Syria, Iraq, and elsewhere, pretending they were coming to fight Israel when actually they were coming for political reasons. Most were given the choice of peacefully leaving the country. Many took that option and were sent, in trucks, into Syria. The Syrians, in turn, kept the *fedayeen* moving into Lebanon. The rest of the Palestinian refugee population stayed peacefully in Jordan. "We had nothing against them and they had nothing against us," my husband told me. "They were

Jordanian nationals. There was no exodus, except for the PLO resistance fighters."

King Hussein had survived. His imminent demise, so widely speculated upon in newspapers around the world, proved to be greatly exaggerated. He had saved his country and, more important, its integrity. Jordan did not descend into the civil war that would rack Lebanon for the next decade; instead it united behind the King. Those who had attacked him for not taking action sooner against the PLO were silenced. Hussein's patience and tolerance, not the premature use of force, had saved Jordan from annihilation.

However, the PLO had not removed Jordan from its sights. A year later, Wasfi Tal, Jordan's Prime Minister and a very close friend of King Hussein's, was assassinated in Cairo by the emerging PLO terrorist cell Black September — the same group that would kill members of the Israeli Olympic team in Munich and was also suspected of shooting Zeid Rifai, the Jordanian ambassador to Great Britain and an old friend of my husband's. The attack in London, which Zeid Rifai, though wounded, miraculously survived, prompted Jordanian security to insist that King Hussein stay outside of London, as his name topped Black September's hit list. Consequently he bought a house, Castlewood, near London in Egham, a beautiful part of the English countryside.

★ ★ ★

Castlewood was where Abir, Haya, and Ali stayed when they joined us in England after Hussein and I returned from the Scotland portion of our honeymoon. There the children could run free while we were occupied in the city. We enjoyed picnics with them in the countryside around Castlewood and took them into London, where we would spend hours feeding the ducks at the Serpentine in Kensington Park. But most entertaining for all were the high-spirited visits to Hamley's Toy Store, when my husband would indulge the little ones, who would scamper down the aisles with the overladen store staff in their wake.

We also visited the Sultan of Oman's mother, Um Qaboos, who was spending the summer in a beautiful house on the Thames River. The five of us were greeted at the entrance by her close friend, Miriam Zawawi, who would become a dear friend to me as well, and escorted to an incense-scented sitting room where Um Qaboos was waiting to receive us. She was an extraordinarily regal presence, hennaed, bejeweled, and dressed in a magnificently embroidered kaftan. Full of curiosity, affection, and good humor, she had prepared generous gifts for everyone. The children, awestruck, accepted theirs politely and then excused themselves. Hussein and I remained, chatting about family and politics. She was extremely knowledgeable on both topics, asking about every family member by name and demonstrating a sophisticated awareness of current events.

Another happy occasion was a surprise visit of Hussein's oldest son, Abdullah, who had just finished his first year of high school at Deerfield Academy in Deerfield, Massachusetts. I was delighted for the two of them. I understood that those few days in London were an important opportunity for Abdullah to be with his father, and for his father to try to make up for not having been able to visit him and his brother and sisters in the United States earlier in the year, before springing a new wife on everyone. Abdullah stayed with us for several days, and in the evenings after dinner Hussein would arm-wrestle or otherwise engage in horseplay with him in our private sitting room on the top floor. Hussein often used to playfully roughhouse with all his children, a way of showing affection, and I tried not to intrude on their private time. It was also perhaps a blessing in disguise that my husband had the distraction of Abdullah's visit because one evening the accumulation of the pressures of the honeymoon took its toll and I broke down. Uncharacteristically calling my mother in tears, I told her: "I feel like coming home."

I meant it, but she knew — and I knew — that I was not a quitter. I felt better after talking to her, and Hussein, otherwise distracted, never knew about my moment of weakness. But the reality of what lay ahead was sinking in. As a young bride I would find the passage difficult and often painful. I was entering a complex world over which I had little control. I was married to a man I adored whose time and attention were stretched to the breaking point. After we returned to Amman from our honeymoon, I realized that I was essentially on my own.

chapter seven

A Young Bride in the Royal Household

All newly married couples go through an adjustment period, and the King and I were no exception. The adjustments were more pronounced for me, of course; I had married into my husband's life much more than he had married into mine. First and foremost was the lack of privacy, which I continued to find very challenging. It was jarring to walk out of even my bedroom to immediately face a valet or a waiter or my husband's aide-de-camp (ADC). Though some people might yearningly fantasize about such personal attention, I found it quite unsettling and intrusive. Over the years to come I would realize that some of this dissonance was cultural — the difference between a Western sense of privacy and personal space and an Eastern emphasis on communal identity and space.

Following the monarchical tradition in most of the world, I was addressed as "Your Majesty" and introduced to other people or referred to in their presence as "Her Majesty." It felt strangely impersonal at first, as if a wall of formality were being erected between me and the rest of the world, including family and friends, and I always thought it was quite a mouthful for those people who were in constant contact with me to repeat the phrase over and over in the course of a conversation. Tradition also dictated that people stand when I entered a room. In no way did I feel entitled to this deference.

Naturally humble and modest, my husband was nonetheless conscious of the symbolism and the essential authority of his position. Unlike some other Middle Eastern monarchs, however, he made himself as accessible as possible and discouraged excessive subservience and formality. When approached by those determined to prostrate themselves or kiss his hand, Hussein would gently help them up and shake their hands instead. I learned from watching him and tried to trust my instincts, sensing that I would be able to strike my own balance.

My attachment to Jordan and Jordanians came very naturally, but it was harder to define exactly what my role should be in terms of contributing to the well-being of the country. I remember one day quite early in our marriage, when I was feeling particularly at sea, I asked Hussein to give me some kind of direction: "How can I be most helpful?" He answered, "I have complete faith in you. You have never made a mistake." It was an unequivocal vote of confidence, and I felt a great wave of affection for him when he said it, but still, he had not answered my question.

As with all new couples we also had to adjust to such basic patterns as our different sleeping habits. My husband was a night person who stayed up very late, a nocturnal rhythm I had barely kept pace with during our courtship when I was still keeping regular office hours at the airline. I did not have that morning deadline after we married, and I tried to train myself to match his routine and sleep later in the morning. Sometimes I managed it, but sometimes not. I remained a day person, naturally awaking almost every day by 6:30 A.M. after staying up with him late into the night.

In truth, life with King Hussein was forcing me to stretch in every direction. Given the constant threats to his life and the political maelstrom that always surrounded him, I had to develop a new approach to life — that, God willing, I would make the best of every day we were granted. There were days, though, that defied such an attitude. As a young bride in a royal household, I began by observing: trying to understand, to tread softly and not upset the daily routine or question the way things were done. However, as I gradually began to express my opinions, I inevitably ruffled feathers. I had several skirmishes with the British chief of the

189

household. His official title was Comptroller of the Royal Household, and I would come to realize that he took his job description quite literally.

Shortly after moving into the palace, I noticed that most lights remained on throughout the night, even after the family retired. Each night I went around turning them off, suggesting we could reduce the waste of energy. My explanation seemed to fall on deaf ears, the implication being that anyone living in a palace should not be concerned with conserving energy. Perhaps our disparate views on the subject were partly cultural; the energy crisis in the United States had made many Americans, including my family, quite conscious of the cost of consumption. The message I took from this exchange was that I could not assume anything about the way the royal household would be run.

Even my husband's diet was a point of contention. During a medical checkup in the United States, the doctors assigned us a top nutritionist, Amal Nasser, a young Jordanian, who urged the King to modify his diet to reduce his cholesterol and triglyceride counts. As hard as I tried to work out a healthier diet with the Controller, I had little success. "Oh, come on, Your Majesty," he once said to me patronizingly. So we struggled, he and I. After all, he had been in his position there for all of two years and did not see why he should make any adjustments to a young, new queen.

My situation was not unique. Negotiating with preexisting staff, as I would learn from sharing stories with other royal consorts, was a universal challenge. A royal spouse's entourage and household staff is often territorial and quite entrenched in their habits. I learned how personally every suggestion was taken, whether the issue was food with the Controller, or clothing with the King's valet, or planning an official meal with Protocol. My suggestions, I began to realize, were often viewed as tacit criticisms of the way things were being done, and occasionally as personal insults. When I tried to liven up Hussein's wardrobe with striped shirts or new ties or more comfortable shoes, they would quietly disappear from the closet; his valet, whom I liked very much, resented my involvement in dressing the King, which he viewed as his job alone.

Once on our aircraft as we returned home from England, my husband mused that every time he would buy himself a pair of Bally shoes, they would vanish. Hussein then noted that his most recent Bally acquisition was remarkably similar to a pair of shoes being worn by a staff member walking past our seats at that very moment, and he complimented the man on his taste. It turned out that the shoes were the very ones Hussein had just bought — passed on to the man by the King's valet, who had reportedly said, "His Majesty will never wear them."

Though some of these early incidents with the staff were more amusing than annoying, I found it puzzling that when I thought I was communicating very clearly and diplomatically, I would discover that I was not. Perhaps we were all a little out of sorts. Certainly both staff and family were living in physically trying circumstances. Repairs had already begun on Hashimya Palace, so we were awakened early every morning by jackhammers on the roof over our heads. The engineering problems at Hashimya would prove to require extensive repairs and renovation. Even before this became clear, Hussein had asked me to begin a quick renovation of Al Diafa, the "guest place" in the Basman compound in the original heart of the city where his grandfather, King Abdullah I, had built the first Jordanian Hashimite Palace, Raghadan. When we moved in around a year later, Hussein changed the name of Al Diafa to Al Nadwa, which identified our home as a place for all to gather.

To be honest, even if we could have fixed all of Hashimya's problems, I am not sure we would have been happy there. My new husband had never really warmed to its formal marble halls and yearned for a more cozy home for our family. From the moment he had walked into Hashimya, he told me, he had felt like a guest, and no doubt it brought back sad memories: He and Queen Alia had just moved in when she was killed, and she was buried on a hillside nearby. I will never forget driving by the gravesite on the way back to the palace with the children, when Abir, who had already lost two mothers, blurted out, "Will Auntie Alexa [my sister] be our mother when you die?"

This period of adjustment was in many ways overshadowed by the politics of the region. Just two months after my marriage, U.S. President Jimmy Carter invited Egypt's Anwar Sadat and Israel's new hard-line Prime Minister, Menachem Begin, to meet with him at Camp David to negotiate a settlement in the Middle East. Abandoned were the plans for the international peace conference in Geneva my husband had been working so hard to arrange. Instead of a united delegation of Palestinians, Syrians, Jordanians, and Egyptians negotiating collectively with Israel, now there would be only Egypt. The announcement brought with it not only the fear that Sadat would negotiate a separate peace for Egypt, but also the suspicion that Camp David was planned to ensure that such a Pan-Arab–Israeli conference never took place; it would be very advantageous to Israel to avoid the pressure of such a public forum.

King Hussein was not included in the invitation by President Carter because he was seen as potentially "complicating the process" by National Security Adviser Zbigniew Brzezinski and by Sadat. Hussein's unwavering insistence on Israel's withdrawal from all territories occupied since 1967 and the right of self-determination for the Palestinians made him a potential obstacle in their eyes, rather than a partner for the political victory they hoped to achieve.

In his preoccupation with the pending talks at Camp David, my husband neglected to tell me about the Sunday family gatherings at the Queen Mother's house, Zahran Palace. Our children had been visiting her regularly on Sunday afternoons with the nannies, and my husband and I would visit more erratically, but it was many months before I discovered that all the Queen Mother's offspring and their families were expected on a weekly basis. Unwittingly, I had made my first family faux pas — at least the first of which I was aware.

The Queen Mother was born Sharifa Zein Al Sharaf in Egypt in 1916 and had married her first cousin, then Crown Prince Talal, at age eighteen. She had raised four children and had been a pioneer for women's rights by sponsoring the first women's union in Jordan and the women's branch of the Jordan National Red Crescent Society. Also, she may well have influenced her husband's contribution to Jordan's 1952 Constitution, which gave full rights to women.

Her husband's descent into mental illness could not have been easy for her, but Queen Zein bore these difficulties with great strength, especially after her father-in-law, King Abdullah, was killed, and her husband was hospitalized abroad. After King Talal abdicated, Queen Zein played a significant role while her seventeen-year-old son finished his schooling, before his accession to the throne on his eighteenth birthday.

Once Hussein became King, Queen Zein focused mostly on her family. When I first began attending the Sunday afternoon gatherings at Zahran I had no idea of what the family conventions were, or what their expectations were of me — I knew only that I was, understandably, the subject of intense curiosity and comment. In the absence of guidance, I followed my own instincts and tried to be polite and respectful, but I had to also be myself; otherwise I would have gone mad.

It was among the children that I felt most natural and spontaneous. One Sunday the children all filed in and kissed Queen Zein's hand, then disappeared into the garden to play while the adults sat with the Queen Mother. I could see that some of the younger children, including our three, were at a disadvantage in the game with their older siblings and cousins. To restore the balance, I leaped in and tackled one of the older boys. The children were startled, needless to say, to see their new auntie suddenly charging across the lawn at them, but I managed to hang on to the twelve-year-old boy, who turned out to be Prince Ghazi, Prince Mohammed's son, just long enough so that the little children could win. I do not know how this affected the adults' impression of me, but I rated high praise from Ghazi and his brother, Talal, who pronounced me "cool."

My husband loved his nephews and nieces as though they were his own children. One story that Talal and Ghazi frequently repeated was the mystery of the missing nephews. It involved King Hussein's first helicopter, then the only one in Jordan, and the boys, who would hear its roaring blades and run out into their garden to wave. King Hussein would land the helicopter on the lawn, scoop them up, and say, "Where do you want to go?" He would then fly them around Amman on a modern magic carpet ride before re-depositing them in their garden. The boys' parents, not unreasonably, would demand to know where the boys had disappeared to. "Uncle took us away in a helicopter," the boys would reply, which would make the parents even angrier. "Don't make up stories," they would scold the boys.

I am astonished, looking back at the beginning of my marriage, at how vulnerable I was to gossip and criticisms of all sorts. The rumor mill in Amman was already churning out what would become a panoply of preposterous stories over the years. On Queen Alia's death, rumors had quickly spread about the cause of her helicopter accident. The most incredible of these insisted that the Queen Mother had somehow arranged the crash. When my engagement to Hussein was announced, I discovered later, rumors had spread that the CIA, in fact, had been responsible for Queen Alia's accident as part of a plan to plant me on the throne. It was also said that I had a black child in America, and my husband was being blackmailed by the father, who threatened to sell the photos to *People* magazine; my sister (who was in law school in Texas at the time) had opened a boutique on Madison Avenue in New York to re-sell my royal wardrobe; I had bought an Asian island on one of our trips to the Far East. And always, there were stories about fantasy purchases of extravagant jewelry, marital turbulence, and pregnancies and miscarriages.

My husband, who was inured to the gossip in Jordan, brushed off these stories, and I struggled to as well. I knew that women in my position in the past, whether in Iran or in Jordan, the United States or Europe, had been similarly gossiped about whether there was cause or not. I also knew that virtually every member of the family was the focus of constant imaginings. Over time I learned that such stories more often than not reflected the values, inclinations, and fantasies of the storytellers and should therefore not be taken personally; however, I never quite adjusted to the fact that people would believe them so readily.

I cannot remember now what triggered it — the gossip, the lack of privacy, the frustrations with the management of Hashimya — but one day I needed a change and persuaded a very reluctant Meliha to assist in my subterfuge. I slid into her passenger seat and averted my face from the scrutiny of the guards as we drove through the palace gates into the freedom of the outside world. Meliha was very nervous. I directed her to our friends, Suha and Khalid Shoman, with whom I then spent a wonderful, carefree couple of hours chatting and drinking tea and not responding to the increasingly frantic calls from the palace trying to determine my whereabouts. When I realized that I was causing our loyal and dedicated Royal Guards a great deal of distress, I returned home and never again indulged myself in this way, but it provided a badly needed respite at the time.

What I really wanted to do was to concentrate on what I could contribute to my marriage and to Jordan. At the beginning finding my way was difficult. Although I fulfilled a few ceremonial roles, I was essentially left alone to set my own priorities. While I disliked artificiality of any kind, I gradually learned to put on a public face for the camera and for the crowd. My husband often explained the importance of body language. "If you smile, you give people confidence. If you don't, they will suspect something is wrong and feel uncertain or worried."

I could not question his reasoning. He had, after all, held his country together through various crises by going out among the people and exuding a confidence that perhaps he did not feel at the time. There were legendary stories about him plunging into near-riotous crowds and defusing their anger, or traveling to army garrisons thought to be at the point of mutiny and winning the support of the troops by dint of his personality. And there was no doubt that his mood influenced the people around him — his family and his countrymen. I had seen with my own eyes the way people smiled when he smiled, laughed when he laughed, tensed when he appeared tense. Still, it had not occurred to me that people would be looking at me in more or less the same way.

From the moment Hussein and I first met I had resisted speaking to anyone about him or our life together. From the beginning I instinctively tried to maintain a zone of privacy in our lives and believed strongly that it was a fundamental right of someone in his position. What I did not realize was that nobody else around him thought that way; they seemed to consider the King and his family public property. That fascination with personalities is, of course, universal, but I did not want to contribute to it, especially in Jordan. In such a small country (about the size of Indiana, with a population in the 1980s of more than 3 million) every tidbit of information about the royal family, especially the King, would inevitably be embroidered or distorted and passed around with great authority. Some people were capable of looking you in the eye while saying with absolute certitude that they had witnessed an event that later would prove to have occurred when they were not even in the country.

On the other hand, there was a negative aspect to trying to maintain privacy. I learned early on that, faced with discretion, some people would speculate even more. In the absence of information, they would simply make things up to give the all-important impression of having insider access and influence. I had to learn to strike an effective balance between my natural inclination to privacy and the practical value of sharing enough of our lives with others so they could understand what we were trying to accomplish.

I still resisted talking to the press. Not only did I feel that my marriage should not be public fodder, but in light of the critical state of affairs in the region I wanted to shift the dialogue in a more substantive direction. I certainly did not want to focus on personal matters, which seemed to be the primary attraction for most of the media. Despite these intentions, I did not get off to a good start.

The Royal Court press secretary was urging me to give an interview to *People* magazine, but I was not convinced that it was the appropriate publication for my first interview. "I do not think this is the right way to go," I told him, but he persisted. I assumed that because the press was his job, he must know what he was talking about.

I was appalled when the article appeared under the headline: "A Blue-Jeaned American in Jordan Says of Her King: 'I'd Be Delighted to Have His Child.'" As my interviewer was leaving the palace, I had responded *"Insha' Allah"* ("If God wills") to a casual question about whether the King and I wanted to have children. But to see that offhand remark become the headline was mortifying. Our press secretary, who became a very good friend and later went on to serve as a distinguished ambassador abroad, was perplexed by my reaction to the article. He did not understand at all why I was so upset. After other similar incidents, I decided to follow my own instincts.

As I became increasingly active in my work, I began to realize that everything I did publicly would be covered by our local media in full. I began to pick and choose what to emphasize, planning my schedule to achieve a balance between my more traditional ceremonial roles and my desire to focus on significant development initiatives — cultural, social, and environmental.

I was not quite sure at the beginning, however, where I wanted to concentrate my efforts. I knew I would need a place to bring people together for meetings, and a small staff to help me follow up on requests for help and to develop new programs. Hussein encouraged me to establish an office in Al Ma'Wa, just up the hill from the Royal Court offices, since it held such sentimental value for him as his late grandfather's peaceful haven, and now for us since our engagement. It was the first such office for someone in my position, and many in the Royal Court were not used to the concept of a Queen who would function relatively independently from the patriarchal Royal Court offices, which were focused exclusively on the King. It was interesting to me that many found it impossible to imagine that I could set out my own priorities, establish projects, and speak publicly on my own initiative. This reflected, I believe, lingering skepticism about women and their professional capabilities that surprised me, considering all the impressive and clearly competent women I had met in Jordan. I would never act independently on issues of political consequence, of course, or interfere with the running of the Royal Court, but I was looking to fill gaps in development programs and promote international understanding at this turbulent point in Middle East history.

While the Royal Court was responsible for media coverage, my office functioned relatively independently in every other area. I ran bold new ideas past my husband and, by trying to promote a broader, more open and liberal agenda, raised issues that might not come to him otherwise. I saw my role as helping to alleviate and complement the burden of responsibility he carried. I did not ask for help or support. I just got on with it with the help of a growing circle of friends and colleagues.

I moved in and adapted Al Ma'Wa's living quarters to function as office space. From the beginning, it was a special place for me, a space of my own. I wanted the office and the projects that would emanate from it to represent the best of Jordan and reflect the country's rich diversity. And I knew it was important to me to have people working in the office who represented different groups and communities in the country: Muslim and Christian, men and women from the East Bank and the West Bank, and from Circassian, liberal, and conservative backgrounds.

My memories of those personally challenging times are inextricable from my memories of the political dramas we were engaged in. In the summer of 1978, we visited Iran. It was a special journey for me. I had not returned since I had lived and worked there in 1976. The revolution that would transform the country into an Islamic republic and send the Shah into exile was only a few months away. When my husband and I stayed with the royal family at their lovely Caspian retreat, there were few signs of the gathering storm. SAVAK, the secret police, and the Iranian military were keeping the rising revolutionary movement in check, and on the surface Iran appeared relatively calm. From people close to the Shah there were murmurings of concern to my husband and others in our entourage about popular restiveness, but there was little sense of the seismic events that would soon shake the country.

I remember trying to fill in some of the picture that my husband was getting. I had a somewhat different perspective about what was going on inside Iran than he did, since his understanding of the situation was coming from his contacts with the Shah and his family, and from official military and intelligence sources. Even two years earlier when I had worked in Tehran, I had become aware of a disturbing degree of polarization and fragmentation within Iranian society.

During this visit, Empress Farah seemed much more vivacious and energetic than her husband, who was either weakened by the devastating cancer that would remain a secret for a while longer or simply very shy. He spent long periods resting and playing backgammon with his doctor, while his family and friends swam, water-skied, windsurfed, and practiced a very impressive *Saturday Night Fever* dance routine at night. We spent a few days at the family compound in what was essentially a wonderfully relaxing extension of our honeymoon. The imperial couple pampered us with such thoughtful hospitality that at times our cares almost seemed to vanish. The family had a tennis coach, and I asked Hussein to play tennis, something I had loved since childhood, and he gamely agreed to try and continued over most of the years of our marriage. In fact, during this visit our only moments of anxiety were recreational, not political.

One of the activities planned for us by the imperial family entailed flying by helicopter over the Caspian Sea, where we were encouraged to jump out of the helicopter into unbelievably high swells. Having grown up on the Pacific Ocean, I had never feared surf when in sight of shore, but bobbing around on those Caspian waves was close to terrifying. They were so enormous that from the troughs we lost sight of land. Our only occasional point of reference was the navy vessel nearby, waiting to pick us up.

By far the most anxious moment for me occurred when the Shah's sister, Princess Fatima, invited Hussein to join her as she piloted a helicopter around the area. She was the widow of a commander of the Iranian air force and was undoubtedly an experienced pilot, but our entourage had the impression that her approach to flying was far more casual and carefree than the by-the-book approach that His Majesty always insisted upon in Jordan. One day she persuaded Hussein to accompany her on a helicopter flight over the compound. We listened to the helicopter buzzing overhead for what seemed like hours, worrying that we would never see him again, praying to God to land him safely.

After we returned to Jordan we kept close track of the deteriorating situation in Iran. We had telex machines in Hashimya and in Aqaba, and I remember reviewing long scrolls of telex news every day. I relished that instant access to news about the region and the world. In those years before the fax machine and CNN, those curled pieces of paper were a critical part of our life and, throughout my early years of marriage, would become part of my nightly ritual as I went through the news briefs, picking out news items I thought might be interesting to Hussein. But the news from Iran in the fall of 1978 was increasingly worrying.

Princess Wijdan, Hussein's first cousin, returned from a visit to Iran a few months after ours and told me that, unknown to her, fourteen people had been killed in an attack on the palace while she and other members of an official delegation from Jordan were inside being entertained by folk dancers. The delegation, which included Crown Prince Hassan and Prince Raad and his wife, Princess Majda, had not learned about the attack or the killings until they were on a plane the next day flying back to Jordan. September 1978, the end of Ramadan — the Muslim holy month of fasting — marked the beginning of massive street demonstrations in Tehran. Fueled by taped sermons of Ayatollah Khomeini sent in from his exile in Iraq, the demonstrators called for the expulsion of the United States from Iran and a return to religious orthodoxy. The government responded by declaring martial law, and shortly afterward, in what became known as Black Friday, the Shah's security forces opened fire on a demonstration in Tehran, killing more than a hundred people and injuring hundreds more.

My husband was anguished by the bloodshed in Iran and furious at the political manipulation of the situation by Ayatollah Khomeini, who in October 1978 left Iraq for France, where he continued to broadcast into Iran. Hussein could not understand, nor could many in the Middle East, why the French would tolerate such open, hostile, political activities on their own soil directed at another country. It prompted considerable suspicion: Why were the French indulging Khomeini? Reports later suggested that commercial or political gains were among the possible motives. If so, it may have worked, but at a terrible cost to the entire region.

My husband and I would make one last trip to Iran at the end of 1978, just weeks before the Shah and the Shahbanou's final departure on January 16, 1979. The four of us dined alone. It was a depressing evening. The Shah barely spoke, and Empress Farah was bravely trying to hold it together. Hussein was convinced that the Shah still had an opportunity to head off the political catastrophe that loomed and urged him to go directly to the people, as Hussein had done so successfully in the past in Jordan: "Talk to the people, talk to the religious scholars, talk to the army, and establish a national dialogue to diffuse the tension." But the Shah would not — or could not — do it.

At the same time, our delegation was dining with the Iranian ambassador to Jordan, who became quite agitated during a discussion and said, "His Imperial Majesty has asked me to go to Qom to meet with the chief mullah to try to calm the situation. Please help me. I have never spoken to any of these religious people before. What should I do?" The ambassador then proposed that perhaps King Hussein could visit several key mullahs with the Shah and, together, see what could be done. "I am sure His Majesty would be very pleased to do so," my husband's cousin, Prince Raad, had told him.

It was not a preposterous thought. The Iranians were Shi'ite Muslims and, as such, had a special respect for King Hussein because he was a direct descendant of Ali, the Prophet's son-in-law, whom the Shi'ites venerated as the Prophet's rightful heir. When Abu Shaker and Prince Raad came to us later in the evening to relay the ambassador's request, Hussein immediately agreed. In spite of the late hour, my husband requested a meeting with the Shah to try to persuade him to go to Qom with him for a last-ditch effort to mediate with the scholars, but the meeting never took place.

If anyone could have influenced the Shah, it was Hussein. Some years earlier, while they were having dinner at the same family compound on the Caspian Sea we had visited in 1978, he had talked the Shah out of precipitating a war. The British had been planning their withdrawal from various countries in the Gulf at the time, when suddenly, out of the blue, the Shah announced his intentions to occupy Bahrain as soon as the British left. "Bahrain is part of Iran, and we are not going to let it go," he had said to King Hussein. A long argument ensued. "You cannot do that," my husband finally told the Shah. "Bahrain is an independent Arab country, and though some of the population is Shi'ite, they are all Arabs, and the Arab world will not let you do that." "Oh, screw the Arabs," my husband recalled the Shah saying, to which my husband replied: "But I'm an Arab." "Oh, no, no, I do not mean you," the Shah said. "You're a Jordanian."

My husband loved to recount this exchange with the Shah to family and close friends, finding the Shah's distinction between the King as an Arab and a Jordanian very amusing, but, in fact, the discussion had a great impact and Bahrain maintained its independence. Sadly, although my husband had helped to save Bahrain from occupation by the Shah, he could not save the Shah from the tragedy of his own country.

chapter eight

Pomp and Circumstance

It was often impossible to reconcile people's fantasies of what a king and queen should be with the everyday reality of our life and work. One experience I always remember with great amusement, not least because it is repeated frequently to this day, occurred upon our arrival to Gymnich Castle, the official German state guest residence outside of Bonn, Germany, on our first state visit in November 1978. Upon exiting the helicopter that had ferried President Walter Scheel, his wife, Mildred, and us from the official arrival ceremony at the airport to what would be our residence for the next several days, we were met by the wife of the castle's owner and their small son, to whom she introduced us as the King and Queen. He was adorably polite but looked up at me with abject disappointment. "But where is her crown?" he asked his mother, who translated his plaintive words. I would encounter that same question and disappointment forever more. Children —

and many adults — crave that fairy-tale presence from royalty.

Many thought a queen should be a glamorous figure on a pedestal, perhaps engaged from a distance in charity work. I had no intention of being just a figurehead and spending my time simply opening bazaars and expositions, which a member of the Royal Court had suggested should be my role. On the contrary, I hoped to contribute to tackling and solving real problems, much as I would have as an urban planner or a journalist. Not uncommonly for someone in my situation, I received enough different opinions — about what my role should be, about how I should present myself, about everything that would be or should be expected of me — that I could easily have been ten different people and never satisfied anyone.

I had to come to terms with the fact that for many people a queen's persona began with how she looked and dressed. I felt particularly awkward about this, but I understood the importance of ceremony and of making a good public impression. Looking back on those first years, I find it laughable how much I had to learn. When our first state visit to Germany was scheduled four months after the wedding, to be followed in December with visits to France, Italy, and the United Kingdom, I had to quickly confront the issue of clothing. My blue jeans and blazer would not do.

The wife of the Controller of Hashimya suggested to my husband that she contact the fashion designer Valentino in Italy to inquire if they might quickly provide us with some outfits for these visits. Valentino, who had designed clothes for Queen Alia and at least one other member of the family, sent his assistant to Jordan with what remained of the design models of their fall-winter collection. I was still very thin, so size was no problem, which was fortunate, as there was no time to have anything made.

It was a relief to know I had something suitable and, needless to say, absolutely beautiful to wear. I looked upon these outfits as work clothes that gave me the freedom to concentrate on the job of representing Jordan in ways that could directly benefit the country.

I also considered the pieces of jewelry I had received as wedding presents, and the lovely diamond tiara from my husband, to be working adornments as well. I did not have any jewelry of my own, save for the sentimental odd silver bracelet or ring, but during the first months of our marriage, my husband returned several times from visits to countries in the region and surprised me with belated wedding gifts of exquisite jewelry from various Arab rulers. As much as I admired these magnificent gifts, I never felt completely comfortable wearing them. Jordan was a poor country, and it seemed inappropriate for me to wear such jewelry at home, even if others did on occasion. It was more fitting for formal occasions abroad, but even that discomfited me.

My husband, however, had a typically Arab appreciation for brilliant color and ornate design, so he encouraged me to wear an exquisite emerald necklace — a wedding gift from King Khaled of Saudi Arabia — to the official banquet on our state visit to Germany. Instead of carrying it off with élan, I spent the entire evening feeling like a Christmas tree and self-consciously attempted to conceal the necklace under the chiffon shawl of my dress. Many other guests that evening were simply dressed, and I did not want the contrast between their attire and mine to create any distance between us. A queen may be expected to present a glittering image, but it was neither my nature nor what I considered useful as a representative of Jordan. Over the years I tried to achieve a balance between an understated style and the need to look regal but invariably erred, in my view, by going to one extreme or the other.

Our state visit to Bonn proceeded smoothly, but I was looking forward to the weekend retreat at the southern Germany resort of Bechtesgaden that our hosts had planned for us at the end of our state visit; we would be celebrating my husband's birthday high up in the mountains. We were treated to rare November skiing on the *Zugspitze* peak high above the town of Garmisch-Partenkirchen. Our first venture on skis together was absolutely comical. My husband had skied only perhaps one other time in his life and was extremely cautious in following his instructor's lead. While I had not had occasion to ski for some years, I had enjoyed the sport since the age of thirteen and expected to pick up somewhere close to where I had left off. This had me skiing quite hard and fast, falling often, picking myself up, and carrying on again. My husband, who never fell, looked at me cartwheeling down the slope as if I were quite mad; I, in turn, looked at him methodically making his way down, surrounded by photographers, his extensive German security detail, and our intrepid Royal Guards, for whom skiing did not exactly come naturally, and thought it was all quite comical. This first ski outing together became a favorite family story as we laughingly recounted the madcap scene and recalled what a huge relief it was to unwind after the intense formality and self-consciousness of the state visit.

There was more formality to come, and again I found that I could not always manage it the way I would have preferred. During our state visit to France my mother-in-law, Queen Zein, insisted that I see her hairdresser, the famous Alexandre, who came to the Marigny State Guest Palace to prepare me for our state banquet at Versailles. Alexandre, who was extremely gallant and flattering, gave me a quick look and began work on an elaborate updo. By the time he was finished, my hair looked like it was wearing me. He then sprayed it with so much *laque* (as hairspray is so appropriately called in France) that my hair became a veritable fortress, impenetrable to my efforts to tone it down after he left. I was practically in tears as we prepared to leave for the state banquet. I felt ridiculous. (Today Marge Simpson might be the best example of my appearance.) My husband sweetly assured me I looked perfectly splendid and that we should leave for the dinner.

It is possible my husband really liked my hair. Certainly he relished it when I represented Jordan by bringing a touch of fairy tale to the all-too-serious affairs of state. I showed him two evening dresses on our first state visit to the United States, one a simple one I planned to wear and the other, a beaded jacket over a long skirt. He immediately chose the beaded jacket, which proved quite a contrast with Mrs. Carter's very simple dress. Whenever I gave him a choice, he would always choose the more elaborate option. Eventually I would incline toward simpler and often ethnic Jordanian dresses that suited both our personal styles.

It has always puzzled me that a woman in the public eye is judged first for her appearance, then for her achievements. Granted, the fashion business is a huge industry worldwide and the clothes a woman in a high-profile position chooses to wear cannot only ensure success for an individual designer but promote the fashion industry of an entire country. Princess Diana, for example, did wonders for British designers and, therefore, for the economy of Britain. This is why French First Ladies wear French designs and American First Ladies wear American designs. It is good for business. Had there been a Jordanian designer I could have showcased, I would have, but at the time there were not any.

Also, at the beginning I did not fully understand the financial value of celebrity to designers. In Rome, during our official visit to Italy, I decided to pass by Valentino and thank him for helping me out with my German visit on such short notice. I left the motorcade behind and strolled as unobtrusively as possible to his office near the Spanish Steps. I was horrified when I turned the corner to find a throng of photographers and reporters, clearly waiting for me. Though I began to appreciate that publicizing celebrity clients was one way designers build and sustain their reputations, I was deeply uncomfortable being used as a form of promotion. It would be a problem for me for years because minimal contact with some designers (or even none at all) was too often exaggerated, creating the distorted impression that I was a major consumer of outrageously expensive fashion.

I would have five pregnancies over the next six years, which would complicate this aspect of my life even more. Eventually I would make use of U.S. mail-order catalogs to cover basic necessities economically and expeditiously.

My lack of interest in fashion produced one very amusing result at the beginning of our marriage. The first state visits I made with my husband to Europe garnered a lot of press coverage, with the emphasis, of course, on my appearance. That same year, Barbara Walters came to Jordan to film us for a television special. During one interview we took Barbara to the Royal Stables with Abir, Haya, and Ali to show her, and her audience, the beautiful Arab horses that were the pride and joy of my husband and his family. I wore jeans and a suede jacket to the stables, which seemed appropriate to me, but evidently not to everyone. At the end of the year, Earl Blackwell chose me for his infamous Worst Dressed List, charging that the jeans and the suede jacket I had worn in the Barbara Walters interview made me look like a centerfold for *Popular Mechanics*! With an irony I relished, I was also listed simultaneously on the International Best Coiffed and International Best Dressed Lists.

In that first year of marriage, issues of public image were of some import because I was just learning my way, but they were nothing compared to our real preoccupations, especially the search for peace in the Middle East. At that time there was no greater challenge to my husband's lifelong dream of bringing stability to the region than what was transpiring at Camp David, the U.S. presidential retreat outside of Washington, D.C. The twelve-day meeting between Sadat, Begin, and Carter and their respective delegations took place in September while we were on a brief working visit to London. When our ambassador, Ibrahim Izzedin, told Hussein that he had received a call from Sadat's secretary in Camp David setting up a time for Sadat to talk to him, my husband was cautiously optimistic.

The call was set for early morning, but it did not come. We waited all day in considerable suspense until Sadat finally called late that night to inform Hussein that he was planning to leave Camp David because, he said, he had not been able to reach an agreement with Begin. The King came away from the conversation relieved that Sadat was adhering to his position not to make a separate peace with Israel at the expense of the Palestinians. The two leaders arranged to meet in Morocco in a few days' time.

En route to the Morocco meeting we traveled to Majorca to visit King Juan Carlos and Queen Sofia of Spain at their beautiful summer house overlooking the Mediterranean. I had just met Queen Sofia's brother, King Constantine of Greece, and his wife, Queen Anne-Marie (daughter of King Frederick IX and Queen Ingrid of Denmark), longtime friends of Hussein's, in London. They had been forced into exile after a military coup in 1967, yet remained actively engaged with the Greek community and in the promotion of Greek culture and education. They had settled into a modest house in Hampstead, where they had successfully started a new life. I liked them both enormously, and we would see them whenever possible on our visits to London and frequently invite them and their family to Jordan.

In Majorca, I was intrigued by Queen Sofia's modern and natural approach to royal traditions. Though the Queen and her family belonged to one of the oldest royal houses in Europe — her full name is Sofia de Grecia y Hannover, and she is related to the czars of Russia, the German emperors, and Great Britain's Queen Victoria — she described how she and the King, Juan Carlos de Borbon y Borbon, were attempting to simplify the private and the public and ceremonial aspects of their life. The couple often drove their own car, mingled informally with their citizens, and moved freely about the country. They had restricted the use of tiaras, elaborate jewelry, and state regalia to exchanges with other reigning monarchs rather than all official occasions.

We were impressed with the way they had chosen to live in Madrid. Instead of residing in the huge, magnificent museum palace, the Prado, the Spanish royal family lived in the Palacio de la Zarzuela, a relatively modest home they had built in a wooded area on the outskirts of Madrid. We loved the long drive to the house, which wound through a wildlife reserve teeming with deer. Hussein often compared their cozy, unpretentious home to the marble-lined, hotel-like space of Hashimya and wished that we could live that way as well.

Hussein and Juan Carlos were great friends. My husband had supported and counseled the King through a decade of dramatic change in Spain, from the restoration of the monarchy in 1969 by the country's longtime dictator, General Francisco Franco, to the establishment of a constitutional monarchy in 1978, three years after the death of Franco. It was King Juan Carlos, together with Franco's holdover government, who reintroduced democracy to Spain and, in 1977, held the first democratic elections in the country in forty-one years. The newly elected Spanish Parliament then adopted a new constitution and designated the reigning monarch as king.

It was Sofie who first noted that I had made an instinctive adjustment to my new life, one that she had never had to make. Sofie is a very accomplished sailor, having been a reserve member of the Greek sailing team in the 1960 Olympic Games in Rome, in which her brother, Constantine, won a gold medal. She and I went out sailing that first summer on a hot, sunny day in a small Laser sailboat in a very private cove. As Sofie frequently recounted, several tourist boats suddenly appeared from around the bend of the coast interrupting our private idyll, and I immediately covered myself. I had lived in a Muslim culture long enough to know that being seen in anything as revealing as a bathing suit in public would be an affront to more conservative Muslims. Sofie said she was struck by how instinctively conscious I was of maintaining a balance between modesty and naturalness.

Our visit to Spain came to an abrupt end. We awoke one morning and, as usual, turned on our shortwave radio to listen to the BBC World Service. To our dismay we heard the terse announcement that Anwar Sadat had reached an agreement with Menachem Begin at Camp David. There was no mention of self-determination for the Palestinians. It seemed that our nightmare scenario had arrived. King Hussein was in a state of shock, especially in light of the reassurances he had received from Sadat a few days earlier. He immediately canceled our trip to Morocco and called our Spanish hosts to inform them that we would have to depart immediately for Jordan. However, as details of the agreement emerged, it would become clear that the damage of Camp David would not be easily contained. Indeed, the fallout would dramatically influence the twenty-one years of our married life and my husband's quest for peace.

chapter nine

One Crisis after Another

My husband rarely lost his temper. When he was vexed, his eyes would darken and the muscles would ripple around his jaw — two expressions that became etched on his face as he was briefed on the details emerging from Camp David. The agreement, signed at the White House on September 17, 1978, was a disaster for the Palestinians and a disaster for Jordan.

Anwar Sadat, under pressure from Jimmy Carter and Menachem Begin, had accepted an accord that was crucially flawed in what it failed to include. There was no specific commitment from Israel to withdraw from the Occupied Territories to pre-1967 borders — the formula of "land for peace" embodied in UN Resolution 242. Menachem Begin refused to even call the occupied Palestinian territories the West Bank. Instead he would insist on, and Jimmy Carter would honor, a definition of the Palestinian West Bank as "Judea and Samaria," and in language inflammatory to the Arab world, he also referred to it as "liberated territory."

There was no mention of Arab or Muslim rights over occupied Arab East Jerusalem. In fact, Jerusalem was not mentioned at all. Nor did the agreement contain a timetable for Israel to dismantle the Jewish settlements that were being steadily and illegally established on the occupied West Bank. In what was probably the most destructive result of Camp David, the language shifted from Palestinian "independence" to Palestinian "autonomy." With one stroke of the pen, the agreement at Camp David made autonomy the most that Palestinians could hope to achieve, and only with the consent of the Israelis over a five-year period. An independent Palestinian state was out of the question.

My husband's sense of betrayal was compounded by the accords' many references to the Hashimite Kingdom of Jordan — without him having been consulted at all. His face tensed furiously as he read what the Americans and the Egyptians expected of him: Jordan, not the PLO, should represent the Palestinians in further negotiations; Jordan, along with Egypt and Israel, would define the terms of "autonomy" for the Palestinians in the Occupied Territories; the provisions of the accord between Israel and Egypt would form the principles for a peace treaty between Israel and Jordan.

The situation was rife with bitter ironies. This "peace" accord was already acting as a destructive force. The Camp David agreement had driven a wedge between the United States and Jordan, and while Sadat was being lionized as a great visionary in America, the leaders of the Arab countries were gathering for a summit in Baghdad to condemn him.

The summit was a momentous occasion for King Hussein, both personally and politically. He had not been to Iraq since his cousin, King Feisal, and other members of the Iraqi royal family were murdered in 1958, during a coup d'état. The cousins had been very close, attending Harrow and Sandhurst together and spending vacations together; they had even been crowned on the same day. My husband told me how he personally had warned the commander of the Iraqi military about the threat of a coup and had been condescendingly ignored. Less than a week after his warning, anti-monarchists seized the palace. Accounts differ on what had happened, but according to one eyewitness report, relayed to a member of the Jordanian royal family, King Feisal was walking down the stairs of the palace with his family, having been promised safe passage from the country, when the insurgents opened fire. King Feisal's grandmother had a Quran in her hand and called out: "Please spare Feisal. Swear by the Quran." But all of them except for one aunt were machine-gunned to death.

My husband never forgave himself for not being more forceful in his efforts to warn Iraqi officials of the danger.

In November 1978, King Hussein joined twenty other countries in the twenty-two-member Arab League for the Baghdad summit. Only Egypt stayed behind. The Arab League decided to send a delegation to Cairo to make one last attempt to dissuade Sadat from pursuing a separate peace with Israel, but the Egyptian President refused to see them. Instead, Sadat fueled the flames of dissent by publicly dismissing the leaders at the summit as "cowards and dwarfs" and announcing that he had no intention of listening to the "hissing of snakes."

During the six months it took for the Carter administration to negotiate the details of the final Egyptian-Israeli agreement, the Americans put extraordinary pressure on my husband to endorse the Camp David Accords. Listening to my husband discuss strategies and responses with his advisers was an invaluable exposure to *realpolitik*. I had seen some evidence of American pressure during my time in Iran and in the Arab world, but to have it brought home to me, literally, was sobering.

March 26, 1979, the day the final peace accords between Egypt and Israel were signed by Begin, Sadat, and Carter in Washington, D.C., was a black day in Jordan. I remember Leila, whose husband was now Prime Minister, glaring at the ceremony on television and saying over and over again to Sadat: "Don't sign. Don't sign it. Please, God, break the pen." But, of course, he did sign, and the inevitable repercussions followed.

The region was already in turmoil. The Shah had been forced out of Iran just two months earlier, and the Ayatollah Khomeini had returned to a tumultuous welcome. The signing of the Camp David Accords created yet another incendiary element in an already volatile situation. For my husband, it represented a terrible setback. He was deeply disappointed by Sadat's opportunism, the shortsightedness of the United States, and the scuttling of the international peace conference that he felt promised the best chance for achieving a comprehensive Middle East peace. Camp David set us on a roller-coaster ride from which the region and we, as Jordanians, have still not fully recovered.

It was a heightened joy for both of us, in this dark period, to discover that I was pregnant. We had never spoken about having children, nor had we spoken about *not* having children. Hussein already had eight, three of whom were living with us, but he had sent a startling signal when I was working on plans for a new home. "Be sure to put in six bedrooms for the children," he told me. "What?" I said, certainly not anticipating three more on top of those we already had. When we received news one day from my doctor that I was expecting, Hussein was, in his own words, "over the moon." We tried to keep the news quiet until the third month, when we told the children, who were thrilled with the prospect of a new brother or sister.

I felt doubly blessed when my husband told me he would soon be making his *Hajj* pilgrimage to Mecca and visiting Medina in Saudi Arabia. In years past he had gone on the lesser pilgrimage, or *Umrah,* usually on the twenty-seventh day of the month of Ramadan, the holiest night of the year. He had never made the full *Hajj,* however, which spans five days of the last month of the Islamic *Hijri* year, which is based on the lunar calendar and therefore is approximately eleven days shorter than the Gregorian calendar used in the West. The faithful gather in the plain of Arafat and pray all day for forgiveness in particular. Every able Muslim is obligated to make the *Hajj* to Mecca once in his or her life, but my husband had never felt the time was right for him. I felt extraordinarily blessed that he felt the moment was right so soon after we married.

During the *Hajj,* my husband wore two seamless, plain white cloths around the waist and over the shoulder, as do male pilgrims, to reinforce the fundamental equality and humility of every man before God. Together he and the multitudes at Mecca would face the Ka'ba, the sacred simple stone structure in the middle of the vast, white marble courtyard of the Holy Mosque, known as the Al Haram Al Sharif. Men and women pray together in the Haram — the only mosque, except for the Prophet's Mosque in Medina, where they are not segregated in prayer. Here my husband's ancestor, Abraham, rebuilt the first house of worship to God 3,000 years ago. And here, some two millennia later, the Prophet Muhammad, Abraham's spiritual and blood heir, smashed the pagan idols of those who had forsaken God.

Hussein's reasons for going to Mecca were always purely spiritual, and he would try to be inconspicuous, but word would get out, nonetheless, that he was there. Because of his lineage, it was not unusual for pilgrims from all over the world to applaud when he entered, saluting him with the words *Ahlan bi Sabt Al Rasoul,* "Welcome to the Prophet's grandson." When he returned from the *Hajj,* I was delighted to see him so peaceful, so restored. He tried to share the extraordinary impact of his spiritual journey with me, but it would be twenty years before I would fully appreciate its transforming power, when I made my own *Umrah* pilgrimage to Mecca. Indeed, his rejuvenated spirit helped us through the losses we were about to face.

I was passing through London in the early spring of 1979 when my husband called to sadly inform me that his maternal uncle, Sharif

Nasser Bin Jamil, had suddenly died of a heart attack. His unexpected death was a shock for us all. Sharif Nasser had been at my husband's side from the beginning of his reign. He had been Commander in Chief of the Armed Forces in the early 1970s and had saved my husband's life on several occasions. They had also been extraordinarily close. Sharif Nasser had been one of the first family members to wholeheartedly congratulate us on our engagement, and he had given us a beautiful piece of land where we hoped someday to build our home. His wife, Hind, a close friend and talented artist, was, like me, expecting a child at the time.

We moved from one trauma to the next. Hussein was preparing to go to Baghdad for what would be a final censure of Egypt for its position on Camp David. The day after his call, before returning to Amman, I had traveled to Hampstead to have lunch with our friends, King Constantine and Queen Anne-Marie of Greece, and Anne-Marie's mother, Queen Ingrid of Denmark. Five months into my pregnancy, I suddenly felt terribly weak. I was introduced to Queen Ingrid as soon as I entered the drawing room, but I had to excuse myself right away. Anne-Marie followed me out of the room in concern as I explained that I was not feeling well. She did not tell me what she feared but took me to her room to lie down. As I began to hemorrhage she went quietly to call her own doctor, George Pinker, the obstetrician of the British royal family. He was away fishing in Scotland, but his assistant agreed to come out as quickly as possible.

Because Constantine and Anne-Marie lived a distance from the center of London, it took ages for the doctor to arrive, and by then the sad realization of what was happening to me began to register. While we waited for the doctor, Constantine came into the room to tell me he was calling my husband. I begged him not to. "He is on his way to Baghdad. This is a critical moment for him; he has all he can handle." We argued, and then he went off and called my husband anyway. I almost broke down when I heard Hussein's voice, but I had pledged to myself from the beginning not to add to my husband's burdens. "Shall I come?" he said. "No, absolutely not," I told him. "Stay there and do what you have to do. I will be fine."

I was not fine, of course. My sense of loss was intensified by feelings of acute failure and guilt. I was far enough along in the pregnancy to have felt the baby moving and had formed a real connection to the life inside me. I felt desperate to get to the hospital and under proper care, but ambulances were on semi-strike in England and operating on a go-slow order, so it would take longer than normal for the ambulance to be dispatched to the house in Hampstead. Then with no siren — not even flashing lights, if I remember correctly — the ambulance crawled at a snail's pace to the hospital. The entire way, the doctor kept telling me to "hold on, hold on" as I struggled with the excruciating pain. Upon arriving at the hospital, everything happened so quickly that I only remember lying in the hospital bed when it was all over; the phone was ringing. When the operator said, "It's Mr. Brown for Mrs. Brown," I thought she had called the wrong room, not knowing that I had been registered under the name of Brown for security. I would soon become used to the name. Forever after, Hussein and I became "the Browns" when we wanted a measure of privacy.

I learned in the hospital, however, that complete privacy would never be possible. Almost immediately news of my miscarriage appeared in the London tabloids. I felt truly violated that this most personal of moments and the tremendous loss we were feeling was being used as fodder for public consumption. My sister must have heard the despair in my voice when she called me at the hospital. She talked to me for a long time, and in our grief we bonded together as adults. I will always be grateful to Alexa for taking leave of her work at a Washington law firm to fly to London to be with me.

My husband arrived in London as soon as he was able after the Baghdad summit and, knowing of my love for skiing, surprised me with plans to visit the tiny ski town of Zurs in the

Austrian Alps for a few days. The last time I had skied there had been as a young teenager with my family. Jordan's Consul General for Austria had kindly made all the arrangements, but my husband and I were never alone. We spent our entire few days there in the company of the Consul General and his wife, as well as our entourage and the people they had met in the hotel. Instead of being able to talk to my husband about our loss and perhaps comfort each other, we were constantly surrounded by people and, of course, had to put on a valiant face for everyone.

I finally broke down on our last night in the Arlberg. We had been taken by sleigh to a small village above the nearby village of Lech to a typical mountain hut for dinner, where young children serenaded us. In the tightly packed, overheated space I became very emotional. I managed to control myself in the public situation, but on the way home I suddenly realized that not once had my husband asked me about the miscarriage, not once had we talked about it. Though I knew that by putting on a brave face I had sent an inaccurate message about my well-being, I also knew that my show of strength and resilience had simply been accepted at face value.

"We can't just pretend this never happened," I said to myself. I became quite angry with Hussein, and perhaps a little angry with myself for concealing my feelings. I told him how difficult our time in Austria had been for me, which evoked an instructive response. "Well, this trip has been difficult for me, too," he said. "The last time I was in the Alps in a sleigh was in Saint Moritz with the Shah and Shahbanou of Iran, and now they have been forced out of their country." I looked at him, dumbfounded by this seeming non sequitur, but I was discovering a pattern of behavior that would hold throughout our marriage. His response to any personal concern I expressed would be to counter with some greater problem that he was suffering from, in order to put my problem into perspective. I also learned that this man, who had the biggest heart in the world, could not talk about things that were personally painful to him precisely because he felt that pain so deeply. He just could not handle it.

We were blessed with another pregnancy six months later. Though many assumed I would have the baby abroad or at least bring in a Western doctor, I had full confidence in our Jordanian obstetrician, Dr. Arif Batayneh. He was the royal family's obstetrician and a colleague of Queen Anne-Marie's English doctor, George Pinker, who had looked in on me after my miscarriage and would consult on the pregnancy. They decided I should not travel outside the country for the first several months, which was a relief. I had more than enough work to do at home.

I had already become involved in a variety of national issues. The United Nations had designated 1979 as the International Year of the Child, and I was appointed chair of Jordan's National Committee for the Child. I invited government ministers and representatives of international and non-governmental organizations (NGOs) working with Jordanian children to Hashimya Palace, where we met to assess the general state of Jordan's children and to begin to identify short- and long-term priorities and strategies.

Child welfare and development was an urgent national priority because our population was so young: More than half of all Jordanians were under sixteen, and one-fifth were under five years old. Our birth rate was exceptionally high — more than twice the average in the developing world — in part because of the dramatic influx of refugees. This population increase put immense pressure on all our services, particularly education and health. There was severe overcrowding in many schools and very high student-teacher ratios. Most schools ran daily double shifts. We had an appalling shortage of children's books and very few facilities and parks, especially for children in poor neighborhoods.

Austria's prime minister, Bruno Kreisky, wrote to me in the early 1980s recommending SOS Kinderdorf International — a network of children's villages for orphans and abandoned children around the world, an initiative that was first developed in the chaotic aftermath of World War II, when so many children were left homeless and without families. After meeting with Hermann Gmeiner, its founder, we began a long and rewarding partnership. Every SOS Children's Village offers a permanent family-style home to children who have lost their parents or can no longer live with them. Four to ten boys and girls of different ages live together with their SOS mother in a family house, and eight to fifteen SOS Children's Village families form a village community.

My husband and I often visited the Amman and Aqaba villages, especially on the occasions of our Eid holidays, when families traditionally gather to celebrate the breaking of the fast. Jafar Tukan, a talented local architect and friend, contributed a unique and beautiful design for our first SOS village near Amman, which Hussein and I opened in 1987 — a charming traditional enclave of stone houses connected by courtyards and flowing gardens. The village design represented our first attempt together to develop a culturally and environmentally sensitive architectural model for Jordan. Jafar and I worked together a few years later on another pioneering design for an SOS village in Aqaba that won the Aga Khan award in 2001, and finally a third in Irbid in the north of Jordan that opened in 1999. I was thrilled in 2002 when SOS Kinderdorf was recognized for its unique contribution to our world's children and was awarded the prestigious Conrad N. Hilton Humanitarian Prize.

In the health sector we began by inaugurating a national immunization campaign, which I launched with the Minister of Health in several rural areas, administering some oral vaccines myself to promote awareness of the importance of the campaign. In 1980 we joined UNICEF's "child survival and development revolution," which led to a reduction in infant and maternal mortality rates through the use of low-cost interventions, such as growth monitoring, oral rehydration, breast-feeding, and immunization.

By the end of the 1980s, Jordan had achieved human development advances that were recognized by UNICEF and other agencies worldwide as exemplary in the developing world in areas such as nutrition, school enrollment and girls' education, and access to health services and water. We ranked among the top forty-five countries in the world to achieve immunization rates above 90 percent.

And so with great pride in 1990, I represented King Hussein at the United Nations World Summit for Children, joining with seventy-one heads of state and governments to sign the World Declaration on the Survival, Protection, and Development of Children. The next year Jordan ratified the Convention on the Rights of the Child, which became the most widely accepted human rights treaty ever, inspiring social change in all regions of the world. (The only nations that have not signed it yet are the United States and Somalia.)

After convening several national conferences on children's rights over the next years, I was asked by King Hussein to establish and chair a National Task Force for Children (NTFC) to monitor and evaluate the status of Jordan's children. To encourage and facilitate cooperation among often competing organizations, we established a National Coalition for Children that coordinated and promoted partnerships among all public and private institutions involved with children's affairs. The NTFC also established a national policy and research center as well as Jordan's first child information system on the worldwide web. The Information and Research Center has focused on critically important issues, such as child labor, urban poverty, youth and culture, smoking among teens, and gaps and priorities in development research and programs.

In those early days, I also assumed an active role with the Royal Society for the Conservation of Nature (RSCN). The society was unique in the region. Founded under King Hussein's patronage in 1966, when few people were talking about conservation, the RSCN was the first, and for a long time the only, national environmental protection organization in the Middle East. I was particularly proud of this because conservation had long been a serious concern of mine. In 1970, while a freshman at Princeton, I had cheered on UN Secretary General U Thant when he declared the first annual worldwide celebration of Earth Day. That sense of global unity and the universal need to balance the health of the environment with the requirements of mankind was as compelling to me then as it is today.

King Hussein and the original founders of the RSCN set a personal example by giving up hunting because their favorite sport was having such a negative impact on Jordan's wildlife. This concern was the seed of the RSCN's growing role over the years in protecting Jordan's fragile natural wonders from the impact of development. In 1978, the RSCN reached out to various international organizations, including the International Union for the Conservation of Nature and the World Wildlife Fund, for assistance in identifying specific areas in the country to be set aside as nature reserves. The RSCN established six protected areas that would generate income for local communities from conservation-based activities. Jordan has also set an example in protected-areas management for surrounding countries and has provided on-the-job training for conservationists around the region.

From the beginning I tried to listen and learn from as many different sources as possible, to develop consensus among my most trusted advisers. I also began to leverage my gradually expanding national and international network of experts, potential partners, and funding support for the country. Once key model programs in education, women's issues, and poverty eradication were successful in Jordan, we began to focus on regional outreach programs.

I urged everyone I worked with to speak freely and offer honest, constructive criticism. I especially valued the straight talkers, who went on to become friends and counselors; there was nothing for me to learn from sycophants who would tell me what they thought would please me rather than the truth. I also wanted to promote the concept of teamwork that would contribute to meaningful and substantive improvements in the quality of people's lives and their opportunities for the future.

By talking to experts, I learned that students in Jordanian high schools and universities were not being given career counseling. The vast majority of students were studying medicine, engineering, and law — fields that were already glutted with graduates seeking employment, yet we did not have enough qualified specialists in a multitude of fields, such as computer engineering, hotel management, traffic engineering, and early-childhood development. In 1979 I established the Royal Endowment for Culture and Education, which conducted the first research on the country's specific manpower needs and awarded scholarships, with special emphasis on outstanding women, to students pursuing graduate studies in fields vital to Jordan's future development. Over the next two decades those scholarship recipients would become leaders in their fields, reinforcing our premise that individuals can make a profound difference in accelerating the pace of development.

My background in urban planning and architecture led me early on to think how Jordan could manage its growth more carefully. I was very aware of my husband's frustrations with the construction nightmare of Hashimya — indeed, with almost every home he had built. Having worked in the country, I was also very conscious of the problems we had had with building projects at the airline. It had become apparent to me that we had a critical need for standardized building codes. Not long after my marriage, I invited the Minister of Public Works to my office at Al Ma'Wa. "Help me understand our building codes," I asked him. Without a word, he opened the suitcase he had brought with him and emptied it out onto the floor. In the heap were books of standard building codes from countries all over the world, but it turned out that we did not have a binding one of our own.

With his encouragement, I called for a meeting of the key engineers and architects in Jordan to ask them what sorts of problems they were dealing with, and what they felt could be done to establish uniform building requirements. There was general agreement that the government and the private sector needed to work together to formulate such regulations. Over the next few years, the Royal Scientific Society produced Jordan's first building code, and I learned a valuable lesson about one role I could play as Queen — as a catalyst for consensus-building and action.

I also proposed a committee of specialists to assume responsibility for the conservation of our architectural heritage and the proper review of designs for new public buildings and spaces. This was a partial success in that it positively influenced a number of key projects, but its effectiveness remained subject to the whims of cabinet officials. This experience caused me to appreciate the challenges the Prince of Wales would face in his efforts in the United Kingdom to promote awareness of the impact and import of public design in reinforcing civic pride and national culture.

I felt that such an approach was particularly vital for Aqaba. If we did not plan that beautiful resort area at the northern tip of the Red Sea very carefully, we would perpetuate the chaotic planning that had existed to date and miss an opportunity to give Aqaba a unique Jordanian character unlike any other resort in the world. If it was going to be a successful tourist destination, Aqaba had to have a distinct personality. We did make some progress in greening the area by planting palm trees along the roads and landscaping part of the city, but the harmony of design that existed in Sardinia, for example, and in the Canary Islands, which reflect a cultural pride and heritage, was never realized. At times of political upheaval, when other ports in the region were closed down, Aqaba would brim with commercial activity, and long-range planning for the city would take a secondary role to economic expansion.

Unfortunately, much of the time our energies were channeled into crisis management. One day a government minister came to my office in great excitement to announce imminent plans to build an elevated tram in Petra and to pave the *Siq*, the ancient, dramatic stone entrance to the site. We were speechless. Very diplomatically, we stopped the project with the King's support, but this was just one instance of last-minute intervention due to lack of uniform planning standards and project coordination in the country.

I met regularly with the Mayor of Amman to explore ways in which we could develop more parks and open space for poorer children and their families. The press of refugees and displaced persons from Palestine, combined with the new affluence from the oil boom in the last half of the 1970s, was leading to the unchecked escalation of development. Open space, so important to the quality of life in an urban environment, was vanishing and being replaced by inadequate housing, high-rise hotels, or oversize, extravagant villas in new upscale districts in the city. In just the few years I had lived in Amman, I had noticed fewer and fewer shepherds on the streets and more and more building on precious arable land.

We also discussed ways to redevelop the downtown area. The original heart of the city had been largely abandoned as more and more people moved to the affluent suburbs of Amman. In our revival efforts we had a number of unique sites to work with. The royal palaces where we lived and worked were downtown, as were the traditional *souk*, or shopping areas, and the magnificent amphitheater built by the Romans. Also central to the downtown area was the ancient hilltop Citadel, layered with all the civilizations that made up the region's history, from Stone, Bronze, and Iron Age settlements beginning in 4500 B.C. through Roman and Byzantine occupation, up through its Islamic flowering in the Umayyad period in the eighth century, when it grew into a city in itself, complete with governor's residence, baths, and mosque.

One proposal called for building a state-of-the-art museum to house priceless artifacts unearthed from around the country and currently stored in what was called a museum on the Citadel. This museum, no doubt once an elegant building, had become essentially a dusty, oversize storage shed. I was not alone in wanting to build an archaeological museum to properly display Jordan's magnificent collection of ancient artifacts. Not only were funds for the museum hard to come by, but also the project was hamstrung by the constant debate among archaeologists and site planners as to how much damage might be done to even more historic treasures by the building construction itself. Many artifacts would end up being dispersed among the small archaeological museums being developed at the time throughout Jordan, a development that created decentralized jewels of museums instead of one prestigious national institution.

Over the years as the Citadel's archaeological excavations progressed, the site began to provide spectacular venues for concerts and cultural events that we also staged across the valley below, in the ancient Roman theater of Philadelphia. Restoring these ancient sites and amphitheaters to the living, artistic spaces they had been centuries ago added an immeasurable sense of continuity to Jordan's history. I took Queen Sofia, Abir, Haya, and Ali to a children's concert at the downtown Philadelphia theater when the Queen and King Juan Carlos visited us in 1979. The atmosphere was electric. Thousands of people from all walks of life joined together to share in the festivities, generating an incomparable spirit of family and community and even civic and national pride. The following year we would inaugurate our first Jerash Festival, which took advantage of an entire Roman city as a performance and exhibition site.

Two extraordinary exhibition spaces that contributed to revitalizing that area of the capital over the next few years were the direct result of perseverance by two of my first and closest Jordanian friends: Princess Wijdan and Suha Shoman. Princess Wijdan succeeded in raising public and private support to found Jordan's National Gallery of Fine Arts, which houses a unique permanent collection of works by contemporary artists from the developing world, with special emphasis on modern art from the Arab and Islamic countries.

Darat Al Funun (Home for the Arts), established in 1993, was the brainchild of Suha Shoman and her husband, Khalid, who purchased and renovated three turn-of-the-century houses overlooking the heart of Amman. The main residence, which houses Darat Al Funun's collection of contemporary Arab art, is typical of the traditional eastern Mediterranean architectural style that prevailed in Amman during the early 1920s and 1930s, and its library and art studios are available to everyone free of charge. Darat Al Funun, which has revitalized Amman's oldest residential district, has brought art to a more populated, lower-income area of the city.

Despite working hard to maintain momentum on various projects of my own, I did not have any trouble with my second pregnancy. After restricting my activities somewhat for the first four months, I resumed my full work schedule and my more ceremonial duties. Various Arab leaders were coming to Jordan to meet with my husband, and often he included me in a private welcome to our home. The first leader I greeted was Saddam Hussein, on his first visit to Jordan. I did not have time to form any opinion of him; I just shook his hand and went on about my business. The second leader I met required more time and attention because he and his entourage were in Jordan for a state visit — a memorable one. The guest of honor was the leader of the Libyan Arab *Jamahiriya,* or Republic, Muammar Al Qaddafi.

I had heard a great deal over the years about this unusual Arab leader who had overthrown Libya's pro-Western monarchy in 1969, replacing it with a strict Muslim socialist Arab republic. He had "Libyanized" the country, replacing every French or English word on street signs and menus with Arabic, and spending billions of the country's oil revenues on Libya's infrastructure, including the colossal Great Man-Made River Project, which was being designed at the time by South Korea to carry underground water from deep under the Sahara Desert 2,500 hundred miles to the Libyan coast. Unfortunately, the hot, dry desert air would evaporate much of the water in the irrigation system's reservoirs, and the project never delivered on its promise, but it was a stunningly ambitious enterprise nonetheless.

We met Qaddafi and his wife Safiyya at the airport. He arrived with an entourage of security guards who all appeared to have the same curly black hair as he did, cut in the same way, and they wore identical safari suits. Sprinkled among the security detail were female guards, a source of great fascination for Jordanians because at the time there were no women active in Jordan's armed services, though I was advocating their inclusion and considered as a model the Women's Royal Army Corps in Britain, which I had visited. Men were required to serve two years in national service at the time, and I saw no reason why women should not be engaged as well in the service of their country. Women did serve in the police but in the army were limited to jobs as nurses, secretaries, and military communications experts, until the late 1980s, when one of my husband's daughters, Princess Aisha, and two female cousins went to Sandhurst and returned to Jordan as trained army officers.

On the evening of the state banquet, my husband hosted dinner for the men and I hosted dinner for the women, including the women bodyguards. The women were all wearing traditional, very brightly colored, flowing Libyan dress and looked quite lovely. In preparation for the visit, everyone in our delegation had been reading Qaddafi's famous *Green Book*, a three-volume manifesto of his political and social philosophy. The senior female bodyguard sitting on one side of me recited long passages from it during the course of the meal, almost as if she were hoping to convert me to its views.

While the first night of the state visit had gone according to plan, the second night was full of surprises. I had spent the day with Safiyya, taking her to various institutions in Amman, in particular to see Jordan's state-of-the-art heart surgery unit. She had been a nurse in a hospital in Tripoli, she told me, and had met her husband there when he had had an emergency appendectomy. They had fallen in love, and she became his second wife and the mother, ultimately, of eight children. I went back to Hashimya at the end of the day quite exhausted, to find my husband equally tired after his long military program with Qaddafi. It had gone well enough, though Qaddafi had expressed his displeasure over and over about the street signs and shop names being written in English as well as Arabic. After that long day of official visits the Qaddafis returned to the guesthouse downtown to rest, and there was no plan for us to meet again later that evening.

While my husband and I were bathing and preparing for bed, our security rang us to say that the Qaddafis were in a car on their way to Hashimya for dinner! We had made no arrangements for dinner. "Take a long scenic route to the house, a very, very long route," I told our security. "Stall for time." Somehow we pulled it all together, including dinner, and when the Qaddafis' car drew up outside Hashimya, we were dressed and waiting to greet them at the front door. We proceeded to have a remarkably pleasant evening. They were a delightful and charming couple, and even my husband was quite taken with how natural and comfortable they seemed and how friendly the dinner was, as if we were the oldest and best of friends.

It would not last. Shortly thereafter, on his return to Libya, Qaddafi started attacking my husband for his dealings with the West and even threw in a gratuitous personal attack on me. Qaddafi was notoriously unpredictable. I was told, though I could not believe it, that he allegedly offered millions of dollars to Syria in 1982 to have Hussein's plane shot down by surface-to-air missiles during one of our trips to Aqaba, although President Hafez Al Assad reportedly rejected Qaddafi's assassination scheme, saying if the assassination were to be successful, no Arab leader would ever be safe in the air. Such was the nature of the neighborhood we lived in.

Still, my husband never stopped trying to maintain open lines of communication with all the Arab leaders, including Qaddafi, no matter how strained relations became. It was extraordinary to me how much faith, tolerance, and stamina he expended to promote cooperative Arab action. A perfect case in point occurred in the fall of 1980 when King Hussein convened the eleventh Arab Summit, the first such summit ever to be held in Amman.

Jordanians were excited and proud that their small and relatively poor country was playing host to the leaders of fifteen Arab countries, including the oil-rich nations of Saudi Arabia, Kuwait, Iraq, and the Gulf states of Bahrain, Oman, Qatar, and the United Arab Emirates. The choice of Jordan was testament to the prominent place King Hussein held in the Arab world by the sheer force of his character and personality, rather than the resources of his country. The preparations were enormous. It was no small job for a country like Jordan to mobilize the finances and the facilities to receive the Arab heads of state and their entourages. We had only one modest guesthouse and limited hotel rooms for large entourages and security, but somehow we made do.

The summit was ostensibly an economic one. Hussein was pushing hard for joint Arab action in developing the economies of all the member states, based loosely on a similar cooperative effort in Europe at the time. Everyone seemed to agree, and a strategy was adopted, though when the leaders left Jordan and went back home, everybody seemed to forget what they had agreed to do.

Despite Hussein's efforts, the Arab world was more fractured than ever. Egypt had been isolated from the Arab community since the

Camp David Accords and was not at the summit. Neither were Libya and Iraq. Almost all the Arab countries, including Jordan, were supporting Iraq in its war with Iran, but Syria, which had an age-old competition with Iraq, and maverick Libya were supporting Iran.

Syrian president Hafez Al Assad, who opposed holding the Arab Summit because he suspected that Jordan was encouraging the Muslim Brotherhood to challenge his regime, massed troops on Jordan's borders, and we found ourselves on the brink of war. The army called up 6,000 members of the Jordanian reserve forces, and another 16,000 citizens volunteered. I saw the overwhelming response myself when I paid a supportive visit to army facilities near our border with Syria during the summit. People were hiring cars and buses at their own expense to join their regiments against the threat of the Syrian aggression. Assad subsequently withdrew his forces, but the situation remained tense.

It all seemed so counterproductive. If ancient enmities and modern slights continued to divide the Arab world, any chance for cooperative efforts for security, progress, and peace would be nullified. How could we break the cycle? It occurred to me one day soon after the summit that the answer might lie in our children. Perhaps we could lay the groundwork for more effective cooperation at every level in the future if we began with Arab boys and girls at an early age and brought them together to appreciate their common bonds.

Later that year, we convened the first annual Arab Children's Congress, gathering children from throughout the Arab world for two weeks of activities designed to promote understanding, tolerance, and solidarity. The children are encouraged to discuss and debate contemporary challenges facing the Arab nations and to appreciate their common cultural and historical bonds. It continues to be a very popular program, and some of the earlier delegates, now young adults, have forged lasting friendships.

I kept up with my work as my pregnancy advanced and, to the consternation of my Jordanian obstetrician, traveled all over Jordan. There were villages to visit to launch the vaccination campaign, urban planning meetings to chair in Aqaba, and conditions in Palestinian refugee camps to check on. I either flew or drove my own car, a four-wheel-drive Jeep that was perfect for the rough roads and steep mountain tracks I often traveled as I visited different communities and projects in rural areas. I loved to drive myself because that was the only solitary respite I could find. My private space became the Jeep, and there I would turn up the music, listening to Fairouz, Bach and Beethoven, Bruce Springsteen and Fleetwood Mac, singing and probably even talking to myself, which must have caused some concern to the security car that always accompanied me.

During the visits to these villages and to other areas of Jordan, I saw that the gap between rich and poor was growing. The economic gains of the business class were most welcome, of course, but having lived in Iran and traveled extensively through the Arab world, I was very aware of the destabilizing consequences of the 1970s oil boom. Hussein and I were both very aware that these new extremes of material consumption and changing lifestyles represented a radical shift in the country's traditions.

When I had first arrived in Jordan it was in the process of becoming a major regional medical and education center. The country's physicians and hospitals were providing services to many other Arab countries, some with far greater resources but without the facilities and the local expertise available in Jordan. For more than a generation Jordan had also provided the educated, specialized manpower to develop the infrastructures of the Gulf states and other parts of the Arab world. Remittances from Jordanians living as expatriates in other countries had become Jordan's largest source of national income, rising to as much as $800 million a year, especially after the oil boom in the mid-1970s, when increased demand and a rising pay scale for Jordanian doctors, nurses, teachers, planners, and engineers brought a new and sudden prosperity. Many people in the business sector were also enjoying windfall profits — and spending them as if there were no tomorrow. Where once they had lived simply but well, many now enjoyed unprecedented wealth and were passing on to their children a completely different set of values than those they themselves had grown up with.

Jordan's prosperity was real, but its economic base was still fragile. The newly privileged were enjoying the lifestyle of an oil-rich country, but without the oil. Money from expatriates in the Gulf countries may have been pouring in, but it was not income that anyone could count on forever. I used to question my husband at length about the insecurity of the way we, as a country and family, were living. I know that, as a family, we did not always set the best example and tried to identify ways we could be more responsible about our own lifestyles. In retrospect I realize that part of the exuberant spending spree in Jordan was fueled by the same regional uncertainty that clouded people's ability to think long-term. Still, it was a troubling trend.

The chief of the Royal Court shared my worry. Sharif Abdul Hamid Sharaf knew the boom was not going to last and made an attempt, at least, to inspire fiscal responsibility. When he became Prime Minister he called on the government to reduce the budget by 10 percent, and he urged the people to ration their consumption of electricity and water, and to save some of their newly acquired money. His directive created an uproar. Many newly prosperous Jordanians adopted the attitude, why should we save? We should be free to spend whatever we want.

The level of indignation was so high that Sharif Abdul Hamid Sharaf and his wife, Leila, became targets of a campaign to discredit them. The Sharafs were building a modest house in Amman at the time, a project that had gotten no further than excavation for a foundation and preliminary cement columns, when reports began surfacing that the house would cost $3 million. The power of rumor was such that people started visiting the site to see the $3 million house. Even though there was little construction yet to be seen, people remained convinced of this excess. Why were these rumors accepted as fact? Because people wanted to believe that Sharif Abdul Hamid was asking the people to save at the same time he was spending a fortune.

Our way of spending was also disturbing. Instead of reinvesting in the Jordanian economy, we were importing luxury goods and furnishings from Europe. Granted there were limited furnishings available in Jordan at the time, and we were importing for our home as well, nonetheless I began to wonder what could be done to allow Jordanians to benefit from their own magnificent Arab heritage.

Women on both sides of the Jordan River, for

example, had traditionally designed and embroidered their own trousseaus, creating the nine or ten dresses they would wear throughout their married life, including a wedding dress that, for some, would also serve in death as a shroud. Finely embroidered cushions were also part of a traditional trousseau, with designs drawn largely from nature — trees, leaves, and feathers. These women were rightfully proud of their handiwork. Each dress and cushion was different; each had fine stitching, and the colors were bright and varied. But what had once been a living part of the Jordanian and Palestinian tradition was rapidly dying out. Were it not for the extraordinary collection of these clothes amassed over the years by a Jordanian friend from Bethlehem, Widad Kawar, I would have known little of this rich heritage.

Leila Jiryes, one particularly enterprising and talented designer, was combining the art of Palestinian and Jordanian needlework with new fabrics like watered silk. I made a point of wearing her lovely kaftans whenever I could in public and on official occasions, and this was not purely promotional on my part. The kaftans also made excellent maternity clothes. I also supported initiatives like the Al Aydi Jordan Handicrafts Center, near the tourist hotels, that featured beautiful traditional textiles, woven rugs, embroidered cushions and clothing, and Hebron glass.

Later I also encouraged two creative and enterprising sisters, Rula and Reem Attallah, who started a handmade ceramics business in Amman using designs and calligraphy from ancient Middle Eastern civilizations and Islamic dynasties. We gave their beautiful glazed pieces, many painted with bas-relief imagery, as personal and official gifts with great pride. One of my favorites from Silsal Ceramics was — and is — the "Health, Happiness and Good Fortune" bowl, which uses the unique Islamic art form of Arabic script to promise blessings on its owner. Another favorite bowl bears the very delicate lettering of an eleventh-century Samarkand proverb that translates to: "Knowledge: the beginning of it is bitter to taste, but the end is sweeter than honey."

Another rich aspect of Arab culture and heritage is language. I had begun learning Arabic as soon as I arrived in Amman, just as I had studied Farsi in Iran. After my engagement I redoubled my efforts to read and become fluent in Arabic, a difficult, demanding language. The King was known and revered throughout the Arab-speaking world for his masterful command of Arabic. Most people speak it in their colloquial dialect, but Hussein spoke classical Arabic with such a beauty and eloquence that Arabs all over the region tuned in just to listen to him on the radio or television. My husband's mastery of the language and his deep, sonorous delivery accorded him special respect.

I had not realized before I came to Jordan how central language is to Arab identity. Arabic is the language of the Quran, which all Muslims, whether in the Middle East, the Far East, Europe, or the United States, need to learn in order to read and recite their daily prayers. My husband's command of vocabulary and nuance was achieved over a lifetime of study of the holy text. Though he knew much of the Quran by heart, he read it over and over again, and he never stopped seeking greater and greater understanding of its message.

I had begun with lessons in colloquial Arabic, which, after my marriage, I expanded to include the classical form used in public speaking. I arranged a heavy weekly schedule with a tutor. Improving my Arabic was my top priority, after my husband and my family. However, Hussein would suddenly show up wanting to go for a drive, visit family, or take the children out, constantly sabotaging these lessons. The tutor and I were unable to refuse him; nonetheless, I continued as best I could with my reading lessons of the Quran, Arabic poetry, the newspapers, and grappling with the impenetrable mysteries of grammar.

My favorite study moments involved helping my stepchildren with their Arabic homework, which was an unexpected treat and boost to my confidence. Abir and then Haya would cuddle up on my bed with me at the end of the day, and we would read their first Arabic textbooks together. Eventually I would learn enough and be secure enough to converse in Arabic and even deliver formal speeches, but it would be a long, difficult process that always left me with a raw feeling of inadequacy. When distractions and other commitments put increasing pressure on my formal lessons, I found some bright, wonderful young women to work with me on special projects and my language skills simultaneously, but I was constantly frustrated by my inability to master the language at a truly sophisticated level of fluency.

Whereas the concern for this pregnancy following my miscarriage had been premature birth, the opposite worry had emerged by the end of my pregnancy. George Pinker, the British obstetrician, had planned his spring holiday in Jordan around the due date in order to assist in the delivery, but the baby had no intention of meeting someone else's schedule. There was some talk of labor being induced, however I did not want to do anything unnatural, so Mr. Pinker left.

To the despair of my doctor, Arif Batayneh, I continued my fieldwork in various communities around the capital. He would often accompany me, complaining that he exercised more vigorously on those trips than he did when working out, and he always returned with an exaggerated account of our adventures to amuse my husband. I kept maintaining that women through the ages had given birth in fields and gone right back to work, and I did not see why their descendants should be less capable (a deeply flawed argument, I know, given the high infant and maternal mortality rates even today in many underdeveloped countries). Over the next six years, Arif must have become quite fit as he supervised all my pregnancies; he also became a great friend.

I had been told over and over again by numerous members of the family that we absolutely had to hire a Norland nanny to help us with the baby. Norland's College, located in England, is internationally renowned from the Gulf to Beverly Hills as the elite nanny training college, providing top-class nannies who have learned everything from handicrafts to nutrition, with a bit of child psychology thrown in. We were lucky to find a great candidate, Dianne Smith, who soldiered on with us in spite of a bomb scare at Heathrow that delayed her first flight to Jordan five hours. My husband tried to put her at ease when he walked in on us during her explanation of the delay. He took her aside afterward and asked: "Are you ready to go to the hospital at a moment's notice?" When she replied, "All ready," he said, "Come and see," and he took her to where he had laid out his clothes long before.

He also shaved off his beard, presumably because he wanted to welcome the baby into the world clean-shaven. His friends and family had been after him for some time to get rid of his beard, but I thought it made him look dashing. I had not advocated either way — it was his face, after all — but seeing him beardless for the first time was a shock. I had come into the bathroom, our private refuge, to chat with him while he was taking a shower. On this particular day we were talking away when I suddenly realized there was a man in the steamy shower who did not look at all like the man I had been married to for the past year. I started to blush and feel very shy. I quickly adjusted, however, for this new person was just as handsome and dashing as his predecessor.

Hussein knew our baby's gender. The first advanced ultrasound machine had just arrived in Jordan, and the technology had progressed to the point that the sex of the baby could be reasonably well determined in utero. My husband, who had an insatiable curiosity, wanted to know. I made him and the doctor swear not to tell me, as I would for all our children.

Our miracle stubbornly refused to happen. One day followed another as the due date passed. My stepchildren were getting very impatient, especially Abdullah and Feisal, who were due to leave Jordan to return to their schools in the United States and wanted to be here for the birth. "Tapioca" became the code word between the boys and us for news of the birth. My husband took me on long helicopter and motorcycle rides, hoping to set something in motion, but all we had was fun. We decided to see if a change in air pressure would start the birth process, so he flew me up to the highest peak in Jordan in his helicopter and then descended rapidly to the lowest point on Earth, the Dead Sea. Nothing. The medical decision was finally taken to induce labor. After six agonizing hours, our son Hamzah finally decided to be born just hours before his older brothers departed for school, on March 29, 1980.

Everyone in the delivery room was so excited when he was born that I do not think I actually met Hamzah until some time later, when he was finally brought into my room after doing the rounds of family and friends and having his first checkup. He was wide awake, and when my husband came in much later, Hamzah and I were in the midst of conversation, which I sincerely believed was not as one-sided as it may have seemed. I could not stop staring at him in amazement. I had never thought of myself as an especially maternal person, and I was stunned by the intensity of my feelings of love for my firstborn child. I do not remember what I had expected, but his large, round, funny face and bald head and wise old soulful eyes took most of my breath away; I expended the rest by talking to him all night.

There were streams of people coming to the hospital to see Hamzah. Everybody in Jordan, it seemed, stopped by my room at some point to say, "*Mabrouk,* congratulations!" Friends, representatives of organizations I worked with, religious figures, government officials, politicians, businesspeople, NGO representatives, tribal leaders, diplomats — all came and sat for a while with Hussein or in the room with me. Their response moved me deeply as a reflection of the unique Jordanian family spirit, but it was also quite exhausting for a new mother. I was just learning to nurse, and I wanted to give this very special baby every bit of my attention and love.

Though this was his ninth child, my husband and Hamzah shared a uniquely empathetic relationship and an affinity for each other, which would bond them in a special way until the day my husband died. Perhaps it was because Hamzah rarely slept as a baby. He would catnap, but mostly he was alert and happy day and night, as long as I was nursing him, which meant we spent an enormous amount of time with him, particularly during the evenings, when he was always wide awake. On those rare occasions when Hamzah actually slept, we would often go into his room at night and just stare at him. Hussein even gave up smoking again after Hamzah was born.

My husband and I chose the name Hamzah to honor a Hashimite ancestor and a favorite uncle of the Prophet Muhammad. Hamzah's story was one of great historical importance. Born in Mecca in 570, he and the Prophet were the same age and very close friends as children. As a young man, Hamzah was known far and wide for his horsemanship and his great strength, which earned him the title "Lion of the Desert" after he killed an attacking lion with a single javelin throw and rode back into Mecca with the lion skin over his saddle. Because of his renown in Mecca, Hamzah's conversion to Islam gave great credibility to the monotheistic belief system that Muhammad was espousing, and he then became known as the "Lion of God and His Prophet." His beliefs cost him his life. Hamzah was cut down defending the Prophet in the religious wars that followed, earning him a hallowed place in Islam as "the Master of all Martyrs" — a name given to him by the Prophet.

Our Hamzah, whose full name is Hamzah Bin Al Hussein (Hamzah, son of Al Hussein), formally received his name in a Hashimite family ritual conducted by the head religious sheikh in Jordan. The male members of the family assembled for the naming ceremony, which traditionally called for the father to hand the baby to my husband as the senior member of the family, who would in turn hand the baby to the sheikh. The sheikh then whispered the call to prayer into each of the newborn's ears so that it would be one of the first things the child heard, and then he would whisper the child's name in both ears and give the baby back to the father. The ritual was only slightly different in our case. Hussein had already named our son privately in our bedroom, as he would all our children. He had the right to do so, being the spiritual leader and head of the Hashimite family.

Beyond Jordan itself, Hamzah's birth prompted extraordinary and unexpected congratulations from Arab leaders and friends, so much so that my husband was slightly taken aback. Congratulatory messages and gifts flooded in from the Arab world, some from leaders whose relationships with my husband had been competitive or conflicted. Our choice of Hamzah as a name was greeted with particular enthusiasm. My husband had named his other sons, predictably, after his grandfather and his great-uncles, and there was one name left, Zeid. Everyone assumed that we would choose it, but there was already a Zeid Hussein in the extended family with a very colorful reputation, and we thought our son should begin life with a fresh slate.

From the moment of Hamzah's birth I spoke only Arabic to him, whatever I had mastered up to that point. Not only did I think it was the right thing to do, I had seen the struggle the other children were having with Arabic when they had first learned English, which is much easier. I decided that Hamzah and I would learn Arabic together, so I shared everything I was learning with him while I nursed him. When he started on his first word some months later, it was in Arabic — *taa taa tayyara* — the word for airplane, prompted no doubt by the constant, overwhelming sound of planes over Al Nadwa.

My husband was so astonished to hear his young son speaking Arabic that he immediately usurped my project. This meant that as my son's Arabic began to outstrip my own, he spoke Arabic with one parent and English with the other — the normal pattern for bilingual children but disastrous to my plans to learn the language with him. At least he and his siblings grew up fluent.

We took the baby with us everywhere, including, in June 1980, our first state visit to the United States since our marriage, when Hamzah was only two months old. I checked with his pediatrician to make sure traveling would not adversely affect Hamzah in any way and was relieved when the doctor validated my maternal instincts by saying it was much better for children under eighteen months to travel with their parents than to be separated from them. He also reassured me that children handle jet travel and time changes much more easily than adults. The net result was that my children would be better traveled by the time they were toddlers than most people are in a lifetime, having been to virtually every country in Europe and Asia, as well as Pakistan, India, the Soviet Union, numerous Arab countries, and, of course, the United States.

We flew the Royal Squadron's Boeing 727, with my husband at the controls for most flights. He was a superb pilot, and he loved to tease his more fainthearted passengers by what I would call his extreme flying. One episode I love to remember involved his approach to the Aqaba airport one day, when he descended so low that we virtually skimmed the Gulf waters between two tankers moored close to our jetty, flying at a level below their superstructure. Sitting behind him in the cockpit, I remember looking up at the tanker towers, and then barely clearing the beach and our home as we began our approach to the airport beyond. Even I was caught off guard! Whenever officials, friends, family, and security guards who were nervous fliers saw Hussein striding toward the cockpit with a certain gleam in his eye, they would hurriedly get out their compasses to identify the direction of Mecca and start to pray.

The children loved flying with him, as did I. He was particularly inventive when flying his helicopter in Jordan, turning the faces of his security guards ashen. Hamzah loved his father's acrobatic flying from the beginning. He would laugh and say, "More, Baba, more," which would bring an even paler hue to the security guards. Sometimes Hussein went a bit too far, as he did once in Aqaba when Hamzah was a tiny baby. He flew so low over the beach before landing at our helicopter pad that he blew all the beach umbrellas out of their stands, the beach chairs into the water, and sand all over

Hamzah, who was on the beach in his big, old-fashioned pram. I found the chaotic scene quite funny, but Hamzah's nanny, Dianne, gave my husband a lecture about jeopardizing his son's well-being. The King was appropriately apologetic, but everyone knew that he would do it again.

We had to take an enormous amount of equipment with us when we began traveling with Hamzah because we never knew if we would find the right kind of cot, bath, sterilizers, and whatever else where we were going. My husband used to joke that Hamzah had more luggage to transport than he did, so Hamzah's nanny eventually learned to hide it in the plane so the King would not see it being loaded.

That first flight to America turned out to be quite trying. We flew to England first, then on to the United States. We stopped to refuel at Gander, Newfoundland, but it was very late at night and the airport was closed. We had to walk up and down the tarmac in the freezing cold until someone arrived to unlock the doors and let us into the airport building. Hamzah caught a cold that lasted our entire stay, and Dianne had so little sleep that she would become ill herself on the flight back to Heathrow and faint. My husband would tease her forever after that she was so nervous about his flying that she had collapsed with fright.

I wondered why I was not more nervous myself when we started to descend into Washington, D.C., in June 1980. I had not been back to America in the two years since we had married. Relations between the United States and Jordan had become so strained since Camp David that when my husband had flown to America the prior fall to address the United Nations, he had not been invited to meet with President Carter. This trip was a first for all of us — my first visit to the United States as my husband's wife, our first state visit together to the White House, and Hamzah's inaugural visit to Washington.

chapter ten

America through New Eyes

I was back in America. In the two years since I had left the United States, I had married and given birth to my first child. Jordan had become home; my life there was fast-paced and always eventful. Between the ever-churning politics of the region and the complex dynamics of the Royal Court, it could not be otherwise. In truth, I had hardly had time to miss America, but now my heart skipped a beat as we approached the runway at Andrews Air Force Base outside of Washington, D.C. — the city of my birth, a place brimming with fond memories of my youth. I was in the cockpit's jump seat behind my husband, who was piloting our plane. My heart fluttered again when the Jordanian and American national anthems were played at the opening lawn ceremony at the White House. Both songs stirred my senses; both countries had a claim on me.

But this was not a sentimental journey. The King and I had no illusions about the hard work ahead. During the stopover in London, we had talked late into the night, considering all the points of contention between the United States and Jordan and how some of these differences might be bridged. This much was clear: President Carter was deeply invested in the Camp David Accords and could not abide my husband's criticism of its failings. My husband, for his part, had his convictions to uphold. He was committed to supporting any initiative that might lead to peace in the Middle East, but he knew that would not be possible without granting self-determination to the Palestinians and the return of the Occupied Territories. It was hard to imagine an easy rapprochement, and harder still to have anticipated what would come next.

We arrived at Blair House, the official guesthouse for visiting dignitaries, located across the street from the White House. We were welcomed with great excitement both because Hussein was already a favorite guest of the Blair House staff and because Hamzah was the first baby ever to stay there. After we were escorted to our rooms, we put the baby to bed and began to unpack. Suddenly, there on the television screen was President Sadat, inveighing against my husband for being an opportunist, blocking the path of peace, and withholding promised support. I watched with openmouthed shock. Hussein had witnessed this sort of display many times, but even he was taken aback. His response was to take the long view: "I know where I stand," he told reporters as we arrived at the White House for the state dinner. "I have always been concerned with life for the generations to come. For me that is more important than today's disagreements." But there was no misunderstanding the timing of Sadat's invective. It coincided with our arrival in Washington, D.C., and I could not help but view it as a deliberate attempt to undermine my husband's talks with the administration and further strain Jordan's relations with Washington.

There was a lot at stake for Jordan. Congress was withholding all military aid to the country — a way of pressuring the King to drop his objections to Camp David. More significant, Sadat's separate peace with Israel had brought a new wave of turmoil to the Middle East. Having successfully neutralized Egypt, Israel had invaded Lebanon in 1978 and was occupying the south of the country, between the Litani River and the Israeli border. Closer to home, Begin had sidestepped the vaguely stated restrictions in the accords by allowing new Jewish settlements to be built on the West Bank. By 1980 the Israelis had expropriated roughly one-third of the pre-1948 Palestinian lands. There were upward of seventy-four settlements and residential areas on the occupied West Bank, the number of settlers in that one area alone having grown from 5,000 before the accords to more than 12,000 in less than two years. We watched in horror while the Israeli government continued to transform the occupied West Bank into a network of armed Israeli camps, connected by new roads that bypassed and isolated Palestinian villages, in blatant violation of international law. How was this policy any less odious than racial apartheid in Africa, which the West had so widely condemned?

Israel was also playing havoc with the region's scarce water resources. By the time of our state visit to Washington in 1980, Israel had seized control of the occupied West Bank's water supply by either confiscating or buying Palestinian land for its own use. What wells the Palestinians still owned were being rendered useless; by boring deeper wells, the Israelis were systematically drying up or salinizing Palestinian water. Israel's unslakable thirst for water to support its ever-growing immigrant population and the expansion of its industry and agriculture had multiplied fourfold since 1948, with no end in sight.

These were crucial issues. But Arab leaders like my husband, who spoke truthfully about them, were demonized in the West for creating obstacles to peace. Lost in the rhetoric was the fact that at the Baghdad summit *all* the attending Arab leaders had reaffirmed their commitment to a just peace only a few months before our state visit to Washington. Hussein, for one, had cooperated with every peace initiative proposed by the United Nations and by the United States during the presidencies of Johnson, Nixon, and Ford. After eagerly embracing the Carter proposal, he had sought to reactivate the Geneva Conference in 1977 by rallying all the Arab countries to participate. He had almost reached that goal when the Carter administration took a separate track with Egypt.

King Hussein was so concerned about the deteriorating situation in the region that, in the fall of 1979, he had addressed the United Nations General Assembly for the first time since the 1967 war, asking the Security Council for its help in finding a resolution to the plight of the Palestinians. "The official Israeli political line has never once provided a glimpse of possible recognition of the Palestinians as a people with a right to a free and secure existence based on self-determination," he said to the members. "Rather it has insisted on smearing the Arab image by projecting the Palestinians as no more than terrorists."

For speaking out in this way my husband was branded as a turncoat by President Carter. "All of us were angered when Hussein subsequently became a spokesman for the most radical Arabs," Carter would write in his presidential memoir. Given this atmosphere of hostility I did not know what to expect when we met the Carters at the White House the morning after we arrived in Washington. I was intrigued by the down-to-earth simplicity that the Carters had brought to the White House. I respected Rosalynn Carter's pioneering role as a First Lady who wanted to pursue serious projects of her own. They were obviously intelligent people with whom we shared similar concerns, if not similar priorities, for our respective countries.

Our first encounter came at the welcoming ceremony at the White House, which was formal and precluded any personal interaction. Joining us at the event were Abdullah and Feisal, who were both attending school in the United States at the time. Afterward the President and my husband met in the Oval Office, and I met with Mrs. Carter, Joan Mondale, the Vice President's wife, and various other wives of officials, Jordanian and American, in one of the White House sitting rooms.

Conversation with Mrs. Carter did not come easily. She seemed quite detached and cool — quite a contrast to the hospitable welcome my husband and I had received on state visits to other countries. I did not know what to think. Although I was surprised by her distance, I realized that Mrs. Carter might be shy, perhaps painfully so. I still carried with me remnants of my acute childhood shyness, and I could easily understand a First Lady feeling the same way.

I had asked for some briefing papers on Mrs. Carter before going to the White House, so I was aware of her keen interest in mental health issues. When I started to make overtures to her about her work with the mentally disabled, she warmed up a little, but the ice was never completely broken. I did not know whether she was just a highly reserved individual or was deliberately expressing the tension created by our different perspectives on Middle East policy. I suspected it was the latter. Understandably, Mrs. Carter was being supportive and protective of her husband, just as I would have been of mine. The closest connection I made with her was over Hamzah. Probably the nicest moments we shared were when Rosalynn walked me from the White House over to Blair House after our first meetings to see the baby. She seemed to relax completely as she cooed to him and we talked about our families and children in that cozy environment.

Hamzah had a soothing influence on his father as well. Hussein would often return to Blair House tense and discouraged. The King had always been such a steady friend to the United States, but this was one of those times when the leaders did not want to hear his point of view. They had their eyes on the prize — the Camp David Accords — and did not want anything to stand in the way of their success. After agonizing rounds at the White House, State Department, and Capitol Hill, my husband would come back to our room at Blair House and seek out our young son. He would take him in his arms, make funny faces, and play with him, all the while talking to him in a mixture of Arabic and English. Caring for Hamzah delighted and refreshed him, reminding us of what the struggle was all about, and helping to keep everything in perspective.

I agreed to give interviews to the press in Washington, with the aim of bridging the gulf of misunderstanding deepened by Camp David. Naïvely, I assumed that I would be able to discuss substantive issues with the reporters who would interview me. It's not that I did not understand where my novelty lay — I was the youngest queen in the world and the only American-born queen — but I hoped to be taken as a credible voice with serious matters to discuss. Unfortunately, *People* magazine persisted in writing about my "storybook romance" and identified me as a "former decorator" for Royal Jordanian Airlines. *The Washington Post* dedicated a whole paragraph to an exaggerated description of what I wore on a tour of the National Gallery of Art.

Perhaps I was being too sensitive, but with all this talk about my appearance I felt my sense of purpose slipping away. It was gallant of President Carter to begin his toast at the state dinner at the White House by saying: "A lot of people have accused me of inviting Their Majesties to Washington just so we could have Queen Noor visit the White House," making an obvious reference to President Kennedy's speech in France about "accompanying Jackie" to Paris. I knew he meant to pay me a compliment with his remarks — and who would not want to be compared to Jackie Kennedy? However, I could not help but feel like a useless accessory. It was not until a luncheon in my honor the next day that I regained a sense of composure. Jane Muskie, the wife of the Secretary of State, hosted the lunch, at which I gave a brief but substantive toast about the importance of U.S.-Jordan relations. Afterward, Leila Sharaf noted that it was the first time that I had displayed my grasp of politics in a public forum, and that I should do it more often. Her encouragement boosted my confidence.

While my husband and his delegation continued their talks with American officials, I carried out a separate mission to meet with Jack Valenti, the president of the Motion Picture Association of America. I hoped to explore ways that Hollywood might recognize the injustice of stereotyping Muslims and Arabs, and help us advocate for a more balanced and realistic portrayal. Anyone in the entertainment industry who reflected any sensitivity to Arab and Muslim cultures ran a great risk of becoming *persona non grata* to the studios. I remember watching the 1978 Academy Awards and being horrified by the near riots prompted by the presence of British actress Vanessa Redgrave. Though she was being honored with an Academy Award for *Julia*, a film in which she played a member of the anti-Fascist underground fighting Nazi Germany, she was reviled at the awards ceremony by the militant Jewish Defense League (JDL) for making *The Palestinian*, a documentary about the siege of a Palestinian refugee camp in Lebanon in 1976. The JDL even burned her image in effigy. Though none of the protesters in Los Angeles had likely seen the documentary — no major American network, not even the Public Broadcasting Service, dared air it — the anti-Arab, anti-Redgrave demonstration outside the auditorium had grown so violent that an LAPD SWAT team had to be called in to disperse the crowd.

In my opinion, Vanessa Redgrave was a brave and sensitive woman, not a public enemy. It had been while she was filming *Julia* in Paris, I learned later, that she had met a young Palestinian couple and learned about the tragedy at Tal Al Zaatar, a Palestinian refugee camp in Lebanon. A right-wing Lebanese Christian militia trained by Israel had killed thousands of men, women, and children there in a fifty-three-day siege. Redgrave was so incensed that she had sold her two houses in England to finance the project, hired a film crew and director, and gone to Lebanon to make the documentary. In the process she had become a spokesperson for the Palestinian cause.

I shall never forget her defiance toward the demonstrators in her acceptance speech for the Oscar. She said she would not be intimidated by "a small bunch of Zionist hoodlums whose behavior is an insult to the stature of Jews all over the world." There had been some boos in the audience and some applause, but from then on she would be targeted by the JDL.

Trying to put a human face on the plight of the Palestinians and presenting a counterpoint to the stereotypical depictions of Arabs and Muslims in the movies would become a theme of my married life. It was so upsetting to be watching a very entertaining film, feeling relaxed and even laughing out loud, and suddenly freeze up whenever an Arab character would be introduced. In the black-and-white dynamic of stereotyping, the media inevitably portrayed Arabs as terrorists or oil-rich gluttons, as religious fanatics or primitive beings. Indeed, some stereotyping continues to this day. In the opening scene of the 1992 Disney film, *Aladdin*, a little Bedouin boy in a cartoon desert happily sings: "Oh, I come from a land . . . Where they cut off your ears if they don't like your face. It's barbaric! But, hey, it's home." Such negative and distorted renderings of Arabs were misleading and damaging to any sort of rational dialogue. Moreover, these depictions bore no resemblance to the Arab people as I knew them. Where were the kind, civilized, hospitable people with whom I came into contact every day in Jordan?

The Motion Picture Association had an office in Washington as well as in Los Angeles.

Beyond championing the film industry world-wide, it was also a lobbying agency and a contributor to the campaigns of several of the congressmen on Capitol Hill who challenged my husband's positions. It was also true that many of the top executives at the major studios Valenti represented were Jewish, and though they were liberal, they were deeply loyal to Israel and Israeli politics, right or wrong.

Jack Valenti was very gracious when we met, and he listened attentively while I talked with him about ways to promote a more balanced portrayal of Arab culture. He let me know that my aims were commendable, but that the film industry would find them more provocative than I might suspect. To make any impact I would need to spend a lot of time in California lobbying the studio executives, he explained. What he said made sense, but California was a long way from Jordan, and my first obligation was to my husband and family.

I am tremendously encouraged to have seen some progress in changing the role of Arabs in films. I was delighted when David O. Russell's 1999 movie *Three Kings*, with George Clooney, Mark Wahlberg, and Ice Cube, portrayed Arabs in a more humane way, and I was heartened when Jack Shaheen recently published *Reel Bad Arabs: How Hollywood Vilifies a People*, a book that generated some media attention for the issue. In my own meetings in recent years with studio executives, producers, actors, and, most recently, board members of the American Film Institute, I have encountered a profound sensitivity to the negative impact of stereotypes, not just in the United States but abroad, where Arabs and others see these films as lingering American biases toward the developing world. I was also encouraged to learn that the U.S. Army bought 100,000 video copies of Akkad's film *The Message*, about the Prophet Muhammad, to show troops preparing for service in Afghanistan. Producer-director Moustapha Akkad did a magnificent job of bringing the Prophet's life to the screen while remaining true to the Muslim belief that Muhammad himself must not be depicted in any way. The main on-camera presence is Hamzah, the uncle of Muhammad, played by Anthony Quinn. State Department employees bound for the Middle East are all required to see that film, as well as Akkad's *Lion of the Desert*, about the twenty-year-old war waged by the Bedouin to combat Italian colonization in Africa.

In the crucial area of bilateral relations, the Jordanian delegation left the United States no further along than when we had arrived but with the sense that the Carter administration had developed a deeper understanding of the issues and was open to considering some specific new proposals to break the post–Camp David stalemate. Nonetheless, it was a low period in Jordan-U.S. relations, and particularly painful for me. I was seeing the land of my birth through new eyes — and the image America was projecting was not a positive one. I had grown up believing in America's commitment to freedom, justice, and universal human rights, but Washington was not exhibiting those fundamental principles in its treatment of Jordan, a longtime friend and partner. I understood then, as I understand today, that U.S. support for Israel is long-standing and inviolable. But why did that relationship preclude other valuable perspectives on achieving the goal of peace in the Middle East? Why did it preclude Arab human rights and the implementation of international law and UN Security Council resolutions?

Confronting the power of the Zionist lobby for the first time was sobering. The Arab-American Anti-Discrimination Committee was founded in Washington in 1980, the year of our state visit, in an effort to promote a more balanced U.S. Middle East policy and to correct anti-Arab stereotypes. But it was a rank amateur compared to groups such as the American Israel Public Affairs Committee. AIPAC's supporters were CEOs of large American corporations and representatives of the top levels of media and entertainment businesses, financial institutions, legal and medical professions, and, increasingly, the highest reaches of government. Their activism at the grassroots level was legendary. I remember hearing about a news program in the late 1980s that was planning a story critical of Israel during the *intifada*, the Palestinian uprising. Hundreds of telegrams poured into the studio protesting the anti-Israel "bias" of the program two hours before it was even aired!

I had first learned about this bias, in the years prior to my marriage, from American correspondents covering the region. They frequently complained about writing dispatches that they considered evenhanded only to find that their editors at home had rewritten them with a pro-Israel slant. Stories casting Arabs in a positive light were greeted with muted enthusiasm, they said.

This tilt was not surprising. More than any other country in the twentieth century, America had witnessed the highly successful migration, integration, and assimilation of Jews from all over the world who achieved influence and power at the highest levels. And their unifying issue — whether they were politically left-wing, right-wing, or centrist — was Israel. By contrast, the Arabs in America were not united behind any one issue. Three million strong, they came from different countries, different religions, and different cultures. Most had blended quietly into American culture and did not want to get involved in controversial issues, while others considered themselves visitors in America until the turmoil in their own countries calmed down. Political activism did not come naturally to them, and, sadly, this lack of cohesion hurt the Arab cause in America.

In this light, it is little wonder that our first meeting with the Carters was so awkward. Our relationship would eventually become extremely warm and respectful, especially after President Carter left office. A generous spirit guides them both. Rosalynn Carter may not have known quite how to approach me — an American married to an Arab leader and living in what was then an Arab world hostile to the Camp David Accords. This was a pity because we had much in common. I think President Carter had a difficult time understanding the reasons my husband had to withhold his support of Camp David. The President had put too much faith in Anwar Sadat's assurance that the Arabs would fall in line with him. As a result, the Carter administration had not really reached out to my husband and other moderate Arab leaders who could have made a difference.

I also suspect that President Carter was even hurt on a personal level by what he viewed as my husband's recalcitrance over Camp David. This was unfortunate because there were affinities between the two men — both were idealistic and spiritual in their outlooks — that might have helped them bridge their differences. At the time there was just too much outside interference. However, once he left office, President Carter became one of the most knowledgeable, sensitive, and balanced voices on our region's search for peace. His esteem in the Middle East and throughout the world has grown enormously during this time, as did my husband's admiration for him — and my own. I myself have had the great privilege of working with Rosalynn on the International Commission on Peace and Food, as well as on a global mental health initiative.

We continued our official travels after returning from the United States, leaving almost immediately for state visits to France, to Austria, and again to Germany. The staff welcoming us back to Gymnich Castle near Bonn were terribly excited about Hamzah, who was now setting records as the youngest visitor to official European guesthouses. He was a lot more fun than the usual round of VIP guests, I suspect. They had never had an infant guest before, as would be the case when we went to France and the Soviet Union in 1982.

Our second son, Hashim, was born on June 10, 1981, the day that historically marks the beginning of the Great Arab Revolt. We named him after the head of the clan of Hashim, the powerful Quraysh tribe in Mecca to which both the Prophet Muhammad and my husband belong (the family's ancestral identification as "Hashimites" stems from these roots). As it was my husband's great-grandfather Sharif Hussein who led the Great Arab Revolt, it seemed fitting to give Hashim that proud family name.

His arrival was equally momentous because it was his decision, and his alone, to be born on that day. All our other children would have to be induced, but Hashim took us all by surprise. Hussein had been in Aqaba hosting the final day of a visit by his close friend the Sultan of Oman. As ever, my husband had exerted an enormous amount of nervous energy on the visit, attending to every detail. Sultan Qaboos, also a meticulous and sophisticated host, always received us in exceptional style in Oman. On this occasion, my husband stayed up until just before dawn to see his guests off, so by the time he returned to Amman he was utterly exhausted.

Before we went to bed that night, Hussein took an antihistamine for his chronic sinus condition. I was having an allergic reaction to the last stages of my pregnancy so I had turned on a humidifier to help me sleep. Nuha Fakhouri, our Jordanian nurse, was sleeping in the children's wing of the house. She had come to help me prepare for the baby in the final weeks of my pregnancy, but there was no sense of urgency. I had seen the doctor that morning, and he had told me that I had at least ten days before the baby would be born.

As soon as he turned off the light, my husband fell into a deep sleep. Minutes later I felt for the first and only time in my life a normal sensation of the beginning of childbirth. Hussein had been through the births of a

287

number of children by this time, so I assumed he would know about the onset of labor. He was not much help. "I don't know," he mumbled. "Go ask Nuha."

I staggered from my bed to the other side of the house where Nuha was sleeping. By this time the contractions were coming almost every minute. I was doubled over by the time I reached her. "Nuha, Nuha," I called, "I think my water has broken." She was sound asleep and, thinking I was talking about the humidifier, responded groggily, "Okay, I'll come in and fill it up." "No, Nuha, that's not what I mean," I said. Mercifully Nuha suddenly comprehended and called the doctor. I went back to rouse my exhausted husband and tell him that we needed to drive to the hospital. He moved out of bed so slowly that I told him I would go without him. "No, no," he said, "there is no question of that." He began walking in slow motion, shaving in slow motion, and dressing in slow motion as I struggled to prepare myself. We finally reached the hospital only slightly ahead of the doctor, who had not had enough time to change into his scrubs. By then my husband was wide awake, ready to greet Hashim.

Nuha helped out at the hospital and continued to care for the baby after I brought him home. Bringing in British and European nannies was an established custom in the family, so my hiring a Jordanian raised eyebrows among some family members. But it was thanks to Nuha and successive young Jordanians that our children became naturally fluent in Arabic.

The summer of 1981 was one of those periods when my husband was consumed with fears for the region. He had begun smoking after a six-month hiatus, and it was easy to understand why. For a year we had watched the war between Iran and Iraq, Jordan's neighbor, steadily worsen. It had begun as a border dispute and a preemptive effort by Saddam Hussein to prevent the new Revolutionary Republic of Iran from exporting their revolution into the region. It had escalated into a bloody war that would last eight years, claim more than a million lives, and bring the economies of both countries to a standstill. By the war's end, more money would have been sunk into the conflict than the entire Third World spent on public health in a decade.

Most leaders in the Arab world and the West saw the war as essential to stopping Khomeini from exporting his brand of revolutionary, politicized Islam to other countries, which is why Saddam was supported by so many in the international community. The King and Abu Shaker, then commander of the Jordanian army, went to Baghdad frequently to visit the Iraqi leader, particularly when there was a setback on the military front.

The senseless tragedy of the Iran-Iraq war

was laced with the hypocrisy that so often marks global politics. At the same time that the United States was punishing Jordan by withholding arms, it was also using Jordan to support Iraq, an enemy of Israel, by covertly sending weapons and intelligence through Jordan. My husband and Abu Shaker regularly received details from the U.S. military about the locations of Iranian ammunition dumps, concentrations of forces, and artillery positions facing the Iraqi front. Jordan would then funnel that information to the Iraqis, who, of course, made good use of it. At one point Abu Shaker discovered that the Americans had also been in direct contact with the Iraqis all along, leading him to conclude that America was using Jordan simply as political cover, if needed, to hide its support of Iraq. He told the Americans to stop putting Jordan in the middle and to send their intelligence to Iraq through their own military attachés, which presumably they did.

Things were almost always not what they seemed in Middle East politics, and Jordan, a small country surrounded by volatile neighbors, was always in the middle. In the early 1980s, a political settlement with Israel seemed increasingly remote. The reelection of Menachem Begin's conservative Likud Party in 1981 escalated Israel's expansionist and reckless policies. Even Israel's staunchest ally, the United States, was alarmed when, in June 1981, Israel violated Iraqi airspace and bombed

Iraq's nuclear reactor at Osirak. We were traveling to Aqaba at the time and my husband noted the unusual direction of the Israeli jets, but by the time he deduced what they were up to, it was too late to intercede. Israel also bombed Beirut, and in December moved into Syrian territory and annexed the Golan Heights, once more violating UN Resolution 242. All the while Menachem Begin continued to order more and more illegal Israeli settlements on the occupied West Bank, leading my husband to worry that the ongoing Israeli campaign to depopulate the West Bank of Palestinians would prolong the crisis by fueling extremism and sending a new and destabilizing wave of refugees into Jordan.

We returned to the United States for a second state visit in November — this time to the Reagan White House. It was a time of terrible turmoil in the Middle East. Not only were Iran and Iraq still at war, but Israel was launching raid after raid against Palestinian targets in Lebanon, bombing and strafing villages along the Lebanese coast. And just weeks before our visit, Anwar Sadat had been assassinated in Egypt by fundamentalist officers in his own army. Hussein and I had been having a late lunch outside Amman when we heard the news on the radio. My husband was terribly shocked and saddened by Sadat's death, despite all the difficulties between them.

My heart had gone out immediately to his wife, Jehan. I had not met her because of the Arab world's isolation from Egypt after Camp David, but I, too, was the wife of a man in a very vulnerable position as head of an Arab state opposed by various forces. Sadat's peace with Israel had inflamed the growing fundamentalist movement in Egypt, and religious extremists reviled him as a puppet of the West. Egypt's economy was also in a downturn, leaving many people without jobs and government services, and allowing the fundamentalists to gain ground by opening health clinics, religious schools, and mosques to preach against the government.

Some said the fundamentalists in Egypt were funded by Iran and others cited Libya. Regardless of the source, there was no doubt their influence was leading Egypt toward civil unrest. There was outrage from the extremists when Sadat had invited the deposed Shah of Iran to Egypt and held a state funeral for him when he died in Cairo in 1980, and fury when Sadat had made a state visit to the United States in August 1981. He had finally cracked down on the religious extremists when he returned from the United States. Two months later he was dead.

"May I at least call Mrs. Sadat to offer my condolences?" I asked my husband that day at lunch. Given the political situation, I knew we could not travel to Egypt, and I wanted to express my heartfelt sympathy. "No," he said, "I will send condolences from both of us. If you call her, the Egyptian media will use the contact to indicate that normalization is going to take place, and that could be used against us." Although I never had a chance to console Jehan Sadat, I grieved for her. Like me, she lived with the constant fear that one of the countless threats against her husband would be acted on — and her nightmare came true.

My husband wrote Mrs. Sadat a very thoughtful letter, which she included later in her memoirs. It was the only condolence she received from an Arab leader. Enmities ran so deep in our part of the world that people actually danced in the streets of Baghdad upon hearing of Sadat's violent death, and both Iran and Libya called on the people of Egypt to seize the moment of Sadat's assassination to overthrow the government and establish an Islamic state. Palestinians, too, celebrated. In their eyes, Sadat had been a traitor for having sold out their cause at Camp David. "We shake the hand that pulled the trigger," said one PLO commander in Lebanon.

During our November state visit to the United States, I had accepted an invitation from my alma mater, Princeton, to address the American Whig-Cliosophic Debating Society. It was to be my first speech in America, and I had spent weeks carefully crafting my remarks. We had no professional speechwriters in the

Royal Court, although well-meaning advisers supplied Hussein with texts, written in the very flowery language of Arabic speechmaking, which resonated better in Jordan than it did for Western audiences. Over the years I urged him to speak extemporaneously — a style of public address well suited to him. For myself, I felt I needed to be more studious in my approach, especially at the outset.

At the dinner before the speech I could not eat and had to excuse myself for a few moments to calm my nerves. I was apprehensive about standing up on a podium and addressing the students and distinguished faculty of a school I had graduated from only a few years earlier. I tried to steady myself by concentrating on the reason I was there: to bridge the gulf between the Arab and American peoples.

From the tenor of most of the questions that followed that speech, I need not have worried. Many were quite trivial, personal, or Princeton-oriented. "Is your husband a Cottage Club kind of guy?" one student asked. However, as the evening neared an end, several people lined up to read statements that amounted to screeds demonizing Arabs and distorting the history of the Arab-Israeli conflict.

I was stunned and did not know how to respond. I could not take time to set straight their accounts of fifty years of history, but I also could not let their inaccurate premises go unanswered. I ended up feeling muddled and on the defensive as I struggled to articulate credible responses. I was informed later that a pro-Israeli political organization in New York had supplied the statements.

The only place I ever encountered these planted distortions was Princeton. The second time, several years later, I was more confident. When my questioner read his statement and immediately started walking toward the door without waiting for an answer, everybody realized what was going on. "Are you staying or going?" I asked from the podium. "Do you want an answer or not?" The audience broke into laughter because the speaker was so obviously a plant, but these episodes at Princeton reflected the lengths that some supporters of Israel would go to to undermine any perspectives other than their own on the Middle East.

For all the hard work, I enjoyed our visits to America very much, not least because they gave me rare opportunities to see my family and old friends. My mother and my father and his second wife, Allison, came to the fall 1981 state dinner at the White House, as did my sister, Alexa, who was at Southern Methodist University Law School in Dallas. My brother, Christian, flew in from California; a lifelong musician, he had founded a pioneering music company producing software used by such artists as the Rolling Stones, Sting, U2, and Michael Jackson. He and I had been separated by geography and our various endeavors for so long that I was particularly looking forward to seeing him.

There was a luncheon the next day at Blair House, given for me by Barbara Bush, to which I invited Marion Freeman, my classmate from Concord and Princeton. When we flew on to Los Angeles, I arranged lunch with my friend Sarah Pillsbury, a film producer who had won an Oscar for her first film, a dramatic short called *Board and Care* played by two actors with Down's syndrome. I wanted my friends to get to know my husband and to understand why I had made the choice I had. Sarah appreciated it immediately. She and her husband had dressed for lunch, thinking it would be a formal affair, but Hussein had heard of an out-of-the-way Mexican restaurant with a great reputation. Sarah would often tell the story afterward of riding with us in a full motorcade — security vans and motorcycle police and secret service — to a little hole-in-the-wall where my husband, as always, greeted our guests and shook hands with the restaurant staff. He thoroughly enjoyed himself, as did we all.

Our next stop was Canada, where my husband wanted to touch base with Prime Minister Pierre Trudeau. We were late leaving an official lunch in Houston and further delayed by bad weather en route to Canada, but we were not overly concerned because we had planned an informal working visit. Somewhere along the line, however, there had been a communication failure, and our first trip together to Canada was on the verge of becoming a fiasco. When we landed in Ottawa, we were surprised to be informed by our ambassador and Canadian protocol at the door of the aircraft that we had delayed the arrival ceremony for our state visit. This was the first we had heard that this was a state visit and we were totally unprepared. Luckily the weather was cold, so we could button our overcoats over our casual clothes for the formal welcome with full military honors.

Once we arrived at the official residence the Governor General pointedly reminded us that we were running late and would have little time to change for the state banquet that evening. "And you will wear your tiara and decorations?" our hostess said to me when she showed us to our quarters. I explained that I did not have my tiara with me, to which she exclaimed indignantly: "What? Don't you always travel with your tiara and decorations?" I was irritated by then. "No, I don't," I said. "We rarely travel with our state regalia, except when exchanging visits with fellow monarchs." She looked horrified, and I wondered what we were getting ourselves into. We managed to make a respectable appearance at the Canadian state banquet that night, but the papers the next day were full of our rudeness for arriving so late, leaving the two of us feeling very much on the defensive.

Two days later, as we prepared for our official departure, I suffered a final indignity. I had put on a new pair of boots and was halfway down the staircase to the ground floor when I lost my footing. I slid to the bottom on my knees, landing at the feet of the stern-faced Governor General, who was standing with his wife, my husband, and his aide-de-camp. I looked up slowly and smiled as if to suggest that stair gymnastics were my usual mode of descent. The aide-de-camp gave me his hand and helped me up. There was a ripple of laughter, and then we carried on as if nothing had happened.

Mercifully, that trip to Canada would prove to be the exception, not the rule. We would return to Canada many times over the years and never again encounter the discomfort that marked our first trip. In fact, Canada is one of the countries for which, to this day, I feel the most affection and affinity because of its progressive and humanitarian support for issues that are particularly important to me, such as global peacekeeping, refugee assistance, and the Ottawa Land Mine Ban Treaty.

The goodwill of the Canadians would be exhibited time and again. It would have to be. For reasons we never quite understood, we usually arrived late for our visits. My husband chose to fly the plane himself on one memorable occasion to make sure we would be punctual, but someone in our party had miscalculated the time-zone changes and we arrived an hour late again! I did not know this until I was in the shower, washing my long hair, thinking I had an hour and a half to get ready, only to be told that I actually had less than half an hour! It was our fault, and we were mortified, but the Canadians were very good-natured about our recurring pattern of late arrivals, at least after the first trip together. It was my husband who was very upset. He was a perfectionist about these kinds of working and official visits, and it was beyond us why we just could not get Canada right.

It was a relief to return home to Jordan, and I was looking forward to the upcoming debut of the Jerash Festival of Culture and Arts in October 1981, in the ancient city's spectacular ruins. First built in the second century B.C. by legionnaires of Alexander the Great, then rebuilt by the Romans in the first and second centuries A.D., Jerash featured two beautifully preserved Roman theaters on its excavated site, set like jewels amid broad, colonnaded streets and plazas rimmed with Ionic and Corinthian columns, massive arches, temples, and baths. I longed to bring the city's ancient splendor back to life and to restore it as a center of culture and trade. Earlier in the year, during a cultural event in an unprepossessing university gymnasium, I had suggested that our magnificent ancient amphitheaters in Amman, Jerash, and Petra could provide superior venues for such performances. Why not make use of them? We formed a steering committee consisting of Adnan Badran, the dynamic and visionary chancellor of Yarmouk University, and other Jordanian intellectuals. We decided that our first festival would feature Jordanian artists performing for a broad cross section of our people, many of whom might begin for the first time to appreciate their rich architectural and cultural heritage.

At the end of the three-day event, we were elated by the overwhelming response. Encouraged by this success, we then began preparations for a ten-day regional festival, which would evolve into an annual event, unique in the Middle East, that would bring artists to Jordan from all around the world.

I was careful to remember lessons learned from the Shiraz Festival in Iran, which made a well-intentioned effort to showcase some of the most avant-garde European and American plays and performers but had been heavily criticized because the selections offended many people. I was hopeful that we could strike a balance between paying tribute to popular traditional Arab and Muslim art forms and introducing contemporary regional and international culture.

Word about the festival spread. Thousands of people would come from all over Jordan, the Arab world, and beyond to attend subsequent Jerash Festivals, which we would move to July to better accommodate the tourist season. The ancient outdoor theaters and monuments would provide extraordinary settings not only for Jordanian talent but also for Arab and European orchestras, Chinese acrobat troupes, Shakespeare performed by the British Actor's Theatre Company, *Rigoletto* (the first opera staged in Jordan, in 1998, sung by an Italian operatic troupe), the Caracalla Dance Theatre of Lebanon, and, my husband's favorite, flamenco dancing performed by Spanish gypsies. The festival was credited with launching the extremely successful international career of Majda El Roumi, a beautiful and talented Lebanese singer who became a great favorite of Hussein's and mine.

In late 1981, I received an invitation to speak at the Center for Contemporary Arab Studies at Georgetown University. "If I speak at Georgetown, my remarks should be fairly substantive, given current circumstances," I told my husband, who had not been to the United States for many months and was deeply concerned about the deteriorating situation in the Middle East. He agreed that I should prepare a speech that was more policy-oriented than usual and encouraged me to accept the invitation. We would work on the speech together, he said.

What evolved was a speech I would deliver in the form of an open letter to the United States

301

from King Hussein, along with my own perspective on the Middle East issues of the day. It would be highly controversial in some circles for the wife of a head of state, especially an Arab state, to deliver a political address rather than focusing on more traditional subjects such as children or culture. Hussein would even be accused of using me, but I was no puppet. He and I shared the same frustrations and the same longing for peace and stability in the region, so I would be speaking from his heart as well as mine.

This was my first visit to the United States on my own since becoming Queen. In my typically obsessive way of working, I rewrote the speech in my Washington hotel room until the last minute, knowing that there would be some 500 people in attendance — diplomats, professors, graduate students, and the press. I had finished polishing what must have been the twentieth draft of the speech, and was dressed and ready to leave for the university when the phone rang. "I've just realized what you're about to do and the position I've put you in," my husband said. "I'm so nervous I've just taken a Valium." "Thanks a lot," I laughed. "That's very comforting."

As I stood before the Georgetown audience, I thought about how much effort I had put into my remarks, and that I would have only one opportunity to present them. I might as well relax and enjoy the experience, I told myself.

My anxiety evaporated. In the course of my comments I referred to the popular myth of Israel as a beacon of democracy. Drawing from recent events, I said: "Israel is a democracy in which a stone thrown by a youth at an Israeli military patrol is reason enough [for that youth] to be fired upon, to be summarily evicted with his or her family from their home, to have that home blown up with all their earthly belongings." I reiterated that any solution to Arab-Israeli conflict would have to be based on self-determination for the Palestinians, on respect for international law, and on repatriation or compensation for Palestinian refugees.

I knew that every word, every phrase, would be parsed and potentially criticized. Any misstep on my part could be used to distort or complicate Jordan's position in the Arab world and its relations with the United States.

The Washington Post sent a reporter from the Style section to cover the Georgetown speech, and once again, the resulting story focused as much on what I was wearing as on what I was saying, but at least I was quoted accurately on substance. I just had to learn to live with the inevitable paragraphs about my appearance and "storybook romance" with my husband. As long as my message came across, I was content. From then on, there was a clear shift in what people expected of me in the public sphere.

Personally, I do not think anyone in the West,

journalist or not, knew what to make of me. I was an anomaly and therefore defied easy categorization. I had been born and raised in America, to be sure, but at the same time I was now a Jordanian citizen, I was addressed as "Your Majesty," and my perspective had broadened to include Arab and Muslim sensibilities. At the same time, I looked like an American, spoke like one, and understood American cultural references. I was married to a head of state who had inherited his position and his commitment to represent Jordan for a lifetime, not merely for four years. And so, as his wife, had I.

In the fall of 1982, my husband embarked on yet another framework for peace in the Middle East, this one generated by the Reagan administration. Variations of the "Reagan Plan" would play out over the next six years, alternately raising and dashing our hopes. In retrospect, I think those may have been the most frustrating years of Hussein's life.

The Reagan initiative grew out of the spiraling violence in the Middle East in the early 1980s and the unchecked expansionism of Israel. In June 1982, two months after my speech at Georgetown, Israeli forces led by Israeli Defense Minister Ariel Sharon, invaded Lebanon, leading to the prolonged bombing of Beirut and the massacre of close to 700 Palestinian men, women, and children at the Sabra and

Shatilla refugee camps.

Hussein and I were sickened by the loss of life and wary of what the Israeli invasion of Lebanon foretold. Israel had invaded Lebanon before, in 1978, and my husband had taken careful note then that there had been no Arab military resistance to the invasion, which had caused some 225,000 Lebanese to flee their villages. The wave of Lebanese refugees — combined with the continuation of Israeli settlement policy and the provocative statements coming out of the conservative government in Israel that "Jordan is Palestine" — convinced him that the West Bank was just as vulnerable to Israeli aggression and Palestinian flight as Lebanon, with the need for a political settlement becoming more and more urgent. When the Reagan administration secretly sent Nick Veliotes, a former ambassador to Jordan, to meet with the King and present him with a new Reagan initiative for peace, Hussein cautiously agreed to it with the stipulation that the United States stand by its provisions.

Hussein was already deeply concerned by his contacts with Reagan. Every U.S. President from Lyndon Johnson on had called the Israeli settlements on Palestinian territory either illegal or inconsistent with international law, but Reagan had not. Two weeks after he took office in 1981, Reagan had abruptly altered American foreign policy by declaring that he disagreed with the reference to the settlements from former administrations as "illegal." "They're not illegal," he said. My husband had immediately written Reagan a letter. "I am amazed you have moved into considering the settlements not illegal," it began.

The so-called Reagan Plan that Veliotes brought did at least call for a freeze on Jewish settlements in the occupied West Bank and a return to the borders of the 1967 war in return for peace. Though it did not call for an independent Palestinian state, it did suggest that the Occupied Territories of the West Bank and Gaza would enter into a confederation with Jordan and that their final status would be negotiated with Israel by a joint Jordanian-Palestinian delegation. Assured that the United States would stand by its word this time, my husband signed on.

Menachem Begin, however, did not. He immediately rejected the Reagan Plan, having no intention of honoring Resolution 242. Moreover, he effectively thumbed his nose at the Reagan administration: Within a week of the announcement of the Reagan Plan, Begin's government allocated more than $18 million to building three new settlements on the West Bank and approved the construction of seven others, adding to the 100 or so armed camps and 30,000 Israeli settlers already illegally in Gaza and the West Bank.

Reagan responded to Begin's expansion of the settlements with mild reproof, betraying the assurances he had given to my husband that the United States would carry through on the provisions of the Reagan Plan. He merely said that Begin's action was "most unwelcome," and that the U.S. government would try to impress on Begin and his government "how damaging the settlements are to peace." This was hardly the language my husband had agreed to in the Reagan Plan, which called for "the immediate adoption of a settlements freeze by Israel."

Nonetheless, the King was still somewhat optimistic as he continued shuttling around the Middle East, trying to build an Arab consensus for the Reagan Plan. He was disappointed when the Arab countries held a summit in Fez a week after the announcement of the Reagan Plan and, instead of endorsing a Jordanian-Palestinian delegation to negotiate with Israel, reaffirmed the PLO as the sole and legitimate representative of the Palestinian people. My husband knew, and the Americans knew, that King Hussein would be an acceptable negotiating partner for both the United States and Israel, and the "terrorist" PLO would not.

But good news also came out of the Arab Summit. Not surprisingly, the Arab nations called for the right of Palestinian self-determination and the dismantling of all Israeli settlements, but for the first time the Arab countries recognized the withdrawal of Israeli troops to the pre-1967 boundaries in Palestine as a condition for peace. And without naming Israel, they called on the UN Security Council to guarantee peace "among all the states in the region." This de facto recognition of Israel was a breakthrough by the Arab countries. Now all eyes turned to the PLO.

The PLO had never recognized Resolution 242 as the basis for peace. To the hard-liners, the very name of their organization, Palestine Liberation Organization, meant the liberation of *all* of pre-1948 Palestine, not just what was being called the Occupied Territories. However, the more pragmatic among them confined their rejection of Resolution 242 to the resolution's omission of the specific right of Palestinians to self-determination. King Hussein and one of his closest aides, Adnan Abu Odeh, himself from a Palestinian family, recognized a loophole in the Reagan Plan that could satisfy the latter group, if not the former. Under the joint Palestinian-Jordanian confederation called for by the Reagan Plan to negotiate with Israel, the Palestinians could have de facto self-determination and the issue would be moot. If my husband could sort that out with Yasser Arafat, peace could be achieved.

Hussein came very close to achieving that breakthrough when the Palestinian National Congress agreed in February 1983 that Arafat should meet with my husband to explore the possibilities. Arafat came to Amman in April, a month I remember well because by then I was nine months pregnant with our third child. The King spent hours with Arafat in Basman Palace in the royal compound, explaining the merits of the Reagan Plan and persuading him to sign on to the joint federation. I was taking a walk in the palace compound with Leila when we saw Arafat finally leave. Hussein looked exhausted when he joined us, but he seemed to have performed a miracle. Arafat had agreed to the plan! I wondered why he did not look more triumphant, and then he explained that Arafat had agreed verbally to the plan but, unlike my husband, had not signed it. Hussein had tried every ruse he could think of, short of locking Arafat in his office, but the PLO leader insisted that first he had to consult with his constituencies in Kuwait and the Gulf and other areas. He had given the King his solemn promise that he would return shortly to Amman with the signed document, but my husband's instincts were right. Arafat left and did not return to Jordan for more than a year.

Our third baby was born three weeks later, on April 24, 1983, in the midst of that agonizing period. I had not planned this pregnancy at all. In fact, I had been quite desperate when I found out I was pregnant again — I had thought that perhaps ten years from now I would have a last child. I had three boys at home — Ali, Hamzah, and Hashim — all running amok through the house, full of young male energy, and then suddenly I was expecting again after little more than a year. I was hoping for a daughter this time, and fate smiled on me. We broke with the tradition of family names and named her Iman, which means "faith" in Arabic. It was simple faith that was sustaining us in the face of the trauma and suffering of so many in the region.

King Hussein would need all that faith and more over the next five years after his talks with Arafat collapsed. All the while he would be under tremendous pressure from the United States to make a separate peace with Israel, as Sadat had done, or at least to meet with Begin face-to-face in Washington. He could do neither, of course. Any negotiations with Israel over the occupied Palestinian territories would have to include the Palestinians, but as a matter of policy, neither the Reagan administration nor the Israelis would meet with any member of the PLO until the Palestinians accepted Resolution 242 and recognized Israel's right to exist. So we were stalemated. Meanwhile, Congress continued to hold hostage the arms and aid Jordan needed because my husband, in the words of AIPAC's spokesman, was not doing enough to "enter the peace process."

It is as difficult to comprehend now as it was then the almost unbelievable disappointment and betrayal Hussein had suffered. But he never let go of his fundamental optimism, his faith in people, and his belief that by giving the best of himself he could bring out the best in anyone or any situation. He always assumed he was negotiating with men of goodwill and that somehow, if he worked at it hard enough, he would be able to achieve peace and reconciliation. In this quest he was often beset by adversaries on every side. But he never, ever stopped trying.

chapter eleven

At Home and Abroad

It was a relief to everyone when we finally moved back into Al Nadwa Palace shortly before Iman was born. For three years we had been living like gypsies in different houses, and all of us were looking forward to settling down. I had enlarged the original attic floor of Al Nadwa during the renovation to accommodate our growing family, but still our quarters were cramped. With the arrival of Iman, we had six young children in the house.

The space at Al Nadwa was half offices, half living quarters. All of us who lived or worked there had more than our share of daily exercise, climbing the three flights of stairs and picking up discarded clothes and toys along the way. We tried to maintain — or perhaps more accurately, cling to — the feeling of an ordinary home. I wanted the children to feel natural and comfortable, even though we had to use the house for official gatherings as well. Distinguished guests — from Queen Elizabeth to the

Sultan of Brunei — would sometimes pass by a jumble of tricycles, bicycles, and prams on their way to the front door.

Al Nadwa was considered quite a modest home for a king. It had no swimming pool, no tennis court, and unpretentious rooms. As one memorable headline in *Paris Match* put it, "The King of Kleenex lives better than the King of Jordan," referring to the fortunes of a leading local businessman living in the affluent new suburbs of the capital, Amman. But we treasured the gracious limestone building, which we considered a happy home. And I also valued our presence in the traditional heart of the capital and in close proximity to diverse groups of people. I loved the city's energy — the call to morning prayers and the sound of animated voices on the streets down the hill from Al Nadwa — and I did not mind the constant sound of traffic on the busy roads around the palace complex or even the roar of planes taking off and landing at the nearby airport. The noise lessened somewhat when a new airport was built farther from Amman, but during the first years at Al Nadwa the scream of jet engines overhead was so loud we had to suspend our conversations or pause in the middle of a state banquet until the plane passed over. In this context it is easy to understand why Hamzah's first word was *tayyara*, airplane.

We lived as naturally as possible under the circumstances, but it was a challenge. I cut back on the household staff to gain some privacy, but still we required a manager, waiters, kitchen staff, and housekeepers to take care of the family and our many guests, from visiting heads of state to personal friends. I can scarcely remember a time when my husband and I were absolutely alone without various family members, waiters setting up or removing meals, and office assistants or government officials with urgent business. We nonetheless made every effort to set aside time for the children in the evenings. Hussein and I often sat with them through their dinner, and then ate in our private sitting room while we helped them with homework or watched videos. We sometimes ordered out for food, usually falafel from a downtown Amman restaurant, as a special treat.

But the fact was that the demands on our time were enormous and we were being called upon constantly to solve the problems of our larger Jordanian family, often at the expense of time and focus on our own children. Even in the evenings, during what should have been inviolate family time, there were constant disruptions: phone calls, meetings, and emergencies. Al Nadwa was only a few meters down the hill from the King's offices, so close that he never really felt he had left the office when he came home.

I never begrudged these responsibilities, but I would often ask myself whether we could find a more successful formula for balancing our disparate commitments. Were we asking too much of all our children? It was a continuous struggle to coordinate our schedules to find time for meals and bedtime stories, even to be with the children when they were sick, but we did our best. And we had help. Although I did not want my children to be raised by other people, however loving, in the end it was a combined effort. It had to be. I like to think our children did have the advantage of growing up in an environment in which the concept of dedication to something larger than themselves was simply a part of life.

Our family derived great pleasure from the innumerable animals that were given to us as gifts. Thanks to the generosity of visiting dignitaries, we had quite a menagerie in Jordan. The Algerian President presented us with a beautiful Barbary stallion, which I loved to ride. Unfortunately, the stallion was banished by my brother-in-law, Prince Hassan, after the horse kicked him when the Crown Prince rode up close to us on a polo pony when Hussein and I were out riding together one day. Then there were the gazelles my husband brought back from Yemen, which we kept, along with rabbits and chickens, in a little zoo we created at Al Nadwa. And there were cats everywhere in Amman and Aqaba. My husband loved cats, as his grandfather had, and he felt he was maintaining a family tradition by allowing the garden around our home to serve as a refuge for strays. Perhaps the most unusual animal given to my husband was the lion from Haile Selassie, the Emperor of Ethiopia. This happened well before I knew Hussein, but he loved to tell me the story of the lion's escape on the flight to Amman and how it had terrorized the flight crew. It lived quite happily in Jordan until it attacked and killed its keeper and had to be put down.

We had just as much of a menagerie inside the house, where hamsters and gerbils kept escaping from their cages. We could catch the children's guinea pigs because they were slower-moving, but it was difficult to keep up with the hamsters. At one point we had a mynah bird that managed to break loose from its carrying case during a plane ride home and bite my secretary as she chased it around the airplane cabin. Much to our frustration and puzzlement, the bird never talked. When it died, an autopsy revealed that the bird had chronic tonsillitis.

Some pets caused us no end of trouble. When our fourth child, Raiyah, was around four years old, she was given a goat when we visited a Bedouin tribe in the desert. She fell in love with the animal, so there was nothing I could do but to bring it home with me in the car to Aqaba, where we built it a pen. The other children teased Raiyah by calling the goat Mansaf, the Jordanian national dish, usually prepared with lamb or goat. One day Mansaf escaped from his pen and was eventually spotted on the beach well on his way to Israel. He was intercepted just before reaching the Israeli border guards. We had similar issues with Jazz, a black Labrador we were given by the Grand Duke and Grand Duchess of Luxembourg. The dog persisted in going into the sea at Aqaba and swimming straight toward the border with Israel. We came close to an international incident several times when Israeli gunboats came out to challenge Jazz, and my husband, who delighted in waiting until the very last minute, roared over in his boat so that the dog could be retrieved.

After one state visit to Germany in the 1980s, as we were preparing to leave the guesthouse for the airport, I opened the door of our suite to find the housekeeper holding a basket with a German shepherd puppy in it. My husband joined me, looking rather sheepish. He claimed he had quite innocently mentioned his admiration for the breed to the German Foreign Minister, Hans-Dietrich Genscher, at the official banquet the night before. We had already discussed the subject several times on our way to Germany, and I had told Hussein that I did not want another puppy at Al Nadwa because living at the top of a four-story house with no elevator was enough of a climb for us, let alone for a puppy. We had already been through countless failures by then, including three Labrador retrievers, another German shepherd, a Saint Bernard, and even a panther Haya had been given. When I looked into the puppy's eyes I relented, and for the next six months I carried him up and down the stairs. We named the shepherd Battal, which roughly translates to "hero" or "tough guy" in Arabic, and his short life was rather tragic. He was very intelligent but he had a violent streak. Two years later, despite our struggle to train him, which included professional help, there were still too many moments in the course of play when he would suddenly bare his fangs and turn into a terrifying, growling creature. He would attack cars coming into the driveway, sometimes puncturing their tires, and all of us had his teeth marks on our arms after we finished playing with him.

We kept thinking it was our fault and that we were not handling him properly. Finally, we contacted the German training center where Battal had been bred to see if they could help. They recommended that we send him back for training. There, sadly, the breeders came to the conclusion that he was an outstanding dog but an extremely aggressive alpha male, that one in a hundred who could not be trained. They had to put Battal down because there was no way to control him and there was the distinct possibility that he would hurt someone.

The children missed Battal, and Iman asked for a dog for her birthday. Soon after, I brought home a smaller, ostensibly more manageable dog — a beagle from England. This dog's story (which has a happy ending) includes one frightening chapter: I inadvertently ran over her one day when she ran between the front and rear wheels of my moving car. I felt my left rear tire hit a bump and heard someone screaming her name. I got out of the car, and there she was on the ground, looking quite flattened. I knelt down to comfort her, certain that she was drawing her last breath, when lo and behold, she slowly began to reinflate. It reminded me of the cartoons I would watch as a child, in which Daffy Duck would be run over by a steamroller and then pop back up. It turned out that our dog had suffered only a fractured hip, protected from worse harm because she was so rotund.

My sister, who had dogs and no children at that point, was furious when she learned of the beagle's near demise. Alexa had decided long ago that we were unfit to have animals, and by the time I finished telling her the story, she was convinced the dog would not survive another minute in our house. "You send that dog over to me right away," she said, and so the beagle has lived with her ever since. And ever since then I have been mercilessly teased for my canine-cidal tendencies.

At least the dogs we were being given were getting smaller. The last one was a ten-week-old Chihuahua, a gift from the former President of Mexico that my husband never warmed to. I eventually gave the dog to our German house manager, who had an apartment in Amman, and the tiny animal caused quite a stir on the streets. Dogs are nowhere near as common in Arab countries as they are in the West, and when Liesa took the Chihuahua, Señor Toki Ramirez, for walks, some people actually ran away in fright and drivers braked to a halt and called out, "What is that?"

My husband loved rescuing our runaway animals and all the general chaos of family life. He was a great tease and I was a favorite target. He never tired of telling the story of a time early in our marriage during a weekend in Aqaba when I asked Manal Jazi, our Jordanian nanny, if she could find my camera. Manal was gone for the longest time and having misheard me finally returned with a camel. My husband laughed uproariously, and the children, utterly delighted, spent the rest of the afternoon taking camel rides.

Hussein personally supported the expenses of our home and of the extended royal family through financial resources he was given from within the Arab and Muslim world. He had a basic allowance from the government that had not changed in all his years as King, and neither of us took any personal money from the Jordanian government. In a crunch, he would sell his assets in order to cover Royal Court bills, which were largely devoted to health and education assistance or to support institutions in need.

Support from Arab and Muslim leaders who valued his stabilizing role within the region was critical in enabling the King to carry out his leadership responsibilities in Jordan, as well as his advocacy efforts for the region as a whole. (Jordan was also reciprocating by contributing to the development of these countries through its expertise and manpower in areas such as education, health, medical research, and military training and security.) However, support from the outside could not always be counted on.

My husband handled his own finances in an openhanded, spontaneous way, based on his faith that God would provide. He believed that if he was a faithful Muslim who focused more on the needs of others than on his own, God would enable him to continue his good works. This was not an MBA's approach to finance, but it could not have been. It was an ethical and humane balance that Hussein struck within the context of an environment that did not function like the West, that was constantly fluid and uncertain and sometimes prone to extremes. The King would never turn away from someone in need. Many a morning, he would listen to a local call-in show called *Live Transmission* and be stirred to offer assistance to someone in dire circumstances. At times his generosity seemed arbitrary, but like a traditional tribal leader he often used it to maintain a complex political balance. In any event, the money went out as fast as it came in, and somehow it all worked out.

My husband's security detail would have preferred us to move out of Al Nadwa, as they were very concerned about its vulnerability. Despite the constant pressure to relocate to a more secure location, it would be fifteen years before we managed it. Site after site that we liked, including beautiful land overlooking the Dead Sea that Sharif Nasser had given to us as an engagement present, would prove to have insurmountable security problems, lack of water, or some other problem, or we would feel it was not the right moment financially. My husband felt an obligation to settle all the members of his family before himself, and we did not have the resources to do both simultaneously. At one point, after ten years of working on countless architectural designs for houses that never came to fruition, I half jokingly suggested, "Let's just live in a tent. If our forefathers were able to do it, why can't we? Think of all that fresh air and waking up in the morning with the sunrise." At least we could have chosen where we wanted our tent to be. (The idyll would not have lasted long, however, since Hussein would have insisted on bringing along a noisy generator, as he did whenever we camped out.)

★ ★ ★

Until school intervened, we included the children in our working trips as much as possible. Iman was barely four months old and still nursing when we took her with us on an ambitious trip through Asia — to China, South Korea, Japan, and Malaysia, with a stopover first in Pakistan. The King wanted to solidify Far Eastern support for a Middle East peace initiative, and to encourage political, economic, and cultural cooperation.

The Chinese ambassador to Jordan, who was helping to arrange our trip to his country, asked me what I would most like to see in China. I told him I had been working on plans for a children's hospital for Jordan for some time. The Arab Gulf state of Qatar had provided support for the planning phase and I had secured a pledge of funds for the project from Iraq in 1981. After the Iran-Iraq war began to drag on and on, however, I decided it would be inappropriate to press Iraq for the funds. The project had been temporarily shelved, one more casualty of instability in the region; still, I was making an effort to study pediatric facilities wherever we traveled the world.

The Chinese ambassador also asked if our delegation had any special needs his government should know about. My husband, knowing that I loved Chinese food, had been teasing me about China's legendary hospitality, which included serving monkey brains and other exotic delicacies to their VIP guests. I decided to avoid the risk of offending our hosts by declaring in advance that I did not eat meat, that I was essentially vegetarian. Forever more Hussein would accuse me of gastronomic cowardice.

As it turned out, we were not served anything as exotic as monkey brains in China, at least not so far as I know. However, one tradition our hosts did maintain involved serving extraordinary banquets of at least ten courses. We marveled at the Chinese presentation of intricately carved fruits and vegetables, and at the quantity of a clear alcohol the Chinese consumed in a steady stream of toasts, not unlike the Russians with their vodka. At one banquet the interpreter and I conspired to discreetly request that the little earthenware jug of alcohol at my place be filled with water instead and I soon had a reputation for being able to keep pace with the increasingly jolly Chinese.

The unfamiliar food, however, was a challenge for some members of our entourage. The second night in Beijing, several close members walked us, as usual, to the door of our bedroom to bid us good-night. As we entered, they stepped inside behind us, which was decidedly unusual. After a moment, it dawned on me that they had heard about my habit of bringing extra food on trips, so I pulled out the plastic containers of date brownies and granola bars I had brought from Amman as emergency supplies. That night, and for many to come, we sat up late together reviewing the day's events and sharing our impressions of that vast and majestic country and its outgoing, resourceful people.

I carried Iman in a backpack along the Great Wall of China, to see the ancient terra-cotta horses in Xian, and on a boat trip down the Yangtze River to Kwelein. At the Children's Hospital in Beijing, I was fascinated to learn about the medical use of acupuncture as anesthesia for even major operations. Traditional herbal remedies were available in Jordan, and Hussein and I had benefited from acupuncture therapy, but this use of acupuncture was a revelation, and I thought it might hold great promise for our medical community. Overall our trip to China was a great success, producing an accord on trade and technological cooperation, as well as an interest-free loan and a pledge of support for King Hussein's initiatives toward peace with Israel.

South Korea was far more troubling to me than Communist China. I was quite unsettled by Korea's militaristic atmosphere and the centralized state control, which reminded me of my first visits to Syria and Iraq in the 1970s before I married. The huge security presence could be felt everywhere, particularly in the city centers and near universities. Everyone we spoke to was exceedingly careful not to discuss government policy. During a visit to a Korean charity, I was struck by the polished presentation of their work, more like a public relations campaign extolling the virtues of the regime than a genuine development enterprise.

Hussein, on the other hand, was riveted by his visits to the Korean military installations, especially our trip to the demilitarized zone, where he and I were briefed on South Korean military readiness. Our hosts pointed out vast expanses of minefields they claimed were an essential line of defense against the enemy. (The United States has long used South Korea's security needs as justification for not signing the Ottawa Land Mine Ban Treaty.) At the time little attention seemed to be paid to the human tragedy caused by the rigidly controlled border between the two Koreas, although I heard heartbreaking stories from Korean families separated for a lifetime from their relatives across the border. Like so many Palestinian families in our area, Korean families were desperate to reunite but could not because of the political situation.

We then continued on to Japan, which, like South Korea, imported 70 percent of its oil from the Middle East and, also like South Korea, was very supportive of the Arab position in general. It was my husband's second trip to Japan in nine months; he had earlier led an Arab League delegation to Tokyo to explain the Arab peace plan. We were warmly received.

I was particularly touched by our meeting

with Emperor Hirohito. I was well aware of the controversy surrounding his role in the Japanese attack on Pearl Harbor in 1941, some claiming he had been powerless to prevent it, others claiming he was the master planner of the attack. Whatever the truth, the man I met forty-two years later was a sweet eighty-two-year-old man who was not in the best of health. Nonetheless, knowing of my background in architecture and planning, he insisted on walking me through the huge Imperial Palace in Tokyo, pointing out design details and the beautiful ornamentation and artwork. I was moved by the effort this required, since he had difficulty walking.

Their son, Crown Prince Akihito, and his wife, Princess Michiko, who became Emperor and Empress on Emperor Hirohito's death in 1989, were also utterly charming and hospitable. We visited them at their home, where I was immediately struck by an alcove in the entrance to their private sitting area that housed a piano and several music stands. It turned out that every family member played an instrument and they often played together. I thought how wonderful it would be if we could get all the members of our family to play music together. Hamzah and Hashim did take up the violin with our National Music Conservatory, but before any talent became apparent, lack of family support, even from their father, dampened their enthusiasm.

The Crown Prince and his wife were a kind and loving couple. She was gentle and serene, a published author and poet. The Crown Prince had inherited his father's passion for marine biology. When I returned to Japan with my son Hashim some years later to open an exhibition on Jordan, the Crown Prince, knowing of Hashim's interest in marine life, presented him with two magnificent volumes of his work in the field, books that my son treasures to this day.

When we returned to Jordan, Hussein redoubled his efforts to jump-start the stalled peace process before it was too late. Settlement creep was continuing unchecked on the occupied West Bank, with new enclaves surrounded by barbed wire and "guarded" by troops effectively and constantly enlarging Israel's military perimeter. Lest we doubt Israel's military superiority, Israeli reconnaissance planes swept over our side of the Jordan River every morning, leaving shattering sonic booms in their wake as a form of intimidation. The Israeli air force also regularly conducted mock dogfights in Jordanian airspace over the farms in the Jordan River Valley, which terrified the animals and sharply diminished their output of eggs and milk. The farmers claimed they could set their watches by the regularity of the Israeli maneuvers and it was even possible to hear them miles away in the capital.

During this period of rising tensions in the fall of 1983, we received foreign visitors in quick succession: former President Carter and Mrs. Carter; German Chancellor Helmut Kohl and his wife Hannelore; a state visit from French President Valéry Giscard d'Estaing and his wife Anne-Aymone; and an official visit from Italian President Sandro Pertini. Given all the problems we were facing, it was difficult to appear serene and carefree with our guests. Hussein was better at it than I, having developed the ability to appear fully connected to the world immediately around him when he was, in fact, focused on something else.

The visit from President Pertini proved quite amusing. A delightful, extravagantly flirtatious older man, Pertini was unaware, or unconcerned, that Jordan's conservative, male-dominated court was not accustomed to my being the object of lavish attention. President Pertini did not do anything outrageous; he just flattered me by making me the focal point of his remarks. My husband accepted this banter with amusement, unlike certain members of the Diwan, who thought the center of attention should always be the King.

The Duke of Edinburgh arrived from Great Britain in October 1983 in his capacity as President of the World Wildlife Fund. To Hussein's great pride and mine, the Royal Society for the Conservation of Nature (RSCN) was about to reintroduce the endangered Arabian oryx into the wild. For conservationists, it was a long-awaited moment of extraordinary significance.

A medium-size white antelope with black patches on its face, dark legs, and two long, curving horns, the oryx once thrived in Jordan and the semi-desert environments of other Middle Eastern countries. By 1962, when an international commission was formed to save this animal from extinction, its numbers had dwindled to fewer than twenty. A small herd of the graceful oryx was successfully bred in captivity at the Phoenix, Arizona, zoo in the United States, and in 1978 Jordan became the first country to be entrusted with eight of these rare animals, which were kept at a reserve in eastern Jordan.

Hussein and I had closely followed their progress and were thrilled when the herd, augmented by a gift from Qatar, grew to thirty-one, a number considered sufficient for release. The fencing around the protected area into which the oryx were to be released had been donated by Sultan Qaboos of Oman, himself an avid environmentalist. This cooperative effort culminated in the release of the oryx on October 18, 1983. My husband and Prince Philip did the honors, opening the pens as the elegant creatures emerged into their new habitat — a moment that was recorded in the *Guinness Book of World Records*. Nearly twenty years later the herd has grown to more than 140, and the program has been extended to include other endangered species such as the ostrich, the onager, and the Nubian ibex. The rescue of the Arabian oryx from near extinction was one of the great environmental success stories of the time, and it provided a blueprint for cooperation among the Arab states and with such international environmental organizations as the World Wildlife Fund. Prince Philip would later invite me to succeed him as president of WWF — the largest privately supported international conservation organization in the world, dedicated to protecting the world's wildlife and wildlands. I considered this offer an enormous honor, but the timing was wrong for me to assume that degree of responsibility. Instead I have served with pride as a member of the board.

These successes were not without opposition. Environmentalists everywhere have to fight against short-term interests, and in Jordan the clash was particularly acute because both arable land and water were in short supply. One classic example involved a confrontation with a government minister shortly after the government created a reserve in Wadi Mujib, the lowest-elevation nature reserve on the planet — a spectacular stretch of land along the Dead Sea that rises dramatically from far below sea level to the peaks of the eastern highlands. By law, nobody could do anything within the reserve without the consent of the RSCN, which had charge of its management, but this particular minister was from the area and was successfully pressured to open the Wadi Mujib Reserve for grazing.

The first I heard about it was from the president of the RSCN, our friend Anis Muasher. The warden in Wadi Mujib had called Anis to report that two bulldozers had entered the reserve to open roads and plant crops. They were under orders from the minister, the men told him. Anis instructed the warden to step in front of the bulldozers to block them and told the minister in question that the decision to make Wadi Mujib a protected reserve had been a high-level cabinet decision and that he would have to appeal to the cabinet to reverse that decision. In response the minister arrested the warden and put him in jail.

Hussein and I were having a late dinner in Aqaba with King Juan Carlos and Queen Sofie and a few other friends, including Anis, when we received word of the warden's arrest. Normally I would not have disturbed the King at a time like this, but I knew he would appreciate the urgency of the situation. In fact, he was furious. He put down his napkin and briefly excused himself from the table. Fifteen minutes later, Anis was called to the phone by no less a ranking official than the national Director of Public Security. "What is going on?" Anis was asked. "His Majesty is very angry. He has just woken me and the Chief of Staff of the army and told us to call you." So Anis explained the situation, and within hours the bulldozers were out of the Wadi Mujib Reserve and our warden had been released. Protecting the environment required constant vigilance, and this time we had been lucky.

My husband loved the natural world. In addition to his beloved Jordan, he had a special attachment to the English countryside, dating back, I imagine, to his first sight of England as a young student, fresh from the arid climes of Jordan and Egypt. I shall never forget a brief visit we made to Martha's Vineyard, off the coast of Massachusetts. We had just attended Prince Feisal's graduation from Brown University, from which we made the short trip to the site of my father's vacation dream house. As my father proudly showed us his little piece of paradise, Hussein looked at the scrub brush and beach plum all around, muttering to me about how the scraggly vegetation contrasted pathetically to the grandeur and nobility of the English landscape.

Jordan's forests were a key focus for the King's conservation efforts. During his reign, Hussein more than doubled the size of Jordan's forests with a national reforestation program, which we participated in each year. The hope, of course, was that the example set by the royal family would be a strong motivator in Jordan. Sometimes this was far less enjoyable than planting trees. On a number of occasions, I took Haya, Ali, and Hamzah with me to pick up litter in Amman's public parks, and I was always so proud of them for contributing without complaint. The RSCN also organized field trips for schoolchildren to Jordan Valley Farms, during which we cleared fields of litter and plastic refuse, which are so dangerous to livestock.

Pollution in Aqaba was also a concern. Phosphate was one of our major exports, and the loading of container ships in Aqaba's port was unleashing huge amounts of dust into the air. Not only was it a waste of phosphate, but also the dust was causing a high incidence of respiratory problems in Aqaba. Company officials repeatedly promised us corrective action, but it took many years before the problem was brought under control.

We did succeed much more quickly in passing a strict maritime law prohibiting the dumping of waste in the port area. To enforce it the King donated a boat to the RSCN to monitor the harbor. The resulting significant fines on miscreant tankers gave Jordan an uncompromising reputation in the shipping industry, which took far greater care thereafter to avoid discharging wastes into our waters.

Hussein loved the sea. While in Aqaba, he personally instructed all of his children in water-skiing as they reached the appropriate age or degree of fearlessness. I remember a tiny Ali insisting on trying, and he set the mark for the youngest to do so in spite of being totally submerged under salty spray as he made his round. My husband also managed to get me onto the skis despite my aversion to the sport, acquired from an excruciating childhood failure on a freshwater lake in Michigan. By contrast, the high salinity of the Red Sea provides maximum buoyancy and is therefore ideal for water-skiing and swimming — even for the reluctant.

The greatest pleasure for all of us who loved him was Hussein's obvious delight in day-long fishing trips along our coastline, past our border with Saudi Arabia, across the Gulf from the Israeli city of Eilat and the Egyptian coastline, and farther down the Gulf of Aqaba. He would captain the boat, sometimes going up on the foredeck to smoke his pipe and meditate for hours, stopping if the excited shouts of children signaled a fish strike, usually tuna. We would return at sunset. Those close to Hussein were used to these bouts of deep contemplation and knew not to disturb him. Ibrahim Izzedin once described the look on the King's face during those periods as the same expression that Hussein assumed when at prayer.

These days, the calm Hussein sought did not come so easily. I tried to help him as best I could, mostly by being available when he wanted to talk, but for the most part he kept his own counsel. In this stalemate of no peace, no war, he began to have trouble sleeping. "Their suffering is becoming intolerable," he told me, referring to the Palestinians. So, I thought, was his. He seemed lost in thought half the time and had started smoking heavily again. He also had an episode of arrhythmia, a condition he had lived with since the 1970s, which required him to take anticoagulants to thin his blood. While his arrhythmia was not life-threatening, the medication was.

It nearly killed him in January 1984. I was in Aqaba with official guests waiting for Hussein to join us from Amman when I received an emergency phone call informing me that my husband was critically ill. I immediately flew back to Amman to find that Hussein had very nearly bled to death. He had been walking from the Diwan to Al Nadwa with his brother, Crown Prince Hassan, when he had suddenly developed a nosebleed. Because of the anti-coagulants, the nosebleed had quickly turned into a full-blown hemorrhage. His doctor arrived quickly, but Hussein's face was already the color of chalk. When he lost consciousness the palace physician could find no pulse. My husband was, for all intent and purposes, dead.

He was stable when I arrived, having been revived after receiving several transfusions. "I felt no pain, no fear, no worries," he said to me later. "I was a free spirit, floating above my own body. It was rather a pleasant feeling, really." He described what is frequently referred to as a near-death experience: He saw a "bright light," felt "relaxed," and realized he was "going." "I must get back," he kept telling himself. "I must get back." And with the immediate medical care he received, he did. The doctors cut back on the anticoagulants, and Hussein never had another episode like that again.

The stress and tension the King had always lived with had taken a definite toll on his body. Shortly after that critical episode in Amman, we went to a clinic in Cleveland, Ohio, where he underwent an intensive physical examination. The doctors there were blunt. After testing all his internal organs, including his heart, they told him: "You have to assume you are ten years older than you are." From then on, my husband lived with a keener sense of his own mortality.

We went to Washington, D.C., following the checkup at the Cleveland Clinic, for a historic moment — King Hussein's first public meeting with Egyptian President Hosni Mubarak since the Camp David Accords, and the first step in the Arab world's rapprochement with Egypt. The arrangements were being made by our ambassador to the United Nations and the Egyptian ambassador, who was his good friend. Both of them wanted the meeting to take place at a public banquet, but Hussein and I preferred to begin with a quiet dinner alone with President and Mrs. Mubarak, given all the years of enforced silence.

Egypt's relations with the Arab world were still extremely tense and fractured, making the

King's decision to break the Arab boycott of Egypt bold and courageous, even dangerous. However, he understood that Jordan's best interests, as well as those of each country in the region, depended upon the degree of unity and cooperation that might be nurtured among them. News of the meeting sent a strong signal to the Arab world that Jordan, at least, thought it was time to end Egypt's isolation. King Hussein would formalize Jordan's reconciliation with Egypt in the fall of 1984, and for the next three years he would lobby throughout the Arab world to repair relations with Egypt.

The Mubaraks became frequent visitors to Jordan after that. In October 1984 we hosted a state banquet for them in Amman. In the course of the dinner, the President spoke to me at length, sharing his concerns about the high profile Mrs. Sadat had assumed as First Lady, and his conviction that it had been inappropriate and counterproductive. He was emphatic that his wife, Suzanne, would assume a much lower profile; he was so emphatic that I guessed he may have been commenting on my own increasingly outspoken role in the areas of Arab-Western relations and national issues. His was a typical traditional perspective. Nonetheless, over the years Suzanne wisely and adeptly assumed a prominent position in her work to promote literacy and a library culture in Egypt, as well as other issues.

Throughout the 1980s I undertook several intensive speaking tours in America, grueling two-week marathons of speeches, interviews, incessant drafting and redrafting of remarks late into each night, struggling with the draining combination of my perfectionism and the often-bewildering complexities of our region's politics to try to achieve a constructive and meaningful assessment of U.S.-Arab relations and policy. Many in the region and in the United States were insisting that I could add a unique voice and perspective from the region for American audiences, in particular because they could identify with me. Only for those reasons was I willing to leave Hussein and the children for such long periods of time. Often I shared our parental responsibilities by taking our youngest, Iman, with me.

Reading over those early speeches now, I smile. I was only too conscious of being the youngest person at these gatherings addressing issues of such political importance. As a result, the speeches were quite dry — the result of my work with academics and experts in Jordan to ensure their accuracy above all else. Only after years of experience and a growing sense that I had established some credibility would I begin to personalize my presentations.

I was not naïve enough to think my speeches could change policy or have a decisive effect on public opinion, but I was tremendously encouraged and motivated by the audiences' response. The American media offered few perspectives on the Middle East other than that of Israel. American audiences and some decision-makers had limited ways of learning about the region, and that was what I was attempting to offer.

My speechwriting ordeals were considerably eased in the 1980s when my stepson, Prince Abdullah, returned from a visit to Taiwan with a very generous gift of a laptop computer. I was delighted by his thoughtfulness, but fairly certain that I would never find the time to learn to use it, remembering my struggles in high school to master the impenetrable Basic and Fortran languages of the MIT computer we were connected to at Concord Academy. However, thanks to my extremely patient secretary, I quickly became completely dependent on the machine for all my speech work and data storage. That laptop became an indispensable mobile office to which I became completely wedded until it literally fell apart years later and had to be replaced.

Just as I was readying myself to address the Commonwealth Club in San Francisco, on March 15, someone handed me an interview my husband had given that morning to *The New York Times*. "The U.S. is not free to move except within the limits of AIPAC, and what the Zionists and the State of Israel determine for it," King Hussein had said as part of an interview enumerating issues of concern. Leila Sharaf, who was traveling with me, groaned when she read the interview. We wondered if we should tone down my speech, but decided to go ahead as planned and encountered no problems with the question-and-answer session after my remarks. Perhaps in California they had not read that morning's *Times*.

They certainly had in Washington, where I attended an Arab-American event to support Lebanon a few days later. I was startled when President Reagan's National Security Adviser, Robert McFarlane, suddenly materialized and asked to speak with me. He sat down, leaned very close, and asked: "Are you trying to lose the President the election?" I was dumbfounded. "No," I replied, "we would never seek to influence your elections, but we do want you to know that Palestinian and Lebanese civilians are dying every day and we cannot ignore that for the duration of your political campaigns." McFarlane, no doubt reflecting the administration's perspective, was preoccupied with one interest alone — the reelection of the President. Our exchange underscored a danger inherent in the American political system. For all its considerable merits and inspirational principles, the American system is based upon a continuous uninterrupted process of election campaigns, stretching out year after year. Lost in the perpetual scramble is any long-term vision capable of addressing the complex tangle of causes at the root of human suffering, especially in the Middle East.

It was on the long flight back to Jordan in 1984 that I decided to make fundamental changes in the protocol of my travel. The Royal Court always booked me into the presidential or royal suites in all the best hotels and provided enormous limousines, in keeping with the traditional view equating status with luxury. I was candid about my view that such extravagant arrangements were unnecessary and inappropriate. One suite booked for me in New York had a living room the size of a ballroom! "I am concerned that we are sending the wrong signal when we are spending so much money," I told the Chief of Protocol. I cut back on the staff that traveled with me and also insisted on flying commercially overseas. On that first speaking tour to America, I had been flown to the United States and back in one of our commercial aircraft that had been refitted with a sleeping area and low-density seating. It was supremely comfortable, but once I calculated the fuel costs and other expenses, I said, "Never again."

I arrived back from the speaking tour just in time for a five-day state visit by Queen Elizabeth and Prince Philip. My husband, in anticipation of the Queen's visit, abandoned his resolve to give up smoking. This was to be Queen Elizabeth's first trip to Jordan during the thirty-two years that she and Hussein had been on their respective thrones, and it was put in jeopardy at the last minute by an explosion in the parking lot of Amman's Inter-Continental Hotel. The Queen gamely ignored calls from the British press to cancel the trip and arrived in Amman with Prince Philip on March 27. Since Queen Elizabeth could travel only with her own crew in her own aircraft, Hussein drove us all to Petra from Aqaba, rather than, as was his custom, helicoptering the royal couple, which would have provided them with breathtaking bird's-eye views of Wadi Rum and Petra.

For all the official trips Western leaders and European royals made to Jordan, my husband was in much closer and more regular contact with Middle Eastern and Muslim leaders. Many became good friends, including Sultan Hassan Al Bolkiah of Brunei, who made a state visit to Jordan at the end of 1984. The Sultan, a very soft-spoken, kind man, had a natural affinity with Hussein. They were both devout Muslims who shared lofty aspirations for their respective countries. They also shared a love of aviation. Brunei is tucked away on the north-western coast of Borneo, and the Sultan frequently traveled long distances to connect his country to the rest of the world. On occasion Hussein advised him on aviation matters.

At the time of the Sultan's state visit, Brunei had just declared its independence from

Britain, and my husband was being as helpful as he could be during the period of transition. Brunei, of course, had a tremendous advantage in achieving its goals: Thanks to rich oil and gas reserves, its population enjoys one of the highest per capita incomes in the world. The Sultan was very supportive of my husband and would even buy his London home in the early 1990s, enabling Hussein to finance the restoration and regilding of the Al Aqsa, or Dome of the Rock, mosque in Jerusalem.

We would make a visit to Brunei ourselves in 1986. The Sultan had two wives, which is acceptable in Islam so long as both wives are treated absolutely equally. He had built two palaces for his wives and their children; one of which, Istana, is the seat of government and sits on 300 acres of beautifully landscaped grounds just above the capital, Bandar Seri Begawan. It has rooms the size of a football field for state functions, and its banquet hall can accommodate 5,000 guests under long double rows of gold and crystal chandeliers.

The Sultan of Brunei would also visit us in England, and on one memorable occasion he vanished. I will never forget the consternation of his security guards as they furiously searched for the Sultan, joined by our own security, who were scouring the grounds for my husband. It turned out that my husband's pilot in England, Richard Verrall, had arrived at the house in a helicopter that was a recent gift to my husband.

As Richard was showing it to Hussein, the Sultan climbed into the captain's seat next to Richard and my husband climbed into the seat behind, and off they flew without telling anyone. The three pilots set down in a nearby airfield, where they practiced hovering and landing on sloping ground and small clearings. They returned an hour later like guilty boys to face their furious security details. My husband apologized profusely, but it was clear to everyone that he and the Sultan had had a very good time.

Since the early 1970s, Hussein had been particularly close to Sultan Qaboos of Oman, who was as generous as he was enlightened. We had first visited his country together shortly after we married and had observed firsthand the extraordinary progress the young Sultan had made in the first few years of his reign. His father, Sultan Said, had kept Oman virtually shut off from the rest of the world. Although plentiful reserves of oil had been discovered in Oman during Sultan Said's reign, the eccentric leader had refused to spend any income on developing the infrastructure of the country or on its people.

When his son, Qaboos, returned to Oman after studying at Sandhurst, his father kept him under house arrest for the next six years. It was not until 1970 that Qaboos took power by overthrowing his father in a bloodless coup and sending him into exile. Qaboos immediately set about building roads, expanding irrigation, and providing housing and electricity to his people. He also opened up Oman to new ideas and culture by creating free primary and secondary schools and establishing Sultan Qaboos University, a particularly impressive institution of higher learning.

What endeared me to the Sultan beyond his investment in his own people was his appreciation and support for the environment, culture, and the arts. When I think of Oman now, I think of music. On our first visit, Sultan Qaboos had just installed a new pipe organ in his palace and was taking lessons from an organ master. The Sultan loved music, and in the evenings we were serenaded, sometimes until dawn, by live performances of the Royal Oman Symphony Orchestra.

The Sultan's mother, Um Qaboos, whom I had met in London on my honeymoon, was an extraordinary example of the very influential role many women play in the Arab world, the Gulf in particular. The role is not public, so many people outside the region do not realize how important it really is. She was invaluable to her son as a link to many groups in Oman society and to ruling families in the Gulf. I liked her very much, and carefully considered what gifts I could bring her and her son from Jordan because they were always so generous to us. And, we were greatly indebted to Sultan Qaboos himself for his support to my husband

and to Jordan. His generosity sometimes weighed on my husband, who felt he could not adequately reciprocate.

While the King and I occasionally traveled to some Gulf countries together, for the most part official visits were exchanged only between leaders. Women visited for personal occasions, such as weddings. These were often lavish, three-day affairs during which the sexes were segregated. The festivities would start late, and long evenings would extend into morning. In vast halls, hundreds of women of all ages would turn out in magnificent couture creations. Even infants were adorned with dazzling jewels.

Occasionally things got out of hand. There was a terrifying moment at one Gulf wedding during an evening performance for the women guests, when several members of the groom's party appeared onstage, waving semi-automatic weapons in the traditional form of celebration. I was seated directly in front of the stage with the wives of other Arab leaders and dignitaries and could think only of the headlines in the newspapers if the revelers accidentally shot us all. Mercifully, they chose to lurch back off the stage and out of the tent.

One of the most colorful weddings I ever attended was the celebration for one of King Hassan II's daughters in Morocco. In honor of his daughter's marriage, King Hassan had offered free weddings to 400 local young women. The King himself orchestrated the entire event.

He was the only man present and, dressed in a dapper white suit, attended to even the smallest details, signaling for the lights to be dimmed, the music to begin, and the food to be served. And what a spectacle it was. The city of Marrakesh was completely closed for the wedding festivities; its streets were lined with exquisite Arabian stallions with riders in traditional Berber garb, and thronged with a sea of well-wishers and entertainers.

A completely different style of wedding took place in Jordan in 1985 when Damian Elwes, the son of our English friend, Tessa Kennedy, was married in the church of Moses on Mount Nebo. The beautiful fourth-century church, from which the Pope would begin his pilgrimage to the Holy Land in 2000, is perched high above the Dead Sea with a breathtaking panoramic view. A deep sense of spirituality pervades the partially restored church and its exquisite sixth-century mosaics. Antique rugs had been laid on the floor of the church along with a few chairs, but that was all. The structure itself was more than enough. As the ceremony ended, white doves were released to soar free over the River Jordan. My husband and I saw the flashes of white as we flew in by helicopter to pick up the bridal party and take them on to Aqaba, where the couple would spend their wedding night cruising up the Red Sea on a boat.

It was a perfect day. Walking back to the helicopter on Mount Nebo, I watched one of the white doves settle on a rotor blade. I saw it as a good omen, a blessing on my husband, the determined peacemaker.

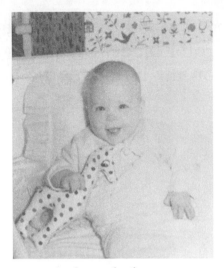

As a baby.

I reluctantly joined the cheerleading squad at Princeton for a few months during my freshman fall at the urging of a coed friend, once it was agreed that we could wear pants and simply lead the cheering like the men. In another break with tradition, many of us would wear black armbands to protest the war in Vietnam.

Shortly after my father became the FAA administrator under President Kennedy, we attend the opening of the Los Angeles International Airport.

In 1975, in the rain forest of northern Queensland, Australia, on a research expedition to find and documument rare birds.

On my first visit to Jordan photographing the magnificent ruins of Petra.

Our engagement.

My first exposure to the glare of publicity at our press conference in May 1978 to announce our engagement.

The marriage ceremony, Zahran Palace, June 1978.

At home in Aqaba, our happiest retreat, with Abir, Haya, and Ali, 1978.

At the royal stables, 1978.

My favorite photo of Hussein with our firstborn, Hamzah, 1980.

With our newborn Hashim in 1981.

Although this is what many people imagined a King and Queen were supposed to look like, we both preferred a more relaxed style.

A rare image of the King and me holding hands. Jerash, 1984.

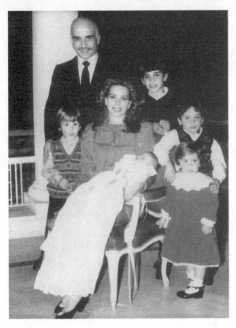

After Raiyah's naming ceremony, with Ali, Hamzah, Hashim, Iman, and Raiyah, 1986.

Iman first visited the Great Wall of China in 1983.

Hussein and I take Raiyah for a ride in the English countryside.

My mother in law's, Queen Zein Al Sharaf's birthday always brought family together. From left: (front row) Prince Rashid, Prince Hussein Mirza, Saad Kurdi, Zein Al Sharaf Kurdi, Queen Zein Al Sharaf, Princess Raiyah, Princess Iman, Prince Hashim, Prince Hamzah; (second row) Princess Muna, Prince Mohammed, Princess Taghreed, Walid Kurdi, Princess Basma, King Hussein, Queen Noor, Prince Hassan, Princess Sarvath, Sharifa Fatima; (third row) Princess Alia Al Feisal, Abir Muhaisen, Princess Haya, Princess Aisha, Princess Zein, Princess Alia, Farah Daghastani, Princess Rahma, Princess Sumaya, Princess Badiya; (back row) Majdi Al Saleh, Ghazi Daghastani, Prince Ghazi, Prince Abdullah, Prince Feisal, Prince Ali, and Muhammad Al Saleh, 1989.

All our children. From left: (front row) Abir, Princess Iman, Princess Raiyah, Princess Haya, Prince Ali; (middle row) Princess Zein, Queen Noor, King Hussein, Princess Aisha, Prince Abdullah; (back row) Prince Hamzah, Prince Feisal, Princess Alia, and Prince Hashim, 1992.

Hussein performing the *Umrah* pilgrimage to Mecca in 1990, shown with Prince Feisal, Prince Hamzah, and Prince Talal.

In Mecca preparing for my own *Umrah* in 1999 with my trusted friend Basma Lozi.

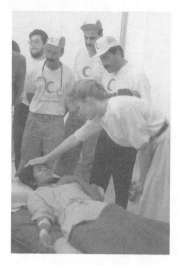

Visiting the Jordan Red Crescent camp for Gulf crisis evacuees near our border with Iraq.

Inspecting land mines with Land Mine Survivors Network and United Nations personnel in Bosnia.

In Amman hosting the Arab Children's Congress organized annually by the Noor Al Hussein Foundation's Performing Arts Center, a unique cultural institution that pioneered the use of arts to promote awareness amongst young people and women on issues related to democracy, human rights, social responsibility, conflict resolution, and good health.

A liberating escape in Wadi Rum.

One of our talented weavers demonstrates her craft at the Jerash Festival.

With Chairman Arafat, 1985.

With President and Mrs. Clinton, and Yitzhak and Leah Rabin, after the signing of the 1994 Washington Declaration.

After the signing ceremony of Oslo II, from left, Queen Noor, King Hussein, Leah Rabin, Prime Minister Rabin, First Lady Hillary Clinton, President Clinton, President Arafat, Suha Arafat, President Mubarak, and Susan Mubarak.

Hussein and me, Sultan Qaboos, and Sharif Zeid bin Shaker in Oman, 1986.

With President Castro during the United Nations 50th Anniversary Celebration, New York, 1995.

On our first visit to Germany with President Walter Scheel and Mrs. Scheel, 1978.

On our first state visit to the United States together. With President Jimmy Carter and First Lady Rosalynn Carter at the White House, 1980.

Hamzah (right) and Hashim followed in their father's footsteps and attended the Royal Military Academy, Sandhurst.

With Princess Raiyah.

With Prince Abdullah, Princess Rania, and their son, Prince Hussein.

King Hussein and me with our children. From left: (font row) Princess Iman, Princess Raiyah, Princess Haya; (middle row) me, King Hussein, Abir; (back row) Prince Hamzah, Prince Ali, and Prince Hashim, 1997.

Our family celebration of King Hussein's 63rd birthday at the Mayo Clinic, November 1998.

January 19, 1999: My husband, in brief remission from cancer, praying upon his return to Jordan.

Iman and me praying at my husband's resting place.

chapter twelve

"Women Hold Up Half the Sky"

In February 1985, after several months of intense negotiations between Jordanian and PLO officials, Yasser Arafat and his colleagues secretly agreed to accept Resolution 242 and the withdrawal of Israel to its 1967 boundaries as the basis for peace negotiations, and with that acceptance came implicit recognition of Israel's right to exist. In return, Arafat wanted enforcement of UN Resolution 181, which called for the partition of British-ruled Palestine into a Jewish state and an Arab state. Among other demands, he also called for an international conference of all parties involved under the auspices of the UN Security Council.

The following month the King and I returned to America on a state visit and Hussein told President Reagan about the secret agreement with Arafat. Reagan was heartened to hear about the breakthrough, and the two leaders even laid out a timetable leading up to the international conference, which was to be held in November. What seemed so promising, however, quickly began to unravel.

Before our trip to Washington, D.C., Arafat had reiterated his promise to accept Resolution 242 to our Prime Minister, Zeid Rifai, but almost immediately upon our return to Jordan the PLO chairman began putting more and more conditions on making the acceptance official and public. My husband's frustration with Arafat was soon eclipsed by news from Washington. Because neither the United States nor Israel would talk with the PLO, my husband and Arafat had sent Washington a secret list of more moderate Palestinians who could serve as potential delegates to the conference. The Reagan administration immediately leaked the list to Israel, where the "secret list" became very public the next day, and the names were announced — and rejected — by Shimon Peres, the Israeli Prime Minister, in the Knesset. Things went downhill from there.

The United States began to balk at proceeding with the international conference. Hard-liners in the PLO began to balk at Arafat's initiative. My husband redoubled his efforts and, with Arafat, sent a joint Palestinian-Jordanian delegation to each of the five permanent members of the UN Security Council, but neither the United States nor the Soviet Union would receive them.

In the midst of all this, I discovered that I was expecting our fourth child. My husband was delighted. He often spoke yearningly of our having another child, and the pregnancy acted as a tonic for him in this period of unrelieved stress. I had mixed feelings. I felt I could barely cope with our six at home already. Also, among our many goals in Jordan was to reduce the high birth rate and I was expecting again. What example did that set?

I focused on trying to consolidate my diverse and expanding development work. I was being pulled in so many directions by projects and programs that I decided to put all my initiatives under one umbrella. In September 1985, the Noor Al Hussein Foundation (NHF) was established by royal decree. The meaning of the name, Light of Hussein, reflected our mission to help realize the King's vision for our people to provide greater opportunity and hope. I had become acutely aware that our most pressing problems of poverty, unemployment, health, education, the environment, and the rights of women and children were all fundamentally interrelated. Because I did not have a vested interest in any one area, and therefore no turf to defend, I hoped the Foundation could provide strategies for integrating efforts for tackling these various issues, which tended to be addressed in isolation by individual ministries and charities.

The Foundation's most significant early contribution to Jordan and the region was through several innovative model projects to fight poverty. Rather than following the traditional practice of charity-oriented social welfare, we developed models that promoted individual and community self-reliance and participatory decision-making, with special emphasis on the empowerment of women. I discussed the mission of the organization with a number of trusted friends and specialists in the field of development, including Leila Sharaf, Adnan Badran, president of Yarmouk University, and In'am Mufti, who had been Jordan's first woman cabinet minister and would become the Foundation's first director. We outlined a plan we hoped would complement and support existing public- and private-sector initiatives without duplicating their efforts, concentrating on people in rural areas and other communities that did not receive enough attention.

One of the first programs we brought under the umbrella of the Foundation was the National Handicrafts Development Project, which we had initiated earlier that year to revive and preserve a unique aspect of Jordan's heritage. When the United States' Save the Children Fund approached me about working in Jordan, we suggested that, because of their successful experience developing handicrafts industries in other countries, they work with us in a rural Bedouin community and in a more urbanized refugee enclave in Jerash. In partnership with that organization we launched two community-development handicrafts-production projects

— Bani Hamida and Jordan River Design.

Successive droughts in the south had forced some 400 Bedouin families to resettle around Bani Hamida, a mountain community an hour or so from Amman. The village was on a spectacular site, looking out across a deep *wadi*, at King Herod's hilltop fortress, where Salome had danced and John the Baptist was beheaded. The tribe itself was very poor. There were very few men at Bani Hamida. Many had been forced to seek unskilled work outside the village, leaving their families behind to tend the family goats and eke out a marginal existence at best. The government had put in roads and built a health center and schools, but the people had no way to support themselves. Many women were in poor health and looked much older than their years.

A representative of Save the Children visited us from the West Bank to assess what we might be able to accomplish in Bani Hamida. "You'd be crazy not to do a weaving project," he said as he stood under a tree and looked out at all the sheep and goats on the slopes of the Rift Valley. "You've got all this raw material walking around on the hoof." He focused the idea even further when he visited the houses scattered around the mountain and saw stacks of rugs the nomadic Bedouin used as room dividers and tent sides neatly folded in the niche of every wall. "Rugs," he said.

We started out by researching traditional

Bedouin designs. We also studied traditional dyes and selected those that were colorfast and would work together, instead of resorting to increasingly prevalent garish, artificial colors. In addition, we asked designers in Amman to create new, contemporary weaving designs. And we established quality controls.

At first the Bedouin women were suspicious of our intentions, which was not surprising. They had been poor and powerless for so long they could not fathom anything else. We provided one young woman with around $180 to buy equipment to set up a dye workshop in the two-room house she lived in with twelve family members, but she refused to take the money. She was collecting and selling goat dung at the time to help support her family, and having $180 was beyond her dreams. It was impossible, she said. She would never be able to pay back the "loan," and besides it was too much wool for her to dye. Rebecca Salti, the first director of the Bani Hamida Women's Weaving Project, had to visit the villager twice to convince her to take the seed money. Finally, with great trepidation she accepted it and went to work. She turned out to be an excellent dyer and so successful that eventually she earned enough money to buy her own house and start a new life.

The signs of progress were thrilling. Not only were the first finished rugs beautiful, but the women who made them were using their money wisely. Rebecca, who went regularly to Bani Hamida to encourage the women and keep the momentum going, would find that the women she had paid the day before had "gone for treatment," as the women at Bani Hamida put it. The same refrain echoed all over the mountain. The women, many of whom had medical problems because of having had so many children, for the first time had money to pay for a bus ticket to go to a doctor and then to a pharmacy to buy medicine, plus a return ticket on the bus. They also had the money to buy pencils, paper, and other school supplies for their children. Some even ended up putting their children through college.

Word spread through the other Bedouin communities on the mountainside, and more and more women started asking for work. In one village we eventually had 150 women participating in the handicrafts project, some making beautiful embroidered pillows and quilts from our designs, others weaving rugs and wall hangings. These women assumed a new role in their communities, thanks to their weaving. Their success reminded me of a favorite saying of mine, the Chinese proverb "Women hold up half the sky," which so concisely captures the universality of women's essential contribution in building society. It was immensely gratifying for all of us to see these industrious women generating income from their homes, thus continuing their traditional role as mainstay of the family while providing a crucial safety net for the community. UNICEF noted that combination of work and family in the project when it ranked Bani Hamida among the best it surveyed.

Bani Hamida, which would become a model for projects in other developing countries, was the first project in Jordan to apply a comprehensive approach to community development using handicrafts production not only as an economic stimulus, but also as an opportunity to provide services in other areas. The project included a family planning program, which reinforced the Islamic approach of encouraging spacing between births for the health of the entire family, and which later expanded to provide much-needed medicines and vaccines.

Once the quality of the weaving stabilized, we realized that we had to develop marketing strategies to ensure the project's long-term sustainability. With the support of Aid to Artisans, a United States nonprofit organization that creates economic opportunities for craftspeople around the world, we began developing contacts at rug fairs and rug outlets in the United States, Europe, and elsewhere, and began to exhibit the rugs internationally. Our first show was at the Jordanian embassy in Washington, D.C., only nine months after we began the project, and we sold out our entire inventory. Katharine Graham, the publisher of *The Washington Post* and a good friend of ours, bought one, which was, of course, an invaluable marketing boost, especially after a magazine photographed her in her living room with a Bani Hamida rug on the floor.

The harder sell, ironically, was in Jordan. Among many in the affluent middle class the emphasis on things European was so well established that changing attitudes was very difficult. I brought Bani Hamida cushions and rugs into my office and into our home, where we received fellow monarchs, emirs, sultans, and other VIPs, to convey the message that Jordan's greatest treasures could be found within our own culture and heritage. The King's obvious appreciation of this handiwork sent the strongest possible signal, and over time attitudes began to change. One of the most satisfying aspects of the project was to see young people beginning to give the rugs and other handicrafts products to each other as wedding presents.

I also broke with convention by wearing traditional dresses to public and official events, even to state banquets abroad. It was difficult at first to find dresses in my size because I was so tall. In time, two sisters, close friends of mine, Fatina and Abla Asfour, began to train local rural women to create beautifully designed contemporary dresses using traditional pieces of embroidery, material, colors, and designs. I have always worn them with great pride and delight, and over the years these dresses have also become extremely fashionable in

Jordan and much sought after in other Arab states. Most significant of all was the transformation of the women in the poor areas the project served. The women in Bani Hamida and the many other communities we went on to work with were generating steady incomes — one of the reasons why they were considered good credit risks for micro-finance initiatives. Small-scale loans act as seed money, and in the hands of women the world over, these investments eventually flower into encouraging advances in education, health, and infrastructure. Women in these projects provided employment for others, sometimes even their husbands, and helped other women start businesses.

Of course, there were always men who did not fully grasp the nature of the changes taking place in the lives of their families. One unemployed husband sat all day watching his wife's prospering weaving business and finally asked whether we could find him another wife like that! He was ignored. Bedouin men were initially skeptical of the enterprise, but as they began to feel its tangible benefits and see that the tribe's name was becoming a proud symbol of Jordan's heritage, they became enthusiastic advocates, even at the Parliamentary level.

Acknowledging the success of these innovative approaches, the World Health Organization contacted us with a proposal to create a Middle Eastern model of integrated community development along the lines of a program that they had used to great effect in Thailand. We began to construct the model, which we called the Quality of Life project, in Sweimah, an isolated, impoverished village in the heart of the Jordan Valley. I was astounded by the conditions I found there on my first visit; some families were sheltered only by trees and had no access to medical facilities, schools, or even clean water.

We had seed money, but we wanted the villagers themselves to decide how to spend it, knowing that taking responsibility on the local level would be the key to the project's success. We helped villagers form a development council to survey households, identify major needs, and come up with potential solutions. We worked with the council, providing information, ideas, and advice, but the decisions were their own. When I attended the first meeting, I was tremendously encouraged to see that women had been included in the formation of the council. The Quality of Life program was one of the most rewarding initiatives of the Foundation. The program expanded to cover seventeen other remote rural communities in Jordan and to offer training and advice to countries throughout the Arab and Islamic world, from Palestine to Afghanistan. Not only did the approach stimulate democratic decision-making, but the village development councils' involvement in every step of whatever projects they chose also ensured their implementation. And for the most part, the projects were self-supporting, generating income for a revolving credit program that would then be used to initiate other projects.

In partnership with the Royal Society for the Conservation of Nature, we contributed lessons from our integrated development experience to Jordan's first ecotourism project. In the mid-1980s we were in a perfect position to take advantage of the boom in ecotourism, to the benefit of both Jordan's ecology and its economy. Our most successful venture was the Dana Wildlife Reserve, a rugged area just two hours from Amman deep in a breathtaking valley that plunged 4,200 feet (some 1,300 meters) through three overlapping microclimates.

Dana is a unique place. I loved visiting the area, and particularly the abandoned village of crumbling stone houses that were gradually being restored, thanks to private donations and help from various government ministries. Once reconstruction started providing training and employment, the villagers began to return, giving new life to the ancient site. By creating productive jobs and alternative sources of income for local people, based on the sustainable use of its natural resources and the subsequent easing of pressure on the land from grazing, Dana became a model for pairing conservation and socio-economic development. Tourism created a natural new market for local products, such as dried organic fruits and silver jewelry with designs inspired from nature. This unique approach enabled the RSCN to mobilize other resources from different donors — including the Global Environment Facility of the United Nations Development Program and the World Bank. The bank's president, Jim Wolfensohn, visited Dana with his wife, Elaine, and said he was "honored" to be supporting the project and would use it as a global model — a vote of confidence that gave the project and its staff an enormous professional boost. Equally encouraging was the steady rise in ecotourists to Dana, some 40,000 annually by the late 1990s, which benefited many in the area, especially our target group of women.

Cultural programs extended the ripple effect of such projects. I saw the arts as a way to provide opportunity for people of varied socioeconomic backgrounds, ethnicities, religions, and political orientations to come together and contribute to a contemporary Jordanian culture that would transcend their differences. Through programs that emphasized pluralism and diversity as well as traditional Arab artistic expression, I believed culture could have great political and even national security value. The more closely people could connect through literature, drama, and art, the greater would be their sense of cohesion in a society made up of often disparate and competing elements.

During an official visit to Washington, D.C., in the early 1980s, I was taken on a tour of the

Capital Children's Museum, which inspired my interest in establishing a similar project in Jordan. As it turned out, the visit gave rise to two of my favorite cultural initiatives: Jordan's Children's Heritage and Science Museum, and its National Music Conservatory. The Children's Heritage and Science Museum is the first hands-on recreational and educational museum in the Arab world. Its mobile outreach program, aimed at poorer families in rural areas, received an unexpected boost during an official visit to Germany, when the King and I visited the Mercedes manufacturing headquarters in Stuttgart. The company had been planning to present my husband with the latest Mercedes, which, of course, would have delighted him. Instead, having learned of my search for a vehicle for our Children's Museum, Mercedes generously responded by presenting us with a magnificent tractor-trailer. Needless to say, my husband never stopped teasing me about his unintentional sacrifice.

While visiting the Washington Children's Museum, I was asked if I could extend my tour to observe a very special musical program. In one of the museum's rooms, a remarkable woman was conducting an orchestra called Young Strings in Action, a diverse group of children aged three to eighteen. Sheila Johnson's violin teaching technique, based on the highly effective Rolland Method, so impressed me that I invited her to bring her young orchestra to Jordan to perform at the Jerash Festival in 1984. Jordan fell in love with the children, and the children fell in love with Jordan. Sheila gave unreservedly of her time, energy, and even financial backing to help us start up our own program — the National Music Conservatory (NMC).

The NMC started out in 1986 with three Jordanian teachers and forty-five students learning violin, but soon expanded to include other classical Western and Arabic instruments. I felt very strongly that the conservatory should encourage and offer opportunities for Jordanian children to explore their own musical heritage as well. Music programs at the Conservatory grew to include choral instruction and courses in music theory and history, and they soon produced the first children's orchestra in Jordan.

Sheila Johnson's Young Strings in Action returned to the Jerash Festival to play with our young orchestra in 1986, which was another great success. In time, growing out of that first inspired moment of Sheila's musical instruction, we developed music curricula for the public schools in Jordan and, in a joint venture with the Royal Schools of Music in England, a three-year diploma program. Children from all over the Arab world come to the Conservatory's summer camp. One of our many individual successes, Zade Dirani, has become an internationally renowned pianist and composer of works that blend Eastern, Arabic scales with

Western classicism.

During Hussein's twenty-fifth year as King he suggested that, instead of spending substantial public and private funds on a national Silver Jubilee celebration, monies be raised for a school that might reflect his long-standing commitment to education. However, adequate resources to fund the entire project had never been raised, so it was shelved. When I was offered those funds to advance our planning for a National Children's Hospital, I insisted that we not abandon that earlier educational dream. The Noor Al Hussein Foundation assumed responsibility for realizing it in 1984, and nine years later the Jubilee School, an independent coeducational secondary school, was established to develop the academic and leadership potential of outstanding students from the country and the region, with special emphasis on students from less developed areas of Jordan. The School provides a unique educational environment that promotes creative thinking, leadership and conflict-resolution skills, scientific and technological expertise, and social responsibility. The Jubilee School's Center for Excellence in Education advances national and regional educational standards through the development of innovative curricula, as well as training programs and workshops for public and private school teachers.

The King was very proud of the School and

its students, and he celebrated their accomplishments and enjoyed their enthusiasm. When my husband graduated the first class, he thanked the students with heartfelt gratitude. "The best times I have spent in my life I have spent with you young men and women, who will hopefully take a lead in the development of the country," he told the students.

Through the King Hussein Foundation, established in 1998, the Jubilee School in partnership with national and international organizations is developing an innovative program integrating state-of-the-art multimedia communications technology into the national curriculum for math, science, and English. In this way and others it serves as a tangible link between King Hussein's dreams for Jordan and the commitment of his son, King Abdullah, to educational reform and modernization.

King Hussein did not look at social and cultural programs in sophisticated development terms. He simply wanted to ensure that every person whose life he could touch had access to the best possible education, health services, and jobs, so they, in turn, could contribute to the nation-building process. It fell to his government, other members of his family, NGOs, and social activists within our society to try to translate that human desire into grassroots programs. Gradually NGOs assumed a greater and greater importance in Jordan as particularly effective, apolitical agents of change.

★ ★ ★

I derived great satisfaction from my work. Now, after seven years as Queen, I had a measure of experience and knew whom to call when I needed professional advice. I had a highly motivated staff, which I counted on to be my eyes and ears when I was away from Amman. When I was in the city, I would meet daily with staff members to discuss new strategies or try to resolve the inevitable logjams that would develop. Although there were always hurdles that required tact and patience, at the end of the day I honestly felt that I was spending my time just as I had always hoped I would, in the service of making a difference. Perhaps it was because my life felt so purposeful and focused that I was thrown off completely when I learned of the personal attacks coming from London.

Nigel Dempster, a gossip columnist at London's *Daily Mail*, began to regularly attack me, starting in 1985. My husband's goddaughter and personal assistant in England, Elizabeth Corke, called me one day to read me an article that Dempster had written under the headline "Nur Needs a Boost" (for some reason he frequently spelled my name incorrectly). The article told readers that I had hired, at great expense, a public relations firm in California to promote me and improve my image. The only possible explanation I could think of was a conversation I had had with a consultant for the

Democratic Party during one of my trips to Washington to see if he could suggest someone who might be interested in doing pro bono work for the Jordanian government as part of our ongoing effort to present a more positive picture of Arabs in America. Our resources were very limited, so there was no way we could compete with well-funded Zionist organizations in America, but I thought that someone, somewhere, might understand the importance of more balanced reporting on the Middle East. Our conversation never came to anything, and I had forgotten all about it until the Nigel Dempster column appeared some months later, quoting a "friend of the mighty monarch" as saying, "Perhaps Nur is trying to gain a separate identity, rather than being seen as a mere appendage to her husband, to whom she owes everything."

My husband, who was well used to the slings and arrows of the press, Nigel Dempster's in particular, told me to ignore it. But I thought that the gossip columnist had been misinformed by his "friend of the mighty monarch" and would appreciate having his column corrected. I called Elizabeth and asked her to inform Mr. Dempster that his column was inaccurate. I was naïve enough at the time to think that no journalist would want his byline attached to something that was completely untrue. Elizabeth was very skeptical, knowing the British tabloid press far better than I, but she went ahead, only to report back that Nigel Dempster's staff insisted that their source was reliable and had even given them the name of the firm I had supposedly retained. I was delighted. All the *Daily Mail* needed to do to clear up the misunderstanding was to call the firm. When we received no further response from Dempster, we tried to track down the firm in California ourselves, only to discover that no such firm had ever existed. Still, the tabloid would not retract the story. Fortunately, my skin toughened, because Dempster's attacks would go on for years — each one more absurd than the last.

It was ironic that at the same time I was coming under media attack, I was arguing for more freedom of the press in Jordan. For although I decried the irresponsibility of certain Western journalists, I felt just as strongly that there should be an outlet in Jordan for differences of opinion. In fact, I had been lobbying my husband and his key officials since the first years of our marriage to reconsider their sometimes restrictive attitude toward personal and institutional freedoms. The press in Jordan, though privately owned, was effectively government-controlled. Truly independent reporting did not exist. Among the more conservative members of our society, there was insecurity about freedom of expression in Jordan, rooted, no doubt, in the sense of high emergency that was the rule, not the exception, in our troubled region. They were apprehensive about allowing the people to read dissenting opinions and about the destabilizing impact of erroneous political reporting.

The conflict over the press came to a head in the mid-1980s. Leila Sharaf had become Minister of Information, and with the King's support she had promised Jordanians more freedom of expression, which I took as a good sign. We were moving in this positive direction when a sensitive debate emerged over the implementation of a decision in 1974 to merge tribal and civil laws, triggering a number of articles critical of tribal traditions.

Tribal leaders complained bitterly to the King, and the extreme sensitivity of the issue prompted Hussein to send the Prime Minister a letter, published in its entirety, chastising reporters on the story for "launching attacks on our social institutions and their values." His rationale was based on lack of professionalism and reliability among Jordanian journalists, whose misreporting could pose a threat to the stability of the country.

Leila abruptly resigned as Minister of Information. My husband was furious with her, but Leila held her ground. She spelled out the reasons for her resignation in a letter, warning the government that "a certain degree of free thinking and free expression" was imperative to "cultural and political development in Jordan." It was hardly a revolutionary statement, but the government-controlled press did not publish it. Instead, the letter and its mildly progressive message gathered more momentum by being widely and privately circulated throughout Jordan.

I was faced with a terrible dilemma. The country was in an uproar over the issue, with everyone taking sides. My husband relied on my total loyalty, as did Leila. I was torn. I could not deny the legitimacy of my husband's concerns, yet I agreed with Leila's position. In private I urged my husband to support a freer press. Of course there would be problems, I argued, but it would be better to face them and develop good laws that would provide accountability; a freer press would prove to be an asset to security, I believed. It would demonstrate confidence, which would, in turn, promote greater confidence in the government. Hussein listened to my arguments but insisted that a strict balance was necessary. Over the years since he had ascended to the throne as a vulnerable teenager, he had developed a strong political intuition, and it had served him well. For many decades he had read the mood of Jordan better than anyone, and he refused to doubt his instincts on this issue.

I could not take a public position against the government; it would have been totally inappropriate. I did, however, appear in public by Leila's side, showing my personal support for her and, implicitly, for her position. I also tried to act as peacemaker between my husband and Leila by helping to clarify for each the concerns of the other. Slowly Hussein began to mellow toward Leila, and although it took five months, they finally reconciled. The restrictions on the press, however, would continue to come and go, although generally Jordan's press corps was far less restrained than the press in other Arab countries.

My support of Leila and others with more liberal views raised eyebrows in Amman. I also came under criticism for another break with tradition. Every year the Royal Court held a series of official *iftars* — evening meals during the month of Ramadan to break the day's fast — but few women were included. I decided to hold *iftars* to bring together influential and dedicated women from different parts of the country to exchange information and share in this communal ritual. This was also a valuable opportunity for women to "network," just as men had always done.

The Royal Court did not agree; women should be home preparing *iftar* for their husbands. That sounded absurd to me. Ramadan lasted a month, and for one night other family members could cook the *iftar*. However, I did not want a showdown with the Royal Court without knowing how other women would react to my idea. The response from most women I contacted was so enthusiastic that I decided we should go ahead. The Royal Court did not give up. At one point they brought such pressure on my husband to discontinue the women's *iftars* that Hussein asked me to suspend them for a while. He was rather surprised when I agreed, but I knew what would happen. So many women complained about the canceled *iftars* that the following year we reinstated them.

Over time, the number of official *iftars* I hosted grew to include diplomats, students, orphans, and people from various organizations, including men and women. Other nights, when possible, my husband and I would break the fast together at home with the children or at Zahran Palace, with the Queen Mother. I loved those family gatherings at the end of each day during Ramadan. First, we would break the fast by drinking water and fruit juices, of which my favorite was *qamareddin,* a delicious drink made out of apricot paste that I had loved since childhood. After we had slaked our thirst, we went on to eat nuts and dates and other light foods before saying our prayers and enjoying a proper meal together. The happiest person at our *iftars* was often my husband, who had not been able to smoke all day and was quick to light up.

Islam is a practical and understanding religion, and during Ramadan expectant mothers are allowed to postpone their fasting. I was grateful for that exemption during my pregnancy in 1985. There was stress enough in our household as my husband continued to negotiate with Arafat, the United States, and, increasingly, Britain's Prime Minister, Margaret Thatcher.

In our part of the world one violent incident after another reinforced the stereotype of Arabs as terrorists. The PLO and Israel traded attacks in April, the Israelis thwarting a PLO infiltration from the sea by blowing up a boat. Two months later, Shi'ite Muslims, whom people in the West wrongly assumed were Palestinians, hijacked a TWA plane in Beirut, holding their hostages for seventeen days and killing an American navy diver. In September, the PLO killed three suspected Mossad agents on a yacht in Cyprus, drawing a characteristic overreaction from the Israelis — the bombing of Arafat's headquarters in Tunis, with the loss of seventy lives. World sentiment ran high against Israel for such an excessive response.

In September 1985, after visiting the Baqa'a Palestinian refugee camp in Jordan and seeing for herself how desperate conditions were, Margaret Thatcher broke ranks with the Israeli and U.S. embargo against meeting with the PLO and invited a joint PLO-Jordanian delegation to London for talks. In October, just a week before the talks in London were to take place, four members of the PLO hijacked an Italian cruise ship, the *Achille Lauro*, and killed a Jewish American, Leon Klinghoffer, who was confined to a wheelchair.

King Hussein was appalled by this senseless violence. Though it made a diplomatic solution all the more imperative, it also made it far more difficult to convince any world leader to talk directly with the PLO. On the eve of the British talks with the PLO-Jordanian delegation in London, the Palestinian members suddenly refused to accept any wording in UN Resolution 242 that implied Israel's right to exist. The talks were canceled, leaving my husband feeling betrayed once again by Arafat, and deeply embarrassed before a very angry Mrs. Thatcher.

In my seventh month of pregnancy, Dr. Arif Batayneh, concerned about my ultrasound readings, urged me to go to England to see a specialist. Because the ultrasound equipment in Jordan was not sophisticated enough at the time for a precise diagnosis, Dr. Batayneh and Mr. Pinker, my British doctor, arranged for me to see a renowned Scottish expert, a protégé of the man who invented sonar in World War II.

The visit to the Scottish specialist was fascinating. He conducted the most detailed and meticulous measurements of an unborn baby's limbs and skeletal structure that I had ever seen and seemed unconcerned during the examination. At the end of the procedure, I bid the doctors good-bye and went on about my business, but not without increasing feelings of anxiety about my Jordanian obstetrician. Dr. Batayneh seemed forgetful at times and confused at others, and he did not give me consistent or direct answers to my questions. I had gone through three pregnancies with him before, plus my miscarriage, but this time he was not himself at all. I remember confiding in my husband several times over the next two months that though Arif was by no means old enough, he seemed to be becoming senile.

My husband, too, acted odd, which I attributed to his ongoing frustrations with Yasser Arafat and the PLO. King Hussein was still working on convening an international peace conference, and both America and Israel had signed on, the latter after a series of secret meetings between my husband and Shimon Peres, Israel's Foreign Minister. The sticking point was Arafat, who once again was balking at the conditions for PLO representation — the acceptance of Resolution 242, the recognition of Israel's right to exist, and the renunciation of violence.

Arafat came to Amman in January 1986, just a few weeks before the baby was due, to meet with my husband. These two men, so very different, had been thrust together by fate. Several of my husband's top advisers had advised him not to deal with Arafat at all, given his history, but King Hussein insisted on trying one last time to persuade Arafat to join the peace process. He also had something new to offer Arafat: a written invitation from the United States to the PLO to attend the conference, provided Arafat agreed to the conditions. Arafat was delighted when my husband showed him the invitation, but he refused to enter negotiations unless Palestinians were guaranteed the right of "self-determination" — that is, statehood. The same issue came up again and again through three drafts of a reply to the United States.

My husband was at his wit's end with Arafat, just as I was with my pregnancy. "Prime Minister Zeid Rifai insisting that the baby wait until Arafat departs," I noted in my journal. Arafat had set everyone on edge. The talks with Arafat broke down on January 26, along with any hope for the international peace conference my husband had been seeking for so long. I thought perhaps the imminent birth of our new baby would offset some of my husband's disappointment, but it seemed as if he was feigning enthusiasm. Dr. Batayneh was also becoming stranger and stranger, so I rather distrusted him when he said he was going to induce the baby, without explaining why. I was also very surprised when my sister, Alexa, suddenly arrived in Jordan. I had no idea how she had managed to just pick up and leave her demanding job at the law firm, although I was very happy to have her with me so close to my due date.

On February 9, I went to the hospital for a routine checkup, only to be informed by Arif that he was going to induce the baby that very day. I would have preferred the birth to be natural, but the doctor was adamant. I stopped him from starting an aggressive induction, and I remember trying to calm him down when he inexplicably ordered the hospital staff to ready the operating theater and organize blood for transfusions. "Just take it easy," I told him. I ended up in the labor room, and four hours later our baby was born. She was a beautiful little girl, a dream come true. Now our daughter Iman had a little sister. It was not until I was taken back to my hospital room that I learned the reason for everyone's peculiar behavior. It turned out that the ultrasound expert's tests in England had determined that the baby was abnormal; her head was far too big for her body and I would not be able to deliver her safely. My husband had summoned my sister to help us all through this impending tragedy.

I was surprised to learn that Dr. Batayneh and my husband had lived under the strain of this dire prediction for two months without telling me. I can handle most anything, but this was one time in my life when I was glad information was kept from me. If they had told me there was something terribly wrong with the baby, it would have meant two months of gnawing concern for me. In the end the baby was perfectly normal. I have a larger-than-average-size head, my husband had a larger-than-average-size head, and our children have large heads. She was just like the rest of us.

We named the new baby Raiyah Al Hussein, which means the "banner" or "flag" of Hussein. We both loved the symbolism as well as the name itself, which we had found in the Hashimite family records. The name had been last used in the seventeenth century. Raiyah did not officially get her name for weeks, however. Her father kept declaring his intention to name her, but like so much in our lives, her naming ceremony kept being thwarted by external events.

After so many false starts and setbacks, my husband decided to sever political relations with the Palestinian leadership. It was not a decision he arrived at lightly. He had spent the last six years trying to form a meaningful partnership with the PLO in order to achieve a comprehensive peace, but it had all kept coming to naught. He addressed the country on February 19, ten days after Raiyah was born, announcing the end of any collaboration with the PLO "until such time as their word becomes their bond, characterized by commitment, credibility, and constancy." With so many Jordanian Palestinians on the East Bank and, of course, on the occupied West Bank, we were anxious about public reaction to his words, but while naturally there was some opposition, much more support poured in from all sectors.

After all the political stress we had been

living with at home in Jordan, it was almost a relief to focus again on international relations. Raiyah was only a month old when we took her with us on official visits to Brunei, Oman, and Indonesia — where my husband and I had a memorable few moments on a hilltop in Bali trying to find Haley's comet in the pitch darkness. Our only concern at that moment was monkeys. Indonesian security had warned us that the monkeys chattering away in the trees and in the bushes would snatch the baby if we were not careful, so I held on to Raiyah as tightly as she would ever be held in her life.

Raiyah survived the monkeys to join us, two months later, on a state visit to the United States, then to Egypt, England, Luxembourg, France, and India. The state visit to India was fascinating. It is a pity Raiyah was too young to appreciate the extraordinary visit we made to the Taj Mahal at sunset, when we had the magnificent marble monument all to ourselves, our hosts having closed it to the public for security reasons. The trip was doubly meaningful because it had been delayed so many times. We had been invited to visit India two years earlier by Indira Gandhi, who was assassinated shortly thereafter. Her son, Rajiv, succeeded her and again extended the invitation. We finally settled on October 1986 and arrived in India only four days after Rajiv himself miraculously escaped an assassination attempt. "It was a goof-up," he said to me at the arrival ceremony, describing how a Sikh gunman had lain in wait for him on the roof of a tiny hut next to the path he was scheduled to cross.

We liked the Gandhis immediately. Rajiv was a rare gentleman — soulful, gentle, and thoughtful — and a meticulous and attentive host, and like my husband he was an enthusiastic aviator and pilot. Sonia Gandhi, his wife, seemed more reserved, which was only natural considering the stunning events that had shaped their lives: her brother-in-law killed in a plane crash, her mortally wounded mother-in-law dying in her arms, the reluctant ascendancy of her own husband as political leader, then the assassination attempt against him. For security reasons, their children rarely left home, not even for school.

Sonia and I became quite close in the course of our visit to India, and she would visit me in Jordan, where I took her up to Bani Hamida to see the handicrafts program. I was grief-stricken for her and her children when Rajiv was assassinated in 1991 by a Tamil suicide bomber at a campaign rally near Madras. I was in a hotel room in California when I heard the news, and I sat down, my head in my hands, utterly distraught that such a gentle, decent man would lose his life that way. Sonia has faced unbearable hardships and traumas with enormous dignity and courage. Neither she nor Rajiv ever wanted to be in politics. They did so out of a sense of duty. I can only imagine the agony she must have felt when she, too, was drafted by the family's Congress Party to stand for national elections.

We ended our trip to India in the state of Goa, a former Portuguese enclave on the west coast. It gave me a chance to introduce Raiyah to the sea, and we spent a luxuriously relaxing time together in the waves. "Brave girl, let's goa, goa, goa," I said to her, laughing as the turquoise waters of the Arabian Sea swirled around us.

chapter thirteen

Parenthood

Raiyah was just three months old in June 1986, when she accompanied the King and me to a ball at Windsor Castle in England. During the evening, Raiyah provided her own unique form of entertainment for some of the younger members of the British royal family when they realized that she was staying in a small room not far from the festivities. My journal entry reads, "Raiyah receives Diana, Andrew, Sarah, and others wreathed in smiles, setting aside Andrew's apprehensions about starting a family, I hope."

In the days before the ball, my husband and I had taken a few dance lessons at our house in London. We were both feeling rusty, so we decided to find an instructor who would come to the house and help us brush up on our skills. We removed all the furniture from our sitting room, which gave us, unexpectedly, a wonderful and liberating space. "Both of us dancing up a storm in our temporarily converted ballroom at Palace Green," I wrote in my journal. "While I do wonder if I am making any progress toward a reasonably credible showing at Windsor, I am also realizing perhaps I am not the only one that has danced left-footed for the past eight years. Nevertheless, I shall always worship my hero."

In the end, we had very little time to dance at Windsor as we left early because Hussein, Hashim, and Iman were scheduled for surgery the next morning. My husband was having minor surgery to ease his sinus problems, and the children were having their adenoids and tonsils removed. All the procedures were expected to be routine. As it turned out, Hussein and Hashim's surgeries were uneventful, but Iman's adenoids were four times the normal size, shocking even the doctor, who jokingly suggested we have them bronzed. The next afternoon she started to hemorrhage. I lay on her hospital bed to comfort her, and eventually we were wheeled together into the operating theater, where they tried to stop the bleeding, but it continued. Over the next few days we wheeled back and forth between the operating and recovery rooms several times. It was a traumatic experience for a three-year-old and heartrending for all of us. Even our Special Branch security personnel had tears in their eyes.

Poor Iman's luck did not improve after she left the hospital and we returned to Jordan.

Five months later she broke her leg when she steered a small car over a 10-foot drop onto a van that was mercifully in a parking lot below in the royal compound. Her nanny downplayed the event, so that at first I did not know that Iman was hurt. I tried to get her to stand, and when she protested I thought she just wanted to stay on my lap, so after a while I tried again to get her to stand. By now it was clear she was in excruciating pain, and when we took her to the hospital we discovered she had a major break in her leg. I felt terribly guilty that I had been unwittingly torturing Iman by trying to get her up on her feet, which she teases me about to this day. Maternal instinct focused all my energy on Iman's well-being, while my husband spent a week or more grumbling about wanting to strangle those responsible. Fortunately Iman's leg healed quickly, but it was a traumatic year for her.

The cumulative psychic and political trauma of this period was slower to heal. In 1986, for the first time, my husband voiced pessimism about the future of the region. Failure to achieve a Jordanian-Palestinian partnership and the severing of relations with the Palestinian leadership had left him deeply disappointed. His ceaseless quest for a comprehensive peace had led nowhere.

His mood grew more somber with the news that the Reagan administration was postponing indefinitely the sale of weapons to Jordan.

Around this time Hussein also learned that the United States was involved in a clandestine arms-for-hostages deal with Iran in order to secure the release of American hostages being held in Beirut by Islamic militants. That the United States was actually arming Iran against Iraq, which it was also supplying with arms, outraged my husband. The additional news that Oliver North was providing Iran with U.S. intelligence in the ongoing war against Iraq was even more disturbing, as Iran had just won a crucial victory against Iraq in the Fao Peninsula in February 1986.

At the same time Hussein began to speak to me about his role and responsibilities as King of Jordan. How could he, with his unique credibility as an Arab and Muslim elder statesman, best put his experience to use? What was the most useful role he might play at this time of his life? He seriously considered the possibility of handing over the throne to someone else, perhaps his brother, in order to assume a less politicized voice for a larger cause.

I was facing my own challenges at the time. Some radical Islamists targeted the Jerash Festival, which they decried as "un-Islamic." I was also having a difficult time on the personal front. My husband, absorbed in his own issues, was oblivious to the mounting tensions of living in a houseful of teenagers. Had I ever imagined the total helplessness I would feel with my stepchildren, I might have reflected more deeply on the advisability of marrying their father. "He might have fared better without yet another wife to serve as a family scapegoat," I wrote in my journal at the end of one obviously dark day.

The hostility in the house was becoming palpable. I could not come home after a hard day's work and find any peace. The family dynamic was further complicated by the fact that as the younger stepchildren in our household grew up, they were being infected by the adolescent restiveness of their older half-brothers and half-sisters.

At one point, the older children drafted a list of fifty-four grievances and elected one of them to present it to us. As we listened to this barrage — which ranged from understandable family dilemmas to truly absurd accusations — my husband and I simply did not know how to respond. Had we been able to talk about each misunderstanding as it arose, the situation would have been simpler. Instead the large group of children traded grievances until their collective reaction blew out of proportion. Extended family members often became involved with varying intentions, which only complicated our quandary. I suggested that we try to talk it all out together, to communicate more directly, but that required trust, which, sadly, was in short supply.

I felt completely helpless, responsible, and

very alone. There were moments during that two- or three-year period when I felt I could not endure the situation much longer. During this bleak time I wondered if I was more of a liability than a help. The stress was such that I felt unable to be a good mother to anybody, including our very young children. I was under so much strain from trying and consistently failing to convert this difficult situation into something harmonious that I felt I had nothing positive to give my husband or the children. He could sense it even if I said nothing — indeed, for the most part I kept my feelings to myself, knowing how helpless he felt as well.

I was able to get through these days by thinking about what Hussein himself had gone through: the many cruel betrayals and his forgiveness of them all, and the jealousy, attacks, and misunderstandings he had endured, his faith and humor intact. Had I married anyone else, I cannot imagine that I would have found within myself the patience and the faith to prevail. Because my husband always focused beyond himself on the greater good, I found myself trying to follow his example.

Still, I was in agony, yet I could not tell anyone, not even my closest friends, not even my own family. I felt it would intrude on my husband's privacy. At one point I considered seeking professional help. I am an optimist and a problem solver by nature, but I felt I needed some direction. What could I do better? What could I do nothing about? In the end, I decided that to discuss our family, given the political situation we were in, was too risky.

This I knew for certain: We loved each other. Hussein obviously needed me. He was taking on much too much to shoulder alone, and however naïve this might sound, I really wanted us to create the example of a successful family. Both of us had grown up in difficult circumstances, and I thought for the sake of all the children in the family — and for our larger Jordanian family — that if my husband and I could somehow find our way together through all of these challenges, and grow together, that would give our children some greater measure of hope, some additional resilience to work with in the future.

As in most families, patience and faith were rewarded over the following years as the older children began to develop their individual talents and interests, became more independent, and then begin their own families. We shared their disappointments and delights, and rejoiced in their marriages and children. These were some of the happiest and most hopeful times of my life.

During those years, I was not able to see my family in the United States very much. The first purely personal trip I took to the United States was in 1987, almost ten years after our marriage. For all that time I had felt I could not in good conscience leave my husband and small children at home, not to mention my other increasingly demanding responsibilities as Queen. However, just days short of her 100th birthday, my grandmother died. My father had been planning a surprise family reunion and birthday party, which instead turned into a memorial celebration of her life in my father's garden in Washington, D.C. Although the occasion was sad, it gave my children a chance to visit with and, in some cases, meet for the first time their American cousins.

That private time in America, without the pressure of speeches, press interviews, or anything political whatsoever, allowed me to realize how much I missed family and friends. I needed to find time for them; otherwise, I would lose touch with my roots and the influences that had shaped my life. In this spirit I decided to stay on for a few days after my grandmother's memorial service to attend the wedding of one of my Concord Academy classmates, Julia Preston.

I had to negotiate intently with the U.S. Secret Service during that week to scale down their arrangements. I would not have gone to the wedding if I thought I would ruin it by being surrounded and creating a distraction. In the end, the head of the security detail made extraordinary efforts to allow me to blend unobtrusively into the wedding party. There was no prior announcement that I was attending, and I arrived quietly and left the same way. Best of all, no one except my close friends knew who I was. It was a wonderful feeling just to be myself, not on display, with old friends.

From then on, I made a concerted effort to invite friends to various official and private events in America. In England I made contact with Carinthia West, my classmate from the National Cathedral School in Washington, whom I had not seen in a decade. Carinthia was somewhat startled when I called out of the blue and she was told by the woman who answered the phone that the Queen of Norway was calling. After we cleared up the garbled message, I invited Carinthia to Jordan. Over the years to come, other friends would visit, and my husband and I would enjoy sharing our Jordanian friends and the rich culture and history of the country with them. For my fortieth birthday, a group of my old friends from Concord Academy camped at Wadi Rum; Raiyah shared a tent with my friend Julia, whose own daughter, around Raiyah's age, had not been able to attend.

Jordan and the region were slipping into recession in the late 1980s as the oil boom ended. Those Arab countries that had been flush with oil revenues in the 1970s were experiencing a downturn, and the aid they had pledged to Jordan slowed to a trickle. The salaries of Jordanians working abroad were either frozen or reduced, and the remittances they sent home began to dwindle. New employment opportunities for Jordanians abroad were curtailed, and the unemployment rate in Jordan rose sharply, especially among university graduates, who would have been in great demand during better times. There was a growing sense of discontent in the country.

In the fall of 1987, Hussein and I made a state visit to Finland. The Finns were incredibly welcoming, lining the streets to wave wherever we went and extending extraordinarily enthusiastic hospitality at every level. Perhaps it was because the King was the first Arab head of state to visit Finland in a decade, or perhaps Hussein was seen as a peacemaker from a region where Finnish peacekeeping forces had been stationed since the early 1970s. Whatever the reason for their fulsome embrace, it was quite overwhelming.

In no uncertain terms, President Mauno Koivisto reiterated Finland's support for a settlement of the Arab-Israeli conflict based on the UN resolutions, and called on Iran to accept a UN-sponsored peace plan to end the bloody conflict with Iraq. And Jordan reached its first tourism agreement with Finland: Once a week from then on, a Royal Jordanian flight would arrive in Aqaba full of Scandinavian tourists from Helsinki, bringing a welcome boost to our economy. It was a phenomenon we had witnessed before. Wherever we traveled, there would be a resulting upsurge in tourism to Jordan from the host country.

To our surprise, this trip also provoked very pointed criticism. Because of Finland's extremely formal protocol, we had been required to wear the most formal state regalia, including decorations and, in my case, a tiara. The press photos of us triggered the reaction back home that we were out of touch with Jordanian reality, a view that underscored the discontent and disaffection that was building as the economy worsened. This was, after all, normal state protocol during a visit that would bring significant economic and political benefits to Jordan.

Throughout 1987 the King continued to press for an international conference with the PLO and all five permanent members of the Security Council. In July he met secretly with Israel's new right-wing Prime Minister, Yitzhak Shamir, at Castlewood outside London to see if there was any hope of making headway with Israel. The meeting was inconclusive. Hussein told me later that the atmosphere at Castlewood had been very tense. Shamir's staff was so suspicious that they wanted to search Hussein's secretary's bags and to examine the food. The Israelis would not even use the house phone. They went into the nearby village to make their phone calls from a public phone booth.

George Shultz, the U.S. Secretary of State,

picked up where Shamir left off and on October 20 visited my husband at our house in London, Palace Green. The U.S. proposal to the King was consistent, virtually word for word, with the Israeli position: Forget any international conference and negotiate directly with Shamir without the PLO or the permanent members of the UN Security Council. The King said he could not oblige. After the U.S. delegation left and we were tidying up the sitting room, we found the briefing notes of one of Shultz's aides behind a cushion on the couch. Marked "Strategies for Dealing with Hussein," it was a point-by-point blueprint for dealing with my husband. Within minutes, a U.S. diplomat rang the doorbell urgently, explaining that the Americans had overlooked some papers on their departure. He recovered the notes in the cushions, where we had returned them after we had made our own copies.

Israel so dominated the U.S. position that there was no negotiating room left for the Arabs. The Arab countries, however, were more unified than ever. In fact, Jordan hosted an Arab summit in Amman in November 1987 and achieved the impossible. Eight months before the conference, the King had invited two archenemies — Hafez Al Assad of Syria, who was supporting Iran in the Iran-Iraq war, and Saddam Hussein of Iraq — to make up their differences, and they had. Now, at the conference, the two men talked for thirteen hours on the first day and seven hours on the next.

The two enemies emerged, if not friends, at least agreeing not to attack each other publicly. Both, miraculously, came to the Unity Summit in Amman, as did the Egyptian leader, Hosni Mubarak, for Egypt's first Arab summit since Camp David. My husband's ceaseless struggle to promote unity in the Middle East was beginning to bear fruit. The summit was, in fact, one of my husband's finest hours. For once the Arab countries spoke with one voice, with even Hafez Al Assad accepting my husband's call for unity by joining the others in announcing "solidarity with Iraq." Arafat was also well received. Indeed, Jordan and the PLO formally restored relations soon after the summit ended.

Saddam Hussein, who almost never left his country, was so worried about his security that he would not stay, as planned, at the Iraqi ambassador's residence. At the last minute we had to ask six families living in a family compound in Amman to move to a hotel so we could house the Iraqi President and his huge entourage, most of them members of his personal guard. Throughout his stay in Amman, Saddam Hussein would eat only food prepared by his own staff.

The unexpected ripple effect of the Amman summit led to a pivotal moment in the Middle East. The Palestinians in the Occupied Territories launched a series of demonstrations against Israeli occupation that reflected a growing cohesion between the Palestinian leadership functioning outside the Occupied Territories and its constituents inside, as well as a mounting desperation. After the past ten years of agonizing stalemate, I could not help but hope that these voices of protest might be heard. The Israelis responded in full force to the demonstrations but went too far in December, a month after the Amman summit, when settlers shot and killed a Palestinian schoolgirl and Israeli authorities demanded that her parents bury her at night without a proper funeral. That inexcusable incident, followed by the seemingly intentional crash of an Israeli army vehicle into a line of traffic, killing four Palestinians, provoked outrage in Gaza and the West Bank. Two days later, the 1987 *intifada*, or uprising, began.

The international media descended on Israel and the Occupied Territories, sending nightly images of boys in jeans and T-shirts throwing stones at Israeli soldiers in full riot gear, who responded with tear gas, beatings, and gunfire. The David and Goliath parallel was unmistakable, and, for the first time, put the human face of the Palestinian tragedy on the front pages of newspapers worldwide and in the television news. Israel insisted the coverage was biased and anti-Semitic, but there was no mistaking the brutality of the images and the rising body count, which over the course of the next four years would reach 1,300 Palestinians and 80 Israelis. Even the Reagan administration took note, leading to a very curious telephone conversation between my husband and the U.S. President in January 1988.

The King had become increasingly aware that his meetings with President Reagan were based more and more on formality and less and less on substance. Conversations that mattered were conducted outside the Oval Office with U.S. officials like the Secretary of State, not with the President. It was as if Reagan was scripted. My husband was deeply concerned because he had always had very direct relations with American presidents, but it was clear to my husband that in this last year of Reagan's presidency his health had become an obstacle.

Hussein's concern was reinforced by a phone call from the White House a month or so after the *intifada* began. What was striking in that particular phone conversation was that after the initial hellos and pleasantries, Reagan went directly into a series of points and then started to say good-bye. When Hussein interjected a question, Reagan was totally thrown off and the conversation abruptly ended. Listening to the playback, it seemed quite obvious that Reagan had been reading the points he was making from note cards and could not sustain any further discussion.

Still, the conversation clearly had an impact. Shortly afterward, Philip Habib, Reagan's former special envoy to the Middle East, arrived in Jordan with the welcome news that the United States would now push "with vigor" for an international peace conference. The new U.S. position was a complete reversal of what the Secretary of State had told my husband just three months earlier.

Although the *intifada* succeeded in establishing an identity for the Palestinian people separate from the stereotype identity of the PLO, the uprising did not lead to a political solution. The United States and Israel still refused to negotiate with the PLO, and the PLO still refused to authorize my husband to speak for a joint delegation. Moreover, a new Palestinian leadership rising out of the *intifada* on the West Bank was just as suspicious of Jordan as of the PLO and, in a March 1988 communiqué, called on the Palestinians in the Jordanian Parliament to resign their seats and "align with their people."

The King was stung. Jordan had been supporting the West Bank since 1967, paying the salaries of teachers and civil servants in both the West Bank and Gaza, and maintaining the holy places in Jerusalem. No one had argued more forcefully or credibly on the world stage for a Palestinian homeland and the right of Palestinian self-determination, all the while resisting enormous pressure from the United States to make a separate peace with Israel.

On July 31, 1988, seven months into the *inti-*

fada, King Hussein severed Jordan's ties to the West Bank. He had decided it was the right moment for Palestinians to assume responsibility for managing their own affairs. His top aides had made a study of Jordan's relations with the Palestinians and recommended disengagement from the West Bank. "Let them have it," the King said to Abu Shaker, then Commander in Chief of the Jordanian army. "Let them carry the burden." He made it very clear, however, that disengagement with the West Bank did not include relinquishing Hashimite trusteeship of the holy places in Jerusalem. Hussein viewed this responsibility as a personal and spiritual obligation as well as a political necessity, since there was no guarantee that the Israelis would allow the Palestinians sovereignty over those disputed sites.

The Iran-Iraq war finally came to an end in August 1988, and in November Arafat persuaded the Palestine National Council to declare a Palestinian state in the Occupied Territories, with Jerusalem as its capital. Events moved rapidly after that. Now that there was no issue of West Bank representation, the Jordanian Parliament was dissolved and restructured and the country prepared for the first free general elections since 1967.

We were able during these demanding times to enjoy rare, peaceful moments with all the children at Buckhurst Park, an English refuge that had come to us through the generosity of a group of Hussein's close friends. Here we had as much privacy as we ever would. We could lead a nearly normal family life, and the children began to think of it as a second home. Where Al Nadwa was full of offices, Buckhurst was a quiet, cozy place to unwind. We would gather to talk or watch television in the sitting room, and sometimes roast chestnuts in the fireplace, a family ritual I introduced that dated back to my childhood winters in New York City. My husband enjoyed chestnuts, and the children would compete over who could peel them faster for him, leaving them all with slightly burned fingers.

We could walk freely through the streets of nearby Windsor with the children, browse in the bookshops and music shops my husband loved, and have meals at the Waterside Inn and nearby restaurants. My husband loved impromptu softball games on the lawn at Buckhurst, in which everyone from the head of the Royal Squadron and the Chief of Protocol to the children and the gardeners would play.

On June 15, Hussein left a beautiful tenth anniversary letter on my pillow at Buckhurst. "This is a very special time, this is a very special month and a very special year," he wrote. "We are ten years older and ten years old. We will never be ten again, but with God's blessings we shall continue to grow and mature together all the more for many other years to come. Silver, gold, who can predict?

"I thank God for our life of love and the children we are blessed to have. I thank you for so much. I know it is not all I would have wished for you or anything close to that. I know myself, I know my shortcomings, and I also know I am blessed to have you by my side, loving, caring, brave, and pure. All the finest things in life grow more valuable as they grow and mature. I hope the times to come will be better than those that have passed, and I treasure all the happiest of memories of our travel through time. For despite the fact that everything changes from time to time and one drives down to start a hill climb, the balance I feel is in the realm of goodness as together we climb through the years.

"This is a special time, a special month and year. I am ever proud of you as you stand by my side. I pray for God to bless you through the years and give us strength and courage, happiness, contentment, and the comfort of sharing and giving of our best. God bless our family. And many thanks to you for being you. The One God blessed me by bringing us together ten years ago to start through life a loving husband and his beloved wife. With you by my side, I celebrate each day. Happy 10th and with God's blessings, many more to come. With all my love, Hussein."

In England Hussein pursued his vision of

preserving Jordan's aviation heritage, and to that end he collected a number of old aircraft to form a historic flight for the Royal Jordanian air force. Among them was the Dove aircraft in which he had learned to fly, the very plane Syrian MiG fighters had tried to force down in the 1950s, as well as several Hawker Hunters that the Jordanian air force used in the 1967 war. These aircraft were displayed at air shows throughout the United Kingdom, the largest of which was the Royal International Air Tattoo, of which Hussein was a patron.

In England we also enjoyed time together in the helicopter my husband had been given as a present. By regulation, our pilot, Richard Verrall, was not supposed to let Hussein take the controls, but of course he did, and we spent some wonderful impromptu moments in the air. My husband also loved flying his fixed-wing official aircraft, particularly for the more challenging takeoffs and landings. He often flew the official TriStar into Brize Norton, a major RAF transport base, where Richard would meet him in the helicopter and fly him the twenty minutes or so to Buckhurst. Flying into Brize Norton was much easier than coming into Heathrow, which was usually backed up because of all the commercial air traffic, but the RAF had strict regulations. Richard loves to tell the story of one of my husband's arrivals at Brize Norton, preceded by a call to air-traffic control requesting permission to do a fly-past before landing. Permission was duly granted, along with a reminder of the strict requirement that he was not to fly below 400 feet. Richard, who was standing with the station commander when the call came in, knew what was coming. "Being a hooligan, all he wanted to do was to rip down the runway at high speed and very low level," he told me. So he was not in the least surprised when the giant TriStar suddenly appeared just over the hedge, closer to 4 than 400 feet, and went roaring down the runway only to veer up very sharply. My husband then came back around, landed perfectly, and taxied in.

Nothing was said at the time, but two weeks later, as the two men were helicoptering into the base, Richard received a call from the Deputy Station Commander: "Would you bring His Majesty in?" After Hussein landed the helicopter, he was asked politely to step inside the station, where he was presented with a royal scolding and the irrefutable evidence of his transgression: a photograph of the TriStar skimming the runway at the height of the hedge, a photograph of which, Richard says, "he was justly proud, no doubt." I would guess that the RAF understood, and certainly Richard understood, that every so often my husband had to let off some steam.

I had one airborne adventure in England on my own. During a formal black-tie event to benefit St. John's Ophthalmic Hospital in Jerusalem, I was persuaded by our host, Robert Pooley, to try out a hot-air balloon. I clambered clumsily into the basket in my formal evening dress, and off we went, with the ever-present Special Branch officer at my side, soaring over the peaceful English landscape. It was the most extraordinary sensation, listening alternately to the roar of the gas jets heating the air to ascend, and to the utter silence when the jets shut off. My only previous experience with ballooning had been watching the film *Around the World in 80 Days*, and I found actual flight absolutely magical. We put down in a cow pasture next to a small farmhouse and knocked on the door to ask to use the phone to send for a car. That is fairly normal behavior for balloonists; you cannot necessarily turn around and go back to where you came from. But it must have come as a surprise to the residents of that house when two men in tails and the Queen of Jordan in formal evening dress appeared at their door.

That exhilarating episode convinced me that ballooning might provide a unique perspective on Jordan's romantic landscapes. Shortly thereafter I approached Richard Branson, the founder and chairman of Virgin Atlantic Airways and an avid balloonist, with my plan. At our invitation, Richard came out to Jordan with a mammoth Virgin Atlantic balloon and helped us explore the possibility of developing ballooning as an adventure tourism activity. I thought Wadi Rum — described by T. E. Lawrence as "vast and echoing and God-like" — would make a unique setting for ballooning, but when Richard arrived to test the conditions the winds were fickle and erratic.

After having to cancel several trial flights in Wadi Rum, Richard scheduled a liftoff for just after sunrise from Amman Airport and invited the children along. My husband, who was normally a late riser, was skeptical enough about the safety of balloon flight that we awoke at dawn to go with the children, and he returned an enthusiast. Hot-air ballooning eventually did catch on in Jordan, even in Wadi Rum. Some years later, a major international ballooning event was held there to celebrate Hussein's birthday. It was an extraordinary sight to see so many colorful balloons, from so many countries, decorating the azure desert sky.

Jordan was soon to be represented in cinematic splendor, and the circumstances behind that event were pure serendipity. In June 1988 my husband spirited me away for a stolen weekend in Scotland, back to Gleneagles for the first time since our honeymoon. Our romantic return coincided with a charity celebrity shoot hosted by our friend Jackie Stewart, the legendary Formula 1 racecar driver. It was there that we first met Steven Spielberg and Harrison Ford, who were filming *Indiana Jones and the Last Crusade* at Pinewood Studios outside of London. Harrison and his wife, Melissa Mathison, were already down-the-road neighbors in Wyoming, where my sister and I had a cabin, but I had not met Steven before. When he told me he was hoping to film part of the movie in Petra, I offered as much help as they needed to simplify any dealings with the bureaucracy or to facilitate arrangements.

For a number of years I had been trying to persuade Arnold Schwarzenegger, who was married to a dear friend, Maria Shriver, and other actors and directors to consider Jordan as a film location. Not only would it be a source of revenue for the country, but it would also provide invaluable exposure and good public relations. There could be no better promotion for Jordan than a George Lucas–Steven Spielberg film shot in Petra.

The day I took Ali, Hamzah, Hashim, and Iman to Petra to see the *Indiana Jones* filming they were starstruck by Harrison Ford and Sean Connery, and I was every bit as thrilled that the directors were very impressed and surprised by Jordan and thought it one of the best locations they had ever worked in.

My interest in the project generated an absurd story in a British tabloid — a detailed story about how I had had a torrid affair with Sean Connery during the filming in Petra, and how my husband had been so enraged that he had sent the Royal Guards to bring me back to the palace, but that I had refused. It was so outlandish that I laughed out loud. My husband, however, was not amused. He, who had always told me before to ignore it when my character was being slandered in the tabloids, promptly said, "Let's get hold of a libel lawyer. I think we should respond to this one." I agreed, knowing that in the Arab world, lies and character assassination are just part of the nasty cycle of gossip, but sexual innuendo about a man's wife involves his honor and is considered an altogether different order of magnitude.

That unpleasantness aside, *Indiana Jones* was a great boon to Jordan, and we were encouraged to learn that Steven was already thinking of filming another project in the country. He had been considering an epic film on Alexander the Great for a long time, Steven told me, and perhaps a film on the Crusades; the conversation quickly turned to Wadi Rum and other possible locations in the country. As their filming came to an end I arranged for Steven and his colleagues to helicopter to Aqaba and make a slight detour up to Hussein's favorite Wadi Rum mountaintop so they could see what an ethereal landscape they would have to work with, if and when they decided to make the Alexander the Great film.

Steven and his crew were impressed and I cannot say I was surprised — Wadi Rum was a location that never failed to stir the senses. One year I gave a birthday party for Hussein there, inviting family and a few close friends to share that occasion on a pink boulevard of sandy desert, rimmed by sheer, lavender limestone cliffs and crags. As the guests mingled, the Bedouin tribesmen in the area quite spontaneously started marching toward our encampment in celebration of the King's birthday. The sound grew louder and louder as they emerged from the inky blackness of the desert night and approached our campfire, where my husband and his sons joined them in the traditional dance, *debkah,* and guttural song.

For one of my favorite parties for Hussein, I asked all his friends and family to attend in traditional Arab dress. Some of our friends, long accustomed to Western dress, had to hunt around for something appropriate for the occasion, but it was worth it. It was the most magnificent sight to see the men in robes and headdresses and the women in their flowing, brightly colored, often richly embroidered kaftans.

In keeping with my wishes, we often celebrated my birthday in a more low-key fashion. August was blazing hot in Aqaba, and besides, there always seemed to be a crisis in our part of the world during the summer. In August 1988 I was looking forward to celebrating my thirty-seventh birthday quietly with my husband and our children in Aqaba when the phone rang during lunch. A woman I did not know very well was calling with a question about my birthday party. Birthday party? When I told her that there were no plans for a party, she insisted that there were. She had heard it from several people in Aqaba. "You know how people gossip around here," I told her. When I returned to the table, sputtering about gossips, I missed the guarded looks on the faces of my husband and several of my stepchildren.

That evening Hussein asked if I would like to cruise down the coast with him in his boat, just the two of us. I readily accepted his invitation, and off we went, down the Red Sea toward the Saudi border. Then, without explanation, we veered off course, heading due west toward the Egyptian coast and picturesque Pharoan Island, site of an ancient castle. Set off the coastline in a beautiful bay with stretches of golden beaches, the island is just beyond the northernmost point of the occupied Sinai, which had been returned to Egypt after Camp David. It was a gorgeous spot, and we had been going there ever since that territory had been returned.

As we approached it in the darkness, suddenly the island burst into light and I could see our children and dozens of family members and friends all standing there, waving at us. I was speechless. Somehow in the midst of all the political crises of the summer, Hussein had managed to pull off the most extraordinary birthday surprise. I could not believe so many of our friends had slipped into Aqaba and made their way to the island — and I did not have a clue.

What an enchanting evening. With the permission of the local Egyptians, my husband had organized an extraordinary buffet dinner and entertainment on a rocky promontory at the base of the fortress, which had loomed majestically since the time of Salahadin, one of the far-flung outposts of his empire. I felt blessed to be surrounded by so many people I loved, and I savored that memory for many years to come.

chapter fourteen

Growing Pains

Hussein and I were on a state visit to Washington, D.C., after the inauguration of President Bush in April 1989 when riots and demonstrations against the government broke out in Jordan. We were shocked by reports we were receiving from Amman and by news images of the turmoil in the southern towns of Ma'an, Tafila, and Kerak. Over the course of the next four days, the violence would even spread to the northern city of Salt.

The rioters' actions were extreme, but the people's discontent was understandable. Several years earlier, the government had adopted measures to fix the ailing Jordanian economy, but by early 1989 the situation had worsened. The country was forced to turn for emergency help to the International Monetary Fund (IMF), which had insisted on draconian austerity measures. The day before we left for scheduled meetings in Washington, King Hussein had learned that the government was planning to raise fuel prices in the coming days to meet the demands of the IMF and that the Prime Minister had failed to inform him that the Central Bank's reserves had dwindled to almost nothing. Jordanians were already suffering from the devaluation of the Jordanian dinar, a high unemployment rate, a drop in the standard of living, and a cut in government services. A sudden government decision to raise the price of fuel and other basic commodities — such as cigarettes, telephone services, electricity, and irrigation water — would be the last straw.

I had begged my husband to appear on television before we left, to explain to the Jordanian people the reason for the price increases: "Explain the hikes so that people understand why belt-tightening measures are necessary. They need to know that you appreciate the extra hardship these measures will impose, and that you will explore every possible way to lessen the burden."

The King, however, was advised against addressing the nation, and there is no way of knowing whether doing so would have made the difference. Instead, we left for our first official visit to the United States in three years. Within forty-eight hours, demonstrations erupted in different parts of the country.

We were kept abreast of every development at home while Hussein carried on with his agenda to request political and military aid from the U.S. Congress, albeit with a heavy heart. George Bush was an old friend and very sympathetic to our position. Congress was less understanding: The King had always been regarded as a leader who could provide stability, and now Jordanians looked like they were joining the *intifada* in the Occupied Territories, throwing stones and burning banks and government buildings. After Hussein's last engagement, we returned directly to Amman.

The riots were quickly contained. What troubled me the most was the willful destruction of health clinics. I understood how some government buildings might become targets of a mob's wrath, but to purposefully destroy buildings essential to humanitarian services seemed so terribly self-defeating. I knew, as did many people around me, that the rise in prices and the resulting riots were indicative of a far larger national crisis in the country. Through my own work I had seen mounting anger and frustration among our people over what they viewed as a lack of responsiveness to their economic hardships. Criticism of the government's autocratic policies, especially restrictions of freedom of expression, had boiled over. There were also charges of widespread corruption. My husband had been only partly apprised of the full extent of the malaise, and now he was criticized for being out of touch. In a sense this was true. His focus on the search for peace and on mobilizing international support for his impoverished nation had consumed most of his time and energy, and he had not been actively monitoring the government, which was responsible for the day-to-day running of the country.

The King acted very quickly in the wake of the disturbances. Within a day of our return to Jordan he accepted the resignation of the Prime Minister and his government and appointed a new, interim government headed by Hussein's trusted and progressive cousin, Sharif Zeid Bin Shaker. Together they forged a blueprint for democratic reforms. Hussein accelerated preparations for the first general parliamentary elections to be held in twenty-two years, and the new Prime Minister lifted martial law and began a process that would ease restrictions on the press. The King announced these changes in a forceful and emphatic speech to the nation.

While we were still in Washington, one opposition group had spread several outrageous rumors accusing me of spending obscene amounts of money on designer clothes and expensive jewelry. That snowballed from my alleged purchase of a ring for $5,000 to buying that same ring for $1 million, then ballooned from a ring to a brooch to a necklace to a whole suite of jewelry for $20 million! Whoever was responsible for the rumor even circulated a supposed photocopy of the check I had written to the jeweler. This, of course, legitimized the gossip because people could say, "We saw the check," although no one was ever able to produce a copy.

I was very upset. For years I had been advocating basic democratic reforms, demands that were at the heart of the unrest, and yet now I was serving as a lightning rod for anger toward the government. I had seen the same pattern played out in other countries and knew that this particular slander was political rather than personal. But, at the same time, I was not used to being targeted politically in such an unstable situation. One wild charge followed another, including the ludicrous report in a U.S. newspaper that my husband had sired an illegitimate child, a dwarf, whom he kept hidden away in America. My husband dismissed all the stories as just one more smear campaign against him.

Nonetheless, I remember vividly going down to Aqaba for the weekend with some of the children at the height of the rumors and feeling truly uncomfortable driving through town to our home, too timid to smile at anyone. What are they thinking? I wondered. Has everyone heard the story of the check, and do they believe it? Could the slander have damaged my relationship with the people, who had inspired and motivated me all these years?

My stomach was churning with anxiety when I summoned the courage to find out a few days later. I had no idea what to expect on my first visit to one of our villages as the riots abated. I drove myself in my Jeep, as I always did. Hundreds of people rushed out to the road to greet me, waving and calling my name. When I arrived at the village, it was as if nothing had happened. Looking at the crowd of welcoming faces, I felt that the weight of the world had been lifted from my shoulders. As they always do, the rumors subsided as it became apparent that they had no substance.

Hussein and I tried to modify our official duties as much as possible after the riots, postponing or canceling most of our scheduled official visits abroad. We knew that during such difficult times Jordanians needed the reassuring physical presence of their leader.

While we curtailed our own international travel, it was more important than ever to continue developing bilateral, economic, social, and cultural relations with other countries. We appreciated the decision of Sweden to go ahead with the planned state visit of King Carl Gustav and Queen Silvia despite what we had just been through. Protocol dictated that full ceremonial dress be worn during official visits by royal families, but the Swedish monarchs were scheduled to visit Jordan only months after the riots, and I did not think such a display would be appropriate. I called Silvia, a particularly thoughtful and wise friend, and asked her if she would be comfortable breaking with the more formal Swedish tradition by not wearing a tiara on this occasion. Silvia was very understanding, and we agreed to compromise by wearing simple ornaments in our hair, which satisfied their needs and was more appropriate for us.

Around that time, we also welcomed Sheikha Fatima, the wife of Sheikh Zayed, the ruler of Abu Dhabi. She is another remarkable First Lady, having pioneered adult literacy and equal job opportunity for women in the United Arab Emirates. She and her husband were also deeply committed to protecting the environment, and they contributed generously to Jordanian charities. Abu Dhabi is a very conservative country, however, which posed challenges for Sheikha Fatima's four-day visit, the first ever to Jordan for a Gulf First Lady. Because of their conservative custom of separating men and women, Sheikha Fatima arrived with a heavily veiled, all-woman retinue. The historic visit had to remain "ladies only" — even our household staff had to be all female. Fortunately, we had women members of our police force and army available to provide security for Sheikha Fatima and her retinue during her official program in Jordan.

I traveled to Iraq in the spring of 1989 to visit Saddam Hussein's wife and cousin, Sajida. I had delayed the trip for some time, despite the government's urging that I accept the long-standing invitation, but I finally seized the opportunity just before our official trip to Washington, D.C. It proved to be a fascinating experience.

In ancient times Iraq was the cradle of civilization, a center for intellectual ferment and discovery. In 4000 B.C., under the Sumerians, early calendars were first used and the first written alphabet was invented. In Babylon, some fifty miles south of the capital, King Hammurabi inscribed his famous code of laws on massive stones in the eighteenth century B.C. In the tenth century B.C., Baghdad was a great center of learning that attracted a dynamic mix of scientists, poets, philosophers, and intellectuals. Some four centuries later, the great King Nebuchadnezzar II built the Hanging Gardens of Babylon. This rich heritage remained a significant part of Iraqi culture, but there was a new political overlay in the country's contemporary art that I found deeply disturbing. When I was taken to the National Art Gallery, most of the art I saw was dedicated to the glory of Saddam Hussein. Perhaps it was the result of the Iran-Iraq war, which no doubt put a damper on creative expression, but the art reminded me of German World War II propaganda.

It was a visit to a kindergarten in Baghdad, however, that affected me most. The extent to which those very young children were being taught to idolize their leader was deeply unsettling. In Jordan the King certainly inspired a personality cult of sorts — a phenomenon not unique to our region — but what I saw in Iraq was extreme. Rather than promoting a sense of national identity, the state was indoctrinating children to view their country through the persona of a single, all-powerful leader.

The Iraqi people's reaction to my visit also surprised me. I was taken to the center of Baghdad to visit a monument erected to martyrs lost in war, where I was welcomed effusively by the mayor, and by all the people with whom I came in contact. The warmth and excitement in the crowds that spontaneously collected around me in different parts of the city amazed me as well. I knew it was not simply my presence that elicited this emotional response, but the affection the Iraqi people felt for King Hussein; still, I was deeply moved by the outpouring of emotion.

When I returned to Jordan after the three-day visit, I told my husband about the extreme cult of personality I had witnessed. For the Iraqi people to have no other choice but to focus all their hopes and dreams on a single person seemed to me to represent an unsustainable future for the country. Saddam Hussein would not always be Iraq's leader, and it was important that generations of young people developed loyalty to the country or its institutions, not simply to one individual.

Summer came and school let out. I had taken to sending the children to stay with my sister in Jackson Hole, Wyoming, for at least part of their summer holidays to get them out of the "royal cocoon," as I often described it. I wanted them to experience the real world and look

434

after themselves without security personnel, household staff, and retainers of any sort. I kept hoping that we would all be able to get away together as a family, but sadly a summer vacation together usually eluded us. When the children returned in August for a quiet birthday dinner for me on the beach in Aqaba, they were full of news about their summer holiday, especially Iman, who had succeeded in becoming the youngest rock climber ever in that region of Wyoming. She had also become a super fisherwoman, to the boys' initial dismay. Hamzah and Hashim loved to fish, and apparently they had not expected Iman to take to it so naturally and so successfully. Once home, however, the boys regaled us with proud stories of her accomplishments.

We were preparing for a historic event on November 8, 1989: the first general elections since 1967. There was a festive air in many of the villages and cities I visited, as young men who had been throwing stones six months earlier hoisted political banners and posters. Candidates for office were running as individuals because, since the destabilizing regional turmoil of the late 1950s, political parties had been banned. The only organized and well-funded political group was the Muslim Brotherhood, which was registered as a charitable society in Jordan.

It was the first time Jordanian women had

been able to exercise their right to vote in a general election since they had been enfranchised in 1974, and on the morning of the election, I was heartened to see so many women at the polls. Quite a few were running for office themselves, though none would win their races. It was the candidates from the Muslim Brotherhood and their allies who would be the biggest winners, gaining enough seats to form roughly one-third of the Parliament.

There was alarm in some quarters at the political success of the Islamists. There were even pronouncements in establishment circles in Amman that King Hussein would dissolve Parliament after the election because neither he nor his ministers would want to deal with opposing views. However, the King was wise enough to appreciate the purpose served by the election of the Islamists. They were now part of the very government they had been challenging. "They have been living on slogans," my husband told me. "Now they are going to have to deliver results." The King also appreciated the positive role the Islamists could play in Jordan. While they emphasized their conservative social agenda, to the dismay of many in urban centers of the country, the Islamists participated in the democratic process and voiced their opinions, part and parcel of the political fabric of the society. Over the years, they have adopted a consistent and usually conservative social posture in Parliament, and they have been allies to the government in many difficult times. Despite the occasional bumps in the road, Jordan's Islamists have been a compelling example of the value of inclusion.

For me, the importance of this day was that Jordan had the self-confidence to risk dissent by opening up debate, not closing it down. By holding democratic elections, free and fair, Jordan was setting yet another example in a region that badly needed participatory decision-making. No one knew at the time where this would lead, but it was the beginning of a process that many of us felt was absolutely vital and necessary. As we drove to the historic opening of the Jordanian Parliament on November 29, my thoughts were focused less on the Islamist presence than they were on the political advances women had made, however slim. "Though the Muslim Brotherhood and others may consider their presence in larger numbers the great significance of the occasion," I noted in my diary, "for me it is Leila's presence as the first woman ever to take a seat in the Parliament's appointed Senate."

King Hussein moved forward determinedly toward a more democratic system of government. He lifted martial law, pledged a freer press, and publicly acknowledged the existence of forces in the society that were not necessarily in agreement with each other or with him. He invited them to debate the state of the country and to put together a new National Charter to reflect all shades of the political spectrum, forming a new basis from which the country could move forward.

In the end, everybody was represented. The National Charter extended the rights of women, defined new policies on the free flow of information, resolved the stance Jordan would take on the Palestinian question, and clarified the relationship between the monarchy and the democratic Parliament. Because Jordanians were so excited about the reactivation and strengthening of the Constitution, almost everybody was willing to compromise. And the compromise came mostly from the socially conservative, who were the single biggest elected bloc in Parliament.

From that time on, my husband's goal was to strengthen the democratic institutions in Jordan and, in so doing, to reduce the natural tendencies in such a traditional society to depend on him as their *Sayidna,* or lord. "I do not want this country to crumble when I am gone," he often said. "Every time there is a problem, the feeling is 'Sayidna can solve it.' Well, Sayidna cannot solve it alone anymore. Everyone has to participate." It would take time, of course, to develop those institutions, especially in a society that was so used to depending on its king, but the historic events of 1989 were a good beginning. "We are on the crest of a new wave of anti-autocratic ideology," I wrote in my journal. "Let us pray we ride it to safety in a new society — dynamic and committed." I had no idea how soon that new society would be put to the test.

chapter fifteen

Prelude to War

Looking back now, as I try to re-create the larger context of the 1990–1991 Persian Gulf crisis, I can find harbingers of trouble as far back as 1977, when I first visited Iraq to gather information on their airline facilities and training requirements for the pan-Arab aviation university project. Saddam Hussein was not yet in power (he would become the country's ruler in 1979), but there was already a palpable climate of fear. It was considered unsafe to discuss anything but the most innocuous subjects. Foreign business representatives or diplomats would feel under tables for listening devices; Iraqis simply assumed they were there.

The Iraqi officials I met with at the airport for my research refused to disclose anything about their commercial aviation operations. The number of regularly scheduled flights was treated like a state secret even though it was a matter of international public record.

Twelve years later, in the spring of 1989, we

observed with concern Saddam Hussein's rhetoric at the February 1989 meeting of the Arab Cooperation Council, formed the year before by Jordan, Egypt, Yemen, and Iraq. Saddam Hussein was increasingly bellicose toward Israel and the United States, stirring confrontational passions when he proclaimed that there was no place in Arab ranks for those who submit to the will of the superpower, America.

The U.S. Congress responded by cutting off wheat sales to Iraq. Much of the Middle East interpreted Saddam Hussein's fiery rhetoric as a bid for regional leadership more than a genuine attack on Israel and Washington. And, increasingly, Palestinians were beginning to feel that Saddam might be the one to finally liberate their homeland, a hope that was becoming desperate in light of the swelling number of settlements in the Occupied Territories.

Soviet Jews started flooding into Israel at the beginning of 1990, having finally been allowed to leave the Soviet Union at the end of the Cold War. The flow of immigrants was staggering — many had applied for visas to the United States, but with a quota system in place there, the vast majority went to Israel — and this influx was of enormous concern to my husband and other Arab leaders. They were arriving at the rate of some 1,400 a week and being settled in the Occupied Territories in violation of the Geneva Conventions. By the summer of 1991, there would be more than

100,000 settlers in the Occupied Territories, plus another 127,000 in East Jerusalem, once again seriously altering the situation on the ground.

Against the backdrop of the deteriorating situation in Israel, King Hussein's frustration grew. There seemed to be nothing he could do to restart the stalled peace process and little he could do to stem Jordan's economic crisis. He traveled to Saudi Arabia in the middle of February to discuss the country's dire economic forecast and his regional political concerns, but King Fahd was not very receptive.

Amid this stalemate came an incident that would heighten tensions for Saddam in the West. Farzad Bazoft, a British journalist from the *Observer* newspaper, was arrested in Iraq, charged with espionage, and sentenced to death. Many in the region speculated that the Iranian-born journalist might very well have been a spy, but the British government insisted on his innocence and called for clemency.

King Hussein telephoned the Iraqi President several times to try to talk him out of executing the journalist, warning that it would be playing right into the hands of those who were looking for an excuse to attack him. Saddam, however, was not about to give in to demands from the West. On March 15, 1990, we received word that the journalist had been hanged. The British outcry against Saddam Hussein was long and sustained. Members of Parliament officially expressed their "total revulsion" at Iraq's "unspeakable brutality" and called the execution an act of "calculated violence by a blood-stained dictatorship." Margaret Thatcher, Britain's Prime Minister, was particularly incensed at Saddam Hussein for denying her personal appeal for the journalist's life, and she became increasingly wary of the Iraqi leader.

On March 22, in the midst of the growing turmoil in the region, the U.S. Senate inexplicably passed a resolution that Jerusalem must remain an undivided city. Though the resolution did not go so far as to recognize Jerusalem as the capital of Israel, it was taken as such on Arab streets — and as yet another provocative move by the United States, in this case to undermine Muslim claims on the holy city. Under international law, Arab East Jerusalem, having been taken by force, was — and is — an occupied city within the Occupied Territories and subject to UN Security Council Resolution 242's call for the withdrawal of occupying forces.

The Senate resolution was strongly denounced a week later at a meeting of the Arab nations, inflaming the growing anti-Americanism on the streets. My husband was discouraged by the apparent lack of interest on the part of the United States in seeking a solution. "Nothing seems to change," he told me. "The openings are not there."

Hussein felt somewhat better when he made

the *Umrah* pilgrimage to Mecca and a visit to Medina in April. As was the custom, many male family members accompanied my husband, including his sons, Princes Feisal and Hamzah, and his nephew, Prince Talal, who kept Hamzah close by them to keep him from being trampled. Hamzah was ten at the time and so small he had to have his white, seamless pilgrimage robes made especially for him. "Hamzah looked like a little angel," Talal told me. Hamzah's first *Umrah* turned out to be quite an adventure for him. The men prayed at Prophet Muhammad's Tomb in Medina, and then at the tomb of Hamzah's namesake. At dinner with King Fahd, Hamzah was evidently enjoying himself enormously, chatting away with the two elderly Saudi princes he was seated between and holding his own with King Fahd himself. "Bring him back and we'll find him a Saudi bride," King Fahd told my husband. Hamzah understood the King's proposal to mean he might have to marry right away, which put a brief damper on his otherwise exciting trip with his father.

Malaise was spreading over the region, and particularly in Jordan. Without some catalyst of significant proportion, I feared we were deteriorating into a cycle of violence that would perpetuate the instability that had affected the region for generations. I was also painfully aware of the pattern, observed by political analysts, that the Middle East suffered a major explosion every decade or so, and in the eleven years I had been married to my husband, there had been no war.

There were certainly violent flare-ups. In May 1990, a lone Israeli gunman suddenly opened fire on Palestinian laborers south of Tel Aviv, killing seven and wounding nine others. I was in the United States on an official visit at the time, speaking at the Eastern Virginia Medical School, which supported our Jordanian IVF program, and meeting informally in Washington, D.C., with various U.S. senators. Protest demonstrations in Jordan over the killings became so intense that I phoned my husband and asked if I should come home, but he insisted that I carry on with the visit. The unrest subsided a few days later, but one never knew which tinderbox might be the one to ignite the entire region. On my way home I stopped in Kuwait for another official visit, not knowing then that this country would indeed provide that spark in just two months time. My visit was uneventful. "The Kuwaiti National Museum is magnificent, especially its Al Sabah collection of priceless Islamic artifacts," I noted in my journal. That same museum would soon be looted by the Iraqis and gutted by fire.

I returned home to find that my husband had been up to mischief while I was away: He had impulsively bought us a new house to live in. One day he had been driving by a villa when someone told him it was for sale, so he snapped it up as a twelfth wedding anniversary gift. The house was close to Hashimya's guard barracks, so I think he felt this would meet one of our logistical requirements. What it did not solve were our personal needs. There was not sufficient room for our seven children or space for the offices and meeting rooms we both needed. "When and if we begin to work like everyone else," I told him, "then we can live like everyone else." I was moved by his thoughtfulness and his yearning to simplify our lives, but the timing was all wrong. With all the crises in the region, we hardly needed a major upheaval at home as well. So we did not move. We would later have the villa renovated for his eldest son, Prince Abdullah, and his wife, Princess Rania, to live in after they married.

As the summer began, my husband paid a routine visit to Baghdad to see Saddam Hussein, who was becoming a very popular figure among Jordanians of Palestinian descent for his financial and political support of the *intifada* and for his unyielding opposition to Israel. There was also some support in Jordan for Saddam Hussein's complaints about Kuwait's overproduction of oil in contravention of OPEC's agreements, a breach that was driving down the price of oil and crippling Iraq's ability to recover financially from the cost of the Iran-Iraq war. His charge that the Kuwaitis were drilling laterally into the Rumaila oil field on the Iraq-Kuwait border, a border that was itself in dispute, also reached a sympathetic audience. Nobody thought, however, that these frictions would lead to war.

In the midst of the growing tension in the region, Ted Turner came to Jordan for a visit. He was, as ever, full of the nonstop energy and limitless imagination that had given birth to CNN. He was spinning all sorts of ideas on this visit, not the least of which took shape on our fishing boat as we cruised down the Gulf of Aqaba. Looking at the undeveloped coastline of Egypt, he suddenly decided it should be the new Palestinian homeland. "Look at all this coastal real estate, " he said excitedly. "Do you know how valuable coastal real estate is? Just bring all the Palestinians down here. This incredibly valuable property would compensate them for leaving Palestine." What Turner did not account for was that relocation was not what the Palestinians wanted; they wanted the right to reclaim their own land from which they had been forcibly displaced. Israel had often suggested that the Palestinians be moved and absorbed by Arab countries. However naïve his suggested solutions were, it was fun to see Turner's mind at work. He did not even try to justify the ideas that came bubbling forth, pointing out that one out of a thousand had led to the creation of CNN. The reality of the unresolved struggle in the Occupied Territories, however, remained the same.

In summer of 1990, some Islamist groups in

Jordan, taking advantage of the unrest permeating the country, made the Jerash Festival their target. They brought incredible pressure on the government to close down the Festival on the grounds that the entertainment was un-Islamic. *The Wall Street Journal* compared Jerash to the Shiraz Festival in Iran that had so inflamed conservative religious sensibilities more than a decade earlier. There was, however, no comparison, and we were not about to give in to extremist bullying, however sinister in this agitated political climate. "Threats made, explosives found," I noted in my journal. "But the Prime Minister has stood his ground."

By July 17, 1990, Saddam Hussein had intensified his rhetoric against Kuwait and in a public speech said, "We have to stand up to those who have come with a poisoned dagger and thrust it in our backs." Seeking to defuse the tension, King Hussein visited the Iraqi leader and then continued on to Kuwait. In his meeting with Sheikh Sa'ad, the Crown Prince, my husband did not water down Saddam Hussein's anger at the Kuwaitis, but at the same time he told Sheikh Sa'ad he did not see any Iraqi military threat to Kuwait. Saddam Hussein had often assured my husband that any differences Iraq had with other Arab countries would be solved in a "brotherly" manner, and he had given King Fahd of Saudi Arabia and Egyptian President Hosni Mubarak the same assurance. It was not until Sheikh Sa'ad told King Hussein that Iraq had massed troops on Kuwait's border that the King began to question Saddam's intentions.

My husband returned home very, very concerned and called President Bush and the British ambassador to warn them that there was a major crisis brewing between Iraq and Kuwait. "Listen," he told them emphatically, "you must encourage the Kuwaitis to sit down with the Iraqis and the Saudis to resolve the border problems, and the oil overproduction, and any other problems that require negotiation." He knew that the issues at hand were not just fabrications by Iraq, but legitimate problems that required political resolution. Inexplicably, neither the American President nor the British ambassador seemed particularly interested. The United States may even have gone so far as to assure Saddam Hussein through its ambassador, April Glaspie, that the United States would *not* interfere if Iraq moved against Kuwait, a charge she later denied. If that assurance was given, it was a critical mistake.

On July 31 my husband told me he was hopeful that a "crucial" meeting between Iraq and Kuwait that was being held in Jeddah, Saudi Arabia, the next day would bear fruit, but it did not. He came to bed very late that night. "I feel terribly nervous for the first time," he told me. We had been asleep only a few hours when my husband received a call from King Fahd, who told him that Iraqi forces were five miles from the center of Kuwait City.

The invasion coincided with my mother-in-law's birthday, and while my husband flew to Egypt to confer with President Mubarak about the crisis, I attended a family gathering for Queen Zein at Zahran Palace. My mother-in-law and I seemed to be among the few there who were deeply concerned about the disastrous consequences for Jordan and the region. Queen Zein had the wisdom to see that this was a very serious issue. She and I had never had a very intimate relationship, but that day we sat together and talked at length about the dangers we all might be facing. As the Gulf crisis deepened and the pressure increased on Jordan, Queen Zein urged me to take an active role in defending Jordan's position, especially in the United States. It would be the one time she strongly encouraged me to assume such an untraditional role. Neither of us could have had any idea how intense the pressure would become.

When Hussein returned to Amman from Alexandria that evening, he told me he had received a pledge from Hosni Mubarak to ensure that the Arab League would not condemn or otherwise confront the Iraqi President until my husband had visited Baghdad to urge Saddam Hussein to withdraw his troops from Kuwait. Mubarak knew that of all the Arab leaders my husband understood his neighbor the best. Time was of the essence. The Arab League was meeting in Cairo, and the foreign ministers gathered there were being pressed by the Kuwaitis and the Saudis, as well as by the Bush administration and Margaret Thatcher, to condemn Iraq. The King knew, however, that Saddam Hussein would not listen to reason if he felt backed into a corner. "Give me forty-eight hours," my husband said to George Bush, Mubarak, and King Fahd. Mubarak not only agreed, but he also said to our Foreign Minister: "Take my plane now and go to Cairo for the Arab League meeting so you are available."

King Hussein's meeting with Saddam Hussein the next morning, August 3, was a success. Saddam Hussein was quite pleased with the intense reaction from the Western powers, my husband told me later, and was already planning to withdraw his forces from Kuwait. As proof, he would immediately withdraw one of his brigades, a symbolic gesture confirmed by the Iraqi news service. "If there are no threats against Iraq or Kuwait, Iraqi forces will start to withdraw tomorrow," the statement read. "A plan to withdraw from Kuwait has already been approved."

My husband called Mubarak to tell him the good news, but to his complete surprise, he discovered that the Jordanian Foreign Minister had arrived at the meeting of the Arab League only to find that the Egyptian Foreign Minister was, in fact, already leading the movement to get the League to condemn Iraq. This under-cutting of King Hussein's mission to achieve an Iraqi commitment on withdrawal would bring Western troops into the region and sow the seeds of radical Islamist terrorist attacks on the United States more than a decade later.

All sorts of explanations would be offered as to why the King's breakthrough with Saddam Hussein was preempted first by Egypt, then by various Arab leaders who, with full knowledge of my husband's successful meeting with the Iraqi leader, nonetheless instructed their Foreign Ministers in Cairo to condemn Iraq. Mubarak may have simply acceded to U.S. pressure; Kuwait suspected King Hussein of having prior knowledge of Iraq's military intentions and concealing them; Saudi Arabia, after being informed by the United States that Iraqi troops were massing on the Kingdom's border, suspected my husband of plotting to merge forces with Iraq's to regain the Hejaz; distrust was rampant.

Within days the Egyptian press would turn against my husband and cast him as the devil, which was incomprehensible to me: It was the Egyptians, after all, who had made a commitment to my husband not to condemn Iraq before his efforts to mediate had been exhausted — and had then ignored it. Although my husband was all too familiar with such broken promises, this one hurt him deeply. "There is no honor in being an Arab head of state," he told me.

In the end, most Arab countries took a hard line against Iraq at the meeting of the Arab League, while Jordan, Yemen, and the PLO tried to keep the door open to negotiation with Saddam Hussein. My husband, who had clearly opposed the Iraqi occupation of Kuwait and called for the withdrawal of Iraqi troops, was stunned when his initial efforts to negotiate a peaceful solution were misconstrued by the United States and Britain as approval of Saddam's occupation of Kuwait. This distortion would be used viciously against King Hussein for years to come.

The consensus in Jordan was that the other Arab countries welcomed a confrontation with Iraq, but they wanted the Americans to fight the war for them. Iraq had always been a sort of Prussia of the Middle East, with its well-organized army led by well-trained, educated officers. That left smaller Arab countries worried about the Iraqi army and about Saddam Hussein himself. As a maverick, he was an unpredictable element in the regional equation. The apprehensiveness of his neighbors was shared by the United States and Britain. The Western powers did not look favorably on Iraq's military strength, though ironically the British, nearly a half-century earlier, had originally trained the Iraqi army.

Interestingly, it was Margaret Thatcher who apparently emboldened George Bush to take military action. At first, the United States was focused on defending Saudi Arabia from Iraq, though none of us in the Middle East believed that Iraq had any designs on the Saudi kingdom. Margaret Thatcher thought differently. She was at a conference in Aspen, Colorado, on August 2, the day of the Iraqi invasion, and when George Bush arrived there the next day she told him in no uncertain terms that if Western forces did not stop Saddam Hussein he would roll his tanks not only into Saudi Arabia, but also into Bahrain and Dubai, and end up controlling 65 percent of the world's oil reserves.

King Hussein called George Bush in Aspen to urge him to support an Arab solution, with no foreign intervention. My husband thought he could still persuade Saddam Hussein to withdraw peacefully from Kuwait and, failing that, motivate him with Arab military force. There was a precedent. In 1962 the Jordanian army, as part of an Arab League force, had protected Kuwait from Iraq when Kuwait, a former province of Iraq, had declared independence and Iraq had not accepted it.

Within a day or so of Iraq's invasion, the Americans and the British were already moving troops into the region, and many more American troops were massing en route. When Defense Secretary Dick Cheney toured the region five days after the invasion, he went to Saudi Arabia and Egypt and bypassed Jordan altogether. This was remarkable in light of the fact that my husband was the last Arab leader to have been in touch with Saddam Hussein, and therefore the one person who might be able to put together a diplomatic approach for dealing with the situation. But the Americans cut him out from the start. A Saudi envoy arrived in Amman soon after the invasion and dismissed as insignificant several satellite images the Americans had produced of Iraqi troops massed on Saudi Arabia's border. The Saudis were not worried about the Iraqis, the envoy told my husband.

U.S. aid to Jordan was cut off. The Arab countries joining the military coalition cut off their aid as well, though it had already diminished considerably due to the regional recession. King Hussein was so anguished that on August 8, six days after the invasion, he talked to me again about abdication. Given the extent to which he was being personally targeted, he felt that Jordan might suffer less if he handed over his responsibilities to a successor. Were it not for the phone calls day and night from many Jordanians telling him the entire country was behind him, my husband might very well have stepped down. I added my voice of support as well. There would be no value in abdicating during this crisis, I told him. Jordanians needed him now more than ever, as did others around the world who depended on his moderation to counterbalance the war fever that was sweeping the region.

I urged my husband to travel to the United States and explain his position to George Bush face-to-face. Our nephew, Prince Talal, was part of the small entourage that accompanied him to Kennebunkport, Maine, and described their reception there by Bush aides as "quite a raw experience." Bush himself was very courteous and understood far better than most the difficult position my husband was in. Nonetheless, he more or less dismissed my husband's negotiations with Saddam Hussein for a peaceful withdrawal. "I will not allow this little dictator to control 25 percent of the civilized world's oil," President Bush told my husband, a remark Sharif Zeid Bin Shaker would remember because of his use of the words "civilized world," "as if there were no civilization except that of the West," Abu Shaker had muttered. The King was quite discouraged when he left the United States and went on to Europe to meet with heads of state there. He was even more discouraged after his meeting in London with Margaret Thatcher, whom he described as bitter and inflexible.

The economic impact on Jordan of the Iraqi invasion was immediate and devastating. Within a week, the United Nations imposed a ban on trade with Iraq, Jordan's biggest trading partner, putting Iraq off-limits to us. Orders were canceled. Tourism to Jordan and the region came to a standstill. In Aqaba, container ships with goods being transported from Jordan to Iraq were turned away.

At the Noor Al Hussein Foundation, we began brainstorming about how to prepare families and communities to cope with the economic and social stress. At particular risk, for example, were the women and their families who benefited from projects like Bani Hamida. The tourist market for their products was dead, although Rebecca Salti devised an ingenious plan to find customers for these handicrafts. Some 800 journalists had flooded into Amman after the invasion, and Rebecca and her co-workers set up exhibits of Bani Hamida rugs at several hotels, visiting them every night at 11:00 to sell rugs to the journalists. As each wave of journalists left with rugs in their suitcases, a new group and potential new market would arrive.

The biggest stress by far of the Gulf crisis came with the mushrooming number of refugees arriving at our borders: Egyptian workers fleeing Iraq and Kuwait, Moroccans, Filipinos, Bangladeshis, Pakistanis, Nepalese, Afghans, Somalis, Thais, and Sri Lankans who had been working as domestics in Kuwait, as well as many Asians. We had no tents or blankets for them at first, and the ground was very rough, but every night 10,000 more evacuees would arrive. By the end of the conflict, an estimated

3 million people had crossed into Jordan, whose own population was fewer than 3.5 million.

During this period, I spent virtually every waking hour meeting with our Interior Ministry and the police, as well as the local and international NGOs that were providing assistance for the evacuees. Some organizations were helping out in the border camps; others were setting up shelters inside Amman. Our family was very much involved as well. My brother-in-law, Crown Prince Hassan, was patron of the Hashimite Relief Organization, which set up an enormous camp inside a fairground in the city. My sister-in-law, Princess Basma, was involved in helping in another camp. Various European NGOs, like Médecins Sans Frontières and the International Committee for the Red Cross, were supporting our efforts to control disease and deal with sanitation and other basic necessities, such as food and water.

We urgently needed humanitarian aid to help with the human flood crossing our borders, but it was slow in coming. The International Organization for Migration took some time to organize transport to return evacuees to their own countries. Something had to be done, and quickly, before the onset of winter. I was reviewing information coming in from the camps one evening when a possible solution came to me — Richard Branson, as chairman of Virgin Atlantic Airways, might be able to provide aircraft to transport evacuees. We also needed blankets and tents immediately for the hundreds of thousands of refugees camped on our borders. Richard was very responsive when I reached him in England the next day, and he promised to do what he could to help.

The refugee crisis had arisen so quickly that there was no time for any comprehensive planning. On September 4, I went out to the border area with Iraq to help plan the new Red Crescent camps, only to discover that in the rush to set up shelters, the site had not been properly studied for its potential environmental impact. When we realized it would adversely affect sources of water vital to our two largest cities, the camp had to be relocated.

That same day, Richard Branson arrived with a planeload of relief supplies and the very welcome promise of continued support. He did not arrive alone. British journalists were aboard the plane to cover the story of the thousands of people who had suddenly lost homes, livelihoods, and belongings.

On that day as well, my husband returned from his long tour of Western leaders and flew right on to Baghdad to try once again to convince Saddam Hussein to withdraw from Kuwait. It was his second of three trips to Baghdad to avoid war in the region. The message my husband brought to Saddam Hussein on this trip was his firm conviction that the Western leaders and their allies were not going to allow Saddam to stay in Kuwait. "Make a brave decision and withdraw your forces," my husband told Saddam Hussein. "If you don't, you will be forced out." But the Iraqi leader was unmoved.

My husband did persuade Saddam Hussein to release some of the hundreds of European hostages he was holding in Baghdad as insurance against an allied attack. Richard Branson wrote Saddam Hussein a letter of request, which my husband translated into Arabic and sent by courier to Baghdad, a request that Saddam Hussein duly honored. Some two hundred British subjects had already been flown out by Iraqi Airways, and another sixty or so would be flown out of Baghdad by Richard during his stay with us. Virgin Atlantic Airways provided the only Western plane allowed to fly into Iraq, an experience Richard described as "eerie" but successful.

Richard Branson continued to fly in supplies for the refugees, as did many other organizations and governments, but we remained overwhelmed. Jordanians extended themselves enormously to help the evacuees, providing shelter, donating blankets, food, and whatever they could. Even the poorest people in the country were giving more than they could afford. It was an extraordinary moment of grace for the people of Jordan. Everybody was involved, giving everything they had and more. There could have been no better demonstration of traditional Arab and Muslim hospitality and humanitarian spirit.

Bernard Kouchner, the French Minister of Health and Humanitarian Action, arrived in Amman to assess the situation. "You need to take the media out to the camps with you to focus attention on this humanitarian crisis," he told me in my office. "You have to use yourself to attract international attention." He urged me so emphatically that, with some degree of self-consciousness, I invited the press to accompany me to the camps. It did help to mobilize the support we so desperately needed. These efforts complemented the very effective media advocacy of the King and Crown Prince Hassan throughout the crisis.

The international community took note and it soon provided supplies and planes to transport the refugees home to their respective countries of origin. When the government of the Philippines ran out of planes to ferry out its evacuees, King Hussein provided eighteen TriStar jets from Royal Jordanian Airlines to help get them home. But the Somali evacuees preferred our desert camps to returning home. I shall never forget sitting with Somali families in their tents, listening to their accounts of the desperate conditions in their homeland. At that time they had nowhere better to go.

The slander directed against my husband continued relentlessly during this time. One day in mid-September we watched in disbelief as Senator Frank Lautenberg was interviewed about the Gulf crisis on CNN. Lautenberg quoted President Mubarak of Egypt as saying that my husband had taken bribes, that he knew about Iraq's invasion of Kuwait ahead of time, and that he had supported — even been part of — the invasion of Kuwait. We decided Senator Lautenberg must have misunderstood or misinterpreted what Mubarak had said, or that the Senator's comments had been taken out of context, but we were mistaken. The King went to Morocco a few days later, on September 20, and learned from the Algerian President and King Hassan of Morocco that President Mubarak was also spreading these stories to the other Arab heads of state.

Hussein responded to this latest round of attacks by writing a letter of correction to CNN, which was duly broadcast, but the damage was already done. Two days after my husband returned from Morocco, the Saudis turned off our oil and expelled our diplomats. I was on my way to the United States for the UN's World Summit for Children and to address the Brookings Institution in Washington, D.C. Our children saw me off at the airport and presented me with a stuffed lion, a symbol not only of my astrological sign, Leo, but also of the courage I would have to muster to meet face-to-face with my husband's critics.

It was vitally important that we dispel the

false impression that Jordan had in any way supported Iraq's invasion and occupation of Kuwait, a view that was becoming ingrained in the U.S., U.K., and Gulf Arab psyches. When I arrived at the UN's opening reception for the Children's Summit, the very first person to approach our ambassador and me was the Saudi Foreign Minister, Prince Saud Al Faisal, an old and respected friend, who greeted me warmly and then brought over the Foreign Minister of Kuwait.

As the four of us exchanged greetings, I debated asking Prince Saud if I could meet with him privately to discuss the diplomatic stalemate that was clouding relations between our countries. My inclination, as always, was to put the issues out on the table and wade through them in the hope that something positive could come from candid discussion. Standing there at the reception, and for some time after, I wrestled with whether I should take a direct approach. In the end I decided to play it conservatively. I did not want anything I said to be used against my husband in any way, and I knew that meeting privately with the Saudi Foreign Minister might be misconstrued and stir up a multitude of cultural and gender issues.

It was much more difficult for me at another event when Mrs. Mubarak came up to me acting as if nothing had happened. "How are you? How is everybody?" she said gaily. "How is His Majesty?" I did not know how to respond because the truth was that we were both completely wretched. "He's fine, Suzanne," I replied. "How is the President? How are your children?"

As our encounter went on, I found it increasingly difficult to maintain my façade. To be fair, Suzanne I am certain had only the best intentions, and I certainly was not holding her responsible for what had been happening to Jordan, but finally I had to say something. "Suzanne, I am sorry, but it is extremely difficult for me to converse as if nothing is wrong when the situation in Jordan is so terrible. So many things have been said and done that have been devastating to us." "Oh, you know the Arabs and their rhetoric," she replied offhandedly. "My God!" I thought. "It's *their* rhetoric!"

I could not let the comment pass. "You know, Suzanne, honesty is so terribly important in the relations between our countries. It is absolutely critical, especially at a time like this." She must have taken my words personally, and our conversation ended abruptly.

Later that afternoon, I debated whether I should just sit down with Suzanne and tell her everything that I knew. After all, we were friends, and, politically, Hussein and I had been the Mubaraks' first Arab supporters. We had spent many hours ruminating together over our roles and the hard questions facing our countries. Suzanne had invited me to Egypt for a wonderful trip down the Nile with all four of my children and my sister, and we had welcomed the Mubaraks to our home many times. I thought that perhaps I should try to talk to her to see if we could clarify matters.

I called Suzanne's hotel room, but she was unavailable. When Hussein and I spoke later, he told me he had already received a message from the Egyptians about my encounter with Suzanne. Then he laughed, saying there had been no better way to handle the situation and that the Egyptians were just looking to justify their actions against Jordan.

In this hawkish atmosphere, I felt it was especially important to focus on the impact of war on children. This was, after all, a global summit on children, and I did not hesitate to point out that more often than not children were the front-line victims of any conflict. During the two-day summit I continued to cite the repercussions of war for these most vulnerable members of society as one more reason to support a nonmilitary solution to the Middle East crisis.

George and Barbara Bush were also in attendance. They were particularly cool, which was not surprising politically, but it was surprising in personal terms. They were old friends. When he was still Vice President, George Bush had played with our delighted boys in the pool in Aqaba, and we had seen them on innumerable occasions since. Mrs. Bush did agree to meet for tea in her hotel, where we had a very interesting exchange that naturally centered on the crisis.

Mrs. Bush repeated the horror stories being circulated by the Kuwaiti embassy, particularly one recounted at a press conference by the Kuwaiti ambassador's daughter, who said she had witnessed Iraqis picking newborn babies out of incubators in the hospitals and leaving them on the floor to die. We had all heard those stories, of course, but we had also heard from doctors who had been in the Kuwait City Hospital at the time that these lurid accusations were not true. It came out later that the ambassador's daughter was not in Kuwait and never saw these things, that Kuwait had hired Hill and Knowlton, a public relations firm in New York, to disseminate the incubator story, but when I met with Mrs. Bush, we had only the refutation of the doctors.

"Jordan opposed the occupation of Kuwait from the beginning," I reminded her, "and we called for withdrawal of the Iraqi forces. There is no question about the fact that a great deal of fabrication and distortion is being used to compound an already tragic situation. We believe Jordan's position has been deliberately misrepresented." I did not bring up the Egyptian misinformation specifically; however I did make reference to the fact that the stories were part of an effort to isolate Jordan, and to prevent any success King Hussein might have in defusing the situation with Iraq and preventing the volatile Iraqi President from becoming even more entrenched in his angry isolation.

My husband was being made out to be an enemy of the United States, when he was anything but. Underscoring his refusal to recognize Iraq's occupation and annexation of Kuwait, King Hussein had stood firm when refugees started coming in from the Iraqi border in cars with license plates that read "State of Iraq — Province of Kuwait." Even though it was customary for Iraqi license plates to indicate the home province of the driver, it was clearly illegal for Iraq to have annexed Kuwait. King Hussein acted immediately and ordered those license plates removed at the border. One of the vivid memories we all have of that time is of the many cars driving around Jordan with temporary black license plates. Hussein also made it clear that the Kuwaiti soldiers undergoing military training in Jordan would continue with their courses and that the Kuwaiti embassy would remain open.

I tried to explain the mounting concern in the Arab world about Iraqi civilian losses and desperate conditions. Mrs. Bush was unmoved. She was a political wife, and she was going to believe what she needed to believe. I would continue to speak out after the war started about the humanitarian consequences of the war and the suffering of the people of Iraq, which evidently so angered Mrs. Bush that she sent a message to me through an American official that she considered me a traitor. I imagine that the message was intended to stop me from talking about uncomfortable issues for the Bush administration.

I enjoyed a warmer welcome on Capitol Hill. Senator Lautenberg came to the meeting, as did a number of other senators, some of whom were old friends of my husband or my family, as well as others who were deeply concerned about the Middle East. I was very anxious to talk to Senator Lautenberg, and I took him aside at one point and said: "Sir, could you clarify something for me? My husband and I saw your interview on CNN, and I am assuming that your comments might have been edited out of context where you were talking about President Mubarak's statements regarding my husband. Was there some misunderstanding or some miscommunication?" "No," he said. "What I said President Mubarak told me about your husband was entirely accurate. In fact, there was much more I did not say." Senator Lautenberg then proceeded to detail the slew of outrageous accusations Mubarak had made against my husband. "Are you sure? Are you absolutely certain?" I asked him. Several other senators had come up while we were having this conversation. "Yes," the senators said, "he told us that too."

I was not at all sure what might have motivated the Egyptian President. There was no doubt that the Egyptian leader was facing a great deal of pressure from fundamentalists and others opposed to Egypt's alliance with foreign powers coming in to fight Iraq. Most people in the region viewed the foreign coalition as anti-Arab and anti-Muslim. They also saw the Western powers, particularly the United States, as baldly hypocritical when they immediately enforced the UN's resolutions condemning Iraq's occupation of Kuwait but had yet to move on the equally binding twenty-three-year-old UN resolutions against the Israeli occupation in Palestine. That hypocrisy was also stirring up the Palestinian population in Jordan, especially after Saddam Hussein promised to move against Israel and liberate Palestine. The streets of Amman were filled with placards extolling his virtues.

My husband looked very strained. We were both exhausted. Every night, after the day's full schedule, we would return to our sitting room to catch up on the events of the day. We monitored all the news out of the United States, which kept us up most of the night because of the difference in time zones. We also tracked everything that was going on in Jordan and throughout the region.

While watching the newscasts, we played with two Game Boys the children had given us. We played endless games of Tetris, piling one brick upon another. We became quite good and very competitive. It was a therapeutic way of channeling our nervous energy and, for my husband, a healthy alternative to excessive smoking, and it helped us stay alert for any late-breaking news. Sometimes members of the family would come over and watch us — no doubt in disbelief — as we sat there, locked on the television set and our Game Boys. But the news only worsened as the war of words escalated and coalition forces continued their buildup in our neighbor, Saudi Arabia.

Those attacks became even more vehement after the King delivered what proved to be a very controversial address at the opening session of Jordan's Parliament on November 17. The government wrote the speech, just as the government in England writes the "speech from the throne" that the Queen reads on the opening of Parliament there. But Hussein was not at all happy with its harsh tone. He asked me what I thought of it during a weekend down in Aqaba. I had been a sounding board for his international speeches since the early days of our marriage, but this was the first time we had deliberated over a speech to the people of Jordan together. "Our people expect your speeches to express your own perspective, and at this critical moment if you are not comfortable with the tone or the message you must change it to reflect your thinking," I told him. There were so many forces he was trying to balance in the country that Hussein gave the speech without much modification, but with instant ramifications.

The King had been trying for some time to speak with George Bush by telephone without success. He had tried again just before the speech and had managed to schedule a meeting with President Bush in Paris. The day after his speech, however, he was told that Brent Scowcroft, Bush's National Security Adviser, wanted to speak to him. Hussein waited four hours for Scowcroft to call, only to have the National Security Adviser tell him that the Paris meeting was canceled because President Bush was upset by the speech. Hussein started to explain, but he was tired of being rebuffed. "Just forget it," he told Scowcroft, and hung up. The abyss widened on November 29, when the UN Security Council passed Resolution 678 authorizing use of force against Iraq unless the country withdrew its forces from Kuwait by January 15.

In England as well we were no longer certain what to expect. My husband had had a long-standing relationship with the British royal family, for example, and at our urging, Prince Andrew and the Duchess of York were staying at Castlewood while they built their own home, but they suddenly vacated the house, apparently under pressure, with no explanation or word to us. It was reminiscent of the British royal family's cold shoulder during the 1967 war, my husband said. In fact, the Prince of Wales was the only member of the royal family who maintained normal relations with us during this period. Prince Charles was remarkably sensitive and insightful about the challenges facing the region, and personally supportive of the King's position. He never said anything that was inappropriate from the British government's standpoint, but, personally, I will never forget the gestures of friendship he made at the time, seeking out opportunities to meet with us and expressing genuine concern for the welfare of the Jordanian and Arab people.

The often-ridiculous news items about my husband and me that continued to run in the world press might also have made it difficult for some to reach out to us. According to one report that made the family laugh uproariously, my husband had bought a fleet of fishing boats and jet skis so that we could make a fast getaway from Aqaba, though where we would go — and exactly why — was not explained. Less amusing was the story in a British tabloid that Saddam Hussein had given my husband a $12 million antique car previously owned by Hitler to persuade the King to side with Iraq. The stories were all rubbish, of course, including speculation about the significance of my husband's new beard, which some interpreted as a sign of his alliance either with the fundamentalists or with Saddam Hussein, when the truth was that my husband had a stress-induced skin condition, which was irritated by shaving.

My husband made one last trip to Iraq to try

yet again to persuade Saddam Hussein to withdraw his troops from Kuwait. "If you do not make the decision on your own to get out of Kuwait, you are going to be driven out," my husband told him. "The whole world is against you." Saddam nodded. "Yes, the whole world is against me, but God is with me and I will be victorious." The King sat quietly, then said, "I can see that you are not willing to change your position, but if you do, all it will take is one phone call and I will come back to help you." There was no phone call.

With time running out on the UN deadline, Hussein and I went to Europe in early January 1991 in a last-ditch effort to mobilize support for avoiding a war. From the beginning of the crisis, the Europeans had generally expressed a far less bellicose position on the crisis than Washington and were supportive of King Hussein's conviction that war would be a catastrophe for the Middle East. Geographically, only an ocean separates America and Europe, but their attitudes toward the Middle East and the use of force to resolve differences are hugely disparate. Many Europeans equate war with devastation and loss, not gain. This attitude is the natural outcome of two world wars on their soil and the arduous rebuilding after each, and it contrasted quite sharply with the prevailing American and Israeli view that armed confrontation and the civilian deaths and destruction of infrastructure that accompanied it were necessary evils in the exercise of national security aims.

My husband was hoping for a miracle from the French or the Germans or the Italians, but they were not in a position to do much. They knew, as did he, that the outcome of the crisis depended on the dynamic between the Americans and the Iraqis, and it seemed the Americans were forestalling the development of constructive dialogue. Nonetheless, my husband was deeply gratified by his meetings with the Germans, especially with Foreign Minister Hans-Dietrich Genscher and Chancellor Helmut Kohl. I was equally encouraged by my contacts with humanitarian organizations eager to contribute relief aid to Jordan for the evacuees and refugees.

Luxembourg was the next country we visited, and it was equally supportive. While my husband met with the Grand Duke and the Foreign Minister, who was then head of the European Union, I visited with our dear friend the Grand Duchess Josephine-Charlotte, President of the Luxembourg Red Cross, and her staff. They were extremely helpful and promised more than $1 million in development aid. The Italians were generous as well. I met in Italy with Maria Pia Fanfani, an Italian humanitarian, and with an Italian NGO focused on development programs for women. They were both very responsive to the needs of refugees fleeing Iraq and Kuwait who had chosen to stay in Jordan and desperately needed to begin generating some income for their families. Princess Irene of Greece, an old family friend and sister of the Queen of Spain, came in and out of Jordan often during this period to help in any way she could. Princess Irene's foundation, World in Harmony, supported projects in the developing world and worked with the Noor Al Hussein Foundation to help the very poorest families in the country.

Hussein also met with John Major, Britain's new Prime Minister, and found him impressively informed and more down to earth than Margaret Thatcher. Hussein was buoyed by Major's insistence that "Iraq would not be attacked if it withdrew from Kuwait," yet the specter of conflict still loomed.

On January 5, the day after Hussein met with Prime Minister Major, he went out to Castlewood, to meet secretly with Israeli Prime Minister Yitzhak Shamir. With war apparently inevitable, my husband had mobilized Jordanian troops on the border with Iraq and on the border with Israel to keep Jordan from being overrun. Shamir said his generals were urging him to place Israeli troops opposite the Jordanian troops, a call he was resisting until he had spoken face-to-face with my husband. "Your Majesty, what we want to know is why your troops are massed on our border and what you will do if Iraq crosses your borders and tries to attack Israel." My husband replied: "My position is purely defensive. If anybody crosses my borders or enters my air space, from Iraq or anywhere else, I will treat that as a hostile act and will act accordingly. And I will not allow anyone to attack anyone else through Jordan." Shamir replied, "Thank you. That's all I wanted to hear."

However, Ehud Barak, the Chief of Staff of the Israeli Defense Forces, was more suspicious about the concentration of Jordanian troops on Israel's border. When Sharif Zeid Bin Shaker, who had spent thirty-five years in the Jordanian army, pointed out that the Jordanian troops were obviously in a defensive rather than offensive position, Barak kept demanding more assurances until Shamir lost his patience. "King Hussein has given me his word," he said, "and that is enough for me."

When my husband returned to Jordan at the end of our European tour, I continued on to Austria with the four youngest children — then ages ten, eight, seven, and four — to leave them for their school holiday with my sister. My heart had never felt as heavy, but it was important that they be distanced from the tension at home as much as possible. I still refused to believe that war lay ahead, but were it to come, the children would be out of harm's way, leaving us to fully focus on our larger Jordanian family.

My time with the children in Austria was all too limited, but as short as it was, it was my first undistracted contact with them during the last four months of deepening crisis. The simple act of reading them a bedtime story reduced me to tears. I tried not to focus on our parting, but it was impossible.

I was going to spend only two days in Austria, but even that short visit proved problematic. I was concerned with how my absence would be perceived in Jordan only a few days before the UN deadline; however, at my husband's urging I stayed on. My apprehension proved to be correct when my husband called to say that yes, indeed, there was a lot of speculation about why I was out of the country. "Of course there is. I should be home in Jordan," I said. I left the next day after discussing with my sister what to do about the children if their father and I did not survive.

The last day I spent with the children was emotionally draining for all of us. "My heart is breaking," I wrote in my journal, "we must be prepared for anything in the event of war." I gave each child a precious, sentimental good-luck gift and promised the children that this would be just a temporary separation, but in my heart I was not at all sure.

chapter sixteen

Fire in the Gulf

As the January 15 deadline for Iraq's with-drawal from Kuwait passed, the tension in Amman was extraordinary. After the U.S. media declared the importance of clear skies for any coalition attack, the weather became a source of constant debate and discussion. The King and I monitored the news without pause as everyone's nerves wound tighter and tighter. Increasingly agitated antiwar demonstrators marched in capitals around the world, reminiscent of the anti–Vietnam War protests during my student days. I felt as though my past was being replayed. "It seems so surreal," I wrote in my journal. "I only pray that whatever happens will be for the best. Let it become indisputably clear that war is not a solution for economic, social or political problems."

Our friends supported us tremendously by calling and sending messages. My family was very concerned, naturally, and called from the States, as did old school friends in America and

England, and leaders from around the world. There was always someone, it seemed, on the phone, but never George Bush or Saddam Hussein.

On January 17, we learned later, Bush called King Fahd and President Mubarak to tell them the air war was about to begin, and James Baker called the Soviets. Hussein and I found out on CNN that the war had started; we sat in front of the television devastated as we watched the opening bombardment of Baghdad. The King acutely appreciated the potential consequences of the assault and the furies it would unleash. Divisions between Arab countries would be exacerbated, and extremists would bring terrific pressure to bear by depicting their governments as puppets of the West. The economic consequences also would be very grave, particularly for poor countries. Saudi Arabia's willingness to accept foreign troops on its sacred soil would be seen as a humiliation to all Arabs, especially in a region that was so sensitive to colonialism. Anti-American feelings on the streets of Jordan and throughout the region would reach an all-time high, fanned by those trying to cast the bombing of Baghdad in religious terms, as an assault by Christian and Jewish forces against Islam. My husband saw the strong possibility of these forces spiraling out of control and was heartsick at his helplessness to do anything to stop it.

Upon hearing the news, Alexa immediately

phoned me and I asked her to take Hamzah, Hashim, Iman, and Raiyah to London to finish their holiday. They were indignant at being kept away from Amman, and they started calling and writing to entreat us to let them return home, but we resisted their pleas. They were in very good hands. They tried to sneak out of bed at night to watch CNN, I learned later, because my sister and my mother thought the images of the bombing of Baghdad would be too disturbing for them and had made the TV off-limits. I was very grateful to my family for responding so quickly and being so sensitive to the needs of my children.

Hussein's eldest sons, Abdullah and Feisal, and his nephew, Talal, were officers in the military, which was called to active duty during the crisis. When the Army Chief of Staff asked my husband what he wanted him to do with the members of the royal family, my husband said: "Absolutely nothing. They will join their units and be treated like any other officer. If any Jordanian soldier is going to be placed in harm's way, so should the King's family." This was not unusual. The entire royal family, men and women, had been brought up to serve the country, and the boys would have felt disgraced if they had been set apart in any way.

Foreigners in Amman felt increasingly vulnerable. I spent part of the second day of the war in the hospital visiting an Italian journalist, Eric Salerno, who had been beaten by a group of Jordanians. He was the exception, for despite the tensions, hundreds of journalists were free to go anywhere they wanted and rarely encountered any hostility. Still, I was concerned, so from the hospital I went directly to the Inter-Continental Hotel, where many journalists were staying, to determine their security needs and make sure they were well provided for.

Other foreign-born Jordanians took their own precautions. Prince Raad's wife, Majda, who was born in Sweden, curtailed her movements outside her home for a period of time, as did the wives of foreign diplomats, many of whom eventually left. Liesa Segovia, our longtime German head of housekeeping, who had lived in Amman for many years, became painfully aware of the transformation in attitudes toward foreigners in her daily dealings with the shopkeepers and market vendors she patronized for the palace. Nonetheless, she felt safe and comfortable in Jordan, and chose to wait out the crisis.

Just as my husband was constantly moving from the situation room in the Diwan to the refugee camps to all the units of the army, where he made it a point to greet and encourage every soldier, I was always on the go myself. Cholera had been reported at one of our refugee camps, and we had an urgent need for more blankets and warm clothing as the winter rains began, so I devoted myself to these tasks.

With each passing day, public sentiment in Jordan became more and more supportive of Saddam Hussein. He became an overnight Arab hero when he launched his first Scud missiles into Israel on January 17. Two days later, the mood on the streets became almost euphoric when at least three Iraqi Scuds hit Tel Aviv, especially since it had happened after U.S. reports that Saddam Hussein had been effectively neutralized. Such overblown coalition claims fueled the myth that Saddam Hussein was invincible.

I clung stubbornly to the hope that it would become clear to all that war was not a solution, only a multiplier of suffering. "Successful missions," as the White House and the Defense Department described them, meant death for Iraqi civilians that we, or people close to us, knew. Those innocent victims were our neighbors.

The Iraqi torching of Kuwait's oil fields in late January created a whole new level of insanity. What could possibly be gained by such senseless destruction? The sight brought my husband, who had spoken out passionately about the potential environmental catastrophe of war, close to tears.

The children arrived home from London at the end of their winter school holiday to begin the new school term. They were as thrilled to be back as we were to have them there, though the danger had not lessened. Scuds were still flying; their school friends had seen them from their rooftops at night. Now school lessons included learning the difference between alarm bells for fire and air raids, and the appropriate procedures to follow: Close the windows for a fire to limit the supply of oxygen, open them for air raids to minimize shattering glass. In case of an air raid on their way home from school, the children were instructed to jump out of the car and get as far away from it as possible, since cars were easy targets.

As the air war continued, every Iraqi Scud launched at Israel or Saudi Arabia raised fears in Jordan that the warheads might contain chemical or biological weapons. Some people hung litmus paper in their houses to determine if there were chemical agents in the air; others taped their windows shut. The demand for gas masks grew. I learned that residents of Tel Aviv were so jumpy that many families relocated to Jerusalem, the assumption being that Saddam Hussein would not risk harming the Al Aqsa mosque and other sacred Muslim sites there.

We were especially vulnerable at Al Nadwa. The palace was very close to the airport, which would be an obvious target if hostilities escalated. Security pressed us to move, but the King and I decided to stay in our home just as other Jordanians were remaining in theirs.

Hussein's greatest preoccupation was the safety of the country. Roads into Jordan were being targeted by allied warplanes, and oil trucks carrying perfectly legal oil into our country were being bombed. A rationing system had already been put into place because of the Saudi decision to cut off our oil; cars with even-numbered license plates were allowed on the roads one day, and those with odd-numbered licenses the next, but still the lack of fuel was becoming a national crisis. So was the carnage along the highway from Baghdad to Amman, with civilian cars and trucks and buses coming under steady allied attacks with a mounting loss of Jordanian life.

The King felt he could not remain silent in light of the ongoing devastation of neighboring Iraq and its effects on Jordanians. The mood on the streets was close to boiling over at the continuing destruction of Baghdad. People were on the verge of taking matters into their own hands. He had to respond, and he did, on February 6, after a coalition bombing of Jordanian oil tankers and trucks on the Baghdad–Amman international highway killed fourteen civilians and injured twenty-six more. In an impassioned speech to the Jordanian people, he condemned the allied attack against Iraq and reaffirmed his commitment to a diplomatic solution to the crisis. He spoke stirringly of the Iraqi people and their reduction to a primitive way of life. Expressing his solidarity with the people of Iraq and of Jordan, he asked: "Which voices will win in the end? The voices of reason, peace, and justice, or the voices of war, hatred, and insanity?"

The speech had an immediate and positive impact on Jordanians, lifting their morale and muting their frustration and anger. There was an almost audible sigh of relief throughout the country as people felt that their concerns and fears were shared and understood by their leader. My husband's stature soared in Jordan and plummeted in Saudi Arabia and in the West. The Saudis angrily wrote off Hussein as having "lost his role" in the Middle East, and the Americans vilified him. The day after the speech, phone calls and faxes poured in from American reporters, members of Congress, and even some of my friends, demanding to know why my husband had thrown his weight behind Saddam Hussein.

I responded as best I could, explaining that the King's sympathy was for the people of Iraq, not the regime. Two days after Hussein's speech, we saw news reports on CNN that Congress was considering postponing its financial aid package to Jordan. My husband got up from the sofa and turned off the television set. "The noose is tightening," he sighed.

I did everything I could to lift his spirits. I reassured him time and again that even when it looked as if everything he had struggled for was in jeopardy, he was still a beacon of light for many in the region. Some might disagree with him; that was to be expected. Yet his was an honest and consistent voice that promoted unity and humanity, not polarization, and the future, not only the present.

The situation only worsened. His speech, so morale-building for Jordanians, sparked a round of vicious coverage in the foreign press. In Israel the *Jerusalem Post* reported that my husband's life had been in danger from his own people before the speech, and if he had not placated the pro-Saddam forces in Jordan he would have lost "not only his throne but his head." *Spy* magazine wrote a disparaging piece about me, claiming to have the "inside story of Jordan's All-American Queen — Mrs. King Hussein — during the countdown to war and exile." Even *The Washington Post* lost its grip on the truth. In the second month of the conflict, the *Post* reported — and other publications around the world picked up the story — that I had visited Palm Beach, Florida, in the midst of the crisis and had acquired a seven-acre estate (there was even a picture of it) for my husband and me when we fled Jordan. Other reports had us refurbishing a house in Vienna in grand style as our exile-in-waiting. Jordan, they all concluded, was doomed.

The truth, of course, was that we had no new home awaiting us. We had no contingency plan at all, and we were certainly not about to go into exile. What we did have were libel lawyers in America and England trying to get these publications to print retractions of these wildly erroneous stories. We did not go after everyone, but there were some accusations out there we just could not let stand.

The slander continued unabated, with accusations that our ships were violating the sanctions against Iraq, and that we were allowing Iraq to use our airspace to launch missiles, when in fact the Scuds traveled through the stratosphere and we did not even have the capability to interfere with them. "So many fires to put out," I wrote in my journal. "I despair of Hussein's depressed spirit. It is becoming more and more difficult to see light at the end of the tunnel."

The war ended six weeks after it began, leaving Kuwait smoldering and Iraq in ruins. American missiles and bombs had destroyed electrical plants, severed telephone lines, and shattered bridges and highways, as well as factories, dams, sewage facilities, hospitals, and schools. No one knows how many civilians were killed, but the toll certainly included hundreds of women and children in the Amariyah bomb shelter on February 13. Some 88,500 tons of bombs were dropped on Iraq, the equivalent of seven and a half atomic bombs the size of the one dropped on Hiroshima. By and large Iraq was reduced to a pre-industrial state, as my husband had forecast in his February speech.

Aside from Kuwait and Iraq, no country suffered more from the Gulf crisis than Jordan.

Because of my husband's neutral stance in the war, the Gulf states, Kuwait, and Saudi Arabia cut off all economic aid. Because of the ongoing UN-imposed sanctions against Iraq, Jordan suffered a shattering $3 billion loss in trade revenue from our largest trading partner, Iraq. Tourism, a major source of revenue, dried up completely, as did foreign investment in Jordan. At the same time, our responsibilities increased enormously. More than 400,000 expatriates, officially called "returnees," came to Jordan after being expelled by Kuwait and Saudi Arabia. (Our family was fortunate that one such family from Kuwait was the Al Yasin family, whose daughter, Rania, would marry my husband's oldest son, Prince Abdullah, in 1993.) Our population grew 15 percent overnight, putting further strain on water and housing, and adding many thousands of new students to our schools. Unemployment soared to nearly 30 percent.

On the Arab street, the war against Iraq was viewed as an anti-Arab war, no matter which governments the Western members of the coalition claimed as their allies. There was absolute certainty among the people in the entire region, including Jordan, that the war was intended to undercut Arab independence, strength, and control over its own resources, especially oil. This led some to an even greater identification with Saddam Hussein, but this was by no means a uniform phenomenon in the region; in fact, many Arabs criticized the Iraqi invasion of Kuwait. There was a general consensus, however, that the suffering of the Iraqi people was completely unjustifiable.

The humanitarian cost of the war was heartbreaking. We had made great strides in Jordan over the previous decade, achieving standards of literacy, immunization, and maternal and infant mortality rates that approximated — and in some cases exceeded — those of far more developed countries. Suddenly the crisis and the war set all that progress back. The immunization programs for which we were renowned began to lag behind schedule, leading to an outbreak of polio in poorer areas. Our schools, which had been models in the region, became impossibly crowded with the new wave of returnees, and we had to establish a double-shift schedule to accommodate them. As poverty rose, we were beginning to see signs of malnutrition.

I remember going down to the Dead Sea with my husband soon after the war ended. "We are at the lowest point on Earth," he said. "It can only go up from here."

chapter seventeen

Test of Faith

Ever so slowly, the black cloud over Jordan began to lift as Britain, the United States, and the other members of the allied coalition gradually eased their political isolation of the country. Though Jordan was returning to normalcy, the country still bore a significant political cost from the war. James Baker toured the region in March 1991, to begin to rally support for a U.S.-initiated Middle East peace process, but he bypassed Jordan, a slight that seemed shortsighted and counterproductive. False charges continued to be leveled at Jordan. The *Daily Mail* and later other news outlets claimed that a CIA agent had irrefutable proof that Jordan had been secretly helping Iraq during the Gulf crisis by supplying Saddam Hussein with ammunition. The story even had photographs, allegedly taken on an Iraqi island, of ammunition crates with the "Hashimite Kingdom of Jordan" stamped on them. The irony was that these crates had in fact contained arms shipments that the United States was sending to Iraq as military assistance during the Iran-Iraq war; Washington had asked to ship them through Jordan. The CIA and the administration were, of course, well aware of this.

Politicized charges like these posed crucial dilemmas for us because they were being used to continue a campaign against Jordan that was destroying us economically, as well as restricting my husband's ability to play any useful role in the Middle East peace process. Because he was overwhelmed with other issues, my husband asked me to contact the CIA's station chief in Jordan to find out what he might tell us about the reports and why the U.S. government had not refuted them.

After looking into the matter, the station chief confirmed the erroneous nature of the key assertions of the article. The CIA did not have an agent stationed in the location cited by the *Daily Mail* reporter, nor did the CIA give any credence to the allegations. I urged him to do what he could to set the record straight, but I knew how difficult it was to rebut published reports. The King wanted to prosecute the *Daily Mail* to the fullest extent of the law, and he managed to get the paper to print a retraction, but nothing could undo the damage that had already been done by the so-called proof of Jordan's collusion with Iraq.

The conflict had cost Jordan billions in lost aid and revenues. Even Royal Jordanian, the national airline that my husband had put his heart and soul into developing, was in crisis. Its financial situation was so tenuous that the airline could not keep up payment on the planes it had leased from Airbus. Without our usual sources of income, we were hard-pressed to handle the social needs of the rapid influx of Palestinians.

The continuing impact on the Noor Al Hussein Foundation's development projects was dramatic and especially disappointing at a time when real sustainability had been within reach. But now, with the economy so burdened, local markets for products such as handicrafts as well as local funding sources had been drastically reduced. Jordanians were suffering a rapid decline in their standard of living and as a result were spending very little on the kind of discretionary goods these projects produced. Tourists, who in the past could be counted on to buy these exquisite indigenous crafts, were returning to Jordan in a trickle.

Just when the women involved in these projects had begun to transform their lives by generating their first real income and having their first real say in family and community affairs, they were having their livelihood snatched away from them. Their families were suffering, too, from the lack of means to provide any sort of balanced diet. Education, the mainstay of Jordan's investment in its people, was also being compromised. Parents who could not afford individual school uniforms for their children were sending the children to school on alternate days so the uniforms could be shared.

During this difficult period of rebuilding, I tried to jump-start the tourist industry by meeting in Amman with European tour operators, tour guides, and travel writers. We also sent abroad a series of traveling exhibitions of archaeological and cultural treasures of Jordan. Fortunately, our ecotourism projects began to draw travelers to Jordan's spectacularly beautiful and environmentally protected sites, providing some income for those in poorer rural areas.

By far my greatest worries were the personal repercussions of the war. The feelings of despair and powerlessness Hussein had experienced when he realized that the leaders of the coalition against Iraq were not interested in attempting a peaceful resolution had grown more acute during the destruction of Iraq and the war's crippling aftermath. In his four decades as Jordan's monarch, Hussein had developed the tough skin necessary to withstand the criticism that inevitably followed his every move; over the years, he had been called both a lackey of the West and an Arab hard-liner. He had shrugged off these unfair portrayals as part of the expected fallout from holding to his convictions, but these days the affronts, large and small, hit him hard.

In the face of these difficulties, one adviser

suggested that the King would cut a more sympathetic image in America if he would be seen holding my hand whenever we were filmed or photographed. Hussein flatly refused, having always felt that such public shows of affection were inappropriate. We both understood that such displays might reap media benefits for politicians in many societies, but we knew that such contrived behavior would be out of character both with our personalities and with our culture.

Some of the slights my husband suffered after the Gulf War were petty and inconsequential, but they carried a sting nonetheless. There was, for example, the "passing out" parade, or graduation of officer cadets, at Sandhurst, Hussein's alma mater and that of his father, four of his five sons, and eventually two of his daughters: Aisha, and later Iman, who entered in the fall of 2002. He had "taken the salute" at the parade on several occasions as the Queen's representative and had maintained very close relations with the Sandhurst administration and staff. During our honeymoon he had taken me to the campus for a visit, followed by many more over the years. Prior to the Gulf crisis, Hussein had been invited to officiate over the parade but later was quietly asked to bow out.

An even deeper affront came from Saudi Arabia. Every year during Ramadan the King went to Mecca and Medina, but the Saudis made it clear to him after the Gulf War that he would not be welcome there either.

Despite his long-standing relationship with the United States, the White House was also giving Hussein the cold shoulder, although we received a Christmas card from the Bushes with a picture of Kennebunkport on it and the handwritten message, "You'll always be my friend."

The one major diplomatic icebreaker was renewed interest in the peace process. The United States recognized that Desert Storm highlighted the urgency of a fresh round of peace negotiations in the region. Together with the Soviet Union, the United States called for direct talks between Israel and the Arab states in the form of a regional conference on the Middle East. James Baker needed my husband to help put this together and requested a meeting with him that we arranged at our home in Aqaba, where the King and the American Secretary of State would be able to clear the air and plan in a relaxed environment. The discussions went well and Hussein was impressed by Baker, judging him to be a decent and straightforward man.

Despite these new and more constructive challenges that once would have stimulated my husband, Hussein's mood did not improve. I was worried because he seemed to be retreating more and more into his own world, as if he were trying to disengage from anything that reminded him of the agonies of the Gulf crisis.

495

Uncharacteristically, he began to avoid dealing with complicated problems. He kept saying he was just too tired, even when it came to resolving parenting issues. He did not shirk his responsibilities, but he became somewhat detached from what was happening at work and at home — a highly unusual development for a man who customarily involved himself 150 percent in everything he did.

It was difficult for me not to take some of this personally. It did not help that during the period that had caused the King so much anguish and frustration, I had been in a position to contribute in ways that were perhaps more tangibly rewarding. And whereas Hussein was still being unjustly targeted, I had been recognized for my efforts on the humanitarian level, due to media focus on the evacuees during the war. This momentary shift in our dynamic may have contributed to Hussein's growing distance and inability to open up to me. I felt unable to help my husband through this difficult period, and the effort was draining me of the energy and optimism I needed for our younger children as well as my stepfamily. I shared my concerns with Leila who emphatically counseled me to wait two years and then reassess the situation, which seemed arbitrary advice at the time, but it was given with love and, it turned out, great wisdom.

New medical problems cropped up. On June 10, after a family birthday party for our son

Hashim, Hussein had an episode of cardiac fibrillation, or arrhythmia. He had suffered from these episodes before, and there was nothing unusual about this one. He usually recovered after a day or so, but we moved him into the hospital for observation, just to be safe. The doctors were concerned by his overall health and wanted him to stay in the hospital and rest for a month, but, of course, he would not do that. I stayed with Hussein in the hospital during his short stay, and his heart quickly reverted to its normal rhythm. His only concession to the doctors was to spend one extra day in the hospital, which gave him the rare luxury of some quiet time alone. When he wanted company, I was there, and other family members would come and go; the rest of the time I worked in an adjacent room editing upcoming speeches or fielding calls.

What was unusual about this minor health event was that we issued a brief press release informing people of the reasons for the King's hospital stay. Israeli radio, typically, had immediately begun broadcasting that Hussein had had a heart attack. It took some convincing, but I persuaded my husband and his reluctant aides that Jordanians had a right to know the truth about their King's health, and to have an explanation as to why he was absent from his scheduled appearances. This approach became policy from then on, and although it did not entirely prevent rumors and conspiracy theories from surfacing, it certainly helped.

Hussein's lack of energy was alarming, however, and I even encouraged him to see an English homeopath recommended to us by friends. The meeting turned out to be more amusing than productive. The homeopath appeared with a box of vials and liquids and several strange machines to assess our health through our feet. The subsequent recommendation that we take a variety of drops and other natural vitamins and enzymes was too complicated, so we quickly abandoned the regimen.

Later I did succeed in persuading the King to visit a specialist in alternative medicine in London who I was already seeing at the suggestion of an old friend. Bob Jacobs's focus on strengthening the immune systems of patients with cancer and HIV or AIDS was proving extremely effective for relatively healthy patients dealing with unusual stress. He placed me on a regimen that cured the insomnia I had suffered from, on and off, for most of my life. That and my daily exercise routine kept me psychologically, mentally, and emotionally strong at times when otherwise I might never have been able to cope with the pressures of our life. My paternal grandmother's fervent belief in the power of the mind to heal was perhaps a source of my own conviction that the right attitude, together with eating properly and keeping physically active, could dramatically contribute to well-being and longevity. How I wish, to this day, that I could have convinced my husband to at least try a complementary approach to his health, but he did not have the patience for it. Instead, he was forever teasing me about my sizable traveling bag of vitamins.

Momentum was building toward a Madrid peace conference in October. What should have been a period of positive preparation was freighted with a sense of foreboding. Over the summer, our intelligence service and that of the United States were reporting a sharp increase in the number of death threats against King Hussein. When Baker visited Aqaba in April, they had discussed photographs of equipment seized from terrorists sent to kill Hussein. One report indicated that my husband's plane was being targeted, and another that a cell of Palestinians was sending a suicide assassin wearing an explosive vest to kill him, much like the Tamil terrorist who assassinated Rajiv Gandhi. I was shown one horrifying set of intelligence photos of an intercepted shipment of child-size garments fitted with explosives. For a time I found myself keeping an eye out for any person, large or small, wearing unusually heavy clothing.

Hussein was a fatalist in the sense that he believed his life — and his death — were in God's hands. He was more stoical than distressed about the threats; however, one intelligence report that did disturb us both very much concerned an intercepted plan to kidnap our young children. We had received similar threats against the family before and always chose not to share them with the children, since we wanted them to live as normally as possible, and they had very good security. This threat was somehow leaked to the local and international media and became general knowledge. "People are shocked and angered, which disturbs me, because the children are bound to hear of it now," I wrote in my journal. While the story was undoubtedly unsettling, the children took it all in stride and continued with their daily routines.

On October 3, the Palestine National Council decided to join the peace process, setting another critical building block in place just three weeks before the American-sponsored Middle East peace conference was scheduled to open in Madrid. Still, the King was focused on domestic affairs, particularly the potential for instability. He was burdened by the pessimistic opinion of his Prime Minister that some of Jordan's cabinet ministers would resign in protest over Jordan's participation in the Madrid peace process. If the enthusiasm for Saddam Hussein that had run so high during the Gulf crisis could be directed against that conference, any incident could spark violence beyond control. As a deterrent, the King presented his case for the peace process to an extraordinary national assembly and achieved a critical, hard-won consensus. Jordan was the first country to accept Madrid, and the first new step toward peace was achieved.

Jordan played a vital role in creating the Madrid conference, but it was also essential to keeping the process going after the conference convened on October 30, 1991. Just orchestrating those preliminary negotiations was dauntingly complex. No Arab residents of Jerusalem or PLO officials or Palestinians from outside the West Bank and Gaza were allowed in the negotiating rooms. Instead, in what was later dubbed "corridor diplomacy," the strategists sat outside the rooms and negotiated everything, right down to the composition of the negotiating teams and when they should meet. "It was like the Vietnam peace talks in Paris, when even the shape of the table was negotiated," our nephew, Prince Talal, commented to me later. "It was all important stuff, though it sounds silly."

The Israelis and Palestinians sat down together for the first time, with Jordan providing the umbrella for the Palestinian delegation, to negotiate a five-year transitional period of Palestinian self-government. Discussions on regional issues were held with the Egyptians, Syrians, and Lebanese. The conference delegates planned forthcoming bilateral and multilateral talks on economics, water resources, arms control, the environment, and refugees. I listened raptly as my husband called me in the

United States, where I was speaking to various Arab-American and other organizations to mobilize support for the new peace initiative, to give me a breakdown of what had happened.

I was heading next to London as patron of the 125th anniversary of the American University of Beirut, where I told the audience: "For the first time in half a century, we may be on the threshold of a truly new and rational regional order. We have an opportunity to shift the momentum in our region from warfare and waste to justice, reconciliation and peace, based on the application of international law and United Nations resolutions. If we can succeed in this endeavor, we shall have destroyed the single greatest obstacle that has stalled Arab political, economic, and cultural development for nearly five decades." I could only hope, and we did with all our hearts.

As the New Year dawned, my husband's fatigue continued, and we discovered a lump on the back of his knee. Our doctors thought it should be attended to right away and put him in the hospital to have it removed. The growth turned out to be inconsequential, but while we were in the hospital, our nephew, Talal, disclosed that he had a swelling on his neck that doctors in London had told him was nothing. I had my own health issues as well. During a routine mammogram a lump had been discovered, and the report was sent on to Memorial Sloan-Kettering, the well-known cancer hospital in New York City, for a second opinion. Only days after my husband's operation and Talal's disclosure, I received a call from a doctor at Sloan-Kettering, who advised me to come to New York immediately for further tests.

I took Talal's X rays and other medical reports with me to Sloan-Kettering for a second opinion on his condition and received the alarming news that they thought he had an even more serious problem — a possible brain tumor. As gently as possible I suggested to Talal that he should come to New York right away. I delayed my own procedure to attend to Talal and Ghida, his young wife of only three months, who arrived shortly thereafter.

My husband and I had become particularly close to Talal when he had a life-threatening accident at the age of sixteen. He was slaloming on water skis in Aqaba when he slammed into the pier. We rushed him to the local hospital, but his internal injuries were so severe the doctors said he had to be transferred to a hospital in Amman, so Hussein and I flew him up to the capital. Talal would fully recover and go on to graduate from Harrow, Sandhurst, and Georgetown University, and eventually serve King Hussein as his National Security Adviser.

More tests were ordered, which revealed Talal's suspected brain tumor to be benign; however, exploratory surgery was recommended for the swelling on his neck. After surgery the doctors appeared pleased with the results, and as I had been away from home for two weeks, I returned directly to Jordan. There Queen Sofie was arriving for a few days before flying with me to Switzerland for the Geneva Summit on the Economic Advancement of Rural Women. In the middle of our meetings in Geneva I took a call from Talal's doctor, informing me that our nephew had been diagnosed with non-Hodgkin's lymphoma and would have to begin a six-month protocol of chemotherapy. I immediately telephoned Hussein with the news. He told me to continue on to New York on our plane, as Amman was blanketed by a blizzard and I could not return home anyway. As I left Geneva, my emotions in utter turmoil, dearest Sofie sent me a thoughtful note: "If we do not manage to see each other before we leave, all my love with you through the awful ordeal you have to go through."

It was an ordeal, not for me so much, of course, as for brave Talal and Ghida. I spent the next several weeks with them in New York while Talal underwent postoperative cancer treatment. Ghida and I went to the gym to work out every morning around 6:00 before going off to the hospital to encounter whatever challenges the day would bring. "I am torn between my children at home and this young couple facing such a terrible challenge," I wrote in my diary at the end of February 1992.

"Thank God they are so incredibly strong." Good news followed bad, in this case. My own tumor turned out to be benign, and Talal would have a full recovery, for which we continue to give thanks.

Apparently, while I was away, rumors had begun circulating in Amman that Hussein was having an affair with a young woman who worked in the Diwan. Such gossip was not unusual. In this case, since we had not told anyone outside the family about Talal's condition, my unexplained absence from Jordan seemed to lend an element of believability to the gossip. Just after I returned to Amman from New York, one of my stepdaughters called me very upset about what people were saying. She laid out the full extent of the stories: that my husband had met this woman's family; that he was planning to divorce me and marry her; that he had already bought her a house; that they were secretly married. "Something has to be done about it," my stepdaughter said. I told her not to worry and tried to calm her down.

There was no reason for me to believe these rumors any more than I had believed the multitude of other stories about my husband and me, although the distance I had sensed between us gave me pause. And I was quite worried that the children would be exposed to this hurtful gossip, since we could not control what they were hearing at school and in their day-to-day lives. They had no way of knowing what was really going on and, like most children, would be hesitant to bring up anything unpleasant with us.

Because of the remote possibility that the reports might carry a grain of truth, I raised the subject with my husband, albeit with a knot in my stomach. "I don't know what is going on," I told him, "but these stories have become very detailed and complicated, and only you can resolve this before they cause more anguish for the family and everyone involved. If there is any truth whatsoever in any of it, and your happiness would lie with someone else, please tell me because I love you enough to let you go. I want what is best for the family, for you, and for all that we have been struggling for."

I had said this to him before, and I meant it sincerely. I loved him very much, but I had been through the tension of my parents' unraveling marriage, and I did not want to maintain a relationship that was not, for each of us and our family, a source of fulfillment and happiness. I had lived an independent life before I married and assumed I could again, if necessary.

Hussein looked at me in genuine surprise. He shook his head, with a baffled expression on his face. "No," he said, "there is no truth to the rumors. These are just stories."

The problem now was how to dispel them. One obvious solution was to remove the young woman from her position, but we both knew how injurious that would be to her reputation in our conservative culture; people would assume the worst. So we decided just to ride out the gossip and to tell the children what was going on. The gossip spiraled out of control, however, and finally our embassy in Washington had to issue a denial, as did the Diwan in Amman.

My husband's depression deepened further over the widely publicized rumors and his inability to put an end to them. He seemed almost paralyzed by the situation, which both worried me and made me very angry. I was furious at him on some level for putting the family through great distress by letting the situation go on to the extent of creating such public damage. As always, I knew his enemies would be quick to exploit any apparent weakness.

In retrospect, I realize now that the whole situation was part of a very difficult period of his life. He talked to me often during that awful time about the final days of his life and his concerns for the family. It was as if he were willing himself to escape it all by dying. "You have to begin to focus again on the long term," I encouraged him. "Take the time to think through what you really need and want."

Yasser Arafat came to Amman in June, and over lunch with the King seemed quite shaky and emotional and complained of headaches.

Concerned that Arafat's fragility might be connected to the plane crash in the Libyan Desert that the PLO leader had survived just two months earlier, my husband arranged for Arafat to have a medical examination that very evening. It was after midnight before Hussein learned that the neurologist had found blood clots in Arafat's brain and recommended that the PLO chief have immediate surgery. Abu Shaker, then Chief of the Royal Court, who had feted Arafat in a state dinner that same evening, passed on the information to Arafat's office right away.

Fortunately for us, given the historic tension between Arafat and my husband, the top neurologist in Jordan was a close friend of Arafat's. Still, were Arafat to die on the operating table, Jordan might well be accused of killing him. "Can't you put him on a plane and send him somewhere outside the country for the surgery?" Abu Shaker asked my husband. But Hussein refused. "The doctors told me he cannot fly in his condition, and I have given them the green light to operate," he said.

I was so worried that I was unable to sleep that night, as was Hussein, who stayed in close communication with the doctors at the King Hussein Medical Center, where Arafat's surgery was taking place. When he received word sometime around 2:00 A.M. that the surgery had been successful, he drove to the hospital. On the way my husband pulled up next to a taxi at a traffic light, and the taxi driver looked over and recognized the King behind the wheel. "Sir, you should not be driving alone at night," he admonished Hussein. "Where are your guards?" "They're coming right behind me," my husband said, shading the truth a bit because he had slipped away from Al Nadwa without disturbing anyone. "Then I am going to guard you until they arrive," the taxi driver said. He then followed Hussein to the hospital and stood guard over his car until the security detail arrived.

Arafat's speedy recovery from the emergency surgery was nothing short of a miracle. His wife, Suha, came to Jordan to be with him, and we put the two of them in Hashimya so they would be comfortable, visiting them often to offer convalescence support. The operation was deemed a complete success. There was no doubt that the emergency surgery saved his life.

My husband would be the next one to have health problems, medical issues that would take center stage, and remain there, for the rest of our life together.

chapter eighteen

A Day Like No Other

One mid-August day in 1992, I was sitting in the hospital with my mother-in-law when my husband unexpectedly arrived for a medical examination. Queen Zein had been quite ill but was now recovering. Hussein was displaying symptoms of a urological problem, and tests showed some questionable cells that needed further study. His doctors recommended that he travel immediately to the United States for a more complete diagnosis and suggested the Mayo Clinic in Rochester, Minnesota, or Johns Hopkins Hospital in Baltimore — both internationally distinguished for their urology departments. Although the King Hussein Medical Center in Jordan had the highest standards, our doctors there were concerned that the King might fall victim to VIPitis, a syndrome facing VIP patients the world over in which medical staff might become overly nervous or emotional as they tended to a famous patient. To avoid such a situation, they would often suggest we seek professional care outside the country for complex medical procedures, while always keeping our longtime Jordanian doctor, Samir Farraj, as Hussein's primary physician. After some discussion we decided that the relatively remote location of Mayo might ensure greater privacy and would provide the opportunity for a comprehensive checkup, for which that clinic is world-renowned. Twenty-four hours later, we were in Minnesota.

Initial tests at the Mayo Clinic confirmed that the doctors needed to operate on a partial obstruction of Hussein's ureter and that the obstruction might be malignant. "I am stunned," I wrote in my journal. "Sidi is quiet and brave, but I know he must be terrified. He speaks fatalistically of being in the process of putting things in order, having sensed this for some time. I do not want to lose him, and he still has so much more to do. He is still needed by so many." It appeared likely that his condition was very serious.

After a sleepless night, I accompanied Hussein to his tests the next day and spent a good deal of time inside the control booth at the hospital while he underwent a CT scan and various other tests. I could not help overhearing the comments of the technicians and drawing all manner of dire conclusions from them. Only later did the doctors tell me the somewhat hopeful news that the scan and a subsequent ultrasound exam indicated that the abnormality was localized. Still, we were all extremely worried. My sister had flown out to be with me, which was a great comfort, but it was very hard to keep my emotions under control.

My husband was also emotional going into surgery and asked me for his Quran, which we always carried with us. He also asked for a photograph of an antique Mercedes he had just restored and presented it to me as an early birthday present. I was surprised and moved by the gift, knowing how proud Sidi was of that particular car, and I was even more impressed that he had remembered my birthday under the circumstances; certainly I had not.

I remained outside the operating theater during Hussein's surgery and accompanied him to the recovery room. When the doctors came out they gave us the news we were praying for: A few precancerous cells had been found in the ureter leading to the kidney, but the cells had not spread. The doctors had removed the associated kidney as a precaution and it contained no signs of abnormality. No further treatment was indicated.

My husband awoke in recovery in his own inimitable way. Still dazed by anesthesia, he began thanking everyone who had cared for him in the operating room, saying he felt grateful and privileged to be in their care, a response that typified the way he would always comfort and praise others even at such personally vulnerable moments.

The days that followed were a turning point in his life. I never left his side during the ten days or so we were at Mayo following the operation. In the first days, until the anesthesia wore off completely, he would often suddenly fall asleep in mid-sentence while we were talking, then awake and carry on with his thought. I had never seen him so weak and vulnerable, and for such a strong man who had always been in charge it was difficult to adjust to such a loss of control over his state of consciousness. The bond of trust between us strengthened. Both of us had been so busy and preoccupied with our work over the past difficult years, but in the hospital he had every reassurance that he, and he alone, was my number-one priority. The cancer scare snapped Hussein out of his depression, and he became once again the eager and engaged person he had been before the Gulf War.

News of Hussein's surgery had spread around the world, and flowers and messages were pouring in, including a particularly touching offer by a young Jordanian boy to donate a kidney to his beloved King, whom he viewed as a father, as did so many Jordanians. At the same time, the rumor mill was churning: In one particularly brazen report, the Israeli press announced he had brain cancer and would be dead in six months. I had to manage the news; we needed to be truthful but not alarmist about what we released. The King was touched by the outpouring of concern and affection from around the world, including the Vatican, the Middle East, Europe, and the United States. Prince Bandar, the Saudi ambassador to the United States, came to the Mayo Clinic to convey messages of support and lavish bouquets of flowers from King Fahd, Crown Prince Abdullah, and other members of the Saudi royal family. "Hussein feels this is a turning point" in the return to normal relations, I wrote in my journal. Our protocol person who accompanied the Saudis to the airport reported that the Prince, who had always viewed my husband as a mentor, had been moved to tears by his meeting with my husband.

In the immediate aftermath of the surgery, the doctors explained to us that there was thought to be a link between urologic cancer and smoking, yet just one day after the operation I opened the door to his room and found Hussein sitting in a chair smoking a cigarette next to a partially opened window. My heart sank, and I quietly went off to the empty sitting room and uncharacteristically burst into tears.

The King was still very, very weak when we left the hospital and began his convalescence at River House, our home right outside of Washington, D.C. Hussein had bought it sight unseen in the 1980s, when Blair House, the official guest residence, was under construction and it was thought that we needed a more se-

514

cure location than a hotel while visiting the United States. One evening, years earlier, he had casually mentioned to me that an old friend in D.C. had recommended he buy a house that had been on the market for some time and so was attractively priced. I replied that I was not sure we wanted the burden of another house, but if he was serious, we should have an engineer do a thorough evaluation of its condition. Hussein then, almost as an afterthought, mentioned that he had already bought it. "You cannot be serious," I said, putting my head in my hands.

River House ultimately did need quite a lot of renovation, including the removal of a significant amount of asbestos, but it had offered us a peaceful and secure home, with a beautiful view of the Potomac River. I had found it the perfect setting to gather my thoughts, especially while I was preparing for difficult meetings and speeches during the Gulf crisis. Now it provided an ideal place for my husband to convalesce. Following the surgery, we made up a room for Hussein on the ground floor since he was too weak to climb the stairs.

I concentrated on nursing him. At first I was nervous about taking on this responsibility, but I found it came very naturally and easily. Although we had a doctor and a superb nurse on staff, I tried to tend to all of Sidi's personal needs, helping him bathe, and helping him dress — and in the process discovering an unknown side of myself that was more capable than I had ever imagined of nursing a loved one, albeit amateurishly. It was very difficult for him to depend on other people, he who was so used to people depending on him, nonetheless, he was lovingly tolerant of my efforts.

After Hussein regained some of his strength, we paid a visit to the White House to have a quiet dinner with the Bushes and the Bakers. Despite the popular support Bush had gained during the Gulf War, he was plummeting in the polls, and 1992 was an election year. I remember Barbara Bush telling me she refused to read any national news because of the criticism of her husband, a stance I understood all too well. We encouraged the Bushes not to pay attention to the press or the polls, and later I called Barbara after her husband lost the election to wish them the best of health and happiness in their new life. I told her I envied the freedom and privacy they could now enjoy, and I meant it.

The doctors at Mayo had urged my husband to make the transition back to work slowly, so on the way home to Jordan we spent a few days in England to rest at Buckhurst Park. Queen Elizabeth kindly invited us for lunch at Balmoral Castle in Scotland, which should have been an easy half-day journey by helicopter but turned out to be anything but. Our plan was to fly first to Gleneagles, refuel the helicopter, and then continue on to Balmoral, which was only another forty to fifty miles. The first part of the plan went according to schedule. My only concern was that Hussein was still weak and that he might catch cold. We wrapped our pilot's big green Barbour jacket around him and took off from Gleneagles, only to run into a lowering cloudbank in the Scottish highlands.

Hussein suggested that the pilot try getting under the clouds by flying through the valleys. It was hair-raising to look out the window of the helicopter and see power lines whipping by almost at eye level. The clouds kept spilling off the 3,000-foot hills, and it became impossible to fly so low, so we decided to divert east to Aberdeen, land at the airport there, and travel by car. When we finally arrived at Balmoral, very apologetic, we were a good hour late and quite famished. After briefly composing ourselves in our rooms, we joined Queen Elizabeth, Prince Philip, Prince Charles, Princess Anne, a few other family members, and a number of the Queen's beloved corgis in the study at Balmoral. The group asked about Hussein's health and about the trip up. After some time we were invited into a small sitting room for afternoon tea, which featured wafer-thin tea sandwiches. I realized at that point that we had missed lunch altogether. My husband was far more polite than I and helped himself to only one or two sandwiches. I took several every time they were passed.

After tea, we went back to the study overlooking the exquisitely manicured grounds. Prince Philip asked me if I would like to see the organic garden. I readily assented, thinking it would be a perfect opportunity for me to supplement my tea with a few vegetables. As the Duke of Edinburgh and I strolled through the garden, Prince Charles and Hussein came up behind us, having noticed my foraging, and quipped dryly that they wished they had eaten salad as well. Soon afterward, fully nourished, we set out for the drive back to Gleneagles.

I became increasingly apprehensive as we prepared to leave for Jordan three days later. The five weeks we had spent away was the longest period my husband had ever spent outside the country, and it seemed from the reports we were receiving that almost the entire population wanted to greet him upon his return. It was heartwarming and exciting, but I worried about Hussein's stamina and whether he was adequately recovered for such an overwhelming event. "Please, he is going to be so tired," I kept telling our protocol officers. "He is stronger now, but you don't want to kill him with kindness." Hussein was susceptible to infection, and now he had only one kidney, which we had to keep healthy.

The view of Amman from the air was astounding. The King was at the controls, as usual, and he flew low over the city, which was reveling in his return. It was estimated later that more than a million people — one-quarter of the total population of Jordan — were already on the streets, having come to Amman from all over the country. I had hoped that just family and a few select officials would be at the welcoming ceremony at the airport, but the entire government, and more, was there. My husband's brother, Crown Prince Hassan, had arranged to drive with Hussein from the airport downtown to the Queen Mother's palace, Zahran. I drove there in my car with Princess Basma, part of a flotilla passing through the most unimaginable sea of human ecstasy.

People were laughing, weeping, waving hand-painted signs, holding up pictures of Hussein and of the two of us, running, screaming, throwing kisses and flowers and even their bodies at the cars, trying to reach in the windows and touch him. The streets were so packed it was impossible for the police to control the crowds. It took us an hour or more to travel the handful of miles to Zahran Palace. It must have been a nightmare for security, but the outpouring of affection dispelled the last vestiges of the King's depression. Over the protests of his security detail, Hussein sat on the car roof as he waved and received the embraces of his people.

Hussein was exhausted but exhilarated when we finally arrived home to Al Nadwa. The air was filled with the particular incense he loved, and the staff was ululating with joy. "I feel privileged," he said to me when I finally persuaded him to go to bed. "There are so many tragic cases of leaders losing their people as time goes on, but to have my relationship with the people grow even stronger after so many years is truly a blessing."

Try as we might, however, neither his doctors nor I could persuade him to stop smoking. When his doctor at Mayo had explained its possible links to certain types of cancer, including urological, grimly alluding to the damage smoking was doing to his body, my husband retorted that if the doctor had as much pressure on him as he did, he would smoke, too. Hussein's children were also worried about their father's health and smoking. He had made an effort to quit from time to time, and we tried to ration the number of cigarettes he could smoke, but even at Mayo he had coaxed his security and even my own aide-de-camp to open the window in his room for an illicit smoke. At Buckhurst, smothered laughter outside our bedroom signaled another surreptitious success at sneaking a cigarette. His goddaughter, Elizabeth, was passing his dressing room one day when she saw an open window — and his legs. Though he was weak, uncomfortable, and using a cane, he had somehow climbed through the window and up onto a ledge to smoke.

Cigarettes aside, my husband's brush with mortality had given him a new purpose and had crystallized his feelings about the legacy he

wanted to leave Jordan. His rejuvenated outlook was a great comfort for the children and
me. He was more determined than ever to advance Jordan along the path to a true monarchical democracy so that the country might
flourish without him. He took a major step a
month after his surgery by lifting the ban on
political parties. He also contemplated changing the succession. As it stood, his brother
Hassan, the Crown Prince, would succeed him,
and my husband's notion was not necessarily to
change that, but to modify it for the next generation after Hassan by the creation, perhaps, of a
family council. He genuinely believed in decision-making through consensus, a long-
standing Arab-Islamic principle, and was convinced that the Jordanian Hashimite family
should participate in such an important choice.
This approach would promote family unity and
help ensure, my husband said, "that they will
not only stand together and work together, but
that the most suitable person *willing* to assume
the responsibility is chosen." That change
would require amending the Constitution,
which specified the eldest son or a brother
since 1965, and he continued to think long and
hard about it.

The more immediate issue was America's ongoing dispute with Iraq. Our intelligence told
us that there was real concern in Washington
about how much of the Iraqi war machine had
actually been destroyed during the Gulf War.

521

Another round of U.S. air strikes against Iraq seemed imminent at the beginning of 1993, when the United Nations Special Commission reported their suspicions that Saddam Hussein was producing uranium for nuclear use.

King Hussein was due to make an official visit to Oman to discuss economic cooperation, but the United States advised my husband to cancel his trip. It was clear something was up: We had already noticed greatly increased air activity in the region. Then he received a message from Washington, telling us a strike against Iraq would occur in six hours. While my husband released his nervous energy through smoking, I gave vent to mine, as I often did, by going through our accumulated possessions and culling out things we did not need. I found it liberating. Given the number of crises we had faced, my husband was fond of saying that pretty soon there would be nothing left for me to discard or rearrange.

Neither the tension nor the air strikes let up. My husband was particularly anxious that there might be a nuclear explosion. An Iraqi nuclear scientist had been assassinated in Amman just weeks before the strikes began. According to intelligence in London, the scientist had been killed before he could divulge details of Iraq's nuclear capability. Was that what the American strikes were going after?

In June 1993 we went to the United States

for a routine medical checkup, which went very well, and for our first state visit to the Clinton White House. Bill Clinton was the eighth American President my husband had met, and in contrast to his immediate predecessors, Bush and Reagan, Clinton was a relative unknown. We did not know what to expect, but both Bill and Hillary were impressive. They were extraordinarily articulate, interested in my husband's views, and eager to learn as much as possible. Hillary confided how unprepared they had been for the ways of Washington, including the intense lack of privacy and the running commentary by the media and political opponents about every aspect of their life.

A few days into our state visit, Warren Christopher, Clinton's Secretary of State, informed Hussein that the United States had launched yet another missile attack against Iraq, this time against intelligence facilities in Baghdad in retaliation for an alleged plot to assassinate former President Bush during a visit to Kuwait in April. We heard Clinton announcing on CNN that he had discussed the attack ahead of time with U.S. friends and allies in the region, but the American President had never mentioned the pending missile strike to my husband, nor had any other U.S. official.

This put the King in a very awkward position. Just before the missile strike, Hussein had visited the Pentagon with full military honors, a moment that had been photographed and reported by newspapers in the Middle East. When we heard about the strike, we thought about the Pentagon ceremony and wondered if my husband had been set up. Were the full military honors to give the appearance of Hussein's complicity or approval of their actions?

The next surprise came from the PLO. The second phase of the peace talks had deadlocked in Washington and had been rescued by a Norwegian diplomat, so the Palestinians and the Israelis had been meeting secretly in Oslo. Suddenly, out of the blue, Washington announced in August that the PLO and Israel had reached a declaration of principles and an interim peace agreement. The King was furious. Yasser Arafat had told my husband that he had been in touch with Shimon Peres, but it turned out that the Palestinians and the Israelis had been meeting secretly for months. Shimon Peres, too, had not said a word about it. "Why not coordinate?" my husband said. "How can we possibly work this way?" Hussein recovered quickly from his shock, however, and within twenty-four hours he endorsed the interim Oslo agreement. "This is what the Palestinians want, and the only thing I can do is support them," he said.

Privately, though, Hussein thought the Palestinians had given away too much. The King had refused to bargain away any Palestinian rights to territory occupied since 1967, yet the wording of the Oslo agreement was so vague that it was unclear what lands the agreement would provide the Palestinians. More troubling to Hussein was that all the truly substantive issues — involving the status of Jerusalem, refugees, settlements, security arrangements, borders and relations, and cooperation with neighbors — were not addressed. Instead they were postponed for further negotiation within three years.

On the positive side, with the announcement of the Palestinian-Israeli interim accord, the way was now clear for King Hussein to work toward Jordan's own agreement with Israel. Because Arafat had made the first move, however flawed, Hussein felt free to proceed.

While talks commenced with Israel, it was with heavy hearts that we began another, more personal transitional event: the delivery of our oldest son, Hamzah, to boarding school in England. Hamzah had been registered at Harrow since the day he was born; the housemaster of Hussein's house, the Park, where he boarded, had been visiting Jordan at the time of his birth and had immediately put Hamzah's name down for the class of 1998. Hamzah's leaving home was an extraordinary wrench for all of us, just as it had been when Abir, Haya, and Ali had left for studies in England, but it was time for him as well to experience life beyond the hothouse of the Royal Court. I had hoped that Hamzah would go to school in the United States because I thought the American educational system was more flexible, but Hamzah wanted to follow in his father's path. Harrow would turn out to be an excellent match for him, however painful it was for us at the beginning.

Hamzah had inherited his father's love of flying, and it was he who flew me into London by helicopter in early September to meet up with his father on our way to Harrow. There were errands beforehand that would become routine — a visit to the orthodontist and the barber, then lunch at the Grill Room at the Dorchester Hotel, where his father introduced Hamzah to his favorite meal from his own student days, hamburgers topped with fried eggs. Neither of them was in the least bit responsive to my maternal comments about cholesterol, and Hamzah immediately adopted his father's favorite student meal as his own.

Hamzah and his father were very much alike, which led later to a great deal of speculation in the country that my husband would choose him as his successor. I discouraged such talk at every turn because I did not think it served any constructive purpose, and it put Hamzah in a difficult position where other family members were concerned. The succession would depend on God's will and my husband's judgment, as well as on constitutional considerations. My responsibility as mother, wife, and Queen was to encourage all the children to develop their own individual talents and to prepare to serve their country in whatever fashion they were most suited, with humility and devotion. No one should expect only a future of royal privilege.

As we prepared to leave him that first day of school, Hamzah waved good-bye to us bravely. It was I who began to dissolve as we drove away, as I had with each of the older children. Hamzah missed us terribly at first, which he tried hard to disguise, but it was obvious to his father. Within a week Hussein and I went back to Harrow after an agonizing debate over whether or not our visit would make life more difficult for our son. Both Hamzah and his father perked up over another meal of hamburgers and fried eggs, and the two of them teased me — a sure sign that Hamzah's mood had improved. All of us felt better after the visit. My husband subsequently wrote Hamzah a loving and affirming letter explaining his plan for a family council to elect a successor and urging him to understand the importance of his education in preparing him for his future role, whatever it might be. It was a private communication from father to son, and no more was said about it, but Hamzah settled down at Harrow and did very well.

We flew back to Jordan from London on September 13, or "Super Monday," as my husband called it, because Arafat and Rabin were in Washington signing Oslo I. Our own peace process was moving forward as well; twenty-four hours later Jordan and Israel signed an agenda for peace at the State Department in Washington, D.C. The spotlight on Arafat shone also on his wife, Suha, who was not in Washington with him but was interviewed extensively on CNN. I had sent her a message of support, and she called me soon after to thank me and to ask for advice in what she described as a very difficult time for her. "She is already being subjected to the same plague of gossip and rumors that all of us cope with in these positions," I wrote in my journal. It was extraordinary how merciless the criticism was. "I have heard that same gossip about so many different people and even about us and I know these kinds of stories circulate with no basis in fact whatsoever," I said to her critics. "Why not give her a chance? Try for once to give the benefit of the doubt."

I tried to share with Suha whatever wisdom I had come by as a twelve-year veteran of Middle East politics. "Focus on what you can contribute and let all the rest of it go," I advised Suha. "Just get in there and do your best. The inevitable gossip and rumors are not important as long as you know you are serving your people to the best of your ability."

Two weeks after Arafat and Rabin signed the interim agreement in Washington, the Israeli Prime Minister came to Aqaba for a secret meeting with my husband. Given the sensitivity of the situation, we kept a minimal staff presence at the house, and our house manager and I attended to every detail of the preparations. My most distinct memory of that meeting was the sound of Rabin's deep, sonorous voice for what seemed hours on end. It was at this meeting that the two leaders would begin to know each other and to establish the personal trust and respect, differences notwithstanding, that would lead to our peace accord with Israel. Jordan had supported every constructive peace effort since 1967, but time and again we had been frustrated or betrayed, sometimes both. We were exhausted by all the turmoil, political upheaval, and suffering of what were now generations of Palestinians, not to mention the corrosive sense of insecurity and all the obstacles to economic development and progress in the region.

Hussein and Rabin agreed not to publicly announce their contact in pursuit of peace, mostly because their positions were so far apart, and they wanted to wait until they had something substantive to offer. Slowly and painstakingly, they examined every position to see where progress could be made.

Our relationship with the Israelis had, at times, bordered on the absurd. At international conferences, we had to be constantly vigilant not to have any inappropriate contact with any Israeli participants and certainly not to be photographed with them. We knew that the Israelis could use those images for political purposes, giving an impression of normalization that would be interpreted on the Arab street as "fraternizing with the enemy." Yet somehow there always seemed to be Israelis poised to ambush us, wherever we might be, with camera in hand.

This sensitivity made for one very awkward international conference of First Ladies, when the de rigueur official group photograph had to be taken. It was customary to arrange the delegates alphabetically by country, which was fine if there were representatives from Jamaica or Japan separating Jordan from Israel. This time neither country was represented. I was placed next to Mrs. Weizman, the wife of Israel's President Ezer Weizman, who talked to me with great animation throughout the entire group photography session. I responded by looking straight ahead into the camera and talking to her out of the corner of my mouth, trying hard not to be impolite.

Avoiding mediagenic contact was absolutely necessary at that point, although we knew dialogue was essential and it was against our natures to have to avoid contact in these ways. A rare exception was the Wheelchair Games of disabled service members the King opened in England in the summer of 1993. We all applauded the entrance of the teams from Jordan, Israel, Britain, South America, and the United States. After the wheelchair games we shook hands with the disabled servicemen and posed for photographs with all of them including the Israelis, despite the taboo. "It seems insane that men must enlist, fight, and be injured in order to communicate with the enemy on a human level," my husband said to me later.

In the last months of 1993 and the beginning of 1994, the situation in the Middle East was particularly unsettled. I was in New York in November addressing a conference on women at Columbia University when an incident occurred that added to the tensions. President Clinton met with Salman Rushdie in the White House, albeit in a corridor, not the Oval Office. Rushdie had been condemned by the Ayatollah Khomeini a few years earlier for the way he wrote about the Prophet Muhammad in his novel *Satanic Verses*, a condemnation of his blasphemy that was widely accepted by Muslims all over the world, although many did not agree with his death sentence. In the West, however, various groups of Western writers, most notably the organization PEN, had sprung to Rushdie's defense, arguing that any censure or even criticism of Rushdie impinged on the constitutional right of everyone to freedom of speech. Clinton's meeting with Rushdie in the White House was obviously not a chance event. No one just happens to bump into the President in a corridor of the White House. Iran immediately blasted the Clinton meeting with Rushdie, and violent demonstrations broke out in other Muslim countries, including Bangladesh and Pakistan. The State Department issued warnings to U.S. citizens living or traveling in Muslim countries, which was hardly helpful to tourism. While Americans were thinking about Clinton's meeting with Rushdie as a constitutional issue, Muslims were viewing it as a gratuitous insult. Even my husband was very upset about it and called me from Jordan. "Hamas and extremists will use it," I wrote in my journal. "We need to ensure that those who might benefit from it and demonize relations between the United States and the Arab-Muslim world are not able to exploit the situation that has been created by the meeting." I called Hillary Clinton to register our concerns, but trying to get anyone's attention was a major challenge in Washington at the time.

Scandals such as Lorena Bobbitt's attack on her husband, Tonya Harding's on a fellow ice skater, and O.J. Simpson's murder trial dominated headlines and made productive dialogue about anything else very difficult. For people living outside the United States, America's extraordinary obsession with what seemed like minor events was puzzling and frustrating. In Jordan and the Middle East we were facing life-and-death issues on a daily basis: Many Palestinians objected to Arafat's peace negotiations with Israel, while others were opposed to Jordan's pursuit of the same goal. Islamic extremists were responsible for a series of explosions in movie theaters. Our first secretary at the Jordanian embassy in Lebanon was assassinated, and on February 25, thirty Palestinian worshipers were massacred by a Jewish settler in the Tomb of the Patriarchs in Hebron.

Nevertheless, negotiations with the Israelis stayed on track. The King had been working directly with Rabin for nearly a year on a workable framework for peace, and by mid-July 1994 the agreement was almost ready. Jordanian-Israeli subcommittees were successfully reaching understandings on water, the environment, and energy. Bilateral negotiations between the two countries were progressing on borders, other territorial matters, and security. On July 25, King Hussein and Prime Minister Rabin were scheduled to sign a declaration of intent to formally end the forty-six-year state of war between the two countries and begin the final path to peace. Even the choice of location was settled.

Hussein had selected Wadi Araba for the signing of the declaration — a fitting choice because of its position on Jordan's border with Israel. Marking this step forward in the region in this way would clearly demonstrate our independent commitment to a comprehensive peace. The King had written President Clinton to give him the still highly confidential news of the agreement and to inform him of the date and site. We thought all was in place, but we were wrong.

We were in Aqaba on July 15, Hussein having visited army units and the specific location for the Wadi Araba meetings, when he heard from Warren Christopher that the United States not only wanted to delay the meeting between the Jordanian and Israeli leaders, but also wanted it to take place in Washington, not Jordan. The King felt that the meeting should take place in Jordan, not at the White House like some media replay of Arafat's meeting with Rabin. "Follow your instincts," I told him. "Don't let anyone hijack this critical historic moment for their own short-term political benefit." The United States responded by dangling all sorts of financial incentives, including the forgiveness of Jordan's crippling $700 million debt. In the end, the King had no choice. "This is the only time I've ever compromised for profit to the country," he said. But I was skeptical about the American offer. Promises of debt relief were one thing, but there were no guarantees, and here we were in the process of losing control over our own declaration of peace with Israel.

Hussein and I were at lunch in Aqaba the next day when we were informed that Clinton was about to break the secrecy of the negotiations and announce the upcoming meeting in Washington. I was so agitated that I could not eat. Neither of us had any idea what Clinton was going to say.

It was surreal to listen to the live television

announcement that Jordan would be signing a declaration to end the state of war between itself and Israel while knowing that Hussein had not been consulted or briefed on the details in advance. Only after the news announcement did we learn that the official trip included a banquet, a White House ceremony, and an invitation for both the King and Rabin to address a joint session of the U.S. Congress, which was especially significant. I had long lobbied for just such an opportunity; it would be a very effective way for Hussein to take his vision of peace directly to U.S. decision-makers.

After months of secrecy, history was made on July 18, 1994, when Fayez Tarawneh, our ambassador in Washington and head of the Jordanian delegation to the peace talks, and Elyakim Rubinstein, the head of the Israeli delegation, appeared together in Wadi Araba to announce the commencement of final peace negotiations between our two countries. "Fayez and Eli Rubinstein trading jokes in shirtsleeves, an amazing sight," I wrote in my journal.

The Jerash Festival opened in the midst of all these historic events, and somehow Hussein found the time to open it officially with me, a remarkable gesture under the circumstances, and a source of excitement for all of Jerash. I think he chose to come to the opening to seize the opportunity to interact with different groups of Jordanians while the meetings were taking place with the Israelis, at a moment when he would be leading Jordan into an entirely new era.

A Jordanian delegation, including our nephew, Talal, had traveled ahead to Washington to lay the groundwork for the upcoming events and to iron out any problems before they arose. Talal, who had become my husband's Military Secretary after the Gulf War, went to the U.S. State Department to confirm the assurances that had been given to my husband and was told that Jordan would indeed receive everything that had been promised, including the squadron of F-16 fighter jets that Congress had been denying my husband now for several years. Talal also went to Capitol Hill, where he received a completely different answer. "Absolutely not," he was told. "You are not getting a thing unless you sign a full treaty with Israel right now, not just an end to the state of war. You are signing a framework for peace for your sake, not ours, so don't expect to receive any rewards from us."

Talal had just sent off an optimistic cable to the King reiterating the assurances from the State Department when he had to quickly fire off a second cable. "Disregard previous message. Congress says no. What shall we do?" It was a critical moment. If King Hussein was to come back empty-handed from Washington, it would be a disaster for Jordan and would almost certainly derail the peace process at the eleventh hour. The King immediately cabled

Talal and said: "I'll speak to Rabin, and you make contact with the American Israel Public Affairs Committee."

Talal was not familiar with the members of AIPAC, so he phoned his doctor, who he knew was well connected and might be able to help. "Yes," his doctor responded. "I know the president of the organization, Steve Grossman. I'll put you in touch." Within minutes, Steve Grossman called Talal, who explained the impasse and its urgency, since the White House ceremony was only three days away. "I would love to help you, but I have to get the go-ahead from the Israelis first," Grossman said.

Hussein had reached Prime Minister Rabin by then, and Talal was very relieved when Steve Grossman called him back to say, "The Israelis have given me the green light. Rabin himself told me to do whatever is necessary to help the Jordanians, and I promise you that Congress will pass your bill. I cannot tell how many votes you'll get, but your bill will pass." It was a stunning example of AIPAC's power. The bill would end up being tacked on to an agriculture spending bill and going quietly before the Senate at 1 A.M. when C-SPAN was off the air. In three days Patrick Griffen, Clinton's Assistant for Legislative Affairs, got the measure passed: one squadron of F-16s for Jordan and a $700 million debt forgiven.

We arrived in Washington a few days before the signing to find ourselves under siege again.

The Middle East experts at the State Department were furiously demanding that my husband show them what was becoming known as the Washington Declaration, but Hussein refused to show the agreement to anyone, including Warren Christopher. So intent was the King to prevent any possible leaks that might endanger the agreement that he waited until late the night before the signing, after all the newspapers had put their morning editions to bed, to send the text to the White House.

We were still working on last-minute edits to Hussein's speech to the joint session of Congress as we sped on July 25, 1994, toward the meeting with Rabin at the White House, where we turned an extraordinary new page of our destiny. We were greeted by the President and Hillary Clinton and taken to our respective Israeli partners for what was, predictably, a media circus. "Mrs. Rabin is quite tough and aggressive," I recorded in my journal. "We eye each other from a distance and keep the conversation social."

It was a typically hot summer day in Washington as my husband and Prime Minister Rabin signed the Washington Declaration, ending a forty-six-year state of war with Israel. Hussein's remarks on the White House lawn were deeply moving. He always spoke best when he did so from the heart, and this occasion was perhaps his finest moment. "For many, many years, and with every prayer, I have asked God, the Almighty, to help me be a part of forging peace between the children of Abraham," he said. "This was the dream of generations before me, and now I see it realized." Among the crowd surrounding the three leaders after the ceremony was Avraham Das- kal, an Israeli who had been invited to Amman fifty-eight years earlier by his friend King Abdullah to celebrate the birth of Abdullah's grandson, Hussein, whom Daskal had last seen as a newborn.

Although the Israelis were jubilant to be signing a framework for peace with an Arab neighbor, my enthusiasm was tempered by worries. While I was elated for my husband, I knew that his mind, too, was thousands of miles away in Jordan. For Israel the Declaration represented the completion of a specific objective, but for us it was simply a continuing part of a process, a landmark on the rocky road toward a comprehensive peace in the region.

The Washington Declaration stated the five underlying principles agreed to by Hussein and Rabin, among them negotiations based on UN Resolutions 242 and 338 and the right of each state to live in peace within secure and recognized boundaries. One controversial principle was the inclusion of Israel's "respect" for Jordan's "special" and "historic role" in the Muslim holy shrines in Jerusalem, and Israel's agreement to give "high priority" to Jordan's continuing guardianship during Israel's permanent status negotiations with the Palestinians.

As we learned at the banquet that evening, this recognition of the Hashimites' continuing spiritual role in Arab East Jerusalem incensed Yasser Arafat. East Jerusalem was, of course, occupied territory, which the Palestinians were claiming as their capital, and Arafat wanted control of the holy sites. But there were no provisions in the Oslo agreements about the sacred sites, and until other arrangements were made for their protection, my husband felt it necessary to ensure that Jordan maintain its historic guardianship of the holy sites where his great-grandfather was buried, his grandfather had been assassinated, and so many Jordanian soldiers had been killed defending Arab East Jerusalem in 1967. As King Hussein said in his address to Congress the next day, he believed strongly that sovereignty over the holy places should reside with God alone and should be extended to all the children of Abraham, be they Muslim, Jew, or Christian.

For the first time, direct phone links would be opened between Israel and Jordan, our respective electricity grids would be shared to conserve resources, an international air corridor would be opened to facilitate commercial exchanges and tourism, and two new border crossings would be opened, one at the southern tip of Aqaba-Eilat, the other to be determined. All in all, the provisions of the Declaration were a very promising step toward the final negotiations still to come.

The joint session of Congress was dramatic; the King's words were greeted by standing ovations. Rabin's speech was also very well received. It was an eye-opener for members of our delegation to see firsthand the seemingly magical hold Israel had on the American political psyche. Representatives and senators were offering warm, enthusiastic congratulations to the King, but they were greeting Prime Minister Rabin as if they were the oldest of friends.

That dynamic was working in our favor, however. Israel was now actively supporting the Jordanian peace initiative. As long as Rabin was alive, our government would have a much easier time rallying the support of Congress. Rabin was consistent in advocating support for Jordan, recognizing that sustainable peace could be reached only with an equal stakeholder, a principle we believed that had to apply to the Palestinians as well. Rabin also knew Jordan. He had fought against Jordan. He also knew Jordanians, having been born and raised just across the Jordan River. Many Israelis did not have this perspective. Whereas members of our government knew a great deal about the Israelis and their internal politics — who was a minister, who was a mayor — their counterparts knew little about us. To most Israelis, we were all just "Arabs." They did not know how different we are from one another, or our cultural terms of reference, or what our concerns are. The Israeli equation was a simple one. The "good" Arabs were the ones who talked to Israel; the "bad" Arabs were the ones who did not. After the signing, our image changed virtually overnight, it seemed, and suddenly even for our traditionally sternest critics, we could do no wrong.

After a brief stop in England, we received news that the Israelis had given us a flight plan to overfly Israel and take the most direct route to Amman. Israeli airspace had always been off-limits. Indeed all of Israel had been off-limits. My husband's closest advisers were extremely anxious about changing our flight plan, but Hussein was determined to do so. We did not tell the crew or anyone else on board the TriStar until we were in the air between the Greek coast and Cyprus, where two Israeli F-15 fighter escorts joined us. Suddenly Tel Aviv and the coastline lay in front of us, unimaginably, stretching north and south. We could see congested traffic on the highways and suburban sprawl, manicured, affluent-looking. As we flew over Tel Aviv, Rabin and my husband gave a joint radio address in which we were heartened to hear Rabin speak of Jerusalem as a city of peace for all future generations. "It gives me hope in the midst of the snowballing pace of events. Hussein appears to be on such a high of emotion that I pray there will be no letdown, that we are not simply pawns in a game in which we may lose our value once we have given everything," I noted in my journal.

As we flew on, leaving Israel behind us, over hills and valleys dotted with settlements, suddenly, gloriously, the golden Dome of the Rock appeared directly ahead. It was an unbelievable sight as we approached it, glowing in the afternoon light — so familiar to me, yet I was seeing it for the first time. Gazing at the Dome was an extraordinary moment for me, and even more so for all the Jordanians on the flight, who had not been able to see or visit the mosque since 1967. Some wept, others prayed. "What feelings must be overwhelming Hussein, so close to the Dome for the first time in twenty-seven years," I wrote in my journal. "In this moment I see none of the ugly new construction surrounding the old city, nor even the house Hussein started building before 1967 that was never completed. I see only the peaceful site of the mosque and its courtyard, which appear to be lit from within." Hussein circled the mosque as we flew lower and lower, until we were barely at 1,000 feet. It was an incredible moment, documented by an Israeli aerial photographer code-named Peace Fox on one of the Israeli jet escorts. It reinforced my sense that we were embarking on a new path with unique spiritual goals. Even now, when I look at the photograph of the huge TriStar flying over Israel with the golden Hashimite crown on the tail and the gray, blue, and red livery, I am overcome with emotion.

I went directly to the Jerash Festival as soon as we landed in Jordan to get a feeling for the mood of the people. So much had happened so quickly and so many miles away that I wanted to see for myself how it was being received. It was Hussein's nature to act intuitively and sometimes impulsively, but always from the heart; perhaps because of his recent physical ordeal I was feeling particularly protective of him during the peace process and very conscious of the different points of view that would influence the vital peace-building after the treaties were signed. I was therefore especially relieved to find at Jerash and elsewhere in the country the usual atmosphere of support and affection. Hussein would need all that and more to lead the country successfully through the negotiations that still lay ahead with Israel, and to accept the dramatic changes that were already taking place.

Less than two weeks after the signing of the Washington Declaration we went to Aqaba to prepare for the inauguration of the first open crossing point between Jordan and Israel. Warren Christopher flew in for the historic event on August 8, along with his wife and several other U.S. officials. Israel sent a huge delegation, including Yitzhak Rabin, Shimon Peres, members of the Israeli army, and the media. Our home was host to an army of Israeli politicians, generals, and journalists. A press conference was held outside the house, and the extraordinary size and unknown makeup of the throng of reporters made our security-conscious sons wary. "Hamzah and Hashim keep a watchful eye on their father, while Mrs. Christopher and the ladies watch the press conference, harem-like, from an upstairs window of the house," I wrote in my journal. Telephone lines between the two countries, mandated by the Washington Declaration, had also just opened. The ceremonial first conversation, which took place on August 6 between my husband and Ezer Weizman, Israel's President, opened floodgates of pent-up communication between families on both sides of the Jordan River.

Israeli and Jordanian delegations immediately resumed negotiations toward a final peace, but despite the progress made by the Declaration, there were no guarantees that they would achieve it. Decades of bitterness and mistrust had to be overcome, along with the aftermath of three devastating wars. My husband and I remained optimistic, but cautious. We had lived through so many failed attempts that made for great media opportunities, but without achieving any lasting peace. We could not afford to repeat that experience. It was critical, from our perspective, that the "areas of cooperation" with Israel outlined in the Washington Declaration produce tangible benefits not only for the Jordanian people, but also for regional progress.

★ ★ ★

Around this time my husband and I finally identified a possible new place to live. The new house was in a royal residential compound just outside Amman where we had stayed for a few weekends with the children to escape the congestion of the city. Known as Darat al Khair, or house of blessing, the house, which had many happy memories for my husband, had a lovely view over the cities of Salt and Jerash, and, most important to Hussein, was far from the Diwan. He had finally settled his siblings, his nephews, and his older children, so the way was clear for the youngest seven and the two of us.

I worked with a renowned Jordanian architect, Rasem Badran, on a design that would allow our entire family to be together without destroying the integrity of the original building. Unfortunately, the final beautiful design, a cluster of family spaces that resembled a traditional Jordanian village, would have required too much time for construction. We decided instead to renovate a slightly larger house that our nephew Talal and his brother Ghazi had grown up in for ourselves, and Darat Al Khair became the home of Talal and his wife, Ghida.

I had worked with a number of architects on plans for a home on various alternative sites. This time I did something different. Instead of making the house big enough for all the children, and thus creating a white elephant for any smaller family in the future, I decided to add a separate building to the plan that would offer the older children a degree of independence. I hoped this would take us all through the years and allow us to adapt to the changing needs of the family once the children began to grow up and leave home. I also developed a landscape design that would give the house the natural outdoor space that my husband loved so much. I worked hard on designing a separate, sunken rock garden for him outside his office, where he could have private conversations or just be alone. Before we moved into it, my husband named the house Bab Al Salam, the Gate of Peace, after one of the entrances to Masjid Al Haram Al Sharif, the Great Mosque, in Mecca.

Meanwhile, the King was working very hard with Prime Minister Rabin on the final details of a peace agreement. We had never been this close to an agreement before, and he would never have a better partner than Rabin. King Hussein described their relationship as that between two military men who dealt directly, and often bluntly, with each other. Rabin and my husband were also able to see issues from each other's perspective. The negotiating question was always, "If I were you, could I live with that?" They both knew that peace was not made between governments but between people, and whatever agreement they arrived at had to answer the needs of both populations in order to stand the test of time. Neither one of them wanted to sign a piece of paper, shake hands, and watch the peace collapse. And by the middle of October, they were very, very close.

On the evening of October 16, I hugged my husband and wished him good luck as he left to meet with Rabin at Hashimya to try to work out the final details. It was a very long night. When the phone rang early the next morning, I had no idea what to expect until I heard Hussein's exhausted but jubilant voice. "I have wonderful news," he said. "We made it!" Hussein touched me greatly when he added that my encouragement had pushed him through to the end.

How far we had all come — and how fast. Life in Jordan had been a roller coaster before, but now it had accelerated to a breathless pace. The intricate, day-by-day negotiations of the Washington Declaration were behind us. Now, after three months of negotiating the painstaking details, the King and Rabin had dotted all the i's and crossed all the t's. The peace treaty to which Hussein had dedicated so much of his life was finally ready.

Within a week we were back in Aqaba, this time preparing for the arrival of the Clintons and a host of dignitaries for the signing of the Jordan-Israeli Peace Treaty on October 26. Hussein and I were both enveloped by a strange calm and sense of destiny.

"This is a day like no other in terms of hopes,

in terms of promise, and in terms of determination," my husband declared. "It is the dawning of the era of peace, mutual respect between us all, tolerance, and the coming together of people here and for generations to come to build and achieve what is worthy of them." Rabin's remarks were no less emotional. "As dawn broke this morning and a new day began, new life came into the world," he said. "Babies were born in Jerusalem. Babies were born in Amman. But this morning is different. To the mother of the Jordanian newborn, a blessed day to you. To the mother of the Israeli newborn, a blessed day to you. The peace that was born today gives us the hope that children born today will never know war between us, and their mothers will know no sorrow."

By attending the signing, Bill Clinton became the first American President to make an official visit to Jordan since 1974. And the day of the signing turned out to be Hillary's birthday. We had learned about it that morning and hurriedly ordered a cake. We celebrated the peace treaty and Hillary's birthday at lunch in Aqaba before going up to Amman, where the President presented a stirring address to a joint session of the Jordanian Parliament. President Clinton's speech struck an important balance between the political and material rewards of the peace treaty — the forgiveness of Jordan's debt, development of the Rift Valley, expansion of trade and investment opportunities — and the spiritual gains. Echoing my husband's life-long belief that what people have in common is more important than their differences, Clinton ended his remarks by quoting Moses' farewell address to the children of Israel as they gathered to cross the River Jordan: "I have set before you life and death, blessings and curses. Choose life so that you and your descendants may live." He then cited a similar message of hope and religious tolerance from the Prophet Muhammad: "There is no argument between us and you. God shall bring us together and unto Him is the homecoming."

The metaphorical breaking down of boundaries was a tremendously positive step. The actual opening of the borders between our two countries, however, posed unforeseen problems. Immediately after the peace treaty, Jordan's archaeological treasure, Petra, was overrun by a massive influx of Israeli tourists. The narrow Siq, or gorge, that served as an entrance to the Nabatean city became crowded with people and horses. The crush of visitors often exceeded the carrying capacity of the archaeological park and accelerated deterioration of the fragile sandstone of the ancient monuments.

UNESCO had designated Petra a World Heritage Site in 1985, and well before the peace treaty I had appealed to Frederico Mayor, the Director-General of UNESCO, to work with us to design a master plan for the entire region. Luxury hotels began to proliferate in Petra — six new four-star and five-star hotels within two years, with many more planned. This uncontrolled development was devastating to the area because there was no requirement for an environmental impact assessment.

Both the site and its income needed to be protected. The local Bedouin communities complained bitterly when we forbade horses in the Siq, so we compromised by allowing them to provide horses for the trip between the tourist center and the entrance to the Siq. The hotel owners were furious when, at UNESCO's urging, we raised the price of admission to around $30, and some foreign tourists were furious when we established a much lower price for Jordanians. Still, for all our efforts, which included the removal of tens of thousands of tons of rubble from the floor of the Siq to stem erosion and reduce the danger of flash floods, by 1998 Petra would be listed as one of the World Monuments Fund 100 Most Endangered Sites, and it remains on that list today.

When my husband made his first public visit to Israel in November for the ceremonial signing of the ratification of the peace treaty, he flew to the southern tip of the Sea of Galilee by helicopter and was greeted by hundreds of ecstatic Israeli schoolchildren shouting, "Hussein! Hussein!" An Israeli journalist commented that night on CNN that if my husband were running for election in Israel, he would win. Such remarks amused my husband but did not sit well with conservative elements in Jordan and in other Arab countries.

The change in Hussein after the success of the peace negotiations was unmistakable. When King Juan Carlos and Queen Sofie made a state visit to Jordan in November 1994 to coincide with Hussein's birthday, the first such official visit we had hosted since the Gulf crisis, he was far more relaxed than I had ever seen him under such circumstances. The Spanish royals presented us with a beautiful Andalusian mare in foal. A terrible sickness had befallen the Andalusians in Spain several years before, but now the breed had recovered enough for Sofie and Juanito to present us with this precious brood mare to join the stallion they had given us years earlier on our state visit to Spain.

Hussein's mood grew even lighter when we returned to Aqaba after saying our farewells and went out on our fishing boat. He decided impulsively to cross the Israeli border into the waters off Eilat. Escorted by dolphins and a flotilla of local boats, Hussein was greeted by crowds of Israelis blowing kisses and cheering. "The atmosphere is electric and very neighborly," I wrote in my journal. "His spontaneity is fun, and our shared enjoyment of so many extraordinary experiences is the greatest gift of the advancing years of marriage."

Later that same year, Queen Beatrix of the Netherlands, another staunchly loyal friend, made a state visit to Jordan. Beatrix, one of the warmest and kindest spirits I have ever known, assumed the Dutch throne when her mother, Queen Juliana, abdicated in 1980. The Queen and Prince Claus had been our first royal visitors in the first years of our marriage and had always shown a deep understanding of the political, economic, and humanitarian challenges we faced.

My husband's spirit remained high in England, where we joined Hashim, who was on Thanksgiving break from school in the United States, and Hamzah, who had come over from Harrow, to spend the weekend with Prince Charles at Sandringham for a shooting party. That Sunday I remember watching my husband and the two boys walking the rolling hills in the requisite breeches and waistcoats and boots, and feeling so proud of my handsome men.

In May 1995, we were back in London, for the fiftieth anniversary of VE Day celebrations. As we pulled up to Buckingham Palace for the opening event, our car was placed first in line because Hussein after so many years on the throne had seniority over every other head of state in attendance. While we waited in the car, my husband reflected with some amazement that the first trip he had made as a monarch to England had been on the occasion of the death of King George, Queen Elizabeth's father. Then he had been the youngest leader, positioned at the end of the line. Forty years later, with innumerable crises and conflicts behind him, he was now the presiding elder statesman of all the guests.

chapter nineteen

The Edge of the Abyss

I was in Swaziland when I heard the news. I had been attending the United World Colleges International Council meeting in Johannesburg, South Africa — where I was officially inaugurated as the global education movement's president, succeeding Prince Charles — alongside President Nelson Mandela, who was assuming responsibility for the movement's International Council.

At the end of the Johannesburg meeting we visited our United World College, Waterford Kamhlaba, in Swaziland, which had provided the best equal-opportunity education for more than a generation of South African and Swazi students during the restrictive years of apartheid, educating, among others, Nelson Mandela's children and grandchildren. The energetic young Swazi King Mswati accompanied me to the school and later hosted a colorful official banquet for us. Upon returning to my hotel suite from dinner I received an urgent message that my husband had called. Moments later I reached Hussein, who told me Yitzhak Rabin had just been shot; nothing more was known. I put down the receiver and sat there alone in the sitting room absolutely stunned, but I clung to the hope that Rabin would pull through. Shortly afterward, Hussein phoned again. Shaken and sorrowful, he said Rabin was dead, assassinated by an Israeli. I tried to comfort him and said I would return home immediately. King Mswati was extremely understanding and considerate, opening the airport at 6:00 the next morning for my departure and to bid me farewell.

The King and I flew to Jerusalem for Rabin's funeral. It was Hussein's first visit there since the 1967 war. As a wife and a mother, I felt deeply for Leah Rabin. I could not help thinking "There but for the grace of God go I," as we condoled her and her stricken family.

King Hussein's words on that day resonated around the world. "He had courage, he had vision, and he had a commitment to peace. Standing here, I commit myself before you, before my people in Jordan, before the world, to myself to continue with our utmost effort, to ensure that we leave a similar legacy. We are not ashamed, nor are we afraid, nor are we anything but determined to fulfill the legacy for which my friend fell, as did my grandfather in this very city, when I was with him and but a young boy."

Later I would be criticized by some in our area for showing sadness at the death of Rabin, an Israeli, but in fact I was not alone. People from all faiths from throughout our region and elsewhere in the world mourned the passing of a statesman who had essentially given his life for peace. Hussein was filled with foreboding over the impact that Rabin's loss would have on the peace process. Hopes had been raised over what was widely being called "the peace dividend," the chance to realize great gains not just in the diplomatic arena but for positive national development as well. Our society, held hostage for so many years by conflict, now had a chance to move ahead, it seemed. My husband and I hoped and expected that this easing of tensions would encourage a broader participation and investment in the building of our country, and the strengthening of its institutions. I returned to Amman deeply sobered by the death of Rabin and all the implications it carried, but more determined than ever to continue my efforts to build bridges between communities and cultures.

King Hussein always emphasized that true peace is not created by treaties between governments, but must be built between people. And to bring people together, we had to begin with our children. The only way to overcome the enmity of previous generations is to enable the next generation, the future guardians of peace, to meet and interact openly and honestly in a secure atmosphere of trust. Education and exposure can impress upon young people the importance of resolving conflicts without violence, teach them the skills with which to do it, and to make their voices heard in issues that affect them. What if we today placed a premium on education for peace, a commitment to it equal to what previous generations devoted to military academies and combat readiness? We might well achieve a more lasting security than war could ever provide.

With these goals paramount, I became actively involved in the 1990s with three inspiring programs that promote cross-cultural understanding and conflict resolution by bringing together young people and potential world leaders from across our region and the world to understand and build on their common humanity.

Since 1993, Seeds of Peace has been bringing children from the Middle East and other conflict-wracked regions together in the summer, to provide them an opportunity to break down the barriers of prejudice and build mutual respect. Its founder, John Wallach, believed that this process would encourage its participants to realize, in his words, that "the enemy has a face." Seeds is producing a significant network of future leaders and activists for peace who value communication over confrontation. One graduate, a Palestinian youngster named Asel Asleh, was wearing his Seeds of

Peace T-shirt when he was killed on a West Bank street by Israeli crossfire. But his family refused to allow their despair to turn to hate, or to abandon what their son believed in. They welcomed his Jewish friends into their home and to the funeral to mourn with them. Other Seeds graduates are reaching out to each other in the midst of the violence. Hundreds of Israelis and Palestinians use the Seeds network to write e-mails or to call each other, whether to trade passionate opinions or to provide comfort over the sound of gunfire, or even to risk their lives to meet at the Seeds of Peace Center in Jerusalem. In their actions and their words, they plead with us all not to give up hope, never to surrender in the fight for peace. Hussein and I often met with the young participants, who were an enduring source of hope for him, especially during some of the most frustrating and painful periods of the peace process.

United World Colleges is a global network of international baccalaureate schools, which foster cross-cultural understanding, peace, and tolerance — ideals even more relevant in today's conflict-scarred world than when the first college opened following World War II. Each campus brings students together from countries throughout the world to live, study, and serve the community together. They break down barriers and weave their regional and national perspectives into a complex tapestry of understanding. As one UWC graduate said,

"When you come into the school you have an idea of how things are. But then you have all your ideas broken down. You start to learn how to pick out the truth, start to see the truth from other people's points of view. That is how you change the world." The enthusiasm, commitment, and solidarity I see in their eyes is my vision of hope and peace.

There are ten United World Colleges spanning the globe, and we were all committed to the dream of a UWC in the Middle East, to bring together students from throughout the region and the world. We chose a spectacular site in Aqaba for its symbolic value as it overlooked Jordan, Israel, Saudi Arabia, and Egypt, and was close to the Palestinian territory. Now, perhaps more than ever, a UWC of the Middle East could contribute to our efforts to educate a new generation of architects of peace.

Such architects were already being trained at the United Nations University International Leadership Academy in Amman, the first global leadership training facility designed to enhance international cooperation through dialogue and intercultural exchange, which we officially launched on the United Nations' fiftieth anniversary. The brainchild of our former Prime Minister, Abdel Salam Majali, the UNU/ILA brought together young professionals to share ideas, experiences, and viewpoints with each other and with current world leaders. In an atmosphere of dialogue and cultural exchange, they gained the skills — but more important, the open, flexible minds — so vital to the leaders of the future.

Jordanian girls and women often excel in these programs, which I find especially encouraging, because in my experience whenever women engage as equal partners with men, development and progress accelerate and endure. I had been deeply involved in women's issues since my marriage, but the scope of my understanding expanded exponentially through such programs as Bani Hamida and the National Handicrafts Development Project, our Quality of Life and micro-credit programs, and the Institute for Child Health and Development, under the aegis of the Noor Al Hussein Foundation. In our women's programs we had worked closely with two national organizations: the General Federation of Jordanian Women, which focused on the political, economic, and social status of women, and the Business and Professional Women's Club, which promoted the advancement of women in the workplace.

Over the decades, the status of women in Jordan had significantly improved. The percentage of women in the workforce had doubled, and gradual legislative improvements were being made. Although men and women receive equal education in Jordan, women still tended to enter the workforce in relatively small numbers.

The obstacles that keep many women in

Jordan from realizing their full potential were a great source of frustration for many of us, particularly the King. The waste of underutilizing half the country's population was not limited to Jordan, of course. Years after the women's movement had made significant gains in the great democracy of America, there were still precious few women in appointed or elected positions. Indeed, it was not until the 1980 presidential elections that brought Ronald Reagan to office that the "gender gap" was first publicly acknowledged.

In Jordan, many women focused their talents and energies on responsibilities at home. The cohesive family environment stemming from this emphasis on motherhood creates a level of social stability that would be the envy of most Western countries. Indeed, the Middle East suffers less random crime and violence than the industrialized world, in large measure thanks to the devotion of women to their families. However, Jordanian women who choose to pursue a professional career are free to do so. Indeed, I have worked with many highly qualified and impressive women in my office and throughout the region.

There were inequities, too, to be sure. We were particularly concerned about our inability to remove the outrageous and legally protected practice of "honor crimes" from Jordan's penal code, which essentially gave men license to kill wives or sisters or daughters whom they accused of having had illicit sexual relations, with little fear of legal consequence. For all the progress Jordan had made in terms of democracy and human rights, our Article 340 remained in place: "He who discovers his wife or one of his female relatives committing adultery and kills, wounds, or injures one of them, is exempted from any penalty."

There were around twenty-five such killings a year in Jordan, and many more in other countries around the world. Crimes of passion are sanctioned in many countries, but we recognized our responsibility to advocate for changes in the penal code. King Hussein condemned violence against women in his 1997 opening address to Parliament, but for all our efforts the elected members of the Jordanian Parliament voted time and again to retain the statute. There was a simple lack of political will, despite the Constitution and the religious law known as *shari'a,* both of which are patently opposed to the so-called honor killings and forbid the taking of the law into one's own hands.

The Jordanian journalist Rana Husseini almost single-handedly brought this problem to the attention of the public in a series of newspaper articles over a nine-year period. Many criticized her work and motives, and some of her detractors even sent hate mail and threats. But Rana persisted. "I kept on going because I knew what I was doing was the right thing and that it did not contradict *shari'a* or the principles of human rights," she told me. Her achievements were given special recognition when she was awarded the Reebok Human Rights Award in 1998.

I was also concerned about women's and human rights issues in other regions of the world, specifically the suffering of women in Bosnia. Jordan had been providing refuge for almost 100 Bosnian refugee families since the outset of the war in 1993, but shockingly little international attention had been focused on the steady stream of Muslim refugees forced from their homes by the Serbian government's policy of "ethnic cleansing." Jacques Chirac, the President of France, was particularly incensed at the indifference shown by Europe and the United States, and had spoken to me on an official visit to France about what we might do to focus attention on the problem.

I contacted other First Ladies and heads of state to urge collective support and to increase relief assistance. Jordan sent planeloads of food, blankets, medical supplies, and reconstruction equipment to Bosnia, and in July 1996 I traveled to Tuzla to meet with Swanee Hunt, the U.S. ambassador to Austria and founder of the global movement Women Waging Peace, and Italian European Commissioner Emma Bonino, my co-chairs of the Women of Srebrenica Project. In Tuzla, 30,000 survivors of Srebrenica were living in temporary, ill-equipped refugee camps, most of them

Muslim women whose husbands and sons had disappeared in the carnage. We met with the refugee women in a huge gym. Many were desperate to know the fate of their missing men and boys and to have those responsible brought to justice. The vast majority of the people collected in the hall were grieving widows, many of whom became increasingly hysterical during the event. At one point, as their moans of grief reached a crescendo, I went up to the stage and was able to calm them somewhat with prayers from the Quran. What could one possibly say in the face of such loss, of such crimes against humanity? The women had hung on the walls and the rails of the stadium thousands of pieces of cloth embroidered with the names of 7,000 missing men and boys. The organizers had even invited Serb and Croat women who had suffered their own losses to join them in commemorating the fall of Srebrenica the year before. "We are all mothers," they explained.

The organizers of the ceremony in Tuzla subsequently toured with the commemorative banner and used the occasion to raise hundreds of thousands of dollars to help the women of Srebrenica rebuild their shattered lives.

Five years later I would return to Bosnia as a member of the International Commission on Missing Persons (ICMP), created in 1996 at the G7 Summit in Lyon, France, and meet with many of the same women. They were still searching for news of their loved ones, unable to rebuild their lives without this knowledge and without assurances that the massacre would be officially memorialized. While the ICMP's state-of-the-art DNA technology has been successful in speeding up identification of remains from mass graves throughout the Balkans — it was also used to assist with identification efforts at New York's World Trade Center site following September 11, 2001 — and while our work with family associations has given these women new hope, it has become painfully clear that conflict recovery and reconciliation in the Balkans will take many years.

In 1996, women in Jordan, Palestine, and Lebanon also continued to suffer the consequences of war and upheaval, particularly those women of Palestinian origin who, like the women of Srebrenica, longed to return home. Sadly, that summer the possibility of a Palestinian homecoming seemed to grow ever more remote.

Jordan's peace with Israel had become increasingly strained after the election of Prime Minister Benjamin Netanyahu. Only two months after he took office, Netanyahu announced that he was lifting the four-year freeze on the expansion of Jewish settlements on the West Bank that was called for in the Oslo agreements. To our horror he approved the construction of 2,000 new homes in the occupied Jordan Valley, an incendiary move that drew condemnation by the Arab League and a stern warning about our peace treaty from my husband. The warning fell on deaf ears. Netanyahu slowed the withdrawal of Israeli forces from Palestinian territory called for in the Oslo accords to almost a trickle, including the planned redeployment of occupying troops from the city of Hebron, which was home to 130,000 Palestinians and only 500 Jews. The tension was palpable to everyone, it seemed, but Netanyahu's hard-liners. The straw that finally broke the camel's back came only three months after Netanyahu took office, when Israel ran a new entrance to a tunnel into Arab East Jerusalem under the sacred Al Aqsa mosque.

King Hussein was furious. The Israelis had not said a word to him in advance, even though a high-level emissary from Netanyahu's government had met with my husband just twenty-four hours earlier. Not only did this action symbolize the presumption of Israel's sovereignty over the entire city, it was also of special concern to my husband as the Hashimite custodian of the holy places in Jerusalem, a role underscored in our peace treaty. Fifty-four Palestinians and fourteen Israelis were killed in the four days of violence that followed in Jerusalem, and Jordan's peace treaty with Israel was almost another casualty. Thirty-eight Jordanian groups, including political parties and professional organizations, signed a statement condemning Jordan's normalization of relations with Israel.

Disillusionment with the treaty was already deepening at all levels of Jordanian society. Israel had not delivered on the trade deals worked out during the pre-peace negotiations, and the peace dividends that so many had anticipated simply failed to materialize. One poll of Jordanians taken at the beginning of 1996 found that 47 percent felt the economy had actually deteriorated in the two years since my husband and Rabin signed the peace treaty. Our national debt was such that the International Monetary Fund ordered us to lift government subsidies on bread, leading to riots in Jordan during the summer of 1996. It was all so predictable — and avoidable. "To build peace, people must not have something worth fighting for, but something to make it worth ending the fighting," I said at an awards ceremony in the United States in the fall of 1996, where Leah Rabin and I were awarded the Eleanor Roosevelt Val-Kill Medal for our work for peace.

The peace process was deteriorating so rapidly that President Clinton invited King Hussein, Yasser Arafat, and Benjamin Netanyahu to an emergency meeting on October 2 at the White House. Hussein did not hold back in his face-to-face meeting with Netanyahu, and the King's list of Israeli transgressions was somehow leaked to Thomas Friedman at *The New York Times*: the illegal expropriation of Palestinian land for Jewish settlements; Israeli-imposed curfews on Palestinians that made it nearly impossible for them to work; the lack of a timetable for withdrawing Israeli troops from Hebron and starting negotiations on final status; the travesty of the tunnel; the counterproductiveness of Israel's fortress mentality when the only real security would have to come from mutual respect. "I speak for myself, for Yitzhak Rabin, a man whom I had the great pride to call my friend, and for all peoples who benefit from peace," King Hussein said to Netanyahu. "All this good will is being lost. We are at the edge of the abyss, and regardless of our best efforts, we might be just about to fall into it — all of us."

It was heartbreaking for us to watch all we had worked to build unraveling so quickly, but my husband was dealing with Netanyahu's right-wing ideology, which not only was uncompromising but also often had no basis in fact. We were in London, returning from a visit to the United States during which many American Jewish leaders had expressed dismay over Netanyahu's approach, when Hussein received a call from the Israeli Prime Minister, who was in the United States, saying that he wanted to meet as soon as possible. He would cut short his U.S. trip to fly to London, apparently having been urged by his U.S. Jewish supporters to meet and repair relations with Hussein.

I was in the shower the next evening when Prime Minister Netanyahu arrived. Our protocol officers had agreed with his people that he alone would be coming to the house, so I was startled to be informed that Mrs. Netanyahu had unexpectedly arrived with him. I came down to the sitting room with my hair half dried, determined to be hospitable and entirely apolitical. However, in my inimitable way, I unintentionally stepped into a minefield. I was trying to stress the positive impact on both our societies — Arab and Israeli — of the institutional, business, and individual contacts that had developed between our peoples over the past several years. As part of the progress in the peace process, we had been very encouraged to see that Israeli and Arab historians and scholars were reviewing textbooks and historical accounts with a view to correcting the propaganda on both sides. She immediately bristled.

"What do you mean, propaganda?" she said. I replied that one example of a myth that had polarized our people was the description of Palestine in the 1940s as "a land with no people for people with no land," when in fact generations of Palestinians had been living in Palestine for thousands of years. She bristled again.

"What do you mean?" she said. "When the Jews came to this area, there were no Arabs here. They came to find work when we built cities. There was nothing here before that."

"I am certain many of your own historians would agree that that is not accurate," I replied.

It was quite an insight for me. Netanyahu was known for his conservative rigidity, but to hear an erroneous version of history stated so emphatically by his wife in private was truly alarming. Did they truly believe myths like this one? And if so, what other misconceptions might impede our working together for a lasting peace?

After the Netanyahu meeting, we flew from London to Amman, and then drove to our new home, Bab Al Salam. For Hussein the house was a refuge from the unrelenting stress and turmoil of the time. He loved the way many of the rooms on the first floor opened onto the terrace and lawn, which made the house light and natural, especially our family kitchen. He loved the small, cozy sitting room with its double-height fireplace decorated by an exquisite mosaic I had commissioned from our school for mosaic arts in Madaba, and the two-story library that also opened onto a terrace. In the entrance hall and dining room I hung his portrait and those of various ancestors, including his father, King Talal, his grandfather, King Abdullah, and his great-grandfather, Sharif Hussein Bin Ali.

The house was not quite finished when we moved in; my office was not ready and we had not started construction on the annex for the older children. So we all jammed in together, but Hussein enjoyed that as well, far preferring to be close to his children than separated by layers of floors, as we had been for so many years at Al Nadwa.

My husband relished watching the garden develop. He loved fragrant plants such as orange blossom and jasmine, and I also focused on drought-resistant, low-maintenance plants. I loved palm trees and bougainvillea, favorites of mine since I had lived in Santa Monica, and put them wherever I could. We fertilized the organic vegetable and herb gardens with sheep manure, and attempted to keep them pest-free with a border of lavender and aubergines. He was particularly enthusiastic about the wooden ties from the old Hejaz railroad that we used to frame the raised beds, and he was curious about every step of the landscaping process. "What on earth are you doing?" he asked our gardener when he came home one day to find a cluster of people picking stones out of the lawn; then he pitched in himself. Generally I designed the garden to be as open as possible so that all the children and grandchildren, who then already numbered eleven, could join together and play games and sports freely.

For all our happiness at Bab Al Salam, it seemed there was little peace elsewhere. Prime Minister Netanyahu and his government did finally follow through on the redeployment of Israeli troops from Hebron, but he immediately precipitated another crisis by approving the construction of 6,500 new Israeli housing units on 425 acres of expropriated Palestinian land on a hill between Jerusalem and Bethlehem. The provocation was as extraordinary as it was transparent. The land, which Palestinians call Jabal Abu Ghoneim, or Green Mountain, and the Israelis renamed in Hebrew Har Homa, or Mountain of the Wall, had earlier been declared part of a protected greenbelt between Bethlehem and Jerusalem, but it had become the last link in Israel's ring of settlements around Arab East Jerusalem. Now the last remaining land corridor between Arab East Jerusalem and the occupied West Bank was to be eliminated, and the vast chain of commercial and fortress-like residential space would effectively tip the balance in Israel's favor in disputed Jerusalem before the final status peace talks, should they ever take place.

The announcement of the Har Homa project triggered increasingly violent demonstrations. "You cannot continue to humiliate a people without some reaction," my husband warned. Israel was condemned for its actions by the world community, with the exception of the United States, which responded by saying that the Clinton administration "wish[ed]" Israel would not build the settlement. But in March 1997, protected by helicopters and soldiers, Israeli bulldozers started their work anyway. The furor was such that the United Nations General Assembly held three emergency sessions, one charging that Israel was violating a provision of the Geneva Convention that prohibits the large-scale destruction of property, the others passing a resolution that the settlement was "illegal" and a "major obstacle to peace." The only two votes against the resolution came from the United States and Israel. The fifteen members of United Nations Security Council also addressed the issue of the settlement, with the same result. When the resolution declaring its illegality came to a vote, not once but twice, in March, fourteen of the fifteen member countries voted in support, while the United States vetoed the resolution both times.

Just when things could not seem to get worse, they did. My husband and I were in Madrid on an official visit on March 13 when he received word that a Jordanian soldier had shot seven Israeli schoolgirls to death and wounded six others on the "Island of Peace" at the Naharayim crossing point. Some of the wounded students were taken to nearby Shuna Hospital in the Jordan River Valley, where Jordanian farmers lined up in the hallways to give blood, saving at least one of them. But nothing could ease the anguish my husband felt as he immediately canceled our trip and turned back to Jordan. "I cannot offer enough condolences or express enough personal sorrow to the mothers, fathers, and brothers of these children who fell today," he said when he arrived.

He then made an unprecedented visit to the Israeli village of Beit Shemesh three days later to offer his personal condolences to the stricken families. He insisted that his visits to each family be shown on Jordanian television, despite the fury he knew this would trigger among the extremist groups in Jordan. He wanted everyone to take note of the price of violence. And it was very moving to see him consoling the mothers. "If there is any purpose in my life it will be to make sure that all the children do not suffer the way our generation did," he said to one of the families.

But the violence continued unabated. The bulldozers at the Har Homa settlement led to more and more clashes between stone-throwing Palestinians and Israeli soldiers shooting rubber bullets. Soon the violence spread through the West Bank and turned into riots in Ramallah. Israeli tanks moved in and surrounded villages on the West Bank. In retaliation, there were more suicide bombings during the summer, more senseless deaths.

Even my husband's optimism was sorely tried by then. I know mine was. We both had trouble sleeping. The shortsighted approach of Netanyahu and the hard-liners in his government had put terrific pressure on the King to reverse the peace process. Everything he had worked for all his life, every relationship he had painstakingly built on trust and respect, every dream of peace and prosperity he had had for Jordan's children was turning into a nightmare. I really did not know how much more Hussein could take.

chapter twenty

The White Bird

Toward the end of 1997, my husband started suffering from the occasional night fever. Our medical team in Jordan gave him a battery of tests but could not find anything. They treated him with antibiotics, which stopped the fevers for a time. Then they would return. The doctors suspected that the fevers were due to some sort of mysterious virus; more than that they could not say. Half in jest I started to call my husband's malady the Bibi virus, alluding to a bizarre bioterrorism episode that fall.

In September 1997 agents from Mossad, Israel's intelligence agency, entered Jordan under forged Canadian passports and attempted to assassinate the head of the political bureau of Hamas, the main Islamist resistance movement in the Palestinian territories, formed after the eruption of the first *intifada* in 1987. They injected the man, Khalid Mash'al, with a deadly chemical agent in broad daylight on the streets of Amman. That a government-sponsored terrorist attack would take place on Jordanian soil so soon after Jordan and Israel had signed a treaty deeply offended my husband. So did the fact that Khalid Mash'al was hovering near death in an Amman hospital and the Netanyahu government was refusing to divulge which chemical agent had been used in the attack. It took the intervention of President Clinton to force Israel to identify the drug it had used, apparently a synthetic opiate called fentanyl, and what the antidote might be. The gravely ill Mash'al was treated and survived. The King was on the verge of canceling the peace treaty with Israel when Netanyahu (whose nickname is Bibi) flew to Jordan in the middle of the night to try to mend fences. Hussein was so angry that he had refused to meet with the Israeli Prime Minister and asked Crown Prince Hassan to handle the contact.

Though I teased about the Bibi virus, one could not help but wonder at times: It was impossible to ignore the fact that my husband was very popular in Israel; many Israelis told us that they would gladly exchange Hussein for Bibi. Might it be politically expedient for Netanyahu to remove a credible moderate Arab voice from the increasingly polarized region?

Hussein's fevers continued on and off throughout the winter. During his annual checkup at the Mayo Clinic in May 1998, the medical staff came up with theories involving various obscure viruses, but they did not identify any other anomalies in his system. We left the clinic and headed for Washington, D.C., where Hussein met with President Clinton and Secretary of State Madeleine Albright to talk about reenergizing the stalled peace process. Then we went on to England for a week, where we celebrated our twentieth wedding anniversary at Buckhurst Park.

We had already celebrated our anniversary with all our Jordanian family and friends in Jordan the previous November. According to the Islamic Calendar, our twentieth year coincided exactly with Hussein's sixty-second birthday, so we had combined the celebrations. We decided to mark the occasion again in England with friends and family who had not been with us in November, and for those few days Hussein seemed to have shaken the fevers and was happy and relaxed. The anniversary celebration took place on a beautiful, balmy evening, and the party seemed to invigorate him. In the series of photographs we took, my husband looks healthy and happy, surrounded by his children. Later, on our return to Jordan, his fevers returned, this time fiercer and more debilitating. His medical staff performed more tests, and this time they found some lab abnormalities that required further study. We decided to return to the Mayo Clinic.

I will never forget the moment at the clinic when I was told my husband had cancer. I was in a private sitting room that the hospital had assigned to the children and me while Hussein underwent the exploratory surgery. After several hours, a familiar face entered the room. Dr. David Barrett, who had successfully operated on my husband in 1992, reported to our group that the surgery had gone very well and that Hussein was being moved into the recovery room. The children relaxed somewhat, and then Dr. Barrett and I stepped outside. In the hallway he turned to me and said that tests had identified abnormal cells in several locations in my husband's body. He said he suspected non-Hodgkin's lymphoma. My mind could only take in so much. I remember standing there, seeing his lips move and dimly hearing his voice while my mind raced at a million miles a minutes trying to process the information in a way that was not dreadful or hopeless. What brought me back to earth was Dr. Barrett's reaction to what he had to tell me. Tears were running down his cheeks as he fought to control his emotions. I ended up comforting him, and while I did, the seriousness of his news sunk in. If there were abnormal cells in multiple locations, did that mean that it might have advanced to the point where we might have only months, weeks, or days left? I could not breathe.

Once he had left, a maelstrom of emotion washed over me. I walked over to a large picture window in the corridor to compose myself before returning to the children. Their father had come through the tests just fine, I told them. I would talk to them about the results, but first I had to go to the recovery room so I could be there when he came out of anesthesia.

I tried just as hard to maintain my composure with our security and staff, and then with my husband as he slowly regained consciousness. As always, he thanked everyone; barely awake, he wanted to make sure that everyone else was all right and knew how much he appreciated their care. I had never lied to him, so suddenly I found myself in unfamiliar territory when he became clearheaded enough to ask, "Well, how did it go?" I mumbled, "The procedure went well, Sidi," as I struggled to keep my face from trembling and tears from welling up in my eyes. "The doctors will have a meeting and tell us about everything," I said, stalling for time.

The Mayo anesthesiologist, Jeff Welna, was sitting at the end of the bed, and when my husband realized he was there, he greeted him. "What did you find?" he asked. "Your Majesty, we think it is lymphoma." My husband blinked hard, clearly startled by the news, while I sat there wishing he had had a few more hours to come out of the anesthesia before hearing the news. But he was always stronger than I. As we reached out to each other for a quick embrace, Hussein was already thinking ahead. "Okay. What do we do next?"

Sidi moved back to his suite and settled in.

While he did, I asked the children to join me and told them what I knew so they could begin absorbing the fearful news and make plans, given their various commitments and schedules. I felt special concern for Ali and Haya, who had already lost one parent and for whom Sidi was the absolute center of the world. I tried to convey the diagnosis in hopeful but honest terms, and it was not easy. I owed them the truth. "Do not sugarcoat it," I remember Haya telling me, as they all reeled from the news.

Not until I was alone that night could I begin to allow the full extent of my own feelings to surface. I felt such fear, such bottomless anxiety at the thought of losing my husband, my best friend, my dearest love and inspiration that it threatened to paralyze me. For twenty years we had been husband and wife, father and mother, life partners through international crises and domestic turmoil in Jordan. I had joined him with all my heart in his quest for peace in the region and experienced with him every achievement and setback. Above all, we shared a love for Jordan and the goal of prosperity for all our beloved people. To lose this man would be a catastrophe on every level imaginable. He simply could not die.

Insha'Allah, we say in Arabic. God willing. My husband believed, as Muslims do, that all things, both good and bad, come from God and that God provides us the shoulders to carry that which we must. I shared that belief and the underlying conviction that King Hussein was not meant to succumb to cancer. At that moment I found the strength to still my panic over his diagnosis. God had willed him this battle with cancer, so we would fight it together. I would devote every fiber of my being to making my husband well, and to protect him so that he could use all his energy to join the battle. "Dear God," I prayed that night, as I would every night and throughout the days for months to come, "please make him well, please make him comfortable, please give him strength, courage, and peace."

Our prayers seemed to have been answered when we met with Sidi's doctors the next day. The doctors were not yet sure whether he did indeed have cancer of the lymph glands, but even if he did, as they strongly suspected, the odds for his recovery were good.

And so began our odyssey into an uncertain future, buoyed with the best that medicine could offer, the goodwill of the thousands of people who called, faxed, and sent cards and letters, and our own deepening faith, which would sustain us in the challenging months to come. The Mayo Clinic became our home, literally. The hospital had just completed a VIP suite that included a kitchen, a dining room, and a little room for me to sleep in next to his. The rest of our family and entourage stayed in a nearby hotel connected to the hospital by a tunnel. All of Hussein's children and various other family members came and went, with the exception of Hamzah, who, fortuitously, was on a break between his graduation from Har- row and the beginning of his first term at Sandhurst; he rarely left his father's side.

Hussein's happiest moments were spent with the children there; laughing and teasing his eldest daughter, Alia, his twins, Zein and Aisha, and Haya, who would have spent the entire time with us if they had not also had their own families to care for and in Haya's case, a successful equestrian career. Somehow they managed both, cheering up their father tremendously throughout his ordeal, as did Ali, Hashim, Iman, and Raiyah, who came on every possible break from school, further lifting their father's spirits. Abdullah and his wife, Rania, and their two children visited, as did his younger brother Feisal and his wife, Alia, when the two brothers were able to take leave of their military responsibilities in Amman.

Between cycles of chemotherapy Hussein and I would fly to River House in Washington or go on day trips around Minnesota in a silver Volkswagen Beetle I had bought for him shortly after our arrival. His treatment plan called for six courses of chemotherapy over five months, followed by a bone marrow transplant. Throughout this time, my husband's optimism never flagged. The doctors insisted that he had to rest to conserve his energy, which put me in a very difficult position. Knowing how exhausted he was from the treatment, it fell to me to try to monitor the amount of time he spent with his visitors. I became the gatekeeper.

For all the agonies of those months, Hussein and I treasured every moment walking, talking, watching the flights of Canada geese through the big picture window, and taking in the small joys of life. Hussein became quite an avid birder at Mayo, something he had never had enough time for in Jordan, which is one of the greatest migratory routes in the world for more than 300 species of birds that pass through the rocky gorges of Dana, Mujib, and Petra, and the Azraq Oasis. It was in Minnesota that Hussein enjoyed some quiet moments to discover these pleasures himself.

We went on one memorable outing in search of baby eagles. After our initial disappointment at not finding any on the lake where we had been told to look, we met two avid bird-watchers who led us to another vantage point. It was there, from a lay-by along the highway, that we trained our binoculars on a small island in the lake and saw the eagles nesting. We must have looked very odd from the road — both of us wearing face masks to prevent infection, looking through our long binoculars at no evident point of interest — but Hussein enjoyed it tremendously.

We also traveled in the silver Beetle to visit various Amish communities in Minnesota. One of our favorite destinations was the hilltop town of Harmony, Wisconsin, where we would admire the beautiful handmade Amish quilts. We would often stop for lunch, and Hussein would shake hands with anyone who approached him, while I worried about the risk of infection. He enjoyed driving the silver "love bug" so much that when I suggested we offer the Beetle to a philanthropic organization to auction off when we left the hospital, he uncharacteristically said, "No! This is a very special car, and we are taking it home with us." I have it to this day.

It was on one of those outings in the VW that my mobile phone rang and we received the long-awaited, thrilling news that on September 17, 1998, the African nation of Burkina Faso had become the fortieth member of the United Nations to ratify the Ottawa Convention banning the use of land mines, thereby automatically putting the ban in force. We may have shattered the peaceful calm of the Minnesota countryside with our cheers. The treaty, the first international arms treaty to encompass humanitarian obligations to the weapons' victims, was brought into force in record time through the unprecedented coalition activism of concerned governments, NGOs, and individuals united in a pledge to win back blighted land, to fulfill our humanitarian duties to the survivors, and to eradicate these insidious obstacles to recovery and peace.

It had given me particular pride to inaugurate the first Middle East Conference on Land Mines the day before our departure for Mayo and to announce in my opening address Jordan's decision to sign and ratify the treaty, to destroy our land mine stockpiles, and to accelerate our effort, which had begun in 1993, to clear the minefields along Jordan's borders. Now we had taken another major step forward.

During our breaks between courses of chemotherapy, Sidi and I also spent as much time as possible with the children, usually at River House. Iman was in a boarding school near Washington, D.C. At the last minute we postponed Raiyah's return to school in Amman and brought her instead to the Maret School in Washington, D.C., where her brother, Hashim, was in his senior year. It was a sudden and difficult adjustment for Raiyah, who was twelve at the time and entering the seventh grade, but the school went out of its way to ease her transition, for which I will always be grateful. Hashim and Raiyah lived with my sister, Alexa, and her family in Washington, D.C., while we were at Mayo. All three would join the rest of us at River House during our respites there.

It was difficult for the children to see their Baba so weak and suffering from nausea. One day Iman called to say that she would have to miss part of one weekend with us at River House because she was participating in the National Coalition for Cancer Survivorship march, "Coming Together to Conquer Cancer." After some thought, I contacted the organizers to see if we might contribute in some fashion, thinking that Hussein might be an inspiring voice to help dispel widespread taboos and fatal ignorance about the disease. Hussein's personal example and courage, I felt, might make a difference. The organizers were enthusiastic. The morning of the cancer rally, my husband awoke feeling somewhat weak and nauseous, but he insisted nonetheless on attending. Unfortunately, once there we were taken to a hot, crowded, tented waiting area, where we were joined by the other speakers — Vice President Al Gore and his wife, Tipper, General Norman Schwarzkopf, various members of Congress, and Cindy Crawford — Hussein felt weaker and weaker. I teased him that Cindy Crawford was taking his breath away, but as time passed and the temperature soared, he finally had to leave, asking me to speak for both of us, as I have continued to do every year since.

There were other breaks when my husband felt quite well. During one of them we had an engaging evening with the Clintons at the White House, eating hamburgers outside on the Truman Balcony. Hussein had developed a close working relationship with Bill Clinton. The Clintons shared our love for Harley-Davidsons, so we sent Clinton an Annie Leibovitz photograph of us roaring around Wadi

Rum on our Harley to remind the President of what he could look forward to at the end of his term. The talk that night was not about motorcycles, however, but about biological warfare and land mines. Hussein had just read with great interest Tom Clancy's book *Executive Orders*, which describes a biological attack on the United States. We were discovering that many in the intelligence and national security community in Washington were quite certain that it was not a question of *if* but *when* someone would launch such a terrorist attack against the United States. My husband discussed the book's realism, and then he turned to the subject of land mines, to give me an opening to discuss the Global Ottawa Land Mine Ban Treaty. At the cancer event, even General Norman Schwarzkopf had offered support in our battle against land mines, as have many other senior retired U.S. military officers. The treaty has been signed by 143 countries, but still the United States is not among them, making it the only NATO member not banning these weapons, and the only Western holdout except Cuba.

The breaks at River House acted as a tonic for my husband. His appetite improved, and our chef supplied him with endless meals of hamburgers, steaks, and falafel sandwiches. Family members and various Jordanian officials arrived to discuss domestic and regional issues, as did U.S. officials and special guests, such as Crown Prince Abdullah Bin Abdul Aziz of Saudi Arabia, who made a special visit to see him, accompanied by Prince Saud Al Faisal, the Saudi Foreign Minister.

The Crown Prince had brought my husband water from Mecca's sacred Zam Zam well, which God created to save Ismael and Hagar from dying of thirst and which has never dried up. The Saudi Prince also brought a gift of saffron, believed to have curative powers. A sheikh recited verses of the Quran over the two gifts, and Prince Abdullah refused to let anyone but himself prepare the water and saffron. He put two teaspoons of saffron in a glass of Zam Zam water and attentively watched His Majesty drink it all, becoming quite emotional. The King was so deeply touched by the gesture of affection that he later wrote an emotional letter to Crown Prince Abdullah.

During my husband's treatments at Mayo, nausea made it difficult for Hussein to eat anything. Sheikh Zayed and Sheikha Fatima of the United Arab Emirates spoiled us during much of our stay there by sending us enormous quantities of Arab delicacies, with the regular shipments of food and supplies they were sending a member of their family who was also receiving treatment at Mayo at the same time. Extraordinarily generous, they kept in touch with us on a regular basis, as did Sultan Qaboos of Oman and his sister, Umaymah Bint Said, who after his mother's death had assumed her caring and generous style. We were the happy recipients of our favorite Arabic dishes and such delicacies as dates and Godiva chocolates, many of which found their way to the children's ward.

Since my husband could not visit other patients at the hospital due to the risk of infection, I visited the children's ward as much as possible for both of us. Halloween was particularly memorable. Bearing in mind how often my unspectacular appearance had disappointed children when they were introduced to "the Queen," I found a large, elaborate Spanish hair comb with gold filigree and turquoise, shaped like a tiara, and I wore a long flowing kaftan. Attired in this way I went to a party in the children's ward with our nurse Burdett Rooney, who was swathed in bandages and telling the children she was the Queen's mummy.

These visits may have meant more to their family members than they did to the courageous young patients. I had learned for myself that understanding empathy and a big hug are sometimes the most helpful support for those struggling with the horror of cancer-stricken loved ones.

One of the renowned cancer specialists that Mayo had enlisted to consult on Sidi's case was Richard Klausner, Director of the National Cancer Institute in Washington. I began discussions with him almost immediately about developing relations between NCI and our newly operational Al Amal Cancer Center in Amman. (Thousands of donations had poured in from Jordan and the region after Hussein's cancer scare in 1992, which enabled us to realize the long-planned project.) The hospital, which had enormous potential to become a regional cancer center, was plagued by organizational and resource problems. Dr. Klausner and I were able to encourage an Arab-American oncologist and cancer researcher at NCI/National Institutes of Health to work with us to develop a plan for an Al Amal/NCI partnership that would exchange expertise and medical personnel, as well as bring us valuable research and development and improvements to our clinical infrastructure, such as telemedicine links to NCI.

My husband never stopped working during his stay at Mayo. A steady stream of government officials from Jordan came through, and he was in constant discussions on the telephone. Jordan was privatizing various institutions at the time, the most critical being the telecommunications network, and many companies were jockeying for position. Various people would attempt to contact the King and often ended up trying to get to him through me. Even while I was Rollerblading on the trails around Rochester, my cellular phone would ring with interested parties persistently asking me to pass on a message to the King.

I had little interest in anything but Hussein's

health, and in trying to conserve his energy for that battle, but the world kept intruding. The amount of news coverage devoted to Washington scandals was appalling. "The television news cannot be a healthy therapy for him, but little else is on," I wrote in my journal. "It is sickening us while we are trying to heal."

More disturbing were the rumors about Hussein's health that were finding their way into the international media. Our daughter Iman called the hospital in tears over a *Time* magazine article in October that essentially wrote off her father. I did not read that article and tried to keep others at bay, because getting well was all that mattered. We certainly did not need to clutter our minds with wild speculation about Sidi's prognosis and intrigue over the succession to the throne. My husband was very much alive, and the doctors kept assuring us that the odds were good that he would win his battle with cancer.

I rarely left Hussein's side, except at his insistence. He urged me to travel to New York in October to announce the fortieth ratification of the land mine treaty at the United Nations, which also gave me some time to spend with one of our favorite persons, UN Secretary General Kofi Annan, who was warm, wise, and supportive, as ever, and stayed in close touch with my husband throughout his hospitalization.

Sidi also insisted that I go through with laser eye surgery that had been scheduled for August with a brilliant, pioneering eye surgeon in Jordan — surgery that I had canceled. The ophthalmic specialist at Mayo recommended a doctor in Atlanta, George Waring, who performed the procedure under the supervision of my Jordanian doctor, Khalid Sharif. I ended up having to undergo the procedure twice, and I never quite achieved 20/20 vision, but my sight improved tremendously, and I was able to stop wearing prescription lenses much of the time. My husband was fascinated by the new laser technology, and he delighted in going through the whole process vicariously with me, even watching a video of the procedure, which I could not bear to see myself.

It was very difficult for Hussein to accept his dependence on others because of his weakened condition, even though he was an extremely undemanding patient. Over and over he would apologize for the trouble he was causing us, and over and over the children and I would respond that we would not be happier doing anything else. We tried throughout to reassure him that there was no greater privilege in life for us than being with him in sickness and in health, and it was absolutely true.

As long as I had known Hussein he had said he would never want to be a burden on anyone as he grew older, and here he was, a relatively young man of sixty-two, already feeling he had become exactly that. The truth was quite the opposite. In fact, he was a constant source of strength and inspiration for all of his family, his friends, and even the Mayo Clinic staff.

Soon after we arrived at Mayo, I had bought my husband a gift of ruby cuff links and studs for his birthday. I had chosen them because rubies are traditionally considered to be healing stones. The children and I started a ritual of sorts, during which we would stand around his bed and gently touch his skin with the rubies. We were willing to try anything. I wore a beautiful ruby ring he had given me, which had seen us through his successful previous treatment at Mayo in 1992, when he had had his kidney removed. This time I never, ever took the ring off, not even to bathe or sleep or wash my hair. It simply reassured him to see me wear it.

We never talked about the possibility of losing the struggle. We were fighting a positive battle for life, not a negative battle against death. We concentrated on what was important about our lives and our work, and the miracle of being on Earth at all, and having the opportunity to contribute to the world around us. We spent much of the time discussing the unfinished business that lay ahead: a comprehensive Arab-Israeli peace, economic stability in Jordan, and global issues such as the environment and weapons of mass destruction. Hussein was preoccupied by what he felt he had not yet accomplished. I tried to reassure him that even though he had not succeeded in reaching all his goals, he had in fact achieved much more than a historic peace treaty by breaking through so many barriers of prejudice and generations-old hatreds. Through his integrity, compassion, and forgiveness, Hussein had always reflected the noblest spirit of Islam and Arab culture. By providing an example and hope for so many, he had truly honored his Hashimite legacy.

In mid-October we were sitting in a VIP suite at St. Mary's Hospital, a separate facility at Mayo, while the staff was preparing the rooms my husband would occupy after the upcoming bone marrow transplant. The phone rang and it was Bill Clinton. I was sitting on the sofa next to Hussein as he spoke to the President, then to Madeleine Albright, then again to Clinton. "Look, if there is anything I can do, no matter what the doctors say, I will be there," I heard him say. It turned out he was referring to the stalled peace talks between Netanyahu and Arafat at the Wye Plantation.

Fortuitously, the doctors felt the King was well enough to leave Mayo at that time, because the impasse was serious. The Israelis were threatening to leave. The Americans were frustrated. And time was running out. Many of the agreements negotiated at Oslo had not yet been implemented. Hope had all but vanished that the timetable of May 4 would be met for the resolution of the status of Jerusalem, the return of the refugees, and a Palestinian state.

The peace process was in shambles.

We flew to Washington on October 18 not knowing whether we would continue on immediately to Wye or pause at River House. We were able to stop, which gave my husband time to rest and visit with the children. The next day we traveled on to Wye Mills on the President's helicopter, Marine 1. On landing we were taken to Houghton House, a lovely private home on the grounds overlooking the Wye River. First the American negotiators and then the Palestinians arrived to brief my husband. "Clinton looks totally exhausted and fed up," I noted in my journal. "The Palestinians are shocked, some to tears, by their first sight of Hussein since his illness began." Arafat and his advisers, who were normally always on the move for security reasons, seemed to be relishing this rare stationary interlude. "Arafat driving golf cart around wildly and trying a bicycle," I wrote.

By contrast, there was an atmosphere of discouragement and resignation among the Americans. "The U.S. thinks they have invested enough time and energy," I noted. "They can't quite believe what they have been put through by the Israelis who, they sense, anticipated an easy time with a President weakened by scandal when in fact he remains very strong in the polls." The Palestinians, however, were praised for being forthcoming. "No one seems certain about the Israeli intentions except to agree that the Prime Minister lacks vision, statesmanship and sound, consistent advice," I wrote.

Meanwhile, I negotiated with my husband that he would rest between appointments if I kept him supplied with jellybeans, one of the few "foods," to use the term loosely, that he was enjoying. We sat together outside the house on two lawn chairs, wrapped in quilts and fleece hats to watch the sunset. We drank hot beef bouillon and gazed at the gaggles of geese settling in for the night and the occasional deer, while Hussein's aides brought minute-by-minute reports of the talks to us. It was a beautiful sunset and a lovely moment full of peace and hope. Canada geese had so much symbolism for us; they had been so much a part of our Mayo Clinic experience and now here they were at Wye. They mate for life, and their elegant beauty was not only romantic but also uplifting to the spirit.

That evening, the King joined President Clinton for a meeting with Netanyahu and the Israelis, including Ariel Sharon, Israel's Foreign Minister. He had hoped that just as Rabin's military experiences had finally convinced him that security could be achieved only through mutual respect, justice, and dialogue, perhaps a former military man like Sharon might also be able to understand that practical wisdom. Hussein's past experiences with Prime Minister Netanyahu had been less promising and, true to form, Netanyahu avoided discussing anything substantive with my husband at Wye. The

Prime Minister said it would be difficult to sell the deal to the Israeli people, but Hussein saw that as a pretext.

We left Wye to return to River House later that evening, over my objections. "Let's not go back home," I said to my husband. "Let's stay here until this is finished." I pressed him because the talks still seemed so fragile, and they had seemed to benefit almost moment by moment from Hussein's seasoned and encouraging presence. But I was overruled. River House was not so far away, and both Burdett and my husband felt that he would be better off sleeping in his own bed. Shortly after we had returned to River House, Sharon and Defense Minister Yitzhak Mordechai sent reassuring messages to my husband that they would make sure the deal was concluded successfully.

At River House, we stayed up anxiously waiting for news, which came in a discouraging series of updates. First, Sharon had left Wye. Netanyahu's plane was being readied for departure, and his delegation, too, was preparing to go. My husband conferred with Clinton, who was back at the White House, and convinced the President not to make a late-night bid to change Netanyahu's mind. If Netanyahu made good on his threat to leave, my husband promised that he would stand next to the President and explain why the deal had gone wrong, so that Clinton would not have to bear the burden alone. We went to bed that night not knowing what the morning would bring, but Netanyahu turned out to be bluffing. "Hussein, having persuaded the President, is vindicated by the morning news that the Israelis are still around, but the roller coaster continues," I wrote in my journal. "By Thursday, we are asked to return to Wye for more last-minute troubleshooting."

Back to Wye we went. "You cannot afford to fail," the King told the two Middle Eastern leaders and their respective aides. "You owe this to your people, to your children, to future generations." The two sides kept working all that day and all that night, and finally, at dawn on Friday, they had a deal. It was a modest one, to say the least. Israel agreed to return 13 percent of the occupied land on the West Bank to the Palestinians and to release some Palestinian prisoners, but one step was better than none. The peace process was still alive, and my husband accepted Clinton's invitation to participate in the signing of the Wye Memorandum at the White House on October 23.

As I watched Hussein stride down the red carpet to the podium in the East Room with the four other leaders, I saw only his steady faith and courage — a handsome and vital presence in our lives. I would learn later that people in other parts of the world were shocked by his appearance, but I was used to his loss of hair and weight and thought he looked and sounded forceful as he presented his case for peace between long-standing enemies. "We quarrel, we agree. We are friendly, we are not friendly," he said. "But we have no right to dictate through irresponsible action or narrow-mindedness the future of our children and their children's children. There has been enough destruction. Enough death. Enough waste. It is time that, together, we occupy a place beyond ourselves, our peoples, that is worthy of them under the sun, the descendants of the children of Abraham."

Hussein would be nominated for a Nobel Prize in 1998 for all his years of effort toward peace in the Middle East, culminating in his leaving his sickbed to go to Wye Plantation to help secure the Palestinian-Israeli accord. That year the prize would ultimately be awarded to the political leaders of Northern Ireland, but the King was honored by his nomination. More important was the recognition he received after Wye for his long-standing commitment to peace and reconciliation in the Middle East.

My husband had a bone marrow tap when we returned to Mayo, his fifth or sixth, but this one was particularly agonizing to watch. He was under a general anesthetic and did not feel anything, but watching them wrench his body around and then violently break through the bone was so disturbing that a new nurse observing the procedure fainted. I empathized with her, shaken myself by the brutal torment that his body had to endure.

Hussein's sister, Basma, and brother Mohammed came from Jordan to donate bone marrow. They were the only two family members whose blood was compatible for harvesting cells for a potential transplant. I would visit them both in their adjacent hospital beds during the process, while they bravely endured the tubes and IV. Hussein was deeply grateful for their loving sacrifice. I nearly wept when, just before leaving, Basma gave me a beautiful gold pin of a pair of Canada geese.

I tried to restore my sense of equilibrium through exercise, especially out of doors. One morning around this time, Burdett Rooney and I were out Rollerblading on an unseasonably warm day. We were crossing a bridge when a flock of birds took to the skies. As they crossed over us, I looked up, and my gaze fell on the single white bird in the flock. Was it a sign, a portent? The bird flew higher and higher in the sky. I watched it soar, unexpectedly moved, until I could see it no more.

We were all very anxious to hear the results of Sidi's latest tests, and I spent another night in constant prayer, beseeching God for Hussein's comfort, confidence, and progress. The tests showed no sign of cancer cells anywhere.

I did everything I could to keep Hussein from seeing a *New York Times* article that appeared a week after Wye with the headline "King Hussein Ails. His Brother Waits." There was a description of my husband at Wye "made spectral by chemotherapy," which had driven home to many for the first time "just how severely cancer has stricken him," along with alleged quotes from Hassan calling my husband "the symbol to the people" and describing himself as "closer to the kitchen," as well as a quote from Hassan's son-in-law, the Minister of Information, saying Hassan had "trained for the job for thirty-three years." That was just the sort of thing Hussein did not need to read, but someone brought him the newspaper and it upset him greatly. Concerned about the repercussions that were already hitting the economy and the stock market hard, Hussein decided to address the Jordanian people directly.

The King gave an interview to Jordan Television on November 13, telling our people that the latest tests showed no trace of lymphoma. "Thank God that everything is proceeding in a good manner," he said. "By God's will, this will be the final stage of treatment, after which I will return home." The Mayo Clinic reinforced his clean bill of health in their own statement. "His Majesty is in complete remission from lymphoma," the clinic said, and went on to explain that my husband would have an autotransplant of his own healthy stem cells, a standard procedure to ensure a permanent remission.

The happiest moment of our stay at Mayo was celebrating Hussein's sixty-third birthday with almost all of his children. Abdullah had called me from Amman saying he needed to remain there for official reasons, asking if his father would understand. I assured him that Hussein, of all people, would understand completely and that Abdullah and his family would be with us in our hearts. Abir was inextricably tied up at school, but Alia, Feisal and his wife, Alia, Zein and Aisha, Haya, Hamzah, Hashim, Iman, and Raiyah surrounded Hussein with love and joy for that birthday feast. The cake, which someone had secretly ordered, pictured the two of us on our lounge chairs in the sunset at Wye. The most special present I could think of for his birthday was a visit from our dear friend Jo Malone, the English skin care specialist and talented creator of fragrances, oils, and skin-care products, who came all the way from New York to give Hussein one of her extraordinary, soothing treatments.

I left Hussein briefly to attend the fiftieth anniversary of the World Conservation Congress in Paris and to join Queen Sofia and the royal family in Spain to celebrate her sixtieth birthday, only to discover that the smear campaign about my husband's health and me had spread over Europe. There were reports that I was Jewish and related somehow to Rabin, and that I, backed by American Zionists, was tirelessly campaigning to have Hamzah replace my husband's brother as Crown Prince. According to other accounts, photographs of Hassan had been posted all over the streets of Amman, replacing those of my husband, and that Hassan's wife, Sarvath, had started redecorating my husband's office in the Diwan. The constant barrage of tales from Jordan drained my spirit and Hussein's. The way in which people were playing everyone against each other and exploiting my husband's illness was dispiriting to all of us, especially the children.

We spent Christmas in the hospital with the children. Raiyah had spent all her money on presents for everyone, and we made every effort to mark the occasion with our extended medical family of nurses, doctors, and other medical workers at the clinic. It was Ramadan and we were fasting, so we did not have any sort of holiday feast, but we were full of gratitude that we were together.

Our time at Mayo was finally coming to an end. "As we begin packing up after five and a half months, I struggle with hopes and fears that have no clear basis," I noted in my journal. "Constant prayer and renewal of faith must be my refuge." We issued another press release before we left the hospital, saying that we were leaving with Hussein's cancer in remission, but that it would take five years for the remission to be considered permanent. Hussein and I felt it was very important for our people that the statement was medically accurate and straightforward, so we consulted with the doctors before releasing it. Our own departure from the hospital was merry and festive. Every doctor and nurse came out to wave good-bye as one of their favorite patients drove away in his silver Beetle, followed by family, security, our Jordanian staff, and our stalwart doctor, Samir Farraj.

We greeted the New Year 1998 at River House with Abir, Haya, Ali, Hamzah, Hashim, Iman, and Raiyah. At the holiday's end we all bid good-bye to Hamzah, who was leaving for Sandhurst. A week or so later, my husband was ready to leave for England himself to continue his convalescence before returning home to Jordan. He was still very weak and took only occasional walks with Iman and me in the garden, wearing his English shooting cap to keep his head warm and his mask against infection. Hussein had also taken to using a cane again, due partly to his weakness and partly to an enduring fondness for walking sticks, which he collected. He also admitted to me with a profusion of apologies that he had started smoking again. All in all, he seemed more his old self again.

We slipped away to visit Hamzah at Sandhurst, and soon after Crown Prince Hassan paid a surprise visit to his brother in London. Because of his many responsibilities in Jordan, Hassan had never visited his brother at Mayo, and consequently his sudden arrival in England prompted a fresh round of press speculation. The succession was definitely weighing on my husband. One of the most burdensome tasks he had set for himself was to put the family and the country's future on a confident path. He had been thinking aloud about the subject for years, and naturally it became a paramount concern at Mayo. He wished that his brother, Crown Prince Hassan, had supported his idea for a Hashimite family council to recommend Hussein's successor on the basis of merit, a change that would have required an amendment to the Constitution, which at the time provided for the eldest son or, since 1965, a brother, to succeed the King.

A few days before our departure to Jordan, Hussein taped a televised address to announce his imminent arrival. "Now that I have fully recovered, by the grace of God, it will be merely the batting of an eyelid before I am again in your midst." The next day he became slightly feverish, prompting Dr. Gastineau, part of the medical team that had traveled with us from Mayo, to recommend that on our final scheduled visit to the hospital in London, St. Bartholomew's, Hussein should have not only the usual blood transfusion, but also a bone marrow tap, which might help explain the reason for his fever. The suggestion had a chilling effect. "Hussein's spirits and demeanor plummeted," I wrote in my journal. "He seemed to sink into himself with dread, especially after having publicly announced his arrival home."

Richard Verrall flew us from Buckhurst to the helipad at Kensington Palace for the medical tests in London. We would not know the results for forty-eight hours, so we went ahead with our planned departure. Hussein clearly felt a sense of urgency about getting back to Jordan while he was in remission, to set things in order. Hashim and Raiyah, then Haya and Iman, arrived to fly home with us for what we knew would be an emotional welcome. Hamzah did not come because he and my husband had decided it would be too exhausting for him to travel in and out of Amman in the midst of his military training at Sandhurst, a decision I agreed with entirely. It would also be better for Hamzah not to have to endure the ongoing speculation about the succession, and his brother Hashim more than rose to the occasion for his father.

We took a last-minute trip to the hospital in London for another transfusion and a last pampering treatment from Jo Malone. The night before we left, Hussein spent hours signing charity letters for a Royal Jordanian Air Force appeal while I spent a prayerful, sleepless night, hoping he would have the strength to descend the aircraft, pray on touching the ground, greet people, and ride in his vehicle without a mishap.

chapter twenty-one

The Skies Cried

We left England for Jordan at 7:55 A.M. on January 19, 1999, aboard a Jordanian Gulfstream 4. We were immediately picked up by an RAF fighter escort from the Sixth Squadron and then, as we passed into France, by a French fighter escort. Over Italy we were joined by an Italian fighter escort, over Israeli airspace by an Israeli fighter escort, and then, for the last leg home, we were accompanied by Jordanian fighter planes. In spite of his immense fatigue, Hussein piloted for the entire trip, with a short break for lunch. The motorcade in the sky was the greatest tribute possible for my aviator husband. Our children were quite excited at times by how close the escorts flew; we could practically read the name tags on their uniforms.

It was raining as we approached Amman, a cold, chilling downpour, which in our part of the world is considered the greatest possible blessing. It had not rained all winter until that moment — a gift that was attributed by many to my husband's special favor with the Almighty. Hussein did a fly-past over Amman to express his delight at being home after such a long time, as we prepared to land to what promised to be a tumultuous welcome. All of us hovered around Hussein in the plane, our daughters and Hashim helping to arrange his scarf and his kaffiyeh. In spite of his frailty, the King descended the aircraft with great dignity and, upon touching Jordanian soil, knelt to the ground and prayed. I stood nearby and joined him, reciting the Muslim prayer known as the Fatiha, to thank God for Hussein's safe return home. We greeted all the family, courtiers, and Arab VIPs waiting on the tarmac and then moved on to a hangar reception for government officials, the press, and special guests.

As usual, I tried to remain in the background when Hussein was the focus of attention. But on this occasion he drew me close to him, and when he made his remarks to the press, I was taken aback, even embarrassed, by his generous personal references to me, which were remarkable because we almost never spoke about each other in public.

We had a draining but euphoric ride home. Hussein asked that the sun roof of the car be opened, in spite of the freezing, relentless rain and wind, and he stood up through it so that he could wave to the crowds along the streets. I tried to dissuade him, but he remained standing, exposed, most of the way to Bab Al

Salam. If the people lining the streets were going to stand in the bitter rain, so would he. I braced his legs inside the car to support him. What other leader in the world had such a rapport with his people? I wondered. What people would show such love? The celebration continued when we finally reached Bab Al Salam, completely soaked but exuberant. The entire palace staff was out on the front steps to greet us. Hanna Farraj, the Jordanian television cameraman, followed us inside and recorded me saying emphatically, *"Yella, Hamaam,"* meaning, "Time for a hot bath," to my sodden husband, which made the nightly news.

We received word the next night that the tests he had taken in England just before we left were negative. We were all elated. The six months at Mayo had been a perpetual roller coaster, however, so I had learned to guard my expectations. "As so often of late, I'm conflicted between celebrating and preparing for any eventuality," I wrote in my journal that night.

Hussein gave a thoughtful interview the next day to Christiane Amanpour, who had asked to cover his return home for CNN. The King warned about the threats to our common security. "Terrorism is one of the most frightening aspects of our lives right now and . . . the potential of weapons of mass destruction was never under less control than now." He was also reflective when asked about his proudest moments. While he said that there had been many, he expressed regret that he had not always been able to prevent the crises he could see coming, despite his best efforts. When Christiane asked him about Crown Prince Hassan, he gave high marks to his brother's contributions over the years. When she pressed him again on the line of succession, he responded: "I have only thoughts and ideas. I've always had to take the final decisions, and although this has been contested at times, it's my responsibility, and I will come to it at an appropriate time."

The repercussions were immediate. Hassan met late that night with officials from the government, the military, and the intelligence services, all deeply concerned about what lay ahead. Princess Basma arrived at Bab Al Salam the next day frantic with concern over the sudden speed with which the issue had taken center stage. My husband was not able to see her, and he and I had not even had time to discuss the subject, but I tried to assure her that her brother would seek the most compassionate, dignified, and brotherly solution for the situation.

Hussein met with Hassan on January 21, two days after our return. Only the two of them know the details of that meeting. I felt great sympathy for Hassan because the succession had turned into such high theater in Amman. While Hussein had repeatedly referred to a variety of options over the years, he now made the decision to designate Abdullah Crown Prince. It was a natural choice to engage the next generation. Abdullah was thirty-seven years old and had studied at Georgetown University's School of Foreign Service and at Oxford University. Like his father, he was a graduate of Sandhurst, and he had risen to the rank of Major General in the Jordanian army's elite Special Forces, which would ensure him the critical support of the military.

"I want Hamzah to finish what I was not able to do in terms of schooling, and let him be the critical partner with Abdullah," my husband told me. I fully supported his decision. Contrary to the media reports that had so upset Hussein — that I had been pressuring my husband to name Hamzah his successor — I had been advocating all along that Hamzah should have an opportunity to attend university and develop his intellectual interests and talents.

My husband met with Abdullah, who then asked to see me. He was completely surprised by the sudden turn of events, he said. Hassan had been Crown Prince since 1965, and Abdullah said that he had assumed that after Hassan his father's choice would be Hamzah, and he had been willing to support that choice. He had never expected to assume the monarchy. I told Abdullah that it was important to me that he know that I fully supported his father's choice and had complete confidence in him. "I will be here for you, and honor my father's wishes toward Hamzah," Abdullah told me. I said I would wholeheartedly support him in every way I could, and do everything in my power to ensure that he and his father had as much time to work together as possible. I hugged him with all my heart as he left, still stunned, to return home and inform his wife, Rania. "I pray for Abdullah, hoping that events will not deny him time with his father," I wrote later in my diary.

In the midst of this wrenching family drama, my husband developed a new and agonizing ailment: chronic and unrelenting hiccups that worsened and became almost constant. Our medical team did everything they could to stop them, and ultimately had to give my poor husband an anesthetic so he could sleep at night.

Sahar, our devoted Jordanian nurse, was in and out of our room most nights checking on him. Hussein was also requiring blood and plasma transfusions on almost a daily basis. But his condition did not improve. Our physicians decided to perform a CT scan and yet another bone marrow tap, through which I held his hand, agonized by the trauma visited yet again on his body. I was called out of the room and informed by Dr. Farraj that Hussein's CT scan had revealed alarming changes. I returned to hold his hand for the remainder of the procedure, but tears streamed down my face under the surgical mask, and I left the room more than once to try to regain my composure. Over all the years of my married life I had tried to project optimism and hope, as my husband had taught me, and at this time I felt it was more important than ever not to appear frightened or in despair, especially now in front of our Jordanian nurses and technicians.

My husband and I met with our team of Jordanian and Mayo Clinic medical experts, who confirmed our worst nightmare. It appeared the cancer had returned. The doctors presented us with three options. One was to keep my husband comfortable and stay in Amman, forgoing treatment; the second was to stay home but try chemotherapy, though this course would not be curative; the third was to return to Mayo and attempt another transplant. This was the most dangerous option, but it was his only chance for remission. Neither one of us hesitated. "We're going back," Hussein told the doctors.

Hussein sat at the dining table in our private sitting room, working through the final details of the change of succession, preparing a public message to Hassan thanking him for his invaluable support over the years he had served as Crown Prince, totally absorbed in his writing, sipping only tea. His aides would check on him, but he would not be interrupted. My husband spent the rest of that evening struggling, with his ebbing strength, to finish the letter he was composing to Hassan. My heart was bursting as I watched him in such pain, unable to write without long, weary pauses. I knew from the doctors that we should be leaving immediately for Mayo, that time might be running out. But Hussein was determined to fulfill his responsibilities to secure a steady, hopeful future for his people. Finally, at midnight, the draft was completed, and as the final page was being typed, he met with his brother Prince Hassan, and his son, the newly designated Crown Prince Abdullah. Immediately thereafter he announced his decision to family elders, the Prime Minister and key representatives of Parliament, the military, and the intelligence services. Finally relieved of this huge burden, he was able to rest for a few hours before our departure.

The letter would be very controversial when it was read on Jordan Television the next day and released to the international media, but it was a first draft, and a miracle of effort at that. It had taken him six hours to finish. He handed me a copy on our return flight to Mayo, but I did not read it until some months later, when I discovered with surprise and considerable emotion that he had also made reference to me: "She brought happiness and cared for me during my illness with the utmost loving affection. She, the Jordanian, who belongs to this country with every fiber of her being, holds her head high in the defense and service of this country's interest. She is the mother who devotes all her efforts to her family. We have grown together in soul and mind, and she has had to endure a great deal of hardship to ensure that I was being attended to. And she, like me, also endured many anxieties and shocks, but always placed her faith in God and hid her tears behind smiles. She also has not escaped the arrows of criticism. Why not? Because there are climbers who want to reach for the summit, and when the fever was getting high some people thought it was their chance."

The next morning, Burdett took me aside to inform me that the morning's blood results were quite worrying. She gently suggested that we arrange for Hamzah to meet us for the return to Mayo. Knowing that Burdett was aware of Hamzah's rigid Sandhurst requirements, I felt my heart sink as I took in her sense of the precariousness of the situation. I retreated to my dressing room and collapsed on the floor in tears. "I am not ready to lose the light of my life," I wrote in my journal. "I must have faith, I must be positive. I will pray and pray and pray for his health, happiness, and peace of mind. If one of us must be called by God, let it be me!"

We set off the next morning, January 26, on the TriStar, one week after we had returned to Amman. We drove to the airport with Abdullah in front with his father and Abdullah's wife, Rania, with me in the back. I tried to calm her intense anxiety and fears about Prince Hassan and others who might attempt to interfere with the succession, expressing my confidence that His Majesty's wishes would not be countermanded. Ashen-faced government officials, members of the Royal Court, and the family were gathered at the airport to wish their beloved monarch Godspeed. Hussein was very tired and weak, yet he shook hands and said something to each of the waiting dignitaries. It took more energy than he could possible have had, but he did it.

The flight seemed interminable. We had arranged for Richard Verrall to pick up blood and platelets in London and meet us at our refueling stop in Shannon, Ireland, along with Hamzah and Raiyah. My husband insisted on being awakened before we arrived in Shannon so that he might dress in a coat and tie to greet his children properly. Again, the effort was considerable, but he met them with hugs and smiles and words of encouragement.

Hussein insisted on doing the same when we finally arrived in Rochester, and steeling himself courageously, he walked off the plane on his own. He remained positive even when we returned to the same room where he had spent most of the last six months. "Okay," he said to the doctors, "let's get started."

The chemotherapy used this time was one my husband had not had before. The danger of this particular treatment was that the rapid destruction of the cancer cells would result in potentially lethal metabolic abnormalities. Because of that potential danger, Hussein was put in the Intensive Care Unit so he could be closely monitored around the clock. This was terribly upsetting to his security guards, many of whom had been with us every day for the past six months, unwilling to take a break or go home to see their families. They would have given their lives for Hussein, but they did not know how to protect him from cancer, and the ICU frightened them. They kept saying that those who went in there never came out alive, so we did our best to reassure them not to be alarmed.

My husband tolerated the new treatment quite well and rebounded enough to be moved back into his room, but little by little he became confused and quiet. He spoke less and less, seeking answers with his eyes and his expressions. Haya, Ali, Hashim, Iman, and Raiyah were there with us, and Hamzah rarely left his side. "My brave children are comforting, soothing, praying for and loving their father as I might never have imagined possible," I wrote in my journal. I was persuaded to take the younger girls and Burdett out for a quick dinner one night but was summoned back by Haya, who was frightened by her father's state. Hussein had begun to talk less and less and seemed to retreat into himself. And then he began to have trouble breathing.

It was Hamzah, at his father's bedside during an early-morning shift, saying the prayers that had so many times comforted him, who noticed the next sudden change. He called Burdett, who in turn alerted the doctors. After speaking to me and explaining the risks and benefits of the procedure, the doctors decided to put Hussein on a respirator. I sat with the doctors for a moment, and then I asked, "Can we take him home?" The answer was "Of course," and my next question was "How soon?" If we are losing this battle, it is not going to be lost in Rochester, Minnesota, I told myself. He belongs at home with his Jordanian family.

Two hours later we were in the air. The entire medical crew, administrative and housekeeping staffs, pharmacists, therapists, and flight crew — all swept into action to prepare us for the journey. We were packed up and at the airport with ten physicians, a flight nurse, a respiratory therapist, and all the equipment and medications we could possibly need. We took off, still praying for miracles, and hoping at least for Hussein to arrive home safely. Once again we had fighter escorts, but no one paid much notice to them this time.

We stopped at Shannon, where we were met by Richard Verrall, who once again had flown in with oxygen, blood, and platelets from London. It was two or three in the morning. Richard said he would never forget the moment when he was standing on the deserted runway and suddenly, out of the gloom, the TriStar came toward him with the logo light shining on the golden crown on the tail. I asked Hamzah to bring Richard aboard so he could say his own farewell to my husband, just as I had invited everyone on the plane to do. We had all been together so long and gone through so much together, it was only fitting. But it was hard on everyone to see my husband, who had been so full of life and spirit, lying so still.

The cold rain beat against the windows of the hospital room at the King Hussein Medical Center in Amman, where my husband lay unmoving. Outside, thousands of Jordanians kept an anxious vigil in the downpour. The day after our arrival home, I walked down to the Medical Center's entrance gates with our sons Feisal, Ali, Hamzah, and Hashim to ask them to pray with me for the King. The nation's despair was palpable. "Every night when I set the table for dinner, I set a place for him," one woman said.

Inside the hospital, my husband's family gathered to say their final farewells to him. His brothers, his sister, his cousins, nephews and nieces, his former wives had all come to pray for him as he lay in a state of unconsciousness, the glorious life that had been his quickly ebbing away.

His deterioration had been so rapid and unexpected that I had asked the doctors to take his sons aside and give them a full prognosis of their father's condition. His eldest son, Abdullah, Hamzah, and their brothers would soon be assuming the responsibility for the country, and I felt they had to know and help make the final critical medical decisions. Throughout the vigil, his children stayed with him praying for him and chanting prayers, *du'aa,* some sleeping on the floor around his bed. I could not help feeling that having his family together gave him peace at the end.

On that last morning, I made my way through the sleeping children to have a last, quiet moment with him. But in many ways, I had already said good-bye. My husband and I had long before peacefully accepted God's will in this battle.

He died in Amman, on February 7, during noon prayers. It had been overcast all morning, and when Hussein's heart stopped, the heavens literally opened up for an unstoppable rain. He was facing Mecca when he died, at the same age as the Prophet Muhammad, *Peace Be Upon Him.* At the moment of my husband's death, I was standing next to his bed holding his hand, surrounded by our children and other relatives. I turned to Abdullah and said, "The King has died; long live the King," and gave him a hug.

The boys and I brought him home from the hospital to Bab Al Salam, the house Sidi had loved so much but had barely had time to live in, and placed his casket in the drawing room. I slept there that night on a couch, by the light of a single candle under his portrait, a calming, fragrant incense filling the air. I was in shock, yes, but I was also imbued with an extraordinary feeling of peace. Words cannot adequately express the serenity and simple faith that sustained me at that time, convinced as I was that this was just another phase of the journey that we would continue to travel together. In the middle of the night, Haya, Ali, Hamzah, Hashim, and Iman came in quietly, supporting one another, to spend a few moments with him.

Hussein's sons came in the morning to take his body into the kitchen for the ritual washing called *ghusl*. Sheikh Ahmad Hllayel, Imam of the Hashimite family, invited me to visit my husband one last time before he led Hussein's sons through the *ghusl*. The boys then wrapped him in the seamless white cloth he had worn on his pilgrimages to Mecca and together said the prayers for the dead. In keeping with Islamic tradition he would be buried immediately.

The funeral brought an extraordinary gathering of world figures to Jordan to celebrate Hussein's life: kings, presidents, and heads of state, friends and foes, royal families and high-ranking delegations. Leaders from the Middle East included President Hosni Mubarak from Egypt, Crown Prince Abdullah from Saudi Arabia, President Ali Abdullah Saleh from Yemen, Sheikh Al Khalifeh of Bahrain, President Omar Hassan Al Bashir of Sudan, the Palestinian leader Yasser Arafat, Syrian President Hafez Al Assad, Taha Ma'rouf, Vice President of Iraq, Arab League Secretary General Esmat Abdul Meguid, and His Highness the Aga Khan. There were four U.S. Presidents: Bill Clinton, Gerald Ford, George Bush, and Jimmy Carter. Prime Minister Netanyahu came from Israel with President Ezer Weizman and a senior delegation. Queen Sofia and King Juan Carlos came from Spain, Prince Charles from England, Queen Beatrix from the Netherlands, and King Albert and Queen Paola from Belgium, as well as Crown Prince Naruhito and Crown Princess Masako from Japan. Political leaders included Russian President Boris Yeltsin, German Chancellor Gerhard Schroeder, Prime Minister of France Jacques Chirac, British Prime Minister Tony Blair, Austria's President Thomas Klestil, Ireland's President Mary McAleese, Interior Minister Mangosuthu Buthelezi from South Africa, UN Secretary General Kofi Annan and his wife, Nane, Czech President Vaclav Havel, as well as many other government officials and friends.

My parents flew over with President Clinton, who had very thoughtfully called them and offered them seats on Air Force One.

After bidding a final farewell to my husband with our daughters and the women of the family, I watched as Hussein's sons carried him from our home and placed his casket on a funeral bier for the long, sad procession through the capital to Raghadan Palace, where Jordanian and international dignitaries would pay their respects before accompanying him to a brief service in the mosque of the royal compound, then up to the royal cemetery for burial. *"Hatta al samaa tabki ala Al Hussein,"* the people in the streets said to one another as they walked through the rain and dense fog: Even the sky is crying over Al Hussein.

I invited Princess Basma to join me at the royal cemetery for the burial. Press accounts at the time said that I was not allowed under Muslim law to attend his funeral, but this simply was not the case. I knew that I should be with him until he was laid to rest, and that this would in no way contradict the teachings of our faith. Societal tradition did not concern me, because I knew that Jordanians had an infinite capacity for compassion, and I will always be grateful to our protocol officers and our Imam, Sheikh Hllayel, for their understanding at such a difficult time.

As Basma and I watched from the entrance of Hussein's parents' mausoleum nearby, his sons laid him to rest near his grandfather, his body wrapped in a shroud, facing east toward the holy city of Mecca. I then returned to Al Ma'Wa to receive Crown Prince Abdullah of Saudi Arabia who had requested a private meeting to convey his condolences, before I continued on to Raghadan Palace to receive condolences from international dignitaries. For the next three days the three generations of women of the family received women mourners from Jordan, the Arab countries, and the world at Zahran Palace. I was in shock, yes, but I felt an extraordinary sense of serenity, imbued with his spirit and faith, that enabled me to reach out and comfort others much as he would have.

From that moment on, I knew I would never fear death but see it as a chance for reunion.

And it is true. Nothing and no one will ever come close to the love and respect I felt, and continue to feel, toward my husband. His humanity, his constancy, his decency in a world of deceit and self-interest — all these are unparalleled. I continue to thank God for the leap of faith I made as a young woman. I will try to bring my husband's spirit of optimism and moral conviction to everything I do. He never gave up, nor shall I. I pray that all our children will someday walk in a peaceful Jerusalem. *Insha'Allah.*

epilogue

Hussein was a true man of faith, and a steadfast believer in peace, tolerance, and compassion. I came to understand him anew after performing the *Umrah* in Mecca, in the year after his death. We had spoken often, especially during his illness, about making the pilgrimage together but the right moment had never come. In 1999, I decided to make my journey in the company of a few close friends and family. While it is customary to pray for the souls of the departed on such an occasion, this was also an opportunity for me to distance myself from the material and temporal world and to reconnect with the purity of faith that had sustained and guided me throughout Hussein's illness and beyond. I also experienced another deeply comforting and uplifting dimension of my faith — solidarity with the larger Muslim community, or *Umma,* a community profoundly unified and at peace in Mecca, the birthplace and heart of Islam.

Upon arrival in the holy city, I was welcomed to the guesthouse suite where my husband had always stayed. As I washed and dressed in simple white I imagined Hussein's impressions and feelings as he made his own preparations there, a ritual of renewal he performed most every year during his adult life. I then joined my family members and friends for prayers before proceeding to the Great Mosque, the Masjid Al Haram Al Sharif. Above us on a hillside overlooking the main entrance to the Mosque, we saw the Hashimite fort that had belonged to Hussein's family — an ethereal golden stone structure that seemed to glow in the waning light of day and the loveliest building in Mecca after the mosque. Inside, we joined a flowing river of humanity — men and women from all corners of the earth, alone or in groups, families and neighbors, all praying to God as Muslims have done since Prophet Muhammad's mission and revelation of the Quran.

Surrounded by the power of their faith and serenity of their devotion, I felt heightened reverence for Islam. In the company of thousands of pilgrims, we circled the Ka'ba — the sacred cube-shaped stone structure, which forms the center of the Great Mosque — seven times. Then in the *Sa'i*, the course of the symbolic reenactment of Hagar's search for water in the vicinity of the Haram between Safa and Marwa, we passed, among others, the Bab Al Salam gate (after which our home had been named) seven times. When the Saudi security gently jostled people aside to clear a path for us, I thought of Hussein, who, as a passionate believer in Islam's message of equality, was always uncomfortable with this kind of preferential treatment.

As hours passed in prayer and reflection, I was imbued with a sense of gratitude for Hussein's extraordinary example — his faith, his patience and calm in the face of conflict and hostility, his vision of peace. I thought about the way he had embraced and sustained not only our Hashimite family but also our entire Jordanian family, with his strength, guidance, and love without reservation.

In our final months together, he taught me that there is power in acceptance, that the path to victory sometimes requires us to submit and trust and so to transcend. As he left on the next stage of his journey, I longed to continue on with him, to give in to the stabbing pain in my heart. But when I was most tempted to let go, I thought of our children — all of them so brave, so comforting to one another and to me. And our beloved people seemed to be looking to me to preserve a connection to their cherished father, son, and brother. It was as if they sought to maintain their ties with him — not with the memory of what he once was but with his ever-present spirit as if I might have absorbed a measure of his wisdom and goodness. I knew that Abdullah and his brothers and sisters would uphold his legacy of Hashimite continuity and leadership. But the extraordinary confidence and trust of our people, was the blessing, privilege and duty that kept me going.

I knew too that faith would sustain me in the days and months ahead, and that I would return to Mecca, *Insha'Allah,* to this living embodiment of Islam's timeless message — piety before God through truthfulness, humility, sacrifice, and empathy for one's fellow man.

Life and death — both are stages in the journey of the spirit, both are entirely in God's hands. Hussein often said that we are mere custodians of a timeless legacy that transcends any single person, country or culture. We are momentary and mortal bearers of eternal, sacred values that have been handed down generation after generation — in our region and elsewhere for thousands of years. These reflections, which so comforted me as I prayed at Mecca three years ago, seem to have fresh resonance today in a world rocked by unspeakable upheaval and violence. Politicians and leaders will seek solutions, peaceful and otherwise, to mankind's ills, but for change to be positive and lasting we must all acknowledge our common humanity and live by the shared values of our faiths, as the Prophet Muhammad, *Peace Be Upon Him,* said: "Not one of you is a true believer until he desires for his brother what he desires for himself."

I know that Hussein's achievements will endure long in history, but it will be the memory of his loving eyes and smile, gentle humor and confident wisdom, his humble, generous and forgiving spirit that will enable me to go on. I pray that his legacy of love, tolerance, and peace lives on in all of us — it is his gift and challenge for which I will be eternally grateful and will seek to uphold in my life and work.

I will not fail you, my love. I will continue on the path we shared, and I know you will be there to help me, as you always were. And when we meet again at the journey's end, and we laugh together once more, I will have a thousand things to tell you.

Noor Al Hussein,
Bab al Salam
Amman, Jordan, November 2002
Ramadan 1423